Lecture Notes in Computer Science   1018

Edited by G. Goos, J. Hartmanis and J. van Leeuwen

Advisory Board: W. Brauer   D. Gries   J. Stoer

Springer
Berlin
Heidelberg
New York
Barcelona
Budapest
Hong Kong
London
Milan
Paris
Santa Clara
Singapore
Tokyo

Thomas D.C. Little   Riccardo Gusella (Eds.)

Network and Operating Systems Support for Digital Audio and Video

5th International Workshop, NOSSDAV '95
Durham, New Hampshire, USA, April 19-21, 1995
Proceedings

 Springer

Series Editors

Gerhard Goos, Karlsruhe University, Germany

Juris Hartmanis, Cornell University, NY, USA

Jan van Leeuwen, Utrecht University, The Netherlands

Volume Editors

Thomas D.C. Little
Multimedia Communications Laboratory, Boston University
02215 Boston, MA, USA

Riccardo Gusella
Hewlett-Packard Laboratories
1501 Page Mill Road, 94304 Palo Alto, CA, USA

Cataloging-in-Publication data applied for

Die Deutsche Bibliothek - CIP-Einheitsaufnahme

**Network and operating system support for digital audio and
video** : 5th international workshop ; proceedings / NOSSDAV
'95, Durham, New Hampshire, USA, April 19 - 21, 1995.
Thomas Little ; Riccardo Gusella (ed.). - Berlin ; Heidelberg ;
New York ; Barcelona ; Budapest ; Hong Kong ; London ;
Milan ; Paris ; Tokyo : Springer, 1995
  (Lecture notes in computer science ; Vol. 1018)
  ISBN 3-540-60647-5
NE: Little, Thomas [Hrsg.]; NOSSDAV <5, 1995, Durham, NH>; GT

CR Subject Classification (1991): D.4, C.2, H.5.1, H.4.3

ISBN 3-540-60647-5 Springer-Verlag Berlin Heidelberg New York

© Springer-Verlag Berlin Heidelberg 1995
Printed in Germany

Typesetting: Camera-ready by author
SPIN 10512287   06/3142 – 5 4 3 2 1 0   Printed on acid-free paper

Preface

The 5th International Workshop on Network and Operating Support for Digital Audio and Video commenced on April 19, 1995 with an audience of over 80 researchers from industry and academia.

The Program Committee selected 23 of the 101 submissions to form the basis of eight technical sessions. In each session, the Chairs dedicated a generous amount of time for discussion. Although there were some differences from session to session to accommodate the nature of the topics addressed and the preferences of the Chairs, in general the discussion centered on a round-table consisting of adjunct papers and various invited speakers.

While the technical program looked at the state of the art in networking and operating system support for multimedia, a ninth session took a broader look at the NOSSDAV workshop charter. Starting with what the workshop has achieved over the last five years from its origin at the International Computer Science Institute, this session explored possible directions for future NOSSDAV workshops.

Because of the limited attendance and the intimate setting of Durham, New Hampshire, the workshop proved to be an exciting and fruitful learning experience for all participants.

We are indebted to our Program Committee, and in particular to the Session Chairs for the work that went into the planning and realization of the workshop. Special thanks to Dinesh Venkatesh and Mary Hendrix for their invaluable support in workshop registration and Proceedings publication. We would also like to acknowledge the support of the IEEE Communications Society, the workshop sponsor, and ACM SIGCOMM, SIGGRAPH, SIGOPS, SIGMM, and SIGIR. Finally, our appreciation goes to Hewlett-Packard Laboratories and Boston University for the resources made available to us to realize the event.

April 1995   Thomas Little and Riccardo Gusella

Program Committee

Workshop Participants

Kevin C. Almeroth	Georgia Institute of Technology
Mostafa H. Ammar	Georgia Institute of Technology
P. N. Anirudhan	Texas Instruments, Inc.
Vivek Bansal	C&C Research Laboratories
Riccardo Bettati	University of California
Ernst Biersack	Institut Eurecom
Paul Bocheck	Columbia University
Jean-Chrysostome Bolot	INRIA
Milind M. Buddhikot	Washington University
John Buford	University of Massachusetts
Andrew Campbell	Lancaster University
Shanwei Cen	Oregon Graduate Institute of Science & Technology
Navin Chaddha	Stanford University
Shih-Fu Chang	Columbia University
Mikael Degermark	University of Lule
Luca Delgrossi	IBM European Networking Center
Alexandros Eleftheriadis	Columbia University
Julio Escobar	Bolt Beranek and Newman, Inc.
Kevin Fall	University of California
Domenico Ferrari	University of California
Valérie Gay	Université Paris VI
David Goodall	University of New South Wales
Pawan Goyal	University of Texas
Amit Gupta	University of California
Wendy Heffner	University of California
Mary Hendrix	Boston University
Ralph G. Herrtwich	IBM Eurocoordination Multimedia
Wen-Jane Hsieh	K200
Kevin Jeffay	University of North Carolina
Michael B. Jones	Microsoft Research
Chuck Kalmanek	AT&T Bell Laboratories
Kiyokuni Kawachiya	IBM Research
Srinivasan Keshav	AT&T Bell Laboratories
Hiroshi Kitamura	NEC Corporation
Edward W. Knightly	University of California
Jim Kurose	University of Massachusetts
K. Lakshman	University of Kentucky
Monica S. Lam	Sun Microsystems Laboratories
Simon S. Lam	University of Texas at Austin
Hugh C. Lauer	Mitsubishi Electric Research Labs
Aurel Lazar	Columbia University
Ian M. Leslie	University of Cambridge
Peter Leydekkers	Bellcore & PTT Research

Christopher J. Lindblad	Massachusetts Institute of Technology
T.D.C. Little	Boston University
Philip Lougher	Lancaster University
John C.S. Lui	Chinese University of Hong Kong
Derek McAuley	University of Cambridge
Shih-Min Mao	K200
Andreas Mauthe	Lancaster University
Darren C. Meyer	Worcester, USA
Mark Moran	University of California
Tatsuo Nakajima	Japan Advanced Institute of Science and Technology
Gerald Neufeld	University of British Columbia
J. Duane Northcutt	Sun Microsystems Laboratories
Max Ott	NEC
Seungyup Paek	Columbia University
Gurudatta M. Parulkar	Washington University
Stephen Pink	Swedish Institute of Computer Science
Kurt Rothermel	University of Stuttgart
Olav Sandsta	Norwegian Inst. of Technology, Trondheim-NTH Norway
Brian Schmidt	Stanford University
Henning Schulzrinne	GMD Fokus
Brian Smith	Cornell University
Ralf Steinmetz	IBM European Networking Center
Scott D. Stoller	Cornell University
Dan Swinehart	Xerox Palo Alto Research Center
Hideyuki Tokuda	Keio University
Dinesh Venkatesh	Boston University
Harrick M. Vin	University of Texas at Austin
Werner Vogels	Cornell University
Jonathan Walpole	Oregon Graduate Institute of Science and Technology
Johan Weilbach	South African Broadcasting Corp.
Ian D. Wilson	Olivetti Research Laboratory
Lars C. Wolf	IBM European Networking Center
Raj Yavatkar	University of Kentucky
Hui Zhang	Carnegie Mellon University

Table of Contents

Session I: Advance Reservation Systems
Chair: Kevin Jeffay, University of North Carolina at Chapel Hill

To date, much of the work on resource reservation in a network has considered only the problem of reserving resources for a network connection that is to be used immediately; the so-called "telephone call" model of network service. For uses that involve a larger number of participants, such as distributed meetings and conferences, or regularly scheduled, recurring events, such as classes, it is highly desirable to be able to reserve network resources well in advance of their actual use. The first session of the workshop considered the problem of supporting advance reservations of network resources.

The first talk, by Lars Wolf from the IBM European Networking Center in Germany, presented on overview of the issues in advance reservation and presented a candidate architecture for supporting such reservations. The issues highlighted in Wolf's presentation included the need to specify the duration of a session that is reserved in advance to be specified and the handling of network failures that occur after an advance reservation is granted but prior to the use of the network. A key issue, and one that differentiated the subsequent presentations in this session, was whether or not network resources are a priori partitioned and reserved for advance reservations and immediate-use reservations. The trade-off is the familiar one between starvation avoidance and potential under-utilization of network resources. The conclusion of the authors was that either resources must be partitioned or the ability for one class of reservation to preempt the other must be provided.

The second talk, by Mikael Degermark from the University of Lulea in Sweden, presented an extension to the service model and admission control algorithm developed by Jamin et al. (presented at NOSSDAV '92 in San Diego, CA) for predicted service. The predicted service model was extended to require that all admission requests (including immediate-use requests) specify the duration of the session. Admission is then based on the resource requirements of reservations whose start times are greater than the present time and on the measured resource usage of active reservations. Simulations of the extended predicted service admission control algorithm showed that network utilization decreases modestly when advance reservations are supported. As expected, the decrease is proportional to the burstiness of the sessions reserved in advanced and the fraction of the overall capacity consumed by advance reservations. Moreover, the addition of advance reservations to the predicted service model preserves the model's property of providing higher network utilization than a guaranteed service model (also with advance reservation).

In the third and final talk, Amit Gupta from the University of California at Berkeley, presented an advance reservation scheme that is being implemented in Suite 2 of the Berkeley Tenet protocol suite. In Suite 2, reservations can be made for both immediate-use, indefinite length sessions, and advance, definite length sessions. It was conjectured that the important distinction to be made between resource reservations was not whether or not the starting time for a session was "now," but rather whether or not the duration of the session was known in advance. In Suite 2, network resources are partitioned into resources to be reserved for definite length sessions and resources to be reserved for indefinite length sessions (although for simplicity the case of indefinite reservations made in advance was not considered). The partitioning of resources is dynamic and is expected to change over time as the capacity required to satisfy reservations of one type dominates that of the other type. A distributed resource reservation mechanism based on a table of reservation intervals was also described. Simulations of the scheme showed that across a range of initial resource partitions, a larger number of sessions can be supported with advance reservations than without advance reservations.

A roundtable discussion following the three presentations focused on charging models for advance reservation systems, and the ability of the proposed Internet resource reservation protocol RSVP to support advance reservations. With respect to charging models, the "restaurant model," wherein reservations are typically respected with a high degree of certainty, and the "airline model" wherein over-allocation of resources is common, were proposed and discussed. It was clear that unknown factors such as how abundant or scarce network resources are likely to be in the future, will determine the outcome of this debate. With respect to RSVP, the discussion centered on the design mismatch between the apparent requirement for persistent state in the network to support advance reservation and RSVP's reliance on soft state.

Advance Reservations for Predictive Service[1]

Mikael Degermark[2], Torsten Köhler[2][3], Stephen Pink[2][3], and Olov Schelén[2]

[2]Dept. of Computer Science
Luleå University
S – 971 87 Luleå, Sweden
{micke,olov}@sm.luth.se

[3]Swedish Institute of Computer Science
PO box 1263,
S – 164 28 Kista, Sweden
{steve,tk}@sics.se

Abstract. We extend a measurement-based admission control algorithm suggested for predictive service to provide advance reservations for guaranteed and predictive service while keeping the attractive features of predictive service. The admission decision for advance reservations is based on information about flows that overlap in time. For flows that have not yet started, the requested values are used, and for those that have already started measurements are used. This allows us to estimate the network load accurately for the near future. To provide advance reservations we ask users to include durations in their requests. We provide simulation results to show that predictive service with advance reservations provides utilization levels significantly higher than those for guaranteed service.

1 Introduction

Real time multimedia applications will share future networks with traditional data applications. To provide quality-of-service (QoS) for real time applications, it is likely that resource reservations will have to be made in the network. Current resource reservation protocols allocate resources just before communication begins, e.g., ST-2 [7] and various ATM signaling protocols reserve resources during connection establishment. This model of communication may not fit the needs of future network users, [6] pp. 44–45.

Resource reservations should be optional and decoupled from the starting time of the session. One should be able to reserve resources prior to or during a network session depending on when a specific service is needed. Users may know far in advance of their needs and would like to plan their activities by making advance reservations to ensure that they are not blocked by the network's admission control mechanism. Imagine some users with busy schedules in different time zones who want to have an important teleconference on a resource-limited network at an agreed time in the near future. They should be allowed to make an advance reservation given that they know when and for what duration their teleconference will take place.

---

[1] This work was supported by a grant from the Center for Distance Spanning Technology (CDT), Luleå, Sweden

In this paper we will look at an important candidate for an admission control algorithm originally proposed at this workshop some years ago [2] and later refined in [5], for a new kind of service called predictive service [1]. Predictive service provides quality of service for applications that can tolerate some loss such as real time digital audio and video applications that can adjust their playback points in response to jitter in the network. The efficiency gain of predictive service comes from allowing more flows into the network than guaranteed service, thus providing more sharing and lower cost. The architecture described in [1] supports guaranteed and predictive service, but not advance reservations.

The possibility of making advance resource reservations should be a part of a communication architecture to provide better service to the users. Whether advance reservations are actually needed depends on future resource scarcity. Where resources are plentiful, not even immediate reservations may be necessary, but where resources are scarce enough to justify reservations at all, it makes sense to be able to make them in advance. In this paper we will show that advance reservations can be provided by the network with little overhead.

2 Framework

The service model and the admission control algorithm suggested in this paper are extensions of those presented in [1] and [5]. In [1], the proposed network service interface offers guaranteed service, predictive service and best-effort (ASAP) service. The service interface is simple and relies on token bucket traffic shaping; the source specifies the bucket size b and the token generation rate r. Guaranteed service provides a minimum transmission rate and the queuing delay bound becomes the bucket size divided by the rate. Predictive service provides K different service classes with widely spaced target delay bounds D_i and it is suggested that the target bounds are spaced by an order of magnitude. The bounded quantity is the queuing delay per hop, so it is necessary to add up the target delay bounds at each hop to find the upper bound on the total queuing delay.

To support this service interface a scheduling algorithm is presented in [1]. The guaranteed service traffic is scheduled with weighted fair queuing (WFQ) [9] so that each guaranteed service client has a separate WFQ flow. All the predictive service flows and ASAP traffic share the spare bandwidth in a pseudo–WFQ flow, called flow 0. The available bandwidth for flow 0 is therefore $\mu - \hat{\nu}_G$ where μ is the link bandwidth and $\hat{\nu}_G$ is the measured bandwidth usage for all guaranteed flows over the link. Inside flow 0, there are a number of strict priority classes: one class for each target delay bound and ASAP traffic at the lowest priority. The strict priority scheme implies that queuing delay experienced by higher priority classes will be conveyed to lower priority classes.

Admission control is performed in each switch along the path of a flow. Admission requests will be carried to the switches by an end-to-end resource reservation protocol such as RSVP [8].

Note that our use of the term "guaranteed service" in this paper is adopted from [1]. There are other ways to provide guaranteed service which may give good utilization, e.g., jitter-EDD [3].

3   Duration Intervals

To achieve an efficient scheme for advance reservations we ask that each request includes a duration interval: $I = [t_s, t_e]$, where t_s is when the requested service will start and t_e when that service will end. The intervals are necessary to determine which requests overlap and when the reserved resources will be released.

We have extended the service interface so that each admission request includes a duration interval. Requests for immediate admission will specify *now* as their starting time. If a requested duration is too short, it should be possible to renegotiate the request by calling the admission algorithm again. If this request is rejected the session may continue but not necessarily with the same service quality.

If a requested duration is longer than needed, resources are over-reserved. This reduces the chances to grant admission to other advance reservations. Fortunately, immediate reservations can be granted to a large extent anyway. This is because the measurement procedure of predictive service automatically detects unused capacity once a flow is active. Therefore, over-reservation has little impact on the total utilization as long as there are some immediate requests for admission. In addition, there is an option for clients to explicitly close the requested service before the duration expires.

4   Admission Control Decision for Advance Reservations

The admission decision for predictive service is based on requested rates for flows that have not yet started and on measured rates for currently active flows. If there are no advance reservations and a request for immediate admission arrives, our extended conditions give the same result as the conditions stated in [5].

Figure 1 is a snap-shot of admitted flows in a time/bandwidth diagram. Flows a, b and c are currently active and we have measurements of their rates and maximum delays which are used as predictions of their future behavior. When a new admission request arrives, admission is granted if the new flow would not cause any delay bounds to be violated or bandwidth limits to be exceeded. The admission conditions only consider flows that overlap with the new flow (b,c,d,e,g,h), using measured bandwidth if they have started or, otherwise, bandwidth requests; we call this the *estimated* bandwidth. The conditions are checked at all points where new flows begin (t_s, t_x and t_y).

For reservations in the distant future the number of currently active overlapping flows is small and admission decisions are based mainly on requested rates. In the near future the number of currently active overlapping flows is probably

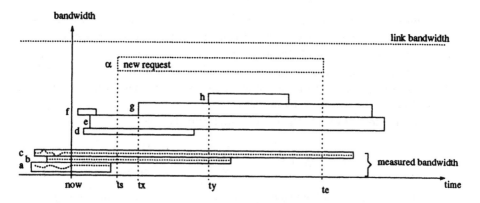

Fig. 1. Snap-shot of reservations

large and admission decisions are based mainly on measured values. So, in the distant future, the admission criteria are conservative, but as time proceeds more overlapping flows will become active and we get better estimates of bandwidth usage. Thus, as we get closer in time to the point at which a flow with an advance reservation is to begin, we have a more accurate knowledge of the network load and more flows can be admitted. Requests for immediate reservation can fill up the remaining bandwidth.

4.1 Admission Criteria

A client may request admission for predictive service in one of the classes 1 to K (where class K packets are scheduled at the lowest priority level), or for guaranteed service. The following notation will be used in the formulas[2] describing our admission criteria:

$\nu_{G(t)}$ estimated bandwidth for guaranteed flows at time t
$\nu_{P(t)}$ estimated bandwidth for predictive flows at time t
$\nu_{P_i(t)}$ estimated bandwidth for flows in predictive class i at time t
$R_{G(t)}$ requested bandwidth for guaranteed flows at time t
$\hat{D}_j$ measured delay in predictive class j
$B_j(t)$ bucket size sum for not yet started flows in predictive class j.

Predictive service: When a client requests service in predictive class k for a flow α, shaped by token bucket filter $(r_k^\alpha, b_k^\alpha, I^\alpha)$, the admission control algorithm performs the following checks:
- Determine if the bandwidth usage, after adding the new load r_k^α, will exceed the available link capacity $v\mu$ during the requested interval I^α:

$$v\mu > \max_{t \in I^\alpha} \left(r_k^\alpha + \nu_{G(t)} + \nu_{P(t)} \right) \quad (1)$$

The available link capacity, $v\mu$, is determined by the link capacity μ and the link utilization target v, that is tunable.

---

[2] These formulas are extensions of those presented in [5]

– Determine whether the worst possible behavior of the new flow and the
other flows that have not yet started can cause violation of delay bounds for
predictive service classes k through N.

The worst case is when all predictive service flows flush their entire token
buckets simultaneously in one burst. The resulting queue will be emptied
according to the available bandwidth.

- check the delay bound, D_k, of the same priority level:

$$D_k > \max_{t \in I^\alpha} \left(\hat{D}_k + \frac{b_k^\alpha + \sum_{i=1}^k B_i(t)}{\mu - \nu_{G(t)} - \sum_{i=1}^{k-1} \nu_{P_i(t)}} \right) \qquad (2)$$

- check the delay bound of the lower priority levels, i.e., D_j where $k < j \leq K$.

$$D_j > \max_{t \in I^\alpha} \left(\frac{\hat{D}_j \left(\mu - \nu_{G(now)} - \sum_{i=1}^{k-1} \nu_{P_i(now)} \right) + \left(b_k^\alpha + \sum_{i=1}^j B_i(t) \right)}{\mu - \nu_{G(t)} - \sum_{i=1}^{k-1} \nu_{P_i(t)} - r^\alpha} \right)$$

$$(3)$$

Guaranteed service: When a client requests guaranteed service for a flow α
shaped by $(r_G^\alpha, b_G^\alpha, I^\alpha)$, the admission control algorithm first performs the total
bandwidth check expressed in (1), then the following checks are performed:

– Determine whether the requested bandwidth of all guaranteed service flows
will exceed link capacity:

$$v\mu > \max_{t \in I^\alpha} \left(r_G^\alpha + R_{G(t)} \right) \qquad (4)$$

– Determine that the delay bounds of each predictive service class is still observed when the remaining bandwidth is decreased (estimated bandwidth for
guaranteed flows and for predictive classes with higher priority is subtracted
from the link bandwidth).

$$D_j > \hat{D}_j * \max_{t \in I^\alpha} \left(\frac{\mu - \nu_{G(now)} - \sum_{i=1}^{j-1} \nu_{P_i(now)}}{\mu - r_G^\alpha - \nu_{G(t)} - \sum_{i=1}^{j-1} \nu_{P_i(t)}} \right) \qquad 1 \leq j \leq K \quad (5)$$

4.2 Operation of Admission Control Algorithm

Figure 2 illustrates how our admission control algorithm operates. At time 1700
a large number of sources start. These sources, which were admitted in advance,
have reserved all of the available bandwidth and all finish at time 1800. There is
a background of sources asking for immediate admission with predictive service.
The figure clearly shows that the number of active flows goes down to zero just
before time 1700 to honor the resource commitments to the previously admitted
sources. At time 1700 the number of active flows increases sharply as the previously admitted sources begin to transmit and then increases further as those
sources are measured and more sources can be admitted.

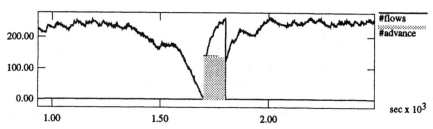

Fig. 2. Plot of number of active flows when there is a large block of flows admitted in advance.

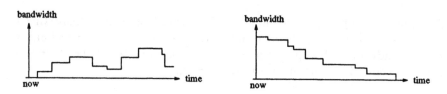

Fig. 3. Cumulative requested bandwidth   **Fig. 4.** Predicted bandwidth use of currently active flows

5   State Requirements

The information needed to make advance admission decisions in a switch is summarized in figures 3 and 4. Figure 3 shows the cumulative requested bandwidth admitted to flows that have not yet started. Figure 4 shows the predicted bandwidth use of currently active flows. Present measurements are used as predictions of future bandwidth use for those flows. We need to keep state corresponding to these diagrams for the guaranteed flows collectively and for each predictive service class individually.

An attractive feature of the original admission control algorithms [2] [5] is that the only state needed is the current bandwidth use for all guaranteed flows plus maximum delay and bandwidth use for each predictive service class. A straightforward implementation for advance reservation would keep an amount of state proportional to the number of active flows plus the number of flows reserved in advance. Aggregation methods, however, can decrease the amount of state needed: flows that start or finish at the same time, or nearly the same time, can be treated collectively.

There is a tradeoff between the amount of state saved by aggregating requests and the flexibility of making requests. A simple way to aggregate requests is to use time slots. Duration intervals may then start and finish only at certain points in time. A disadvantage with this scheme is internal fragmentation: clients may have to reserve longer intervals than they will actually use.

6 Simulations

Our simulations aim to show that adding advance reservation capability to the admission control algorithm for predictive service does not decrease utilization levels very much. We have simulated a single link topology using two different source models. We have done simulations of scenarios with immediate reservations only, and with both immediate and advance reservations. We have also examined the effects of aggregating state for active flows with similar finishing times.

6.1 Simulated Topology

The simulated topology is a single 10 Mbit/s bottleneck link connecting two routers. A number of sources are connected to one of the routers with links with infinite bandwidth. All sources send data to a sink connected to the other router. Our data comes from the upstream router R (fig 5).

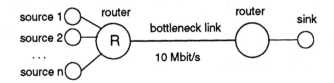

Fig. 5. Simulated topology

6.2 Source Model Parameters

We use two kinds of sources, both generate packet trains at some peak rate p. The train length is exponentially distributed with mean N. The time between packet trains is also exponentially distributed with mean I. The ratio between the peak and average rate, p/a, can be calculated from those values.

All sources regulate their output with a token bucket filter with token generation rate r and bucket depth b. Each token is worth 1000 bits which is equal to the packet size; sending one packet consumes one token. The token bucket filter is designed so that there should always be a token available when the source wants to output a packet. However, if the bucket is empty the packet is queued until a token is available.

All source parameters are listed in table 1. In the table, D is the maximum delay for a guaranteed flow, calculated from the token bucket parameters. D_j is the requested delay bound when the source asks for predictive service. The router supports two predictive service classes, one with a delay bound of 16 ms and the other with a delay bound of 160 ms.

Model Name	Model parameters				Token bucket		Delay bounds	
	p pkts/sec	I msec	N pkts	p/a	r tkns/sec	b tkns	D msec	D_j msec
EXP1	64	325	20	2	64	1	16	16
EXP2	1024	90	10	10	320	50	160	160

Table 1. Source model parameters

6.3 Flow Generation

Sources ask for admission according to a poisson process; the times between admission requests are exponentially distributed with a mean of 400 ms. The requested duration intervals are also exponentially distributed with a mean of 300 seconds. For sources that ask for admission in advance, the times between the admission request and the start of the duration interval are exponentially distributed with a mean of 300 seconds. Note that with these parameters, the offered load is much larger than the available bandwidth, so most admission requests are rejected.

A source requests admission by sending a setup packet containing the desired service type and token bucket parameters towards the destination. If all routers along the path grant admission, the source transmits during the requested interval and then it stops.

6.4 Measuring Process

The measuring process estimates current bandwidth utilization $\hat{\nu}$ and experienced maximum delay $\hat{D}$ in the same way as in [5]. When deciding whether

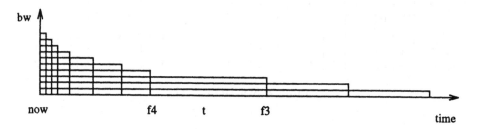

Fig. 6. Estimated future bandwidth use for currently active flows

to admit an advance reservation, the algorithm needs estimates of bandwidth utilization in the future, e.g., at time t in fig 6. This is done by continually estimating current bandwidth utilizations and using these as predictions of future utilization. The estimates are obtained by a straightforward extension of the measuring process in [5]. The packet rate of every active flow is sampled; these rates are then used as in [5] to obtain estimates of bandwidth utilization between finishing points of flows. The sum of the rates of the bottom three flows in figure 6 are used to estimate $\hat{v}$ between *f3* and *f4*, i.e., the finishing points of flows three and four from the bottom. This procedure ensures that the estimates are conservative in the distant future and accurate in the near future where many currently active flows will still be active.

In a straightforward implementation, calculating the estimates is linear in the number of flows. To avoid keeping track of every individual flow and reduce the overhead in calculating the estimates, we have experimented with aggregating flows that finish at about the same time. The bandwidth utilization of the aggregated flows is then estimated collectively.

6.5 Simulation Results

To verify our simulation environment we first replicated some relevant results from [5] in our simulator. In this first set of simulations, all sources in a single simulation conformed to the same source model and all requested immediate admission for the same type of service. The results of these simulations are summarized in table 2 under IMM. In table 2; *util* is the utilization of the

Name	Model	Serv	util %	delay (ms)	# sources (avg)			Measuring params		
					act	adv	adm	T (s)	S (s)	A (s)
IMM	EXP1	G	45	2.6	140	—	—	5.0	0.80	—
ADV	EXP1	G	44	2.3	137	137	282	5.0	0.80	—
IMM	EXP1	P	78	2.3	244	—	—	5.0	0.80	—
ADV	EXP1	P	68	1.9	213	160	265	5.0	0.80	—
GRA	EXP1	P	70	1.9	219	164	249	5.0	0.80	32
GRA	EXP1	P	75	2.5	232	153	240	5.0	0.80	128
IMM	EXP2	G	28	9.3	28	—	—	1.0	0.12	—
ADV	EXP2	G	27	8.4	27	27	109	1.0	0.12	—
IMM	EXP2	P	76	37.0	75	—	—	1.0	0.12	—
ADV	EXP2	P	59	13.4	58	37	124	1.0	0.12	—
GRA	EXP2	P	54	11.1	54	37	122	1.0	0.12	32
GRA	EXP2	P	50	11.5	49	33	123	1.0	0.12	128

Table 2. Simulation results

bottleneck link and *delay* is the maximum experienced queuing delay. *# sources* are averages of flow counts; *act* is the average number of sources that were transmitting. The *measuring params* are the size of the T and S windows used in the measuring process (see [5]).

The utilization target v was 90% in all simulations. All simulations ran for at least 3000 seconds simulated time. The data in table 2 comes from the second half of the simulated time. Visual inspection confirmed that no startup transients remained at that time.

In the simulations with advance reservations, 50% of the sources asked for immediate admission and 50% for admission in advance. The choice was random. All sources conformed to the same model and asked for the same type of service. These simulation results are summarized in table 2 under ADV. There, *adv* is the average number of sources that were transmitting and were admitted in advance, and *adm* is the average number of sources that were admitted in advance but have not begun transmitting.

The GRA simulations are similar to ADV, the only difference being the measuring process: all flows that finish within the same A seconds are aggregated and measured collectively. This also implies that for purposes of admission control, finishing times are rounded upwards to the nearest A seconds. In the table, A is the granularity of the measuring process.

6.6 Discussion

Our simulations clearly show that predictive service with advance reservations provides higher network utilization than guaranteed service with advance reservations. They also show that adding advance reservation capability to predictive service decreases bandwidth utilization. The levels are not much lower though for smooth traffic, but for bursty traffic the utilization level decreases more. When the fraction of sources asking for advance admission is lower the decrease in utilization is lower. E.g., in simulations when 10% of the sources (instead of 50%) ask for admission in advance, the utilization is 69% for the bursty EXP2 traffic.

The reason for the decrease in utilization is that advance reservations will block requests for immediate admission. This blocking effect is larger when the sources are bursty since the token bucket parameters are larger. Moreover, when token buckets are deep the admission decision is based on delay considerations more than on available bandwidth. To make a good admission decision in this case, the algorithm would need to know how much each flow contributes to the current queuing delay. This would enable the algorithm to estimate future delay since it knows which flows will be active at any future time. Instead, the algorithm uses the current delay as an estimate of future delay. Since this is a very conservative estimate, network utilization suffers.

An interesting and somewhat surprising result is that when there was aggregation of flows in the measuring process utilization increased for the smooth traffic generated by EXP1 sources, but decreased for the burstier EXP2 sources. It is easy to see that utilization might decrease since the durations of active flows are virtually extended by the aggregation in the measuring process. This gives less room for new flows.

Utilization will increase when there is less blocking, i.e., when fewer flows that were reserved in advance become active per time unit. The utilization increase for smooth sources may thus be due to a decrease in the fraction of active flows that were reserved in advance or to a higher rejection rate of short lived flows. The simulation results are not conclusive on which effect dominates.

An interesting observation is that for guaranteed service, sources asking for immediate admission are almost completely shut out by sources asking for admission in advance. This is due to the fact that for guaranteed service the admission decision is based on requested values only, regardless of estimated bandwidth use. The sources asking for admission in advance are admitted first and so can starve out sources asking for immediate admission since no bandwidth is freed when the sources with guaranteed service begin to transmit.

7 Setting up Advance Reservations using RSVP

With some minor changes, RSVP [8] could be used to set up advance reservations. RSVP is a receiver initiated reservation protocol supporting unicast and multicast reservations along a distribution tree. It can be used for setting up advance reservations in almost the same way as it is used for setting up immediate reservations. To establish an advance reservation for a multi-party session the senders have to announce their session by periodically sending announcement messages (in RSVP terms, "path" messages) down a multicast tree. Receivers respond to those announcements by sending reservations towards the senders. The resources have at this point been reserved for some time in the future. At the time the session starts, resources are allocated and the service to each session participant increases from best-effort to the requested quality.

For reservations made far in advance, there is potentially a very large number of path and reservations messages that must be sent before the session begins. To reduce overhead, the frequency of sending these messages should start low and increase as the time of the session approaches. RSVP could support advance reservations efficiently while allowing the admission control algorithm and measuring process to aggregate sessions if the following two minor changes are made:

- To support advance reservations the flow specification carried by RSVP path and reservation messages should include session durations. A sender will state a duration for the session and the receivers are free to reserve any interval within that duration. Since senders may lengthen or shorten durations, special wildcard durations can be used by the receivers to follow the changes made by the sender.

- To cancel a reservation, RSVP should provide the original flowspec in the interface between RSVP and the admission control mechanism. This is because our admission control algorithm aggregates requests for sessions of similar duration to save state and for measuring purposes. We propose that RSVP provide the original flowspec when making a call to the admission control mechanism to delete a session.

8 Related Work

There are few papers on advance resource reservation in the literature. The earliest mentioning of advance reservations in packet switched networks we have found is from 1992 [6].

[4] describes a scheme for advance reservations. Their simulations show network wide utilization gains since conference sessions (that share resources) get priority by being reserved in advance. No link level utilization gains are reported. [10] describes a general model for resource reservation in advance.

9 Conclusions

We have shown how the predictive service admission control algorithm developed in [2] and [5] can be extended to support advance reservations provided that requests for admission specify the duration of their reservation. The extended admission control algorithm proposed in this paper relies on knowledge of which flows overlap in time with the flow that requests advance reservation, measuring those overlapping flows that are active, and assigning the requested rate to the flows that have not yet started. Thus, more requests for a certain duration of time can be granted as we get closer to that duration of time increasing sharing and lowering cost for those flows that occupy that duration. We have also suggested ways to minimize the amount of state information necessary to provide advance reservations, and to simplify the measuring process that estimates future bandwidth use.

Our simulations show that predictive service with advance reservations provides higher network utilization than guaranteed service with advance reservations. They also show that adding advance reservation capability to predictive service decreases bandwidth utilization. The levels are not very much lower though, and they are still significantly higher than for guaranteed service. The decrease in utilization is due to the fact that advance reservations will block sources asking for immediate admission. This blocking effect is larger for bursty sources which request more resources.

References

1. D. Clark, S. Shenker, L. Zhang: *Supporting Real-Time Applications in an Integrated Packet Services Network: Architecture and Mechanism*. Proc. ACM SIGCOMM'92, 1992.
2. S. Jamin, D. Clark, S. Shenker, L. Zhang: *Admission Control Algorithm for Predictive Real-Time Service*. Proc. 3rd International Workshop on Network and Operating System Support for Digital Audio and Video, November 1992.
3. D. Ferrari: *Real-Time Communication in an Internetwork*. Journal of High Speed Networks, 1(1), 1992, pp. 79–103.
4. D. Ferrari, A. Gupta, G. Ventre: *Distributed advance reservation of real-time connections*. Proc. 5th International Workshop on Network and Operating System Support for Digital Audio and Video, April 1995.

5. S. Jamin, P. Danzig, S. Shenker, L. Zhang: *A Measurement-based Admission Control Algorithm for Integrated Services Packet Networks*. Proc. ACM SIG-COMM'95, 1995.
6. C. Partridge, S. Pink: *An Implementation of the Revised Internet Stream Protocol*. Internetworking Research and Experience, 3(1), March 1992, pp. 27–54.
7. C. Toplocic: *Experimental Internet Stream Protocol, Version 2 (ST-II)*. RFC 1190, October 1990.
8. L. Zhang, S. Deering, D. Estrin, S. Shenker, D. Zappala: *RSVP: A New Resource ReSerVation Protocol*. IEEE Network Magazine, September 1993, pp. 8–18.
9. A. Demers, S. Keshaw, S. Shenker: *Analysis and Simulation of a Fair Queuing Algorithm*. Journal of Internetworking: Research and Experience, 1, 1990, pp. 3–26.
10. L. Wolf, L. Delgrossi, R. Steinmetz, S. Schaller, H. Wittig: *Issues of Reserving Resources in Advance*. Proc. 5th International Workshop on Network and Operating System Support for Digital Audio and Video, April 1995.

Distributed advance reservation of real-time connections

Domenico Ferrari, Amit Gupta, Giorgio Ventre*

E-mail: {ferrari,amit,ventre}@icsi.berkeley.edu
Tenet Group
University of California at Berkeley, and
International Computer Science Institute

Abstract. The ability to reserve real-time connections in advance is essential in all distributed multi-party applications (i.e., applications involving multiple human beings) using a network that controls admissions to provide good quality of service. This paper discusses the requirements of the clients of an advance reservation service, and a distributed design for such a service. The design is described within the context of the Tenet Real-Time Protocol Suite 2, a suite being developed for multi-party communication, which will offer advance reservation capabilities to its clients based on the principles and the mechanisms proposed in the paper. Some simulation results about the performance of these mechanisms are also presented.

1 Introduction

Some of the important multimedia applications of integrated services networks require that advance reservations be possible. The clients who wish to set up multimedia multi-party meetings (i.e., meetings involving multiple human beings) need to schedule those meetings in advance to make sure that all or most of the participants will be able to attend; at the time the meeting is scheduled, they must also be certain that the network connections and the other resources required will be available when needed and for the entire duration of the meeting. Unfortunately, distributed multimedia applications must be supported by real-time communication services, which are to provide the necessary quality-of-service (QoS) guarantees, and these services cannot admit an arbitrary number of connections. Thus, there is no guarantee that the resources for a pre-scheduled meeting will be available at the time the meeting is expected to start, unless they can be reserved in advance. To our knowledge, advance reservation services are not available within any of the existing schemes for real-time communication (see for example [1, 3, 4, 13, 14, 15]).

---

* Now with Dipartimento di Informatica e Sistemistica, Università degli Studi di Napoli "Federico II", Napoli, Italy

This paper presents a scheme for advance reservations of real-time connections. It is organized in the following manner. Section 2 discusses the service requirements for advance reservations. In Section 3, we describe the distributed advance reservations mechanisms we have designed for, and are implementing in, the Tenet Suite 2 [11]. The principles on which our mechanisms are based, however, are easily portable to other approaches and protocols for real-time communication. We also present some simulation results in Section 4.

2 Client requirements

The only true requirement network clients with multi-party applications have, in the area we are investigating here, is that they be allowed to specify in advance their needs in terms of real-time channels, and to obtain a guarantee that the resources for those channels will be available at the future time they have specified. Clients will accept the necessity to reserve channels in advance if they can convince themselves that this is the only way to avoid the risk of partial (or total) rejection of their requests at the time they need to use the network.

The service model in the existing proposals and realizations of real-time communication services, including that in the Tenet Suite 1 [1], assumes that real-time channels are requested (and established) for an indefinite duration. Clients are not asked to specify for how long such channels (to be called *immediate channels* in the sequel) will be alive, and this non-negligibly simplifies their tasks. The current establishment model, in which channels are to be created immediately (i.e., as soon as possible), coincides with that of a normal telephone call, whose expected duration never has to be specified by the caller.

When advance reservations are introduced into such a service, the provider has to do some planning for future allocations of resources, and this planning would be easier if the expected durations of the channels were known. A limitation of this duration would also allow more clients to reserve channels in advance, thereby increasing the sharing and the utilization of the resources. This modification of the service model for channels reserved in advance (henceforth to be called *advance channels*) is consistent with the practice of booking other types of facilities, for example, meeting rooms, which may never be reserved for an indefinite amount of time. For this reason, clients should be expected to accept this service model and conform to it without too much difficulty, especially if negotiating an extension of a channel's duration is sufficiently easy and inexpensive.

The same meeting-room analogy can be used to argue that, if the service provider found it useful to adopt a coarse granularity for time, i.e., to accept only starting times and durations that are integral multiples of, say, five minutes, clients would find it fairly easy to conform. Similarly, clients would accept reasonable values for the minimum and maximum advance notice with which reservation requests can be submitted (e.g., not less than one hour and not more than six months) if such limits were imposed by the provider.

Even with advance reservations, there is the possibility that a request be rejected. The significant difference with respect to the case in which a request for the immediate creation of a channel is rejected is that there is still time to reschedule or cancel the meeting without any great disruption of the participants' lives. If one or more of those channels needed by a multi-party application cannot be reserved in advance for the time interval specified by the client, the client would certainly appreciate being informed by the service provider about other values of the time or of the other parameters that would make it possible to set up all the channels requested.

One way the provider could encourage advance reservations is to offer lower charges for an advance channel than for the equivalent immediate channel. These discounts could be justified with the same arguments that are the basis of similar discounts for airline tickets, i.e., easier and more effective planning.

Thus, to summarize, an advance real-time channel will be requested by specifying, besides the parameters that define an immediate channel, the following two quantities: (i) the starting time, and (ii) the duration. These two times may have to be (or to be transformed into) integral multiples of a *time granule*, and the starting time may have to satisfy the constraints (if any) on advance notice, as mentioned above. In the case of a rejection of the request, the client should be notified of the reason for the rejection, and of what changes to which parameters, including (i) and (ii) above, would be effective in getting the request accepted.

3 An advance reservations service

In this section, we describe the design of an advance reservation service for a real-time (or integrated-services) network. While this description is presented in the framework of the Tenet protocols, the underlying ideas and techniques are also applicable to other schemes and protocols.

3.1 Design alternatives and decisions

Since clients are expected to accept rather easily the requirement that advance channels be created for a definite amount of time, we have chosen to enforce this requirement in our design due to its expected beneficial effect on the utilization of network resources, whereas immediate channels will normally be created for an indefinite duration.

In the establishment of immediate channels, which in the scheme described in [9] only considers the situation at the time the request is made, we must now look at all the future situations as well: Figure 1 shows a case in which no immediate channel can be created through a server (i.e., a network component that has resources to be allocated) at time t_1 even though the resource in question is fully available in the server at that time. This complication can be avoided, and the establishment of immediate channels still kept as fast as possible, by separating the two types of channels so that the admission tests for a new channel only take into account the channels of its type in each server. Resource partitioning [7, 10], a service the Tenet Suite 2[2] will offer network managers, is an almost perfect solution for this problem. The *immediate partition* treats any new request exactly as described in [9]. The *advance partition* must instead use a different mechanism (to be presented in Section 3.2) to test new requests for admission.

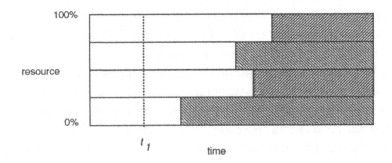

Fig. 1. A request for an immediate channel cannot be accepted at time t_1, even though the resource is 100% free at that time. The shaded areas represent fractions of the resource that have been reserved in advance.

The partition-based solution raises, however, a problem: each resource has to be allocated statically to each partition, and this may cause inefficiencies due to fragmentation [10] and, worse, to poor allocation decisions; one of the two partitions for a resource may be saturated while the other is almost empty. Since choosing *a priori* allocations suitable for the types of requests that will arrive is hard, the implementation of a movable boundary between the two partitions must be explored; mechanisms for obtaining this result will be described in Section 3.2.

As for the minimum advance notice required for an advance reservation, which was mentioned in Section 2, it seems reasonable to set it to zero: if there is enough room for the requested duration in all the servers to be traversed within the advance partition, why should the network not accept such an "immediate reservation"? This argument suggests that the crucial distinction between the two partitions might be not so much that between advance and immediate channels, but that between channels of definite and indefinite duration. In fact, it would perhaps be useful to allow for the advance reservation of indefinite-duration channels, but in our design, for simplicity, we ignore this possibility, and do not allow advance reservations of indefinite-duration requests. Thus, all such requests are immediate, and belong in the immediate partition, while all definite-duration requests are tested against the advance partition, even if their starting time coincides with the current time.

Finally, a decision is to be made concerning the organization of our advance reservation service. A centralized solution for a real-time network running the Tenet protocols is feasible, but would suffer from the problems usually associated with centralization: the creation of a performance and reliability bottleneck, poor scalability, and the need to keep in the central reservation agent an up-to-date view of the present and future resource allocations throughout the network. The last problem could be solved by centralizing all channel setups, including those of the immediate channels; however, this would be a major departure from the Tenet approach, which, being targeted to large internetworks, has always tried to maximize distribution of control operations. We have therefore adopted a distributed procedure also for the establishment of advance channels, which is described in Section 3.2.

3.2 A distributed advance reservation mechanism

In a distributed approach, the advance reservation information must be stored in the servers of the network: each server has to keep track of how much of each of its resources has been reserved at various future times, besides knowing how much of each resource is set aside for those channels that already exist at the present time. This increase in the amount of state information to be recorded in each server certainly makes fault recovery more complicated and time-consuming; however, this important problem is outside the scope of this paper, and its discussion is therefore postponed to a future publication.

Having divided each resource in a server into at least two partitions, we can just concern ourselves with the amount of each that is allocated to the advance

partition. Since the boundary between the two partitions is movable, we allow this amount to vary from time to time; however, we subdivide the future-time axis of a server into *intervals* characterized by the following two properties: (i) an interval does not include any instant at which a channel traversing the server starts or ends its life; these events delimit intervals but never occur within them; (ii) the allocations of resources to the advance partition are constant throughout an interval; they can only change (i.e., the boundaries for some of the resources in a server can only be moved) at the transition point from an interval to the next.

The basic mechanism used to manage the advance partition in a server is the *interval table*, which lists all the advance channels that will traverse the server during a future interval, together with the requirements for each of the server's resources. The interval table, an example of which is shown in Table 1, includes also the amounts of each resource that are available to the advance partition during the interval, as well as the totals that have been allocated to advance channels.

Channel id	Buffer space	Processing power
312	14	800
174	8	144
586	11	650
Resources allocated	33	1594
Resources available	50	2000
Start time	002041735	
End time	002641735	

Table 1. An example interval table in a server

In the table, buffer space is expressed as a number of packet-sized buffers, and processing power in Kbits/s; times are measured in milliseconds. We have omitted several columns that contain local bounds and other channel parameters.

When the advance partition in a server is empty, there is only one interval table; its top row is empty, its start time is the current time (as we have decided not to require any minimum advance notice), and its end time is "infinity". When an advance channel request is received from a client, the source[2] sends out an advance establishment message containing, together with all the usual traffic and QoS parameters, the start and end times of the reservation.

---

[2] The Tenet suites allow receiver-initiated as well as sender-initiated channel establishment. We describe only the sender-initiated procedure here to simplify the discussion.

The arrival of this message at our server causes the only existing interval to be subdivided into three intervals: (current, start), (start, end), and (end, current + max advance notice). For each interval, the corresponding interval table is created; the first and the third have the top rows empty, whereas the second has just the requested channel in it (assuming the available resources are sufficient to accept the channel, i.e., assuming that the request passes all the tests against the available resources).

The situation remains as described until a message relating to the same channel comes back from the destination(s), assuming, for simplicity of description, that no other establishment request is received by the server before this time. If the returning message is a *channel-accept* one (i.e., at least one destination has accepted the request), then the reservation is confirmed; only some of the values in the second table are modified to adjust the reservations and set the local bounds. If, on the other hand, the returning message is a *channel-reject* one, then the three tables are re-merged into the initial empty table.

This procedure is repeated at the arrival of every successive request at the server. In general, such an arrival will find the future-time axis of the server subdivided into n intervals, and its expected lifetime will cover completely a fraction of them, but its birth and death may split up to two of the existing intervals; for example, in Figure 2, tables T_{01} and T_{56} will not be affected by the addition of the new channel, while T_{12} will be relabeled $T_{11'}$ (its end time will change from t_2 to $t_{1'}$) and T_{45} will be renamed $T_{4'5}$ (its start time will become $t_{4'}$ instead of t_4); T_{23} and T_{34} will be updated by the simple addition of a row corresponding to the new channel, and $T_{1'2}$ and $T_{44'}$ will be created from T_{12} and T_{45}, respectively, in the obvious way.

Thus, after the arrival of the new request, the server will have two more interval tables; to put a curb on the proliferation of tables, we use the time granules that have been mentioned above, with the provision that a client-specified time not satisfying this rule will be modified to coincide with that of the nearer inter-granule transition. Of course, if the return message is a *channel-reject* one, the new interval tables (e.g., $T_{1'2}$ and $T_{44'}$) will be deleted, and the others restored to their previous state.

If clocks are kept in approximate synchrony throughout the network, those advance channels whose start time coincides with the start time of the current interval, i.e., with the current time, can spring to life automatically in all the servers they traverse without any need for establishment, thereby producing the illusion of being connectionless, while in reality they were established in advance. Note that the intervals have variable lengths so as to minimize the number of

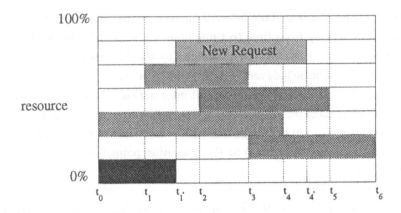

Fig. 2. Effects on the intervals and interval tables of the addition of an advance channel

tables in a server. In fact, this number at any time is bounded from above by twice the number of advance channels established in the server at that time.

We shall now sketch mechanisms for moving the boundary between the two partitions, as mentioned in Section 3.1. First, suppose that in a server one of the interval tables is full when a new advance request is received. Instead of sending a negative return message back towards the source, we may choose to reduce by the needed amount the current allocation of that resource to the immediate partition. This reduction could be *temporary*, i.e., from the current time to the end time of the interval in which the advance partition was saturated, in which case the relevant "Resources available" entry in each of the tables chronologically preceding the saturated one and in the saturated one would have to be increased by the same amount; or the reduction could be *permanent*, in which case all tables in the server would be updated. Of course, if the boundary is moved only temporarily, we have to make sure that the allocation of the resource to the immediate partition is re-increased at the time the table that was saturated is deleted. As long as there is a mechanism that can move the boundary in the other direction on demand, such as the one to be described in the next paragraph, we may be tempted to favor a permanent reduction; however, it may be necessary to put curbs to the expansion of the advance partition, since advance reservations might sometimes be too aggressive and leave too little room to the immediate ones.

Conversely, let a request for an immediate channel be received by a server in which the immediate partition is out of one of the resources. Then, instead of rejecting the channel, the server could look at the interval tables kept by the advance partition to determine whether a sufficient amount of that resource is available there. If such an amount is available in all of the tables, the server can allocate that amount to the immediate partition by reducing the appropriate "Resources available" entries accordingly; again, the "borrowed" amount could be returned on demand using the above mechanism. If, on the other hand, a table is found in which the required amount is not available, the server may reject the request or accept it for a limited time. The latter option introduces a third type of channel, the *immediate channel with definite duration*; however, this is not a channel that may be requested by a client (who can request an advance channel with an immediate start time instead), but a restriction imposed by the network on an immediate channel for lack of resources. We favor this option, and have included it in our design, since we want to maximize network utilization and minimize the blocking probability. A watermark to protect the advance partition may be necessary too, and network managers may find it useful to create only immediate channels with definite duration once this watermark is exceeded, so as to leave room for farther-future reservations while using near-future resources for requested immediate channels instead of keeping them for unlikely advance requests.

All the dilemmas we have mentioned above without resolving them are policy choices. We have designed mechanisms that allow network managers to specify the policies. The evaluation of the possible policies is a topic for future research.

4 A simulation-based evaluation

We performed a number of simulation experiments to evaluate the performance of the resource partitioning algorithms. Because of space limitations, we present only two sets of simulation experiments here (see [8] for many more results). In the first set, we ran simulations of resource requests for a simple traffic characterization, with and without the advance reservation mechanisms, while the second set evaluated the effect of time granularity on the performance of advance reservation mechanisms. In each case, we ran many experiments on a topology reproducing that of the NSFNET backbone, with varying workload parameters, and averaged the results thus obtained.

The main metric we adopted for evaluation and comparison was the *acceptance ratio*:

$$\text{Acceptance ratio} = \frac{\text{Number of destinations reached with advance reservations}}{\text{Number of destinations reached without advance reservations}}$$

In all experiments, we created a partition for non-real-time traffic containing 20% of the resources in each server. The main result of these simulations

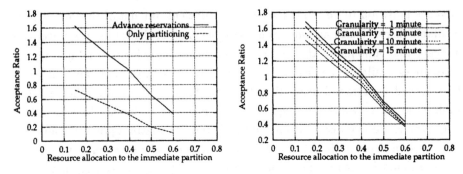

Fig. 3. Acceptance ratio for advance reservations, and the effect of time granularity

is that our distributed mechanism works, and its cost is affordable. Figure 3 presents some of the results of the two sets of experiments described above. The percentage of resources allocated to the immediate partition is reported on the horizontal axis in both diagrams.

In the first set of experiments, we compared the following three scenarios:

- 10 50-person conferences, and 50 10-person conferences, all in the same partition, which was allocated 80% of the network's bandwidth; we call this the *without advance reservations* case;
- two partitions: the first partition empty; 10 50-person conferences and 50 10-person conferences in the second partition, where resources are not reserved in advance; we call this the *only partitioning* case; and
- two partitions: the first partition empty; 10 50-person conferences and 50 10-person conferences in the second partition, where resources are reserved in advance; we call this the *advance reservations* case.

In this workload, there exist resource sharing relationships among the conference channels (only up to 2 of the channels constituting a conference may be active at any given time) so that they can share resource allocations [12].

In Figure 3, there is a large region in which the acceptance ratio is higher than 1, i.e., in which the acceptance rate is higher with advance reservation mechanisms than without these mechanisms. However, there is also a large region in which the ratio is lower than 1. Thus, moving the resource allocation boundary is necessary whenever the workload is such that the boundary falls in an area with low acceptance ratio.

In the second set of experiments, we ran the tests on the *advance reservations* and the *without advance reservations* scenarios while varying the granularity of start times and durations from 1 to 15 minutes. As shown in the figure, the acceptance ratio and the overhead ratio decrease slightly as we increase the time granularity. However, the lower acceptance ratio may be due to the assumption made in the simulations that the start times are completely random within a small time interval. So, we conclude that time granularity does not appreciably affect the performance of our mechanisms.

5 Discussion and conclusion

We have presented a fully-distributed scheme for advance reservations of real-time connections. The experiments have shown that our distributed mechanisms work, and their cost is affordable. An interesting feature of our advance reservation mechanisms is that they favor channels that belong to conferences (and, because larger conferences usually have larger advance notice periods, our mechanisms favor larger conferences over smaller conferences). Conferences may not be held if there are no advance reservations; for example, a conference may not be held at all if all its channels, or a substantial fraction of them, are not established.

Reinhardt[14] proposes a signaling mechanism for advance reservations with the ST-II protocol; the signaling approach used here is somewhat similar to ours, except that it uses fixed-size intervals, with the accompanying extra overhead (for example, with five-minute granularity, the overhead for a two-hour video conference would be approximately twenty-four times the overhead for an immediate reservation, which is the extremely unlikely upper bound for overhead in our case). This proceeding also includes two other papers that discuss advance reservations for real-time communication: Delgrossi et al.[6] discuss the design issues encountered when trying to support advance reservations in ST-II, while in [5], the authors propose an advance reservation mechanism for *predictive service* [4].

This research was supported by the National Science Foundation and the Defense Advanced Research Projects Agency (DARPA) under Cooperative Agreement NCR-8919038 with the Corporation for National Research Initiatives, by AT&T Bell Laboratories, Digital Equipment Corporation, Hitachi, Ltd., Mitsubishi Electric Research Laboratories, Pacific Bell, Tektronix, and the International Computer Science Institute. The views and conclusions contained in this document are those of the authors, and should not be interpreted as representing official policies, either expressed or implied, of the U.S. Government or any of the sponsoring organizations.

Issues of Reserving Resources in Advance

Lars C. Wolf, Luca Delgrossi, Ralf Steinmetz, Sibylle Schaller, Hartmut Wittig

IBM European Networking Center
Vangerowstr. 18
D-69115 Heidelberg

{lars, luca, rst, schaller, wittig}@heidelbg.ibm.com

Abstract: Resource management offers Quality-of-Service reliability for time-critical continuous-media applications. Currently existing resource management systems provide only means to reserve resources starting with the reservation attempt and lasting for an unspecified duration. However, for several applications such as video conferencing the ability to reserve the required resources in advance is needed. This paper explains a model for resource reservation in advance. We identify and discuss issues which must be resolved in resource reservation in advance systems. Some of the possible scenarios to be considered are described and we show how the resource reservation in advance scheme can be embedded in a general architecture.

1 Introduction

Computer systems used for continuous media processing have to be able to cope with streams with data rates of several Mbits/s and to provide timely processing guarantees, for instance such that an endsystem shall synchronize audio and video streams up to a granularity of about 80 ms [11].

Since available system resources are not abundant, applications have to be 'protected' such that they have access to the required resources in time because otherwise the user will notice a drop in the presentation quality. Hence, a means to manage the available system resources is necessary.

Resource management provides a way to offer applications reliability with respect to *Quality-of-Service* (QoS). A resource management system controls the access to scarce system resources needed for audio and video data processing. It checks whether additional service requests can be satisfied, if yes, the required resources are reserved for that application, if not, the request is rejected. The importance of resource management and the need of respective techniques is now widely accepted in the research community [9].

1.1 Motivation

Today existing resource management systems, for instance, HeiRAT [13], offer functions which only allow to reserve resources for a time interval which starts with the reservation attempt and which usually lasts for an unspecified time.

For several application scenarios this model of immediate reservations is not appropriate. Consider, for instance, a meeting room (conferencing) scenario which has to be supported by multimedia systems. Traditionally, a meeting will be scheduled for a specific time in a selected room in order to allow for arrangement of all participants. To be sure that the room will be available at the scheduled time, a reservation is made, in some form of a meeting room calendar, *before* the meeting starts. The time between

References

1. Anindo Banerjea, Domenico Ferrari, Bruce Mah, Mark Moran, Dinesh Verma, and Hui Zhang. The Tenet real-time protocol suite: Design, implementation, and experiences. Technical Report TR-94-059, International Computer Science Institute, Berkeley, California, November 1994. Also to appear in IEEE/ACM Transactions on Networking, 1995.

2. Riccardo Bettati, Domenico Ferrari, Amit Gupta, Wendy Heffner, Wingwai Howe, Quyen Nguyen, Mark Moran, and Raj Yavatkar. Connection establishment for multi-party real-time communication. *Proc. 5th NOSSDAV*, Boston, MA, April 1994.

3. Robert Braden, David Clark, and Scott Shenker. Integrated services in the internet architecture: an overview. Request for Comments (Informational) RFC 1633, Internet Engineering Task Force, June 1994.

4. David Clark, Scott Shenker, and Lixia Zhang. Supporting real-time applications in an integrated services packet network: Architecture and mechanism. *Proc. ACM SIGCOMM'92*, pages 14–26, Baltimore, Maryland, August 1992.

5. Mikael Degermark, Torsten Kohler, Stephen Pink, and Olov Schelen. Advance reservations for predictive service. *Proc. 5th NOSSDAV*, Boston, MA, April 1995.

6. Luca Delgrossi, Sibylle Schaller, Hartmut Wittig, and Lars Wolf. Issues of reserving resources in advance. *Proc. 5th NOSSDAV*, Boston, MA, April 1995.

7. Domenico Ferrari and Amit Gupta. Resource partitioning in real-time communication. *Proc. IEEE Symposium on Global Data Networking*, pages 128–135, Cairo, Egypt, December 1993.

8. Domenico Ferrari, Amit Gupta, and Giorgio Ventre. Distributed advance reservation of real-time connections. Technical Report TR-95-008, International Computer Science Institute, Berkeley, California, March 1995.

9. Domenico Ferrari and Dinesh Verma. A scheme for real-time channel establishment in wide-area networks. *IEEE Journal on Selected Areas in Communications*, 8(3):368–379, April 1990.

10. Amit Gupta and Domenico Ferrari. Resource partitioning for multi-party real-time communication. Technical Report TR-94-061, International Computer Science Institute, Berkeley, California, November 1994. Also to appear in IEEE/ACM Transactions on Networking, 1995.

11. Amit Gupta, Wendy Heffner, Mark Moran, and Clemens Szyperski. Multi-party real-time communication in computer networks. *Collected abstracts of 4th NOSSDAV*, pages 37–39, Lancaster, UK, November 1993.

12. Amit Gupta, Winnie Howe, Mark Moran, and Quyen Nguyen. Resource sharing in multi-party realtime communication. *Proc. INFOCOM 95*, Boston, MA, April 1995.

13. Craig Partridge and Stephen Pink. An implementation of the revised internet stream protocol (ST-2). *Journal of Internetworking Research and Experience*, pages 27–54, 1992.

14. Wilko Reinhardt. Advance reservation of network resources for multimedia applications. *Proc. ICAWA 94*, Germany, October 1994.

15. Lixia Zhang, Steve Deering, Deborah Estrin, Scott Shenker, and Daniel Zappala. RSVP: A new resource reservation protocol. *IEEE Networks Magazine*, 31(9):8–18, September 1993.

the reservation and the meeting itself can vary from short intervals, e.g., hours or few days, to very long periods, e.g., months. In addition to 'one time events', meetings such as department meetings occur periodically. To support these 'virtual meeting room' scenarios the resource reservation system must offer mechanisms to reserve in advance the resources needed during the conference, i.e., network, router, and end-system resources.

Resource Reservation in Advance (ReRA) is not only needed for conferencing but for other scenarios such as video-on-demand as well. This resembles a video rental scenario where a user 'orders' a video for a specific time which means for video-on-demand that the resources necessary to retrieve, transfer and present the video have to be reserved in advance, i.e., video server, network, router, and end-system resources.

1.2 Related Work

Despite the fact that the necessity of mechanisms for ReRA seems to be accepted in the research community, at least to our knowledge, only few work has been done so far in the field of ReRA.

Ferrari, Ramaekers and Ventre are among the first who notice in [6] that ReRA is a useful concept. They describe the parameters for the start and duration of a reservation but go not further into the requirements of ReRA nor do they discuss design aspects.

Campbell, Coulson and Hutchinson describe in [1] their Quality of Service Architecture and specify start and end time parameters for 'forward reservations', however, they also state in the article that these parameters have been omitted so far and remain for further study.

Reinhardt gives in [10] a straight-forward extension of the resource reservation protocol ST-II [12] to exchange, within the flow specification, the necessary information about start and end time of a reservation in advance and describes shortly some problems to be solved within ReRA. He does not discuss a general model and possible scenarios.

This proceedings contain two other articles about ReRA. Ferrari, Gupta and Ventre from the Tenet group at the University of Berkeley describe in [5] a scheme for advance reservations of real-time connections. They concentrate on connection establishment, resource partitioning, and a mechanism to manage effectively the table of all set advance reservations, but do not give a general architecture.

Degermark, Köhler, Pink and Schelén show in [3] an extension of the admission control algorithm for predicted service suggested by Jamin, Clark, Shenker and Zhang [2, 7]. A general model or architecture is not presented in their work.

1.3 Contents and Outline of this Paper

This paper discusses a model for ReRA, identifies the issues to be resolved and describes some of the possible scenarios to be considered. Since ReRA seems to be a complex topic, we believe that a complete solution to all its related problems requires deep understanding and discussion within the research community. We hope to brighten the discussion on this interesting and important research field.

The paper is organized as follows: Section 2 provides a short description of a common resource management scheme; Section 3 introduces the notion of ReRA and presents the base model; Section 4 deals with issues of ReRA and Section 5 shows how the ReRA scheme can be embedded in a general architecture.

2 Resource Management

A complete discussion of resource management is, due to space limitations, out of the scope of this paper (see, for instance, [8] for a discussion of resource management). Here, we only describe shortly those parts relevant to the ReRA scheme.

The resource management component on each system which is part of an application must provide certain functionality for each "active" resource (i.e., CPU, network adapter):

- *Interpretation and translation* of the application specified QoS in metrics applicable to the affected resources.
- *Capacity test* to check whether the available resource capacity (taking the existing reservations into account) is sufficient to handle the new request.
- *QoS computation* to calculate the possible performance the resource can provide for the new stream.
- *Resource reservation* to reserve the required resource capacities.
- *Resource scheduling* to perform the scheduling of the resource during data processing such that the QoS guarantees are satisfied.

Figure 1 illustrates how this functionality can be distinguished into two resource management phases. In the set-up phase (also called 'QoS negotiation') applications specify their QoS requirements (e.g., throughput and delay). These parameters are used for capacity test and QoS computation which finally results either in resource reservation or in rejection of the reservation attempt if the QoS cannot be met due to a lack of resources. After the negotiation phase has been successfully completed, in the data transmission phase, the resources used to process the user data are scheduled with respect to the reserved resources (also called 'QoS enforcement').

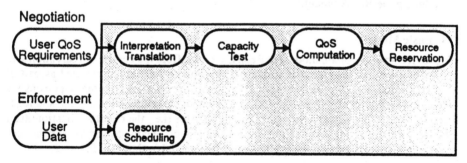

Figure 1: Resource Management Phases.

In a ReRA system, the negotiation phase is not in close vicinity to the enforcement phase and the resources are not reserved for immediate but for delayed use.

To achieve QoS provision for a distributed multimedia application, resource management is applied to all resources on the transmission and processing path, from the sending host via gateways or any other computers and networks to the receiving host. Resource reservation protocols such as ST-II [12] and its more recent version ST2+ [4], and RSVP [14] offer the functionality for QoS provision in distributed systems.

3 A Model for Resource Reservation in Advance

This section introduces the notion of ReRA and presents a basic ReRA model. To distinguish ReRA schemes from other reservation schemes, e.g., existing reservation techniques, we classify reservations based on two key factors:

- whether the resources are exploited at reservation time, and
- whether the reservation duration is known at reservation time.

This leads to the simple matrix presented in Table 1:

Table 1: Classification of Reservation Schemes.

		Reservation Duration	
		Known	Unknown
Resource Usage	Immediate	non-ReRA / ReRA	non-ReRA
	Deferred	ReRA	?

Traditional resource management systems (non-ReRA) assume that the resources are immediately used after they have been successfully reserved and no assumptions are made on the duration of the reservations. A ReRA scheme, on the contrary, is characterized by deferred resource usage and reservations of known duration (which might possibly be enlarged).

We feel that it is difficult to implement ReRA schemes if the duration of the reservation cannot be determined at reservation time. Therefore, we include a question mark in the correspondent table entry. In case of immediate usage and known duration, both schemes can be realized. We clarify this point at the end of this section, after introducing the ReRA model.

3.1 Basic Model

To provide an appropriate model for ReRA, we start from the common reservation scenarios of everyday life. In such scenarios, appropriate actions are required as part of the reservation, e.g., we have to specify at what time and for how many persons we intend to reserve. Here, we introduce a simple model to define these actions and regulate the interaction between the reservation requestor (i.e., the client application itself or a ReRA agent acting on behalf of the application, cf. Section 5) and the service provider (e.g., network and server applications). The model is shown in Figure 2.

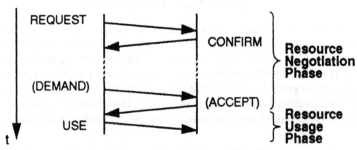

Figure 2: Reservation in Advance Primitives.

The ReRa scheme consists of two parts:

* resource reservation in advance
* usage of reserved resources

In the first part of the ReRA scheme, the client issues a REQUEST and it specifies the nature of its request by indicating how much of the resource capacities will have to be reserved for its application, i.e., it gives a *workload specification*. It also specifies the points in time that define *beginning* and *duration* of the reservation. The service provider may then CONFIRM the reservation. As part of this confirmation, it possibly provides the client with a *reservation identifier* for later client identification. This terminates the first part of the ReRA scheme.

The second phase begins shortly before the client intends to exploit its reservation. The client contacts the service provider to DEMAND the previously reserved resources. It may be requested to show some form of identification, which the service provider will ACCEPT. After receiving this acceptation, the client eventually exploits its reservation by making USE of the reserved resources.

It is possible to further simplify this scheme by eliminating DEMAND and ACCEPT. In this case, the client attempts directly to make use of the allocated resources and client identification can be associated with USE. However, we feel that the scheme described in Figure 2 is more convenient because it provides for the management system the ability to prepare the resource usage phase and generally allows for higher flexibility. For instance, it is often necessary to change reservations at the very last moment. A common example is a couple of unexpected guests for dinner making a larger table necessary. With the DEMAND and ACCEPT scheme, DEMAND can be used to adjust reservations appropriately when possible. Also, an explicit ACCEPT from the service provider is desirable because it informs the client that everything is set so that its requirements can be met.

3.2 Timing

In order to appropriately define a ReRA system, it is important to analyze the temporal relationships among the events. Consider the events in Figure 3.

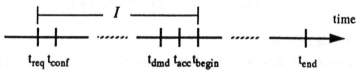

t_{req} t_{conf} t_{dmd} t_{acc} t_{begin} t_{end}

Figure 3: ReRA Model Temporal Sequence.

In our view of a ReRA system, we assume that the distance between t_{req} and t_{conf} is short, about the order of delay tolerated by Remote Procedure Calls (RPC). The same holds for t_{dmd}, t_{acc} and t_{begin}. On the contrary, t_{req} and t_{begin} are possibly very distant, possibly in the order of weeks or months. Let us call I the time interval between resource reservation and exploitation:

$$I = t_{begin} - t_{req}$$

When I is too small, making a ReRA reservation is pointless and a normal reservation scheme can be adopted. A ReRA system may define a value for I, say I_{min}, such that requests with:

$$t_{begin} - t_{req} < I_{min}$$

are rejected. In the same way, an I_{max} value for I can be defined to prevent applications to request their reservation long ahead of time, e.g., to prevent storing too much reservation state. These definitions help clarify Table 1 when both non-ReRA and ReRA are possible, the I_{min} value can be used to decide which of the two schemes to adopt.

4 Issues in Resource Reservation in Advance

4.1 Resource Management

Assuming non-ReRA and ReRA schemes will have to coexist on future systems, there are two ways of managing the resource capacity:

- the capacity is *partitioned* into two parts so that a portion is assigned to non-ReRA and the other to ReRA reservations (cf. [5]).
- non-ReRA and ReRA reservations make *shared use* of the resource capacity.

The two alternatives are briefly sketched in Figure 4. Partitioning a resource's capacity makes it easier to implement the system at the price of a non-optimal exploitation of the resources. The latter can be possibly reached by sharing the available capacity, but the system realization is in this case more complex because of the additional need of a reservation pre-emption scheme. Note that if the durations of all reservations are known (which can be achieved by the introduction of a default duration value), then it would be possible to apply the sharing strategy without preemption.

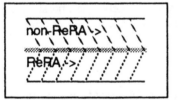 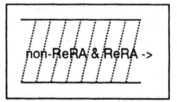

Figure 4: Examples of Resource Capacity Allocation Strategies: Resource Partitioning (left) and Sharing (right).

4.2 Reservation Duration

ReRA schemes require that the applications reserve resources over a certain time interval. The problem is, it is difficult to predict in advance how long some applications may need their reservations. In a video-on-demand system, it is usually possible to foresee the duration of a movie. Still, the user may increase this duration by pausing playout or even by stopping and rewinding to watch his favorite sequence a second time. In the same way, meetings take often longer than expected. Note that also shorter durations may be induced, e.g., by skipping through movie sequences or by rapidly adjourning a meeting.

When the actual duration does not correspond to the reservation, several issues arise:

- if the *duration is shorter*, exceeding resources should be freed and made available for other applications. In this case, resources are more likely to be made available for immediate use and for traditional reservation requests than for new ReRA requests, because of the short notice (which is likely $< I_{min}$).

- if the *duration is longer*, the system may or may not have a sufficient amount of resources to serve the application with its needed QoS. If enough resources are available, one possibility is not to interrupt the service and to provide the application with the means to extend its previous reservation. If insufficient resources are available, the system may still attempt to serve the application on a best-effort basis with a degradation in the QoS.

Means to extend a previous reservation are desirable for a ReRA system, i.e., in addition to the primitives discussed in Section 3.1 a CONTINUE primitive to enlarge an already established reservation is necessary.

Sometimes, the delay can be foreseen, e.g., it becomes clear that the meeting will take longer than expected. In such cases, it may be possible to extend in advance, i.e., before it expires, a previous reservation. This will only be successful if sufficient resources are available, e.g., if no other reservation overlaps with the extended reservation. For the prolongation of the reservation, we differentiate two alternatives, (i) the management system informs the application/user that the reservation will expire and queries whether the reservation should be extended or (ii) the application has complete responsibility about the reservation state and must take appropriate action to lengthen the reservation.

The ability to extent reservations encourages applications not to book resources over too long time intervals in order to be guaranteed against unpredicted longer durations. In a cost-based ReRA system, this can also be imposed by adequate payment policies of the associated reservation costs.

If it is known before the beginning of usage that the needed reservation duration is different to the originally specified length, the DEMAND mechanism can be used to adapt the reservation to the required duration. If the duration shall be shortened, the reservation requestor might be charged for preventing other reservations. For prolongation, the necessary resources might be unavailable, however, due to the earlier request, the risk is lower than during the usage phase of a reservation.

4.3 Failure Handling

We believe that failure handling is one of the most difficult topics within ReRA, here we outline only shortly some aspects. For the handling of failures, we must distinguish when the failure occurs:

- after the reservation, but before the usage (between REQUEST and USE), or
- during the usage phase.

The second case is not different from failures within traditional reservation-based systems. The former case, however, requires special attention.

The reservation state information stored at nodes might be needed for long lasting time periods. State information must be stored in stable storage not only to protect against failures, but also since any node may be restarted between REQUEST and USE also regularly, e.g., for maintenance.

In opposite to failures occurring during data transmission, no client is running when a node notices a failure. Hence, means to inform the clients explicitly about the failure situation and whether it can be resolved in time must be provided. The failure itself might, however, not be detected at the failing node but only at a neighbor which has only partial information about the reservation state stored at the node.

4.4 Relation Between ReRA and Scripted Presentations

For presentations, e.g., specified via a script, the information is available about which parts of the presentation are needed at which time, e.g., when a particular video must be presented[1]. This information can be used to perform ReRA for all presentation parts. Support from the ReRA system for the presentation application should be available to ease the applications task, additionally such support functions also provide more information to the ReRA management which can lead to better scheduling decisions.

5 An Architecture Exploiting ReRA Mechanisms

In addition to services needed for non-ReRA systems, e.g., multimedia communication system and resource management system, the following components are required as shown in Figure 5:

- a *ReRA agent* at each system participating in the processing of the stream, i.e., enhancing the 'standard' resource manager,
- a *user agent* providing the front end for users to inform them about incoming ReRA attempts, hence, it interacts with the ReRA agent. An incoming ReRA attempt is also combined with the announcement of a data stream, e.g., the invitation to a video conference.

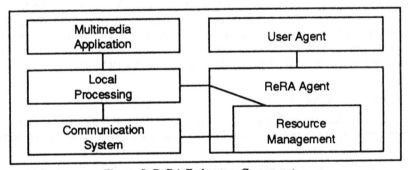

Figure 5: ReRA Endsystem Components.

5.1 ReRA Agent

The ReRA agent is illustrated in more detail in Figure 6. Compared with a traditional resource management system it contains the following extensions:

- time parameters in the flow specification exchanged via the used resource reservation protocols,

---

1. This information is only available if later parts of the presentation do not depend on user input. In that case, heuristics can be used to determine the most likely presentation path. However, use of ReRA beyond points where user input is required seems to be questionable.

- time parameters in the reservation database, and
- new resource management algorithms in the resource manager.

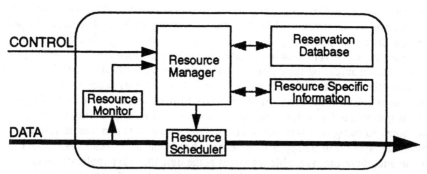

Figure 6: ReRA Agent.

In the used resource reservation protocol, the flow specification transmitted as part of the reservation setup PDUs must be extended by the parameters *start_time* and *duration*. While these PDUs are exchanged between the systems participating in the final transfer of the data stream, the resource management systems of these nodes are informed about the time and QoS parameters of the reservation request.

The reservation database has to be enhanced to store the time parameters of a reservation in advance. This includes the date for the start of a reservation and its duration. If the resource manager receives a reservation request it uses these time parameters to check the available resource capacities against the requested capacities in the time period given by the request. If requested resources exceed the available resources the resource manager rejects the reservation request.

5.2 User Agent

The user agent is similar to the user agent of a mail system. It provides the interface for the user to handle resource reservations in advance. An incoming invitation to a multimedia application (to be started sometime in the future) is presented to the user who can acknowledge or reject the invitation. Using this agent, users can also start reservation attempts themselves. The user agent should provide the ability to start automatically the application at the time the data stream has been scheduled, i.e., just before the conference begins.

5.3 Scenarios

Considering distributed multimedia applications, two different scenarios can be distinguished:

- the sender of the data stream has complete knowledge about the set of receivers, i.e., their identities,
- the sender has no knowledge about the set of receivers, i.e., the sender knows neither identity of receivers nor even whether anyone is listening.

The former scenario occurs in point-to-point communication or in multicast communication using a sender oriented communication setup, this is the case, for instance, in

ST-II. The latter scenario is used in multicast communication where the receivers are not specified by the sender and is typical for IP multicast communication.

In both cases, the human users who will consume the presentation of the transmitted data must be informed about the intended transmission of the multimedia data and accept or reject the stream. While it would be possible, in the first scenario, to perform the announcement phase together with the reservation attempt, it should be avoided. The reason is the severe drawback that until the user decided about the delivery of the stream, the resources on the complete path from the sender to the receiver must be set aside (for the future time frame) for the case that the receiver accepts the stream. However, the reaction of the user might be delayed for an unknown amount of time – the user might even not be at the computer for days or weeks, e.g., during business trips or vacations. Keeping resources reserved for such a long time can lead to rejected reservation attempts for other applications even if finally the user decides not to receive the stream and, therefore, available resources at the time the other applications intended to run. Additionally, it complicates the implementation of the ReRA components and the recovery from system failures. Altogether, it becomes clear that a distinction into the *announcement* of the data stream and ReRA for that stream is necessary.

6 Summary

While current resource management systems provide mechanisms which offer reliability with respect to QoS, this is not sufficient since not all application scenarios we are used to from our daily live can be supported.

ReRA mechanisms are needed for several important classes of applications. However, ReRA is more than a simple extension of current resource reservation systems. As part of the development of ReRA systems, several issues must be solved.

The integration of current reservation schemes and ReRA requires resource partitioning or the ability to preempt resource usage. Applications must be offered a variety of mechanisms to prolong and adapt reservations. Failure handling raises difficult questions and must be carefully integrated into the system architecture. The provision of reservation mechanisms is only one part of a complete ReRA system. Agents to interact with the user, for reservation request generation as well as for the presentation and handling of incoming invitations, are necessary.

Acknowledgments

The description of the relationship between ReRA and scripted presentations is based on the hint of one of the anonymous reviewers.

References

1. A. Campbell, G. Coulson, D. Hutchinson: "A Quality of Service Architecture", ACM Computer Comunication Review, Vol. 24, No. 2, April 1994, pp.6-27.
2. D. Clark, S. Shenker, L. Zhang: "Supporting Real-Time Applications in an Integrated Packet Services Network: Architecture and Mechanisms", SIGCOMM 1992.

3. M. Degermark, T. Köhler, S. Pink, O. Schelén: "Advance Reservation for Predicted Service", Fifth International Workshop on Network and Operating System Support for Digital Audio and Video, Durham, NH, USA, April 19-21, 1995.

4. L. Delgrossi, L. Berger (Ed.): "Internet STream Protocol Version 2 (ST2) – Protocol Specification – Version ST2+", Internet Draft – Work in Progress, IETF ST Working Group, March 1995.

5. D. Ferrari, A. Gupta, G. Ventre: "Distributed Advance Reservation of Real-Time Connections", Fifth International Workshop on Network and Operating System Support for Digital Audio and Video, Durham, NH, USA, April 19-21, 1995.

6. D. Ferrari, J. Ramaekers, G. Ventre: "Client–Network Interactions in Quality of Service Communication Environments", Proceedings of the Fourth IFIP Conference on High Performance Networking, University Liege, Belgium, December 1992, pp. E1-1 – E1-14.

7. S. Jamin, D. Clark, S. Shenker, L. Zhang: "Admission Control Algorithm for Predictive Real-Time Service", Third International Workshop on Network and Operating System Support for Digital Audio and Video, San Diego, CA, USA, November 1992.

8. K. Nahrstedt, R. Steinmetz: "Resource Management in Networked Multimedia Systems", IEEE Computer, Vol. 28, No. 4, April 1995.

9. NOSSDAV4: "Panel Discussion (D. Ferrari, K. Jeffay, D. Northcutt, J. Rosenberg)," Fourth International Workshop on Network and Operating System Support for Digital Audio and Video, Lancaster University, UK, November 3-5, 1993.

10. W. Reinhardt: "Advance Reservation of Network Resources for Multimedia Applications", Proceedings of the Second International Workshop on Advanced Teleservices and High-Speed Communication Architectures, 26.-28. September 1994, Heidelberg, Germany.

11. R. Steinmetz: "Human Perception of Audio-Visual Skew" in "Hochgeschwindigkeitsnetze und Kommunikationssysteme" W.Effelsberg, A.Danthine, O.Spaniol (Ed.), Kluwer, 1994.

12. C. Topolcic: "Experimental Internet Stream Protocol, Version 2 (ST-II)," RFC 1190, October 1990.

13. C. Vogt, R. G. Herrtwich, R. Nagarajan: "HeiRAT: The Heidelberg Resource Administration Technique - Design Philosophy and Goals," Kommunikation in Verteilten Systemen, Munich, Germany, March 3-5, 1993.

14. L. Zhang, S. Deering, D. Estrin, S. Shenker, D. Zappala: "RSVP: A New Resource ReSerVation Protocol," IEEE Network, September 1993, pp. 8-18.

Session II: Operating Systems Support
Chair: Duane Northcutt, Sun Microsystems Laboratories

The presentations in this session spanned a wide range of levels of abstraction, from novel low-level subsystem designs, through entirely new operating systems, and up to high-level distributed system architectures. However, the presentations all touched on various aspects of how operating systems can be made to provide enhanced support for digital audio and video. There are a great many ways in which system software can be made to actively support the unique requirements posed by applications which include continuous digital media. One should not expect operating systems to simply "get out of the way" and permit applications direct access to the underlying hardware. There are still a number of valuable things that can be done at the system level to meet the needs of multimedia applications.

The session's first full paper was presented by Valerie Gay of the University of Paris and described how industry standard distributed object system architectures can be augmented to permit the specification of interfaces for objects that possess timeliness constraints. In particular, the suggestion was made to modify OMG-IDL to include a means of specifying streaming constructs, as well as including the notion of "computation environment contracts" which provide the additional information needed to capture all of the (higher-level) quality of services requirements of objects. The speaker made a case that it is becoming increasingly important to incorporate the means to express the needs of real-time multimedia applications into the formalisms and tools for architectural specification of development of large-scale, object-based, distributed systems.

The second paper of the session was presented by Mike Jones of Microsoft Research, who described a novel approach to real-time system resource management being implemented in the Rialto operating system. This work illustrated how an operating system can be devised which provides a new set of abstractions that reflect the needs of time-critical (e.g., multimedia) applications. Specifically, the Rialto OS provides a means for effectively resolving the forms of contention which occur when independently-developed real-time applications compete for shared system resources. The presentation suggested that abstractions provided by Rialto, in conjunction with the (local) resource planning modules, provide a simple, yet effective means by which successful resolutions to difficult resource allocation problems can be achieved.

Kevin Jeffay of the University of North Carolina presented the final full paper which described an approach to real-time computing that defines application timeliness requirements in terms of execution rates – which is translated to the allocation of a given amount of computational resources, over a given interval of time. Included in this presentation was a description of some initial results of the application of this rate-based technique to a desktop teleconferencing application. The benefits of the proposed computing model included a straightforward method of expressing the timeliness behavior of applications, as well as a means for applications to dynamically adapt to changes in system resource availability.

In the first of the adjunct paper presentations, Chris Lindblad made some suggestions as to how operating systems could better provide support for multimedia applications. These suggestions were made from the perspective of the designer and implementer of a substantial, application-level, multimedia system (i.e., the VuSystem at MIT). The suggestions for operating systems support included a desire for additional resource availability feedback to the applications from the system, as well as for finer-grained processing control for applications.

Next, Guru Parulkar of Washington University presented a proposal for a new programming interface for I/O subsystems that provides support for multimedia applications in the form of reduced system overhead and improved application performance. The proposed operating system enhancements focussed on the creation of mechanisms to reduce (or better manage) the number of system calls, interrupts, and instances of memory-to-memory copy operations involved in each instance of I/O.

Finally, Hiroshi Kitamura of NEC discussed his interest in high-performance network interfaces, his analysis of TCP performance that led to the observation that memory copying incurs a significant cost, and his experience with an implementation of a zero-copy TCP interface on an OC-3 ATM network. The results presented supported the view that zero-copy TCP implementations can provide performance gains (where packet checksums need not be computed in software).

Broadly speaking, the round-table discussions centered on issues related to interactions between the application and the operating system, the problem of maintaining a connection between user-level views of quality of service and system-level resource allocation decisions, and the nature of user expectations and their impact on system software.

A Computational and Engineering View
on
Open Distributed Real-Time Multimedia Exchange

Peter Leydekkers[1,3],Valérie Gay[2] and Leonard Franken[3]

[1]TINA - Core Team, 331, Newman Spring Rd, Bellcore, Red bank, NJ 07701, USA
[2]Université Paris VI, Laboratoire MASI, 4, place Jussieu, 75252 Paris Cedex 05 - France
[3]PTT Research, P.O. Box 15000, 9700 CD Groningen - The Netherlands

Abstract. *An important requirement for distributed multimedia applications is the support of real-time communication and the means to specify real-time aspects. The aim of this paper is to extend RM-ODP and TINA-C computational and engineering views on distributed systems for the specification and support of real-time communication. It is expected that these bodies have a major impact in the area of distributed processing. However, concepts and mechanisms to support real-time communication are not yet fully included or detailed in these standards. In particular this paper addresses Quality of Service (QoS) specifications for continuous dataflows. These QoS specifications are described from the ODP computational and engineering viewpoint and the repercussions of these QoS specifications for functions located in both the computing and telecommunications environment are discussed.*

Keywords. Distributed Multimedia Architectures, QoS, ODP, TINA-DPE

1. Introduction

In the near future, distributed multimedia applications such as video-on-demand and multimedia conferencing services will operate in a Distributed Processing Environment (DPE). The DPE is a distributed platform that offers important properties such as heterogeneity and distribution transparency. In a distributed environment heterogeneity may include: equipment heterogeneity due to a multi-vendor environment, operating system heterogeneity due to different operational contexts (office, factory), and authority heterogeneity (e.g. co-operation between separate network providers).

In a distributed multimedia context, an important requirement for the DPE is the provision of real-time communication and the means to specify real-time aspects for distributed applications. This paper addresses this real-time communication aspect from both the ODP computational and engineering viewpoint. It is closely aligned to RM-ODP, TINA and OMG since it is expected that these 'standardisation' bodies will have a major impact in the area of distributed processing. However, in the area of multimedia communication these 'standardisation' bodies have some weak points:

– They do not specify a complete language to specify real-time interaction at the computational level. OMG defines a language which is used as a basis by TINA-C and RM-ODP but it does not incorporate the streams concept that is used to model continuous dataflows which is essential for real-time multimedia communication. They also do not provide a language to specify the non-functional properties of objects. In particular QoS specifications are required for stream interfaces to guarantee real-time multimedia communication.

- They do not provide (complete) mapping rules to relate a computational real-time specification to an engineering configuration which can be executed.
- Concerning the engineering configuration, even if their architecture is flexible enough to integrate the functionalities required by the real-time application, there is still the need for further research to define and design the functions required for an open real-time platform.

This paper addresses these issues using the TINA DPE platform as a basis and proposes solutions for real-time multimedia communication based on concepts defined in RM-ODP.

2. TINA-DPE and RM-ODP

The Telecommunications Information Networking Architecture Consortium (TINA-C) is a world-wide initiative that consists of members from the computer industry, telecommunication network operators and telecommunication vendors. TINA-C is defining an open architecture which will enable the rapid deployment of telecommunication services. The TINA-architecture is based on techniques such as object-orientation and distributed computing and it uses as much as possible concepts and standards from both the telecommunication and computing area. One of the main goals of TINA-C is to define a platform that supports the execution of distributed telecommunication applications. This platform is called the TINA Distributed Processing Environment (TINA-DPE).

In this paper we present two views on the TINA-DPE as shown in Figure 1, i.e. a computational view and engineering view. These viewpoints are derived from RM-ODP [1] and adopted by TINA. RM-ODP identifies five viewpoints from which a distributed system can be described. However, the computational, engineering and technology viewpoint are of primary interest for the specification of real-time multimedia exchange in a distributed environment.

The *ODP computational view* on the TINA-DPE (upper plane in Figure 1) specifies a distributed application in terms of computational objects that interact with each other in a distribution transparent way. A computational object provides a set of services that can be used by other objects. To enable other objects to access a service, an object offers a computational interface which is the only means by which other objects can use the service thereby providing data encapsulation. Complexities introduced by the distribution can be hidden from applications in this view on the TINA-DPE. This can be done using transparencies which are used to hide aspects of systems that arise through their distribution. The applications using the DPE platform may select those transparencies they need and handle other aspects of distribution characteristics as they want. The DPE platform supports, for instance, location transparency which implies that applications are not concerned with communication aspects and on which nodes the (computational) objects are located. This implies for example that applications that interact with each other do not need to be aware of the physical locations of each other.

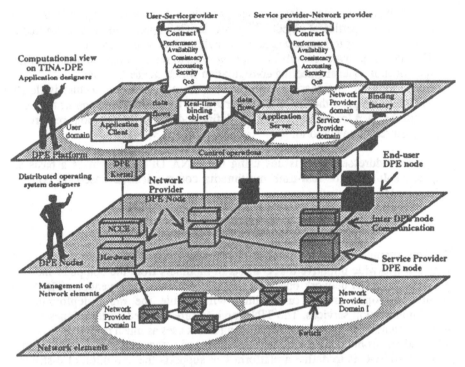

Fig.1. TINA Distributed Processing Environment

For computational objects to interact in a meaningful way the specification of well-defined interfaces in TINA and *contracts* are important. A contract can be specified between objects describing the agreed non-functional properties which should be observed in order for the application to operate properly. Several contract classes exist addressing different issues (e.g. security or accounting) but in this paper we focus on the *QoS contract* in relation with real-time interaction for continuous flows such as audio and video. A QoS contract provides a specification of the service provided and 'level of service' agreed between the involved computational objects.

The *ODP engineering view* and corresponding engineering language describe the mechanisms and functions required to support distributed execution and interaction between (computational) objects. The ODP engineering view on the TINA-DPE (middle plane in Figure 1) shows a collection of *DPE nodes*, a user node, service provider node and a network provider node each having different characteristics. A DPE node provides the mechanisms to support distribution transparency as assumed in the computational view and hides the native computing and communication environment from the application designer. For applications to be capable of interoperating with applications on the other DPE nodes there should be a (minimum) agreed set of functionality that is available on each DPE node.

A DPE node is composed of three parts, i.e. the DPE kernel, the Native Computing and Communications Environment (NCCE) and Hardware. The *DPE kernel* is a software layer that is available on each DPE node. It is a software layer between the local operating system and application components. It provides a set of basic functions such as communication, storage and processing capabilities. The *NCCE* describes the local operating system and basic communication functions that are used by the DPE kernel. The *Hardware* describes the devices and hardware resources available on a DPE node. The description of the hardware and NCCE is part of the ODP technology view on a system and is often vendor specific.

The network provider provides communication services (bottom plane in Figure 1) to interconnect the user and service providers that are geographically distributed. The network provider has access to and controls the network elements for the purpose of set-up, release and maintenance of network connections. Network elements represent the resources in the telecommunication network and consist of elements such as switches, cross-connects and video-bridges.

It is worth noting that the elements in the DPE platform plane and DPE node plane in Figure 1 need not to have a one-to-one relation. Computational objects in the DPE platform plane may correspond to one or multiple (engineering) objects in the DPE node plane and may also be distributed over multiple DPE nodes.

3. Computational view on real-time exchange

Focusing on the computational view on the DPE (upper plane of Figure 1) real-time aspects are mainly reflected in the ODP computational concepts of *stream interface, explicit binding object* and *environment contract* [1]. Stream interfaces are used for objects to exchange real-time continuous data (e.g. voice, video). For real-time exchange it is important to be able to specify QoS as part of the binding between computational objects (interfaces). QoS properties can be specified in a static way by means of declarations attached to the object and its stream interfaces (expressed in an environment contract).

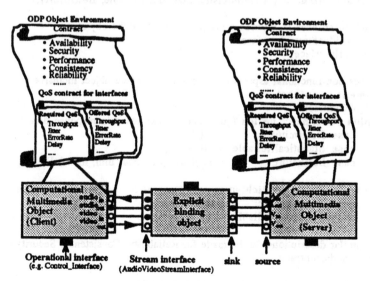

Fig. 2. Object environment contract, stream interface and binding object

In a dynamic way QoS properties are handled by the *explicit stream binding* process. Figure 2 highlights and relates the computational concepts of concern for real-time specifications.

3.1 Static specification of real-time exchange

The stream interface concept in RM-ODP can be used to describe continuous flows that have tight real-time constraints. Stream interfaces represent a communication end-point that may be a source or sink of continuous flows. Stream interfaces are described in detail in [9] using the TINA-ODL (Object Definition Language) specification language. TINA-ODL is an extension of OMG-IDL (Interface Definition Language) [11] that enables to express telecommunication and multimedia oriented computational specifications. Based on the syntax template for stream interfaces as proposed in [9], a simplified TINA-ODL specification for a multimedia computational object is shown in Table 1 and the related stream interface specification in Table 2.

A *computational object template* [1] comprises a set of computational interface templates which the object can instantiate, a behaviour specification and an environment contract specification.

The QoS specification is inspired on [4] which allows the separate specification of the guarantee level required for each QoS parameter. In general, three classes of guarantee level are identified, i.e., deterministic, statistical reliable and best effort. For each guarantee level this results in different commitment specification of the QoS parameter.

```
object template Computational_MultiMedia_Object;
typedef enum guarantee { Deterministic, StatisticalReliable, BestEffort};

supported interfaces /* interfaces that are offered by the object. */
        AudioVideoStreamInterface;
        ControlInterface;

/* Describes non-functional aspects that apply to the whole object inclusive interfaces. */
environment  contract
 struct QoSContract {
        union Performance switch (guarantee) {/*expressed in response time in seconds*/
            case Deterministic:      real Peak;
            case StatisticalReliable: real Mean;
            case BestEffort:          struct interval {real min, max;} Bound;
        };
        union Availability switch(guarantee){/*expressed in mean time between failure*/
            case Deterministic:      real Peak;
            case StatisticalReliable: real Mean;
        };
        /* similar descriptions can be made for Reliability, Consistency, Security etc. */
 }      multimediacontract;

behaviour /* describes the behaviour of the object */
```

Table 1. TINA-ODL specification of a MultiMedia terminal object template

A *computational stream interface template* consists of a finite *set of action templates*, one for each flowtype in the stream interface. Each action template for a flow contains the name of the flow, the information type of the flow and an indication of causality for the flow since flows are unidirectional (producer or consumer but not both), a *behaviour* specification and an *environment contract* specification.

```
interface template AudioVideoStreamInterface;
typedef struct VideoFlowType {...};  /*A VideoFlowType describes the characteristics
of video and attributes are e.g. codingtype, resolution, colordepth. */
typedef struct AudioFlowType {...};/*AudioFlowType  characteristics are e.g
                                   compressiontype, samples/s. See [9] for details. */

typedef enum guarantee { Deterministic, StatisticalReliable, BestEffort};
environment contract
   struct StreamQoS {
      union Throughput switch (guarantee) /* expressed in samples/s or frames/s */
         case Deterministic:       real Peak;
         case StatisticalReliable: real Mean;
         case BestEffort:          struct interval {real min, max;} Bound;
      };
      union Jitter switch (guarantee) /* expressed in samples/s or frames/s */
         case Deterministic:       real Peak;
         case StatisticalReliable: real Mean;
      };
      /* similar definitions for Delay and Errorrate */
   } requiredVideoQoS, requiredAudioQoS, offeredVideoQoS, offeredAudioQoS;

sink    display        VideoFlowType with requiredVideoQoS;
sink    speaker        AudioFlowType with requiredAudioQoS;
source  camera         VideoFlowType with offeredVideoQoS;
source  microphone     AudioFlowType with offeredAudioQoS;

behaviour /* This part describes the behaviour of this AudioVideoStreamInterface */
```

Table 2. TINA-ODL specification of a Audio video stream interface template

In RM-ODP the *environment contract* concept can be used to specify the QoS attributes of a computational object and its interfaces (Table 1, 2). The values in an environment contract are specified between a set of objects which are possibly located in different domains (Figure 1). Such a contract provides a specification of the service provided and of the 'level of service' agreed between the involved objects. It expresses the requirements and obligations which have to be fulfilled and it addresses issues such as the performance, availability, and security aspects of the objects and indications of behaviour which invalidates the contract (e.g. severe QoS-degradation). An environment contract between computational objects is determined during the set-up phase. QoS negotiation is possible during this phase and once agreement is achieved the QoS values can be monitored by a QoS manager.

Based on this contract, specific object environment contracts can be determined for each involved computational object (Figure 2). For each interface a contract is specified. We distinguish between *offeredQoS* contract (i.e. for outgoing flows) and *requiredQoS* contract (i.e. for incoming flows) for stream interfaces since the QoS requirements may be different for each flow [13].

The offeredQoS specifies the values by which the stream interface will transfer its output to other objects. These parameters are described in the QoScontract of the AudioVideoStreamInterface (Stream_QoS in Table 2). The requiredQoS specification is similar to the offeredQoS specification and represents how the object expects frames or packets to be delivered at its input.

The guarantee level agreed should be obeyed by the object. Three classes of service commitment are distinguished, deterministic, statistical and best effort. If the object can not maintain the agreed service commitment the involved objects should be informed.

3.2 Dynamic specification of real-time exchange

In addition to the specification of stream interfaces and QoS contracts, it is important to check the compatibility of stream interfaces prior to data exchange and the ability to express some real-time control on the set of stream interfaces that are bound.

The *binding object* is a suitable ODP concept to describe these aspects of real-time exchange. It represents an end-to-end association between two or more computational objects. The binding object is used to abstract over end-to-end connections and is responsible for compatibility checks between the stream interfaces (in particular the non-functional aspects such as QoS). It provides several operational control interfaces for monitor and control purposes during the exchange of continuous media. These control interfaces may be used by other computational objects such as the QoS manager (Figure 3).

A binding object is of a certain type that defines its configuration possibilities and its characteristics. Its type influences the engineering configuration and in [2] an example is described of a 'multiparty' binding object. In this paper, we consider a *real-time stream binding object*.

Figure 3 shows an example of an explicit binding action to create a real-time binding between three computational objects similar to the configuration shown in Figure 1. In our example, the server object interacts with the binding factory object. It asks for the creation of a binding object of type 'real-time' to link and control three stream interfaces, each of them having non-functional parameters specified. The binding factory creates the real-time stream binding object to enable the data exchange necessary for the binding. The binding object is an abstraction of the connection(s) set-up in the telecommunication network (lowest plane in Figure 1). The binding factory functionalities are compatible with those supported by Communication Session Manager as described in TINA and Eurescom P.103 [12].

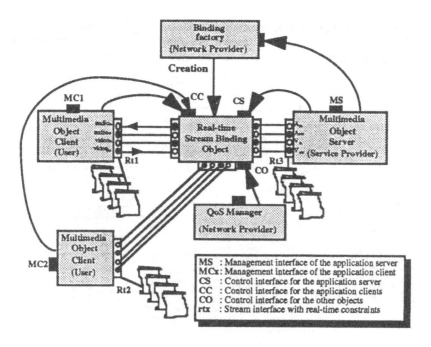

Fig. 3. Binding process

Client and server stream interfaces are linked and controlled by a real-time stream binding object and exchange of data is now possible. The binding object has several control interfaces used by the application server (CS), the application clients (CC) and other computational objects (CO). The CO interface will be used for example by the QoS manager (owned by a network provider) to monitor the network QoS and to initiate operations (e.g. QoS-renegotiation) in case of QoS contract violations. The binding object may also invoke signal operations on the clients and servers to notify particular events (e.g. synchronisation events). The binding object should provide the QoS guarantees between the interacting interfaces as described in the QoS environment contract.

4. Engineering view on real-time exchange

In the engineering view (Figure 1 middle plane) functions and mechanisms are identified which are required to support real-time stream communication. Many functions of a DPE node are derived from RM-ODP. RM-ODP contains general descriptions of functions fundamental to the construction of ODP systems (like the TINA DPE), but it does not define detailed mechanisms for these functions. The functions defined in RM-ODP are management, co-ordination, repository and security functions [1].

In general, each DPE *node* contains a *nucleus* that co-ordinates processing, storage and communication functions for use by other engineering objects within the node to which it belongs (Figure 4). Engineering objects (e.g. Video object, QoS manager) are grouped into a *capsule* which is a configuration of objects forming a single unit for processing and storage. Functionalities such as capsule creation, deletion and checkpointing are supported by the capsule manager. The ODP *channel* concept [1] provides engineering mechanisms that enable communication between engineering objects that are either located in the same DPE node or on a remote DPE node.

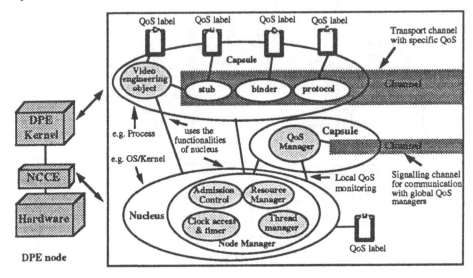

Fig. 4. RM-ODP engineering view on a DPE node

For the support of real-time multimedia exchange, specialisation is required (e.g. thread manager) and additional functions are needed to be included such as QoS management and resource management (section 4.2).

4.1 Computational QoS contract related to engineering QoS labels

The computational QoS specification provides an abstract expression of QoS which does not make any reference to engineering or technology mechanisms. A translation has to be made onto the engineering configuration that realises the QoS aspects as specified in the (computational) contracts. A computational QoS specification covers both the end-to-end aspects as well as the QoS aspects of the end systems DPE node. To check if the suitable amount of resources from the nucleus are allocated to the capsules we introduce *QoS labels* to guide the allocation process. The labels describe the QoS aspects of the engineering components. The values of the QoS labels specify the available capacity of the nucleus, and the required capacity by the capsules. The QoS labels associated to the channel objects guide the allocation of communication resources in order to realise the required throughput, delay and jitter [6].

For example, the specification of throughput expressed by the number of frames/sec in the computational QoS contract will be translated to throughput in Mbit/s for the protocol object and compression/decompression speed of the stub object in the engineering viewpoint. Furthermore, the video engineering object needs per invocation (for the processing of a frame) a number of milliseconds on a certain CPU type located in the nucleus. It is important to realise that a computational QoS parameter may influence several QoS parameters in the engineering viewpoint. The computational throughput can be derived from the combination of engineering objects using queuing theory or operations research [7], [8].

The check if the engineering objects can fulfil the required throughput depends on the capacities available of the hardware components such as CPU, memory, storage and communications. These descriptions should be expressed in a technology viewpoint description of the system.

The approach described above is in its initial stage and subject to future work in TINA-C.

4.2 Functions required for real-time support

The DPE node that deals with real-time dataflows accounts for several functions that can monitor and control the resources available on a DPE node.

The *resource manager* should be available on each DPE node and has a view of the available resources on a particular DPE node (CPU, memory, etc.). In case of a network provider DPE node it has an overview of the network resources available that are located in his domain. Resource allocation is based on special mechanisms which might be different for each DPE node. In general resource allocation for the object is based on the object's *QoS labels* and the computational QoS contract. Especially for real-time services it is important to have strict resource management policies so that real-time QoS contracts can be not only met at service instantiation but also during the life-time of the service.

The *QoS manager* checks if the DPE node can and, will fulfil the computational contracts as agreed. The QoS manager uses monitoring and control functions to perform its task. It requests the resource manager for certain resources (e.g. buffer, CPU-time, Audio-device etc.) that can be allocated to a particular application. The QoS manager in the DPE node uses the QoS labels to check if the specified contract can be realised. Global QoS managers have the task to check if the computational contracts between user and service provider can be met in relation to the network provider.

The *Node management* function manages the threads in a DPE node. Several threads will be active to deal with real-time flows on a DPE node. (In general for each flow a separate thread will be running since the devices are located in different capsules [9]). Due to the timeliness of these flows, threads have to be scheduled in some manner to satisfy the timeliness constraint. Customised *thread scheduling* algorithms can be used for real-time exchange. Pre-emptive scheduling is most appropriate for real-time flows, where a running thread can be stopped and another thread allowed to run. Different pre-emptive policies can be applied such as First In First Out, Round Robin or Time-sharing [14].

Admission control functions are needed to decide whether new (engineering) objects can be executed without offending the existing QoS contracts that are already established for other objects running on the DPE node. The admission control functions have a different scope for each type of DPE Node. In case of an end-user DPE node the admission control checks the CPU, memory and devices that are in use and makes decisions upon this workload. For a network provider DPE node the admission control function checks the workload of the network elements, available bandwidth etc. The allocation policy of network resources should be in accordance to the guarantee level that is requested for the binding (i.e. statistical, best effort or deterministic).

As indicated above different engineering configurations will exist depending on the concerned operating environment. For instance, the DPE kernel of an end-user DPE node will have different mechanisms described for its QoS managers than the network provider DPE node.

5. Conclusion

From the computational viewpoint, this paper describes how the RM-ODP concept of environment contract can be used to specify real-time requirements for objects and interfaces. It also shows how real-time requirements are handled by a real-time stream binding object. The approach described in this paper to assign an environment contract to each flow can also be applied to operational interfaces. We suggest to extend OMG-IDL with the concept of *stream interface* and *environment contract* since they are important for the specification of applications operating in a telecommunications environment. An outline is given of QoS specifications using the computational environment contracts. Further work is needed to complete the specifications and to provide 'standard' contract environment descriptions which can then be used to specify the non-functional aspects of distributed applications.

A lot of open issues still remain and future work is needed how to make the appropriate QoS translation from a computational to an engineering specification. This translation is very complex since it also depends on the engineering configuration of objects that represent a computational object. With respect to QoS this paper presents the first ideas of relating computational QoS specifications to engineering objects and associated engineering QoS labels. In order to enable the mapping, QoS labels have to be refined for all engineering objects and functions.

In the engineering view, we added several engineering functions necessary for DPE nodes that need to deal with real-time multimedia applications. It shows how they fit in the RM-ODP and TINA-C engineering view on distributed systems. Future work remains to be done to describe the functions in the context of ODP standardisation. This paper may serve as an input for the RM-ODP standardisation group on the work item 'QoS in Open Distributed Processing'.

6. References

1.   Basic Reference Model of Open Distributed Processing:
      'Part 2: Foundations (IS)', ITU/T X.902-ISO 107046-2.
      'Part 3: Architecture (IS)', ITU/T X.903-ISO 107046-3. February 1995.

2.   V. Gay, P. Leydekkers, R. Huis in 't Veld, *'Specification of Multiparty Audio and Video Interaction Based on the Reference Model of Open Distributed Processing'*, Computer Networks and ISDN Systems - Special issue on RM-ODP, 1995.

3.   K. Nahrstedt, R. Steinmetz, *'Resource Management in Multimedia Networked Systems'*, submitted to IEEE Computer, Special issue on Multimedia, April '95.

4.   A. Campbell, G. Coulson, D. Hutchison, *'A Quality of Service Architecture'*, ACM SIGCOMM, Computer Communication Review, June 1994.

5.   R. Gopalakrishna, G. Parulkar, *'Efficient QoS Support in Multimedia Computer Operating Systems'*, Washington university report WUCS_TM_94_04, August 94.

6.   L.J.N. Franken and B.R.H.M. Haverkort, *'The Performability Manager'*, IEEE Network: The Magazine of Computer Communications, Special Issue on Distributed Systems for Telecommunications, volume 8, 1994

7.   L.J.N. Franken and R.H. Pijpers and B.R. Haverkort, *'Modelling Aspects of Model Based Dynamic QoS Management by the Performability Manager'*, In Lecture Notes in Computer Science, Springer-Verlag, Volume 794, Proceedings of the 7th International Conference on Computer Performance Evaluation. Modelling Techniques and Tools, Vienna, Austria, 1994

8.   L.J.N. Franken, P. Janssens, B.R.H.M. Haverkort and E.P.M. Van Liempd, *'Quality of Service Management in Distributed Systems using Dynamic Routation'*, Proceedings of ICODP'95, Brisbane Australia, February 1995.

9.   A.T. van Halteren, P. Leydekkers, H.B. Korte, *'Specification and Realisation of Stream interfaces for the TINA-DPE'*, Proceedings of TINA'95 Conference, Melbourne Australia, p.299-312, February 1995.

10.   M. Jacobs, P. Leydekkers, *'Specification of Synchronisation in Multimedia Conferencing Services using the TINA Life-Cycle Model*, Proceedings of SDNE'95, Whistler Canada, June 1995.

11.   The Common Object Request Broker: Architecture and Specification, OMG Document Number 91.12.1, Draft edition, December 1991.

12.   M. Zweiacker (editor), *'Network Resource Model'*, Eurescom Project P103, Technical report 7, December 1994.

13.   J.B. Stefani, *'Computational Aspects of QoS in an object-based, distributed systems architecture'*, 3rd International Workshop on Responsive Computer Systems, Lincoln, NH, USA, September 93.

14.   M. Kudela, K. MacKinnon, *'Engineering Modelling Concepts (DPE Kernel Specification)'*, TINA document TR_KMK.001_1.1_94, restricted distribution, November 1994.

Support for User-Centric
Modular Real-Time Resource Management
in the Rialto Operating System

Michael B. Jones, Paul J. Leach, Richard P. Draves, Joseph S. Barrera, III

Microsoft Research, Microsoft Corporation
One Microsoft Way, Building 9S/1
Redmond, WA 98052

mbj@microsoft.com, paulle@microsoft.com, richdr@microsoft.com, joebar@microsoft.com

Abstract. This paper describes ongoing investigations into algorithms for user-centric modular distributed real-time resource management. These investigations are being conducted in the context of the Rialto operating system – an object-based real-time kernel and programming environment currently being developed within Microsoft Research.

A primary goal of this research is to develop appropriate real-time programming abstractions to allow multiple independent real-time programs to dynamically coexist and share resources on the same hardware platforms. Use of these abstractions is intended both to allow individual applications to reason about their own resource requirements and for per-machine system resource planner applications to reason about and control resource allocations between potentially competing applications. The set of resources being managed is dynamically extensible, and may include remote resources in distributed environments. The local planner conducts resource negotiations with individual applications on behalf of the user, with the goal of maximizing the user's perceived utility of the set of running applications with respect to resource allocations for those applications.

1. The Need for User-Centric Modular Real-Time Resource Management

One of our major research goals for the Rialto operating system is to investigate programming abstractions that make it possible for multiple independent real-time applications to dynamically coexist and share resources on the same hardware platforms. In particular, just as it is possible to today to purchase or write time-sharing applications that successfully coexist with other time-sharing applications, we are researching a real-time software architecture that is intended to make it possible to purchase or write real-time applications that can successfully coexist both with other real-time applications and time-sharing applications. Furthermore, the techniques we are developing are designed to be applicable not just for single-machine applications, but also to distributed applications that make use of remote resources through remote object invocations.

To be usable in a tractable fashion, it is our belief that resource management must be *modular*. By this, we mean that it should be possible to write and use software components (classes, modules, libraries, etc.) that have real-time resource requirements as components of larger real-time modules or programs without having to understand their implementations in order to reason about their real-time resource requirements. This allows the traditional benefits of modularity (abstract interfaces, information hiding, the ability to reimplement, etc.) to be carried forward into real-time programming.

As well as applying to software components, we believe that this kind of modularity of resource requirements must also extend to entire real-time applications. This allows a system *resource planner* application to reason about and participate in overall resource allocations between applications, just as an application can reason about its own internal resource requirements. The planner makes resource allocation decisions between applications on behalf of the user with the goal of maximizing the user's perceived utility of the set of running applications with respect to resource allocations for those applications.

2. The Problem Being Solved

This paper focuses on one aspect of the real-time programming model provided by and used within the Rialto operating system. This aspect is:

- An extensible modular distributed real-time resource-management scheme. This scheme allows programs to reason about their own real-time resource needs and negotiate for resource reservations based on those needs. It also allows a system resource planner to arbitrate between applications' resource requests on behalf of the user.

2.1 Research Context

This research is being conducted in a larger context of real-time systems work. While not the focus of this paper, it is nonetheless useful to have an overview of this larger systems context so as be able to better understand our resource management strategy. Other features integral to the programming model are:

- A constraint-based real-time scheduler. Time constraints contain a deadline, a time estimate, and an earliest start time. The scheduler notifies the application if a constraint is unlikely to be met, providing for proactive load shedding in cases of transient overload. Actual time taken is reported back to the application, providing the basis for a realistic real-time feedback mechanism. This is a simplification of the mechanism described in [Jones 93].
- An object invocation mechanism that propagates a thread's real-time scheduling constraints to remote object invocations, both to remote processes and to remote machines. (The object invocation mechanism is a real-time implementation of the Component Object Model (COM), the invocation mechanism used by OLE2 [Microsoft 94].) Taken together, these three facilities enable a consistent end-to-end treatment to be applied to real-time scheduling decisions.
- An I/O system that also schedules I/O operations using the same real-time scheduling constraints.

- A set of I/O and RPC abstractions designed to avoid data copies when transmitting and operating on large quantities of data. This mechanism is derived from Fbufs [Druschel & Peterson 93].

2.2 The Rialto Approach

Resource management can be viewed as a generalization of admission control. Unlike CPU or I/O scheduling decisions, resource management decisions occur infrequently – typically at program startup, exit, or mode change. Programs negotiate for the resources needed to operate on an ongoing basis in a given mode, and then operate in that mode until either exiting or changing modes.

The Rialto programming model is designed to permit incremental development and refinement of the resource management code used by real-time programs. First, the application can be developed (or ported) and its gross real-time resource needs determined. Next, resource management calls can be added to cover the gross real-time resource requirements of the application, which is still a relatively non-invasive change. Finally, real-time scheduling constraints can be added to fine-tune the behavior of critical sections of code in the application.

The model carefully separates mechanisms and policies. This allows varied or dynamic resource management policies to be used without modifying applications.

We intend to use this flexibility to implement user-centric, rather than application-centric, resource management policies. By user-centric, we mean that they attempt to dynamically maximize the user's perceived utility of the entire system, rather than the performance of any particular application. We expect this to lead to policies which focus on maximizing expected normal-case resource utilization, rather than always limiting resource allocations to account for worst-case behavior.

3. Resource Management Design

This section describes our approach to modular real-time resource management, giving examples to help clarify how it would be used in practice.

3.1 Resource Management Abstractions

The following abstractions are used by our approach to real-time resource management:

- **Resource:** A limited hardware or software quantity provided by a specific machine. Individual resources might include CPU time, memory, I/O bus bandwidth, network bandwidth, devices such as video frame buffers and sound cards, or higher-level software-defined resources, which may themselves manage or use other resources.

- **Resource Amount:** An abstraction representing a quantity of a specific resource. This is represented by a number between zero and one, with one representing 100% of a particular resource. Resource amounts are derived by resource providers (see below) from interface-specific quality-of-service specifications supplied by interface clients.

- **Resource Set:** A set of (resource, resource amount) pairs.

- **Activity:** The abstraction to which resources are allocated and against which resources usage is charged. Normally each distinct executing program or application would be associated with a separate activity. Activities may span address spaces and machines and may have multiple threads of control associated with them. Threads execute with rights granted by secured user credentials associated with their activity. Examples of tasks that might be executed as distinct activities are playing a studio-quality video stream, recording and transmitting video for a video-conferencing application, and recording voice input for a speech recognition system.

- **Resource Provider:** The object that manages a particular resource. Operations include allocating amounts of the resource to activities, performing resource accounting as the resource is used by activities, and notifying the resource planner of activities exceeding their resource allocations. The resource provider object would typically be implemented by the device driver that manages the physical resource, by the scheduler (which manages the CPU resource), by other parts of the system software (which manages other physical resources, such as memory), or by the module that implements software-defined resources.

- **Resource Planner:** A server that arbitrates access to the resources of a machine among different activities. Rather than reserving resources directly from the specific resource providers, applications negotiate for resources with the resource planner. The planner, at the conclusion of a successful resource negotiation, in turn contacts the resource providers to grant specific resource amounts to the requested activity, which can then use up to that amount.

  The planner's job is to implement the resource arbitration policy between competing activities. The expected policy goal is to maximize the user's perceived utility of the system as a whole – the policy is user-centric rather than application-centric. The planner makes all resource allocation policy decisions between activities (on behalf of the user); this allows for a clean separation between mechanism and policy.

- **Preferences:** Input from the user to the resource planner as to the desired behavior of the system and of particular applications. Preferences may be either retrieved from a database, or in extraordinary cases, obtained by directly querying the user. Example preferences include statements that a video-phone call should pause a movie unless it's being recorded and that video should be degraded before audio when all desired resources are not available.

These abstractions are designed to make it possible to reason about application and overall system behavior.

Abstractions

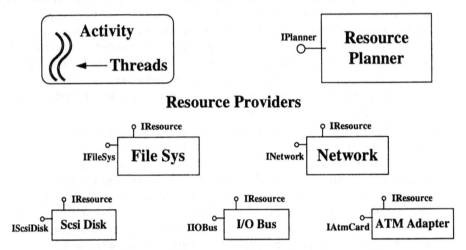

Figure 3-1: Resource Management Scenario

Figure 3-1 shows an activity that uses a set of abstract resources (file system, network) which themselves use other physical resources (SCSI Disk, I/O Bus, ATM Adapter). Exported interfaces are depicted as labeled circles. Note that software modules export both their usual functional interfaces, as well as resource manager interfaces. Also shown is the resource planner service. This scenario will be used to illustrate several aspects of resource management in later figures.

3.2 Modules and Resource Interfaces

Within our resource management framework, software components (classes, modules, libraries, etc.) that have real-time resource requirements provide interfaces exposing those requirements to clients of those components. This allows clients to query the module about the resources needed to perform the operations they will use, so that the client modules can, in turn, make their resource needs known to their clients.

For example, consider a module M which implements a network read operation. As well as exporting the network read operation, M would also export an operation for determining the resources needed to perform the network read on an ongoing basis. In particular, it would allow client modules C to ask M questions of the form: "What resources are needed to read N bytes every T time units" with the response being a resource set S enumerating the needed resources. In this instance, S might indicate an amount of CPU time, an amount of network bandwidth, an amount of bus bandwidth, and an amount of memory.

Note that resource queries are in terms of operations exported by the modules, and may contain whatever qualifications are necessary to sufficiently specify the operations being asked about. For instance, to accurately quantify the resources needed for a series of network reads, M might also need to know the source address from which the data would be read and might need to know acceptable jitter bounds.

58

If so, the corresponding resource query operation would accept this qualifying information as parameters.

Also, note that C, in general, does not (and need not) understand the contents of the resource set S. To determine their own resource requirements, client modules just add together the resources required by each of the modules (such as M) that they use, and add in any resources required for operations directly implemented in the client. Indeed, it is the fact that clients do not need to understand what resources are in a set returned from a resource query that makes the resource management scheme modular. Implementations may change to use different resources without requiring changes in clients.

This gives us a modular algebra for reasoning within a program about the program's resource requirements. As a starting point, resource providers are aware of and understand the resources needed to do their jobs. Client modules subsequently determine their own resource requirements in terms of those of the modules they use. Finally, this permits a program to determine its own resource requirements for the various modes of behavior which the program might choose to exhibit.

This ability for a program to reason about its own resource requirements forms a basis for it to negotiate for the these resources.

Translating Application Requirements to Resource Sets

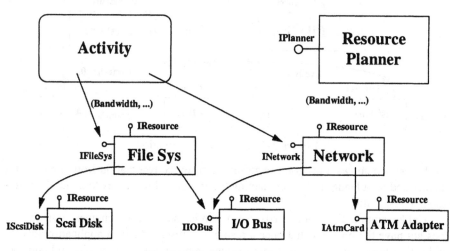

Figure 3-2: Resource Queries

Figure 3-2 shows resource queries being made by the program to its resource providers. Note that some of the providers themselves make queries to other resource providers as part of this process. Resource sets are returned in response to these queries.

3.3 Resource Negotiation

Once an application has determined what resources it will need (either through resource queries, as described above, or by consulting a database of cached resource requirements taken from past runs) it negotiates for those resources with the local resource planner. If the requested resource reservation is granted by the planner, the planner in turn contacts the resource providers on behalf of the program's activity and makes the actual resource reservations. At this point, the application is free to use at least the reserved amounts of the requested resources until such point as it is notified to the contrary by the resource planner.

If, however, the requested resource reservation cannot be granted, either due to conflicts with other programs or because of insufficient capacity, the planner will notify the application of this fact, telling it what quantities of the requested resources the program could successfully acquire. Then, the program either makes a modified resource request (probably based on reasoning about its own resource requirements for running in a different mode than originally negotiated for) or it may decide that there are insufficient resources to function in any mode, and will shut itself down.

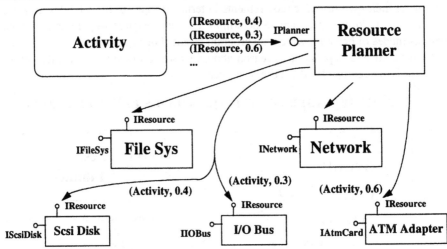

Figure 3-3: Resource Reservation

Figure 3-3 shows a program requesting a resource reservation from the resource planner and the planner in turn contacting the individual resources to make the actual resource reservations.

Unlike simple first-come first-served admission control schemes, our scheme does not have the property that once a resource is reserved for an application that the application is guaranteed at least that resource amount until it explicitly relinquishes it. We view this as an application-centric policy. Instead, we have opted for a user-centric policy – ideally the resource planner allocates resources among the competing applications in the way that provides the most perceived value to the user. (Of course, the planner *can* implement irrevocable reservation for some resources or some applications if it is deemed appropriate, but this is merely a special case of more flexible policies.) Design and implementation of these policies is an important area of future work.

Under our scheme, there are several different scenarios where resource re-negotiation may occur. First, a program may modify its own behavior or enter a new mode, causing its resource needs to change. In this case, the program contacts the resource planner to request that its resource reservations be revised.

Second, another program may have been started, may have exited, or may have changed its resource usage pattern. In this case, the planner may contact running programs, requesting that they modify their resource usage in specific ways (or notifying them that they may request more resources if they choose to do so).

Third, a resource provider may detect a persistent overload condition, at which point the resource provider would contact the resource planner making it aware of the activities that are exceeding their reservations.

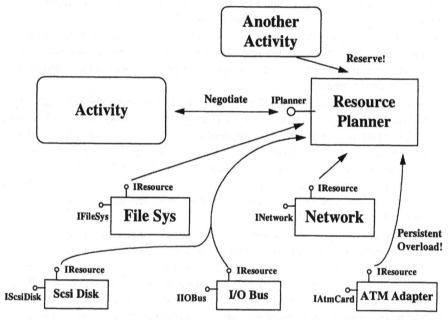

Figure 3-4: Resource Negotiation

Figure 3-4 depicts several scenarios under which resource re-negotiation may occur. First, a program may modify its own behavior or enter a new mode, causing its resource needs to change. Second, another program may have been started, at which point resources may be reallocated by the planner among existing activities. Third, a resource provider may detect a persistent overload condition, at which point it would contact the resource planner making it aware of the activities that are exceeding their reservations.

3.4 Distributed Resource Management

In our scheme, each resource is represented by a resource object that is registered with a resource planner that is (typically) running on the machine where the resource resides. Resource queries for locally implemented objects return references to local resource objects and resource reservation is done via the local resource planner. Thus, most resource management decisions require only local object invocations.

However, resource queries to remotely implemented objects will cause remote object invocations and will consequently return references to the remote resource objects needed to implement the requested service. Applications in general are not aware of which resources are local or remote, but the local resource planner is. If a reservation request is made to the local planner for remote resources, the planner forwards this portion of the request to the remote planner. Because the planners cooperate to transparently manage remote resource reservations, application resource management code is resource-location-independent.

3.5 Simplifying Assumptions

A number of simplifying assumptions underlie our resource management model. This section describes and motivates these assumptions.

- Linearity of resource amounts – For most resources this should be a reasonable approximation to reality when not close to overload. This assumption permits the resource planner to manage resource allocations without deep understanding of individual resources.

- Independence of resources – Like linearity, we believe this to be reasonably true for many resources. Where not true (for instance, reading from disk causes DMA, which can reduce effective processor speed) we may need to handle this at the resource provider level by explicitly modeling interdependencies (for instance, by also reserving some "CPU" time for DMA transfers). This assumption permits the resource planner to manage allocations of different resource independently (even though resource providers and consumers may be aware of the interdependencies).

- Application resource self-awareness – We believe that cost in complexity of having applications be aware of their own resource requirements and usage is reasonable in comparison to the benefits gained. This self-awareness permits applications to reason about their own behavior in the presence of different resource allocations. Note also that an incremental approach can be taken, adding refinements of resource awareness to a program on an as-needed basis.

One of the research goals of this work is identifying which simplifying assumptions yield reasonable results, and under what circumstances they hold.

4. Related Work

This section examines the relationships between this work and other related work.

Mercer [Mercer et al. 94] has advocated a "temporal protection" scheme in which enforcement of CPU and possibly other resource reservations is provided between competing programs. Our resource management strategy is largely independent of whether hard enforcement of resource usage is provided, but is compatible with it. Indeed, if both are present, resource amounts derived from resource negotiation would be used to choose the values used for resource enforcement.

Unlike Mercer, Compton and Tennenhouse believe that resource protection is inappropriate and that applications should dynamically and cooperatively shed load when necessary [Compton & Tennenhouse 93], but they bemoan the crude measures available for deciding when to shed load. Rather than shedding load reactively, our work provides a means for programs to cooperatively reason about their resources in advance, proactively avoiding most dynamic load shedding situations.

A number of mechanisms are currently being proposed for reserving network bandwidth and related resources such as RSVP [Zhang et al. 93] and a number of ATM-specific schemes. This work is complementary to such mechanisms. Indeed, one result of distributed resource negotiation can be using these mechanisms to allocate any network resources needed by the activity.

Anderson described a system for trading off buffer space and variabilities in network latency when delivering continuous media streams [Anderson 93]. The application resource self-awareness needed to analyze these tradeoffs is an example of the kind of self-awareness needed to be able to negotiate for and make tradeoffs among resources in our more general setting.

One important aspect of this work is that it provides a more flexible admission control scheme than the first-come first-served or priority schemes that are common today. Admission policy is controlled by the resource planner, which is able to redistribute resources among both existing applications and new applications in a user-centric rather than application-centric manner.

Finally, it should be stated that this work is intended to be complimentary to, and not a replacement for, algorithms which provide fine-grained CPU scheduling, whether classical priority-based schemes or more flexible schemes, such as those employed by Northcutt [Northcutt et al. 90, Wall et al. 92]. Even given sufficient resources, fine-grained scheduling decisions still must be made correctly to ensure that application deadlines are met.

5. Status

The Rialto operating system kernel, including its real-time constraint-based scheduler, has been implemented and is in use as a research testbed for a number of kinds of real-time applications. The implementation of resource management is under way. We expect to report initial results at the workshop.

6. Conclusions

This paper presents a design for modular resource management within and between applications. The set of resources managed is dynamically extensible and may include remote resources in distributed environments. The design carefully separates mechanisms and policies, allowing varied or dynamic resource management policies to be used without modifying applications. We intend to use this flexibility to implement user-centric, rather than application-centric, resource management policies.

While ambitious, we believe that the goals of this research are both attainable and practical. We believe that dynamic resource management will allow combinations of independently authored real-time applications to nonetheless coexist and be concurrently executed on the same platform. Resource management can be an enabling technology for a free market in independently authored real-time components and applications for widely available home multi-media information platforms.

References

[Anderson 93] D. P. Anderson. Metascheduling for Continuous Media. In *ACM Transactions on Computer Systems*, 11(3):226-252, August, 1993.

[Compton & Tennenhouse 93] Charles L. Compton and David L. Tennenhouse. Collaborative Load Shedding. In *Proceedings of the Workshop on the Role of Real-Time in Multimedia/Interactive Computing Systems*. IEEE Computer Society, Raleigh-Durham, NC, November 1993.

[Druschel & Peterson 93] Peter Druschel and Larry L. Peterson. Fbufs: A High-Bandwidth Cross-Domain Transfer Facility. In *Proceedings of the 14th ACM Symposium on Operating Systems Principles*. December, 1993.

[Jones 93] Michael B. Jones. Adaptive Real-Time Resource Management Supporting Modular Composition of Digital Multimedia Services. In *Proceedings of the Fourth International Workshop on Network and Operating System Support for Digital Audio and Video*, pages 11-18. Lancaster, U.K., November, 1993.

[Mercer et al. 94] Clifford W. Mercer, Stefan Savage, Hideyuki Tokuda. Processor Capacity Reserves: Operating System Support for Multimedia Applications. In *Proceedings of the IEEE International Conference on Multimedia Computing and Systems (ICMCS)*, May 1994.

[Microsoft 94] *OLE2 Programmer's Reference, Volume One*. Microsoft Press, 1994.

[Northcutt et al. 90] J. D. Northcutt, R. K. Clark, D. P. Maynard, and J. E. Trull. *Decentralized Real-Time Scheduling*. Final Technical Report to RADC, RADC-TR-90-182, School of Computer Science, Carnegie-Mellon University, August, 1990.

[Wall et al. 92] Gerald A. Wall, James G. Hanko, and J. Duane Northcutt. Bus Bandwidth Management in a High Resolution Video Workstation. In *Proceedings of the Third International Workshop on Network and Operating System Support for Digital Audio and Video*, pages 236-250. IEEE Computer Society, San Diego, CA, November, 1992.

[Zhang et al. 93] Lixia Zhang, Steve Deering, Deborah Estrin, Scott Shenker, and Daniel Zappala. RSVP: A New Resource ReSerVation Protocol. IEEE Network 7(5), Sept., 1993.

A Rate-Based Execution Abstraction For Multimedia Computing*

Kevin Jeffay, David Bennett
University of North Carolina at Chapel Hill
Department of Computer Science
Chapel Hill, NC 27599-3175 USA
{jeffay,bennettd}@cs.unc.edu

Abstract: Process models for multimedia computing must allow applications to adapt their pattern of execution as resources become scarce or abundant. As processes adapt, it is natural to express their desired performance in terms of a processing rate of application-defined data units or events. We propose a process model wherein processes execute according to a general rate specification of x process executions every y time units. In addition, a separate parameter is used to specify the desired response time for the completion of each execution. In all cases the real-time performance of a rate-based process is predictable. The model is general enough to encompass or extend many of the existing models proposed for multimedia systems. Our model of rate-based execution is described along with an implementation that detects when processes should adapt their execution rate and minimizes latency in interprocess communication.

1 . Introduction

To be effective, distributed multimedia applications require operating system support to ensure real-time, low latency acquisition, processing, delivery, and playout of audio and video streams. Within the domain of process management, numerous proposals have been made for thread and process models, scheduling algorithms, and IPC mechanisms for supporting multimedia computing [1-8]. From these discussions, several themes and preliminary requirements have emerged. These include:

- *Deterministic execution.* At some level, services must be provided for applications to execute in a predictable manner. This is typically manifested in guarantees of bounded response time to events (*e.g.*, interrupts, message arrivals), or in some form of periodic execution [2, 4, 5].

- *Adaptive resource management.* Processing and communications resources can become saturated in the face of the demands of multimedia applications. Mechanisms for allocating resources to processes must allow applications to dynamically alter their desired service parameters to optimize their execution for the current perceived state of the system [2, 6, 7, 8, 13]. (An implicit assumption here is that applications can provide acceptable user performance across a range of resource requirements.)

- *Feedback on actual performance.* To best adapt to changing execution conditions, applications must be able to determine their actual execution performance in terms of desired service parameters. Operating systems must

---

* This work supported by grants from the Intel and IBM corporations.

support a mechanism for an application-kernel dialog on performance parameters [2, 6, 7, 8].

- *Integrated resource allocation and IPC.* The real-time performance of an application should not be a function of its process structure. In principle, the guaranteed real-time performance of an application should be the same when the application is structured as a set of communicating sequential processes as when it is a single monolithic process. This implies that when processes communicate, either on a peer-to-peer or client-server basis, the desired service parameters of the initiator should be propagated to and inherited by, the recipient [1, 16]. This is to ensure, for example, that priority inversions do not occur in interprocess communication.

- *High-level specification of service parameters.* There is a general desire to allow applications to specify desired service parameters in a context that is removed from low-level operating system mechanisms (*e.g.*, priority) and ideally tied to application or system-level concepts such as a *capacity, utility* or *added value* function for real-time execution [2, 6].

In this note we describe a "new" process model based on the concept of *rate-based execution (RBE)* that addresses each of these requirements. In an *RBE* system, processes specify their desired rate of progress in terms of the number of events they desire to process in an interval of specified duration. Examples of rate specifications include processing two audio frames every 16.6 ms, one video frame every 33 ms, or 30 packets every second. Our *RBE* model is based on a formal resource allocation model that indicates both on-line scheduling and admission control algorithms to use. A process in an *RBE* system is guaranteed to make progress at at least its specified rate whenever work exists for the process. When insufficient resource capacity exists to admit an *RBE* process, the process can either negotiate with the operating system for a reduced rate of progress or wait for sufficient resources to become available. Resources can be made available in two ways. A user can explicitly reduce their performance expectations for an application and request an application to scale back its resource usage (*e.g.*, lower the frame rate of a videoconference). Alternatively, the operating system can request that a process reduce its resource requirements when the system perceives that the process is continually using less resources than they reserved.

We conjecture that the notion of processing rate is a natural and useful abstraction for multimedia systems. Our particular *RBE* model is general enough to encompass the majority of the traditional real-time task models based on periodic or sporadic tasks, as well as several of the models previously proposed for multimedia computing. Moreover, it also allows the specification and integration of soft- and non-real-time activities with hard-real-time activities. The model has been implemented in an experimental microkernel and is presently being ported to the Real-Time Mach kernel. Initial experiences with *RBE* indicate that it is easy to support and provides a simple but effective means for applications to communicate, monitor, and adapt their desired service. While not a panacea, we believe the *RBE* process model is a simple yet powerful paradigm of process execution that is suitable for generic real-time computing in general, and multimedia computing in particular.

In the following, we provide an overview of the *RBE* abstraction and briefly compare it to existing real-time and multimedia process models. We then discuss how *RBE* processes can be used to manage latency in applications and how *RBE* processes can adapt their execution rates as resources become scarce or abundant.

2. The Rate-Based Execution Concept

Our formulation of rate-based execution is designed to integrate three paradigms of repetitive real-time execution. The first is the concept of *software phased-locked loops* as embodied in the Synthesis Kernel [10]. Here the operating system monitors each process's event queue and uses a control theoretic scheduling policy to schedule the processes so as to minimize their event queue length. This mechanism has been demonstrated to execute processes in soft-real-time. Execution is soft-real-time in the sense that all resource allocation is best-effort and no guarantees of performance are possible. The second paradigm is the *linear-bounded arrival process (LBAP)* model as defined in the DASH system [5]. Here processes specify a desired execution rate as the number of messages to be processed per second and the size of a buffer pool used to store bursts of messages that arrive for the process. When *LBAPs* are independent it is possible to state conditions under which a collection of *LBAPs* will execute at their desired rate. The third paradigm is the *real-time producer/consumer (RTP/C)* process model used in the YARTOS kernel [11]. Here applications are expressed as networks of processes that execute in response to message arrivals. The arrival rate of messages is assumed to be uniform in that the difference between the expected message interarrival time and the minimum interarrival time is small. When this assumption holds it is possible to state conditions under which *RTP/C* processes will execute in real-time (each process will process each message before the next one arrives).

Our model of rate-based execution takes as its starting point the linear-bounded arrival process model and generalizes it to include a more generic specification of rate and adds an independent response time (deadline) parameter to enable more precise real-time control of the execution of *RBE* processes. An *RBE* process is described by three parameters:

- two rate parameters x and y, where x is a number of events to be processed and y is the length of an interval in which x events are expected to arrive.

- a response time parameter d which specifies the desired maximum elapsed time between the delivery of an event to a process and the completion of the processing of the event.

Informally, an *RBE* process (x, y, d) will execute at a rate sufficient to ensure that x events are consumed every y time units and that each event is processed within d time units after its arrival whenever possible. The actual execution rate of an *RBE* process is determined by the rate at which events are actually generated for the process. For example, if events are generated at the rate of no more than one every x/y time units or no more than x events are generated in any interval of length y then every event will be processed within d time units after its arrival. If events are generated at a higher rate (*e.g.*, an unanticipated burst of work arrives), then in the worst case these events will be processed as if they had arrived at the desired rate. (As is the case with unexpected bursts of work for *LBAPs* in DASH.)

More precisely, for all $j \geq 1$, if t_j is the arrival time of the jth event for an *RBE* process, then that event is guaranteed to be processed before a deadline of time $T(j)$, where

$$T(j) = \begin{cases} t_j + d & \text{if } 1 \leq j \leq x \\ MAX(t_j + d, T(j-x) + y) & \text{if } j > x \end{cases}$$

If events are generated at the rate of x events every y time units, then every event will be processed within d time units after its arrival. If events arrive at a faster rate then their guaranteed completion time is based on that for the x previous events and not (directly) on the parameter d.

We have developed a general theory of rate-based execution that gives conditions under which a set of *RBE* processes are guaranteed to execute in real-time [14]. Real-time here means that the jth event for an *RBE* process is guaranteed to be processed before time $T(j)$. The theory is used both by the operating system for admission control and by a programmer to understand which rate specifications are more likely to result in an admissible process when resources are scarce.

Beyond *LBAPs*, our model of rate-based execution is general enough to encompass traditional real-time process models. For example, when $x = 1$, events are separated in time by exactly y time units, and $d = y$, then the above reduces to the commonly held definition of a periodic task [9]. The primary distinction between a rate-based process and a periodic one is that in the rate-based case, no assumptions about the interarrival times of events are made or required (however, in any implementation of an *RBE* process, the set of allowable execution rates for a process would be limited by the number of event buffers available to the process). A secondary distinction between the two models is that for a rate-based process, no assumption is made about the distribution of processes' execution time within an interval of length y.

RBE processes can be used to emulate software phased-locked loops, however this is less a function of the *RBE* model *per se* and more a function of the implementation of the model. This is described next.

3. Supporting Rate-Based Execution

We have implemented *RBE* processes in the YARTOS (*Yet Another Real-Time Operating System*) kernel [4]. Here we describe three interesting aspects of the implementation: admission control, the use of *RBE* processes to manage end-to-end latency, and the paradigms and mechanisms used for adapting execution rate.

Programming Model and Admission Control

YARTOS supports a simple data-flow model of computation. Processes receive events, process them, and generate events for other processes. We distinguish between two types of *RBE* processes in YARTOS: *internal* and *source* processes. A source *RBE* process is a process that receives events directly from an external device.

Its rate parameters are the expected rate at which the device will generate work and are specified when the process is created. An internal *RBE* process is a process that receives events generated by other *RBE* processes. For example, a server process would be an internal *RBE* process. Internal *RBE* processes are created without a rate specification and at run-time (transitively) inherit the rate specification of their event generators. That is, at an internal process, the deadline for processing each event is computed using the rate specification of the event's generator. This inheritance of rate parameters is done to ensure that all internally generated events (and by transitivity, all externally generated events) are processed at the rates at which they are generated.

A source *RBE* process is created by specifying:

- a program to execute in response to event arrivals,

- an event type — an input descriptor (port) specifying the logical device that generate events for this process,

- a rate specification — the parameters x, y, and d,

- an optional event queue length — the number of buffers allocated for events,

- an execution cost — the estimated worst case execution time for processing an event,

- a rate adaptation callback — a function called by the kernel to suggest that the process either speed up or slow down.

There is an event queue for each source process that contains events to be processed. By default, for a process that executes at the rate of x events every y time units, the queue will have x entries. If events for this process are never generated at a higher rate than x events every y time units, then events will never be lost. If event generators (devices) are expected to be ill-behaved, then larger queues can be specified.

An internal *RBE* process is created by specifying:

- a program to execute in response to event arrivals,

- an event type — an input descriptor (port) specifying the other *RBE* process(es) that generate events for this process,

- an execution cost — the estimated worst case execution time for processing an event.

The port descriptors of processes are used by the kernel to construct a directed graph of interprocess communication that is used for admission control. When a new process is created a topological sort is performed on the graph and each internal process (an internal node in the graph) is assigned a rate equal to the sum of the rates of all its immediate predecessors in the graph. The resulting set of rate specifications along with the execution cost parameters of all processes are then used as input to the schedulability test described in [14]. If the result of the test is positive then the *RBE* process is created. If the result is negative then the creator must either reduce the rate specification (in the case of a source *RBE* process) or reduce the rate specification of a source *RBE* process that will generate events for the process to be created.

In general, two useful strategies for gaining admission of a rejected process are to (1) relax (lengthen) the response time parameter of either the process itself (for source processes), or that of a source *RBE* process that will generate events for the rejected process, or to (2) reduce execution rate of either the process or its event generators. When a process is rejected, the kernel can provide hints to the calling process in the form of possible reduced rates or relaxed response times.

Finally, we support non-real-time processing by allowing processes to be created with event queue lengths of zero. In this case the system will enqueue events for the process on a space-available basis and schedule the process so as to minimize its event queue length. As the event queue grows for an adaptive *RBE* process, the system increases the rate at which the process executes (if possible); as the queue shrinks, the rate is decreased. The size and frequency of rate manipulations is controlled by a simple control theoretic model borrowed from the Synthesis Kernel [10].

Minimizing Response Time

A second benefit to having internal processes inherit the rate specifications of their event generators is that it enables the kernel to minimize its guarantees of worst case response time for the processing of events that propagate through a chain of *RBE* processes.

Response time guarantees for event processing are based on the response time parameters of source *RBE* processes and are contingent upon the accuracy of the rate specifications of these processes. If a source *RBE* process S is admitted into the system with rate and response time parameters (x, y, d), then so long as events arrive at S no faster than x events every y time units, each event is guaranteed to be processed by S within d time units of its arrival.

The response time guarantees for internal *RBE* processes are determined as follows. If whenever S receives an event e, it generates an event e' for an internal *RBE* process I, then the processing of events e and e' is guaranteed to be completed within d time units of the arrival of e at S. That is, the worst case guaranteed response time for processing events that propagate through processes S and I is the same as the worst case guaranteed response time would be at a process S' that combined the functions of processes S and I and had *RBE* parameters (x, y, d). Thus, the guaranteed response time for an event that propagates through S and I is given by the response time parameter of S. In the general case, the worst case guaranteed response time for an event that propagates through a chain of *RBE* processes is not a function of the length of the chain; only of the response time parameter of the source *RBE* process at the head of the chain.

Note that strictly speaking, this technique of minimizing response time is orthogonal to the concept of rate-based execution. It has been applied to other non-rate-based systems [1, 16] and is related to the concept of priority inheritance. We have demonstrated, however, that it is also applicable in a rate-based framework. Minimizing response time is particularly important in a rate-based system as it is important to be able to control throughput and response time independently.

Adapting Execution Rate

Once admitted, *RBE* processes are guaranteed to execute at a rate that is sufficient to process their events in real-time. Here the interpretation of "real-time" is ultimately given by a set of rate specifications that describe the expected behavior of processes external to the computer. Whenever the external environment deviates significantly from these rate specifications, source *RBE* processes should adapt their execution rates to reflect the changes in the environment.

If work is being generated faster than a source *RBE* process's rate specification, its event queue will overflow and events will be lost. When an event queue overflows the system can use the source process's callback function to suggest that the process increase its execution rate. Rate adjustments are performed by the affected processes since the interpretation of a rate for each process is application dependent. Rate decreases are always accepted (provided that the response time parameter is not reduced), however, rate increases are subject to the admissibility test and thus are not guaranteed to succeed.

The system can monitor the execution rate of a source process by simply keeping a count of the number of times the process has been scheduled in the recent past (a system parameter). Whenever an *RBE* process cannot be admitted into the system, the kernel can check if there exists a source process with a rate specification that is higher than the rate at which work is currently being generated for the process (*i.e.*, the process is executing below its rate specification because of a lack of events). The process can be contacted and requested to reduce its rate specification. Since internal *RBE* processes are reactive, no mechanism is needed to adapt their execution rate.

These rate re-negotiations naturally handle the case where processes need to adapt the rate of input processing. A slightly different form of rate adaptation is required when output cannot be performed at a fast enough rate to satisfy *RBE* processes. For example, consider a videoconferencing system. At some point in time video frames may be generated by a camera at a faster rate than they can be transmitted across the network because of network congestion. The symptom of such a problem is the same as in the input case — a queue overflows — however, because of the way output must be handled in a real-time system, the queue is not an event queue.

In a predictable real-time system, it is not possible, in general, to synchronize individual output devices with input devices. For example, a video digitizer for NTSC video will generate one video frame every 33 ms. For an application such as videoconferencing, ideally one would like to transmit 1 video frame every 33 ms. However, on current local-area networks, one cannot guarantee that this will be possible at all times. Thus, given the variability of sustainable network transmission rates and the determinism of the NTSC video generation process, it is not possible to synchronize the camera with the network so that video frames are transmitted as they are generated. That is, events generated by the camera cannot be guaranteed to be processed by the network in real-time. Therefore, events generated by the camera cannot be treated as events for a network process.

Because of this (generic) inability to synchronize input and output devices, somewhere between the camera and the network there must exist a set of buffers that are written by a process whose execution rate is derived from events generated from the camera/digitizer (*e.g.*, vertical blanking interrupts) and read by processes whose execution rate is derived from events generated by the network (*e.g.*, transmission complete interrupts). (Operations on this buffer must be non-blocking to ensure response time guarantees are met.) It is this buffer that overflows when frames are produced faster than they can transmitted. Since this buffer cannot serve as the event queue for a network process, a separate mechanism is required to detect and respond to overflows of this buffer.

In general it is difficult to systematize these interactions. The buffer can either be constructed to return its current length when items are deposited or removed, in which case processes can learn of rate mis-matches themselves, or system processes (*e.g.*, device drivers) can be designed to report buffer overflows to the operating system which can in turn notify the appropriate processes.

Finally, applications themselves may choose to adapt their execution rates on their own. For example, a videoconferencing application that is able to sustain a sub-optimal frame transmission rate may attempt to increase the frame rate in hopes of producing a higher quality conference. Similarly, the application may receive application-level feedback from a conference receiver that data is being lost in the network and thus the application may elect to reduce its frame transmission rate [12].

4. Using Rate-Based Execution

Our *RBE* system has been used to re-implement a desktop videoconferencing system [12, 13]. The original system used a more traditional hard-real-time process model based on sporadic tasks [4]. In that system, events were required to have a minimum inter-arrival time in order to guarantee real-time performance. Since conferences spanned internetworks made up of existing local-area networks, it was not possible in general to guarantee that network packets containing conference data arrived at a receiver with a non-zero minimum interarrival time. Therefore, to ensure that packet processing did not consume all available processing cycles, the system effectively polled the network interface for packet arrivals using a variation of the periodic server concept [17].

There were two immediate benefits to using *RBE* processes in this application. First, the *RBE* system resulted in substantially lower latency media playout in times of severe network congestion. Figure 1 compares the latency of media playout in a simulated conference using *RBE* processes to read data from the network interface versus a periodic server. A trace of packet arrival times was recorded during an actual conference and used to simulate the arrival of events at conference receiver based on *RBE* processes and one using a periodic server and sporadic application tasks. Both systems were executed under a variety of system loads. The conference processes in both cases consumed approximately 25% of the processor. In the *RBE* system, the rate specification for the network's source process was 10 arrivals every 550 ms with a response time parameter of 550 ms. In the periodic server based system, the server executed with a period of 55 ms. No rate adaptation in the *RBE* system, and no period adaptation in the periodic server based system was used.

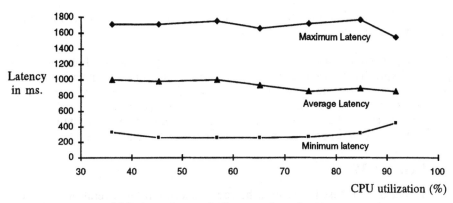

(a) Latency in a periodic server based system.

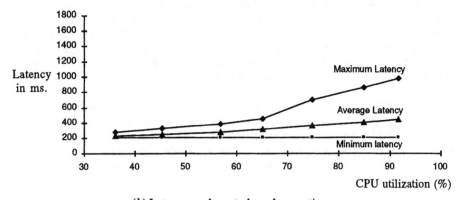

(b) Latency under rate-based execution.

Figure 1

The performance of the periodic server based system was consistent across system loads. Average latency was approximately 1 second with significant deviation. The relatively high latency is due to the fact that a periodic server can only serve its event queue at a constant rate. Thus, once a queue builds up, if work continues to arrive at the expected rate then the server can never work off its backlog of work. In this environment, there were several periods of bursty arrivals that led to the formation of a queue of packets at the server. In fact, the queue overflowed on several occasions resulting in approximately 4% of all packets being lost.

In the *RBE* system, the average latency was well below the desired response time of 550 ms, however, as the CPU utilization reached approximately 70%, arrival rates that exceeded the rate specification caused some events to be processed with latencies of close to 1 second. No packets were lost in the RBE system.

In the periodic server based system, the processing of events that arrive in a burst are spread out over time as if the events arrived periodically. In contrast, the *RBE* system schedules all events (assigns them deadlines) when they arrive. Thus, it is possible for events with deadlines far off in the future to actually be processed well before the time at which a periodic server would first see the event.

The second benefit of using *RBE* processes was a less pessimistic admission control policy. Typically, to achieve low response times for events one must configure a periodic server to execute at a higher rate than work is expected to arrive. The excess CPU capacity that is reserved for the server but rarely used, cannot be allocated to other processes. In the *RBE* system, by specifying the desired aggregate processing rate, a process reserves only the capacity that it expects to actually use.

5. Related Work

Our model of rate-based execution borrows concepts from several other systems including, RT-Mach [1, 2, 7], DASH [5], Synthesis [10], and Concord [15]. Thus, while our system is an amalgam of others, we believe our primary contribution to be a demonstration that *RBE* processes are a simple and effective primitive for constructing multimedia systems and conjecture that the same holds for generic real-time applications. The *RBE* model encompasses those in each of the related works. Moreover, it has a formal underlying model of resource allocation that accommodates interprocess communication and synchronization.

We also believe the *RBE* to be a more natural and easy to use abstraction than those previously proposed. For example, the *reserve* abstraction for a task proposed by Mercer *et al.* [2], is essentially a specification of the processor utilization of a task. We claim that unlike the concept of execution rate, the notion of a reserve is inherently not a natural (or portable across hardware platforms) application-level concept.

Our work represents a counter-point to the work on *imprecise computation* by Lin *et al.* [15]. The imprecise model of computation was developed to primarily deal with the case of insufficient processing resources. The model provides a framework for real-time tasks to dynamically control which sections of their code are executed when the system is overloaded. By executing only fragments of the complete task, an "imprecise," but nonetheless useful, partial result can be obtained in a statically defined interval. Rather than directly controlling the execution of task code, an *RBE* system manipulates the interval in which task executes.

6. Summary and Conclusions

Process models for multimedia computing must allow applications to adapt their pattern of execution to make the best use of the resources currently available to them while not sacrificing their ability to execute predictably in time. Moreover, applications should be able to express their desired performance in terms of application-defined data units or events. We have proposed a new process model wherein processes execute according to a general rate specification of x process executions every y time units. In addition, a separate parameter is used to specify the desired response time for the completion of each execution. The model is general enough to encompass or extend many of the existing models proposed for multimedia systems.

We have implemented a prototype of processes that adhere to this rate-based execution (*RBE*) model. In the implementation, the system identifies processes whose input events are arriving at a faster or slower rate than expected and requests these processes to modify their rate specification. Moreover, interprocess communication is implemented so that the response time guaranteed for processing an event in the worst case is not a function of the number of processes involved in processing the event.

Preliminary experiences with rate-based execution in the YARTOS kernel indicate that an *RBE* rate specification provides a convenient means of expressing the desired performance of a videoconferencing system and allows the system to easily adapt its execution in response to changes in its environment such as changes in network congestion. We conjecture that the same will hold for other multimedia applications. A comparison of the performance of *RBE* processes and traditional periodic processes shows that the *RBE* model offers significant advantages in terms of both accuracy of admission control and average and worst case response time for the processing of events.

We presently have a primitive rate-based process model implemented in the Real-Time Mach kernel and are working on expanding the implementation and comparing *RBE* processes (threads in Mach) to the real-time threads already present in Mach in an effort to confirm our initial findings of *RBE* performance.

7. References

[1] *Integrated Management of Priority Inversion in Real-Time Mach*, Nakajima, T., Kitayama, T., Arakawa, H., Tokuda, H., Proc. 14th IEEE Real-Time Systems Symp., Durham, NC, December 1993, pp. 120-130.

[2] *Processor Capacity Reserves: Operating System Support for Multimedia Applications*, Mercer, C.W., Savage, S., Tokuda, H., IEEE Intl. Conf. on Multimedia Computing and Systems, Boston, MA, May 1994.

[3] *Scheduling and IPC Mechanisms for Continuous Media*, Govindan, R., Anderson, D.P., Proc. ACM Symp. on Operating Systems Principles, ACM Operating Systems Review, Vol. 25, No. 5, October 1991, pp. 68-80.

[4] *Kernel Support for Live Digital Audio and Video*, K. Jeffay, D.L. Stone, F.D. Smith, *Computer Communications*, Vol. 15, No. 6, (July/August 1992) pp. 388-395.

[5] *Support for Continuous Media in the DASH System*, Anderson, D.P., Tzou, S.-Y., Wahbe, R., Govindan, R., Andrews, M., Proc. Tenth Intl. Conf. on Distributed Computing Systems, Paris, France, May 1990, pp. 54-61.

[6] *Adaptive Real-Time Resource Management Supporting Modular Composition of Digital Multimedia Services*, M.B. Jones, in Network and Operating System Support for Digital Audio and Video, Proceedings, Fourth Intl. Workshop, Lancaster, UK, November 1993, D. Shepherd, *et al.* (Eds.). Lecture Notes in Computer Science, Vol. 846, pp. 21-28, Springer-Verlag, Heidelberg, 1994.

[7] *Dynamic QOS Control Based on Real-Time Threads*, H. Tokuda, T. Kitayama, in Network and Operating System Support for Digital Audio and Video, Proceedings, Fourth Intl. Workshop, Lancaster, UK, November 1993, D.

Shepherd, *et al.* (Eds.). Lecture Notes in Computer Science, Vol. 846, pp. 124-137, Springer-Verlag, Heidelberg, 1994.

[8] *System Support for Time-Critical Applications*, J.D. Northcutt, E.M. Kuerner, in Network and Operating System Support for Digital Audio and Video, Proceedings, Second Intl. Workshop, Heidelberg, Germany, November 1992, R.G. Herrtwich (Ed.). Lecture Notes in Computer Science, Vol. 614, pp. 242-254, Springer-Verlag, Heidelberg, 1992.

[9] *Scheduling Algorithms for Multiprogramming in a Hard-Real-Time Environment*, Liu, C.L., Layland, J.W., Journal of the ACM, Vol. 20, No. 1, (January 1973), pp. 46-61.

[10] *Fine-Grain Adaptive Scheduling Using Feedback*, H. Massalin, C. Pu, *Computing Systems*, Vol. 3, No. 1, (Winter 1990) pp. 139-173.

[11] *The Real-Time Producer/Consumer Paradigm: A paradigm for the construction of efficient, predictable real-time systems*, K. Jeffay, Proc. 1993 ACM/SIGAPP Symposium on Applied Computing, Indianapolis, IN, ACM Press, February 1993, pages 796-804.

[12] *Two-Dimensional Scaling Techniques For Adaptive, Rate-Based Transmission Control of Live Audio and Video Streams*, T.M. Talley, K. Jeffay, Proc. Second ACM International Conference on Multimedia, San Francisco, CA, October 1994, pp. 247-254.

[13] *Transport and Display Mechanisms For Multimedia Conferencing Across Packet-Switched Networks*, K. Jeffay, D.L. Stone, F.D. Smith, *Computer Networks and ISDN Systems*, Vol. 26, No. 10, (July 1994) pp. 1281-1304.

[14] *A Theory of Rate-Based Scheduling*, K. Jeffay, University of North Carolina, Department of Computer Science, Technical Report, *in submission*.

[15] *Imprecise Results: Utilizing Partial Computations in Real-Time Systems*, Lin, K.-J., Natarajan, S., Liu, J.W.-S., Proc. of the Eighth IEEE Real-Time Systems Symp., San Jose, CA, December 1987, pp. 210-217.

[16] *On Latency Management in Time-Shared Operating Systems*, K. Jeffay, Proc. 11th IEEE Workshop on Real-Time Operating Systems and Software, Seattle, WA, May 1994, pp. 86-90.

[17] *Enhanced Aperiodic Responsiveness in Hard Real-Time Environments*, J.P. Lehoczky, L. Sha, J.K. Strosnider, Proc. of the Eighth IEEE Real-Time Systems Symp., San Jose, CA, December 1987, pp. 261-270.

VuSystem Performance Measurements [*]

Christopher J. Lindblad [†]

Telemedia Networks and Systems Group
Laboratory for Computer Science
Massachusetts Institute of Technology

Abstract

In this paper I discuss some performance measurements made of the VuSystem, a programming system for the software-based processing of audio and video data. The VuSystem is designed to run on ordinary Unix workstations with no specific support for the manipulation of multimedia data. Measurements made of processing times of representative filter modules demonstrate the viability of the approach.

Introduction

There is a class of multimedia applications in which the computer performs tasks requiring the direct processing of multimedia data, as well as the capture, storage, retrieval, and display tasks of traditional multimedia applications. Members of the class are best called *computer-participative* multimedia applications, because in them the computer directly participates in the interpretation of the multimedia data. These applications require more support than is provided by traditional multimedia toolkits. They require an extensible in-band media processing component.

To support their development, I designed and built the VuSystem [1, 2], a prototype software environment for applications that directly manipulate temporally sensitive data. The system provides simple scheduling and resource management functions to allow intelligent media-processing applications to run on ordinary Unix workstations. Because it includes an easy-to-program extensible in-band processing component, it is uniquely suited for rapid development of applications that perform intelligent processing of live media.

VuSystem applications [3] combine intelligent media processing with traditional capture and display. Some process live video for more responsive human-computer interaction. Others digest television broadcasts in support of content-based retrieval. Both classes demonstrate the utility of network-based multimedia systems that deliver audio and video data all the way to the application.

Following the construction of the VuSystem prototype, I performed a series of experiments that demonstrate the system can manipulate digital video with low overhead and high throughput. In this paper, I report some of the measurements made.

---

*This research was supported by the Advanced Research Projects Agency of the Department of Defense, monitored by the United States Air Force (AFSC, Rome Laboratory) under contract No. F30602-92-C-0019, and by a grant from Nynex.

[†]The author can be reached at: MIT Laboratory for Computer Science, Room 504, 545 Technology Square, Cambridge, MA 02139; Tel: +1 617 253 6042; Email: cjl@lcs.mit.edu.

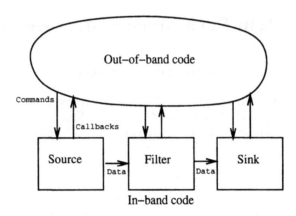

Figure 1: The VuSystem Approach.

The VuSystem

VuSystem applications include The Room Monitor, The Whiteboard Recorder, and The Video Rover. They provide more responsive human-computer interaction through the intelligent processing of live video. Other applications that manipulate pre-recorded video include The News Browser, The Joke Browser, and The Sports Highlight Browser. They demonstrate the practicality of automatic extraction to support content-based retrieval of produced video.

VuSystem applications have two components: one which does traditional *out-of-band* processing and one which does *in-band* processing. Out-of-band processing is that which performs the event-driven functions of a program. In-band processing is that performed on every video frame and audio fragment. In-band code is more elaborate in the VuSystem than in traditional multimedia systems such as Apple Quicktime or Microsoft Video for Windows because VuSystem applications perform sophisticated analysis of their input media data.

In the VuSystem, the in-band processing component is arranged into processing *modules* that pass dynamically-typed data *payloads* through input and output *ports*. The out-of-band component of the VuSystem is programmed in the Tool Command Language, or Tcl [8], an interpreted scripting language. Application code written in Tcl is responsible for creating and controlling the network of in-band media-processing modules, and controlling the graphical user-interface of the application.

The VuSystem is implemented on ordinary Unix workstations as a program that interprets an extended version of Tcl. In-band modules are implemented as C++ classes and are linked into this Tcl shell. Simple applications that use the default set of in-band modules are written as Tcl scripts. More complicated applications leverage customized modules that are linked into the shell.

VuSystem programs have a *media-flow* architecture: code that directly processes temporally sensitive data is divided into processing *modules* arranged in data processing *pipelines*. This architecture is similar to that of some visualization systems [9, 10], but is unique in that all data is held in dynamically-typed time-stamped *payloads*, and programs can be reconfigured while they run. Timestamps allow for media synchronization, and dynamic typing and reconfiguration allows programs to change their behavior based on the data being fed into them.

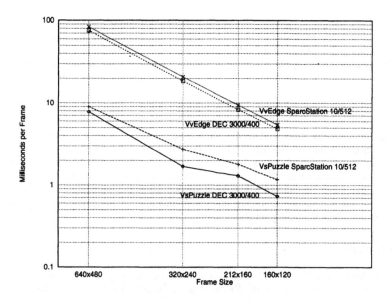

Figure 2: Processing Times of Representative Filter Modules.

frame size	puzzle frames/sec	edge frames/sec
640x480	12	6.67
320x240	30	25
212x160	15	15
160x120	30	30

Table 1: Rates of VuSystem Applications.

Performance

To verify that the overhead of the module data protocol is low, I measured the amount of time a simple transparent filter took to process a payload. It was approximately 12 microseconds on the Sun SparcStation 10/512 and approximately 3 microseconds on the Digital DEC 3000/400. Similarly, to verify that the run-time scheduler has low overhead, I measured the amount of time a mimimum filter takes to process a payload. It was approximately 150 microseconds on the Sun SparcStation 10/512 and approximately 115 microseconds on the Digital DEC 3000/400.

To demonstrate that media processing modules in the VuSystem are able to perform their functions with perceptual-time granularity, I measured the amount of time two representative filter modules took to process a video frame (Figure 2). On both the Digital DEC 3000/400 and the Sun SparcStation 10/512, a filter module that rearranges video frames for a puzzle program can scramble a 320 by 240 pixel, or half-sized, frame in approximately 2.5 milliseconds. An edge-detecting filter module can highlight edges in a half-sized frame in approximately 20 milliseconds. These times indicate that elaborate pixel-based operations can be performed efficiently on standard computer workstations.

I measured the total system throughput of two VuSystem programs based on two representative filter modules (Table 1). The video puzzle example application can process half-size live video at fully 30 frames per second with system capacity to spare. The edge highlighting application can process 25 frames per second of half-size live video.

Conclusion

In this paper I briefly discussed some performance measurements made of two VuSystem filter modules on two popular Unix workstation models. These measurements hint that it is possible to perform in-band media processing and still retain the temporal sensitivity that multimedia requires. VuSystem applications that perform visual processing can easily do so at 15 half-resolution frames per second. This is an acceptable level of performance for today, and will improve with advances in workstation technology as the system is portable.

References

[1] C. J. Lindblad, D. J. Wetherall, D. L. Tennenhouse, "The VuSystem: A Programming System for Visual Processing of Digital Video," *Proceedings of ACM Multimedia 94*, October 1994.

[2] C. J. Lindblad, "A Programming System for the Dynamic Manipulation of Temporally Sensitive Data," MIT/LCS/TR-637, MIT Laboratory for Computer Science, Cambridge, MA, August 1994.

[3] C. J. Lindblad, D. J. Wetherall, W. F. Stasior, J. F. Adam, H. H. Houh, M. Ismert, D. R. Bacher, B. M. Phillips, D. L. Tennenhouse, "ViewStation Applications: Intelligent Video Processing Over a Broadband Local Area Network," *Proceedings of the 1994 USENIX Symposium on High Speed Networking*, August 1994.

[4] D. L. Tennenhouse, J. Adam, D. Carver, H. Houh, M. Ismert, C. Lindblad, W. Stasior, D. Wetherall, D. Bacher, and T. Chang, "A Software-Oriented Approach to the Design of Media Processing Environments," *Proceedings of the International Conference on Multimedia Computing and Systems*, May 1994.

[5] J. F. Adam, H. H. Houh, M. Ismert, and D. L. Tennenhouse, "A Network Architecture for Distributed Multimedia Systems," *Proceedings of the International Conference on Multimedia Computing and Systems*, May 1994.

[6] W. Stasior, "Visual Processing for Seamless Interactive Computing," *The ViewStation Collected Papers*, MIT/LCS/TR 590, MIT Laboratory for Computer Science, Cambridge, MA, November 1993.

[7] J. F. Adam, "The Vidboard: A Video Capture and Processing Peripheral for a Distributed Multimedia System," *Proceedings of the ACM Multimedia Conference*, August 1993.

[8] J. K. Ousterhout, "Tcl: An Embedded Command Language," Computer Science Division (EECS), University of California, Berkeley, CA, January 1990.

[9] C. Williams and J. Rasure, "A visual language for image processing," *IEEE Computer Society Workshop on Visual Languages*, Skokie, Illinois, 1990.

[10] C. Upson, T. Faulhaber, Jr., D. Kamins, D. Laidlaw, D. Schlegel, J. Vroom, R. Gurwitz, A. van Dam, "The Application Visualization System: A computational environment for scientific visualization," *IEEE Computer Graphics and Applications*, 30-42, July 1989.

Design of Universal Continuous Media I/O*

Charles D. Cranor and Gurudatta M. Parulkar

Washington University, St. Louis MO 63130, USA

Abstract. The problem this research addresses is how to modify an existing operating system's I/O subsystem to support new high-speed networks and high-bandwidth multimedia applications that will play an important role in future computing environments.[2]

1 Introduction

The current Unix I/O application program interface (API) is a cross between file I/O and socket IPC I/O. While this API is flexible and compatible with older versions of Unix, it has a number of weaknesses that need to be addressed for future applications. These weaknesses include the API's unwieldiness, performance problems in the I/O subsystem (due to data copying and system call overhead), and little support for continuous media.

Thus, our objective is to design and implement a universal continuous media I/O (UCM I/O) subsystem with the following features:

- a clean and uniform I/O API
- a high performance I/O subsystem with minimal data copying and system calls
- support for continuous media including QOS specification and periodic data transfer support

The four most significant ideas behind UCM I/O that will contribute to UCM I/O's meeting of its objectives are:

- *a new* I/O API that has a small number of functions, can support a variety of I/O devices (traditional as well as continuous media), can work with different underlying buffer management systems, and can support all the I/O semantics of application programs
- the use of *clock interrupts for polling* I/O devices and user programs in order to support periodic data transfer and to reduce the number of asynchronous interrupts and system calls

---

* This work was supported in part by ARPA, the National Science Foundation, and an industrial consortium of ascom Timeplex, Bellcore, BNR, Goldstar, NEC, NTT, Southwestern Bell, SynOptics, and Tektronix
[2] This paper is an extended abstract of [1].

- *a supercall mechanism* that allows the kernel to run an I/O program on behalf of an application, thus reducing the number of system calls and data copying operations performed
- *a buffer management system* that works with different I/O devices and allows efficient page remapping and shared memory between user programs and the kernel (and the devices controlled by the kernel)

The last three ideas lead to efficient support for continuous media devices and significant performance improvements for the I/O subsystem as a whole. The first three ideas are briefly described in the subsequent sections.

2 New I/O API

The UCM I/O applications program interface consists of a small number of functions that take general data structures as arguments. The two main I/O system calls are called import and export. The import function takes data from the I/O system and imports it to the application. The export function sends data from the application to the I/O system. These calls support vector based I/O, and both connectionless and connection-oriented I/O with the same interface. Other functions include functions which start and stop continuous media I/O, buffer allocation functions, and functions that open and close UCM I/O descriptors. Also, note that simpler backward compatible functions can be implemented as library functions rather than systems calls to keep the kernel interface focused.

UCM I/O provides flexibility to applications and devices. This is done by absorbing some complexity in the buffer management of UCM I/O. When the application or device driver sends data into UCM I/O subsystem there are three options:

1. The application can force the UCM I/O layer in the kernel to copy data between application and kernel memory.
2. The application can allow the kernel to remap the data (in effect the application is giving away its buffer).
3. The application can allow the kernel to choose whether the data buffers should be remapped or copied.

When data is in the UCM I/O system, the I/O system owns the data buffers. This allows it to let the outside layers either copy or remap the buffers depending on the size of the data (UCM I/O can provide a hint as to which is more efficient). Note that to use the new features of UCM I/O the application's semantics may change.

UCM I/O also supports continuous media by providing for QOS specifications in the API. These specifications are given at I/O descriptor creation time. This allows for multimedia applications and for application oriented flow and error control in protocols. To meet the requirements, resources must be allocated on the network and on the host, and enforced within the OS using a soft real-time scheduling mechanism. There also needs to be an interface for changing the attributes of a descriptor. This can be combined with normal file system attributes. It should be noted that QOS enforcement is beyond the scope of this effort but is being explored in a related project [2].

3 SuperCall

UCM I/O also improves application performance by reducing the number of system calls by allowing them to be aggregated into "super" system calls or SuperCalls. This is useful for applications such as data transfer programs and daemons whose execution time is spent mostly in system calls. A SuperCall is a short program passed into the kernel for interpretation. This program can include multiple system calls.

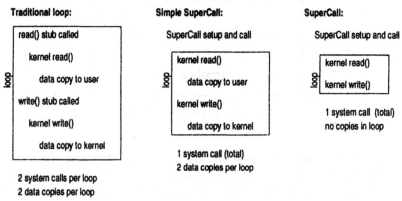

Fig. 1. SuperCall

Figure 1 shows how a SuperCall can reduce the cost of a file transfer loop. The left-hand side of the figure shows the cost of the file transfer loop if a SuperCall is not used. The cost consists of two system calls and two data copies per loop. The number of loops executed depends on the size of the buffers being used and the size of the data being sent. A system call consists of a stub that is called by the user program and a function in the kernel (usually with the same name as the stub) that is called on behalf of the user to perform the system call. A naive implementation of a SuperCall would simply take the SuperCall program and call the kernel routine directly, as shown in the middle of Figure 1. While this is not difficult to implement, it is still expensive because the kernel routines will still be copying (or mapping) the data into and out of the user space. A more efficient scheme would be for the SuperCall to only copy the data between the user and kernel at the ends of the SuperCall, as shown in the right-hand side of the figure. While this is more efficient, it is also much harder to implement because the kernel usually defers copying until the data is actually needed.

4 Clock Interrupt for Polling

UCM I/O adds support for continuous media to the operating system. In traditional I/O, the only way to trigger a data transfer is with a system call. This is not efficient for continuous media because it does not take advantage of the periodic nature of the data stream. UCM I/O provides a way to take advantage of the periodic nature of continuous media to transfer data. It uses a circular pool of data buffers, as shown in Figure 2. The buffer pool can be used to trans-

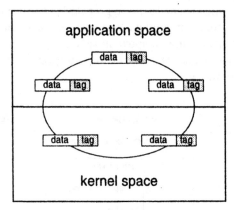

Fig. 2. A pool of buffers

fer data between the application and kernel without the need of a system call. It is accessed by both the application process and the kernel at the same time. The application arranges for the kernel to check the circular buffer on a periodic basis. The application can ask the kernel to operate in one of two modes. In one mode of access, the kernel polls a tag in the shared buffer area to see if data needs to be sent. In the other mode, there is no tag and the kernel always sends the data at the polling interval. The main difference in cost between the two modes is that the first mode requires one access to the tag area per polling interval, and the second mode does not. However, in the second mode, if the application does not meet the polling interval the kernel may send an invalid data buffer. By folding the polling of the tag into an already existing interrupt, cost is minimized.

References

1. Cranor, C., Parulkar, G., "Universal Continuous Media I/O: Design and Implementation," Washington University Department of Computer Science, Technical Report WUCS-94-34, 1994.
2. Gopalakrishnan, R., and Parulkar, G.M., "Application level Protocol Implementations to provide Quality-of-service Guarantees at Endsystems," Ninth IEEE Workshop on Computer Communications, Duck Key, Florida, Oct 1994.

A New OS Architecture for High Performance Communication over ATM Networks
– Zero-copy architecture –

Hiroshi KITAMURA, Kunihiro TANIGUCHI,
Hiromitsu SAKAMOTO, and Takeshi NISHIDA
E-mail: kitamura,taniguti,sakamoto,nishida@nwk.cl.nec.co.jp

C&C Research Labs. NEC Corporation

Abstract A new OS architecture, referred to as *Zero-copy architecture*, for high performance communication is proposed. This architecture dissolved memory copy bottleneck that is a major overhead in protocol processing. This can reduce CPU processing overhead, in addition to realizing high speed data communication. This architecture is shown to be suitable for large volume of data communication like video and image transfer.

1 Introduction

This paper focuses on the communication performance improvement on the end systems ("host" is used hereafter). As many researchers pointed out in their papers [1-6], protocol processing overhead mainly comes from memory copy of both transmission and received data within a host. Although several researchers have tried to overcome this problem [7-9], they have some limitations.

In the paper, we propose a new OS kernel architecture, referred to as *"Zero-copy architecture,"* for high performance network communication. This architecture eliminates data copies between applications (user space) and OS kernel (kernel space). Combining *"Zero-copy architecture"* and our experimental ATM NIC (Network Interface Card), which is devised to be able to transfer data directly from and to main memory using DMA, provides high performance end-to-end network communication. Application data can be directly transferred to (from) a network.

This paper discusses some limitations of the other methods for reducing memory copy costs. *"Zero-copy architecture"* and its implementation method are presented. Some experimental results are also shown.

2 Research Background

Jacobson proposes a simple I/O interface (WITLESS)[7], which minimizes both memory copy and control cost between the OS and the network interface. This advanced I/O interface design is adopted by HP's *Afterburner* architecture[8]. The *Afterburner* design aims at avoiding data copy between interface board and main memory. However, data copy between kernel and user spaces is not removed. In addition, since interface and OS kernel share local memory in the *Afterburner* network interface board, a communication application is restrained by this structure. For example, bulk data communication is difficult, because large memory area is needed.

Another interface design for reducing data copy cost is to utilize "*Copy-on-Write*" technique[5], but this technique includes many constrains. Since *Copy-on-Write* technique was designed originally for the same domain memory management, it is difficult to apply this to reduce copy between user and kernel space. Moreover, if an application changes the data, it must be copied onto the other memory area.

3 Design of Zero-copy architecture

"*Zero-copy architecture*" avoids data copying between kernel and user spaces in main memory at transmission and receiving processes. Essential characteristics of *Zero-copy architecture* are as follows:

Transmission data in user space is transferred to a network interface driver program without copying. Received data in kernel space into which a network driver program stored is transferred to a user program without copying. In addition, user programs can directly access these memory areas.

Design criteria in "*Zero-copy architecture*" are as follows;

1. Application independent platform: The existing applications, in addition to new multimedia applications, can be easily implemented.
2. Easy migration: The existing major OSs, e.g., UNIX, are easily migrated into the new architecture with minor modifications.
3. Reliability: The new kernel should be reliable in terms of data management.

In order to avoid copy management between kernel and user spaces in communications, memory areas must be shared between the kernel and user processes. The *Zero-copy architecture* realizes this using the memory mapping mechanism.

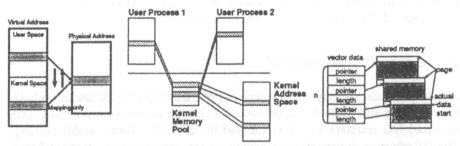

Fig. 1 Zero-copy
architecture   Fig. 2 Memory sharing method   Fig. 3 I/O vector
format

As shown in Fig. 1, *Zero-copy architecture* only performs memory mapping in the virtual address space. In *Zero-copy architecture*, virtual addresses of communication data in both the kernel and user spaces are mapped onto the same physical address. The single physical address can be accessed from different virtual addresses by controlling the mapping translation rules of the virtual memory systems. Fig. 2 shows the memory sharing method in the *Zero-copy architecture*. Some areas in the kernel memory pool are exclusively mapped onto multiple user process's user space. A specific area allocated to the kernel space is mapped onto a process's user space temporarily. The control information is exchanged between kernel and application, e.g., pointer to communication data location, in a form of *I/O vector* format shown in Fig. 3. *I/O vector* format is flexible, and it is easy to treat scattered data.

An application interface for *Zero-copy architecture* is as follows. In transmission, an application requests the kernel to allocate and map shared memory area, fill data into the area, and then release the area. On the inbound side, an application requests the kernel to map shared memory area to user space, and release the area after completion of data processing.

4 Implementation and Performance Evaluation

Fig. 4 illustrates our experimental implementation of *Zero-copy architecture* onto the typical UNIX workstation with ATM interface.

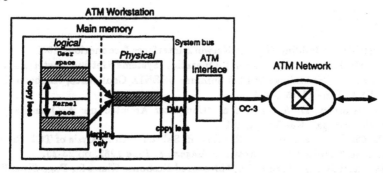

Fig. 4 Zero-copy architecture over ATM LAN

"Mapped device segment" in UNIX is used for data mapping address space. Since the "mapped device segment" has simpler structure and has enough capabilities to implement *Zero-copy segment*. Using "mapped device segment," *Zero-copy architecture* can be realized by a device driver. This leads to enhance portability and extendibility of *Zero-copy kernel*.

The ATM interface hardware can transfer data from and to main memory directly using DMA. That is, there is no local buffer within the network interface.

In order to evaluate the performance of *Zero-copy architecture* itself, it was carried out using a *loop-back interface*. The host processor is RISC CPU with about 130 MIPS power. A user process transmits 3 GB data using a TCP socket. Fig. 5 shows the throughput in changing TCP packet size. Since the TCP checksum computation causes another memory access, we eliminate this in the experiments. The results are **over twice faster** and **220 Mbps throughput**.

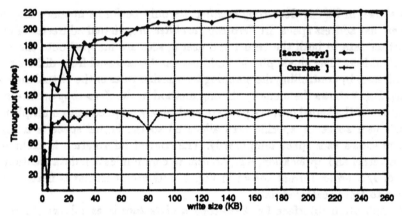

Fig. 5 Zero-copy architecture performance (TCP checksum-off)

5 Conclusion

In this paper, we proposed and explained the design concept and implementation methods of a new OS kernel architecture "*Zero-copy architecture*," to achieve high performance computer communication. This architecture avoids communication data copy on hosts, which is a major bottleneck in a communication process.

References

1. C. Patridge, "Building Gigabit Network Interfaces." connexions 1993.
2. J. K. Ousterhout, "Why Aren't Operating Systems Getting Faster As Fast as Hardware?" Proceedings of 1990 Summer USENIX Conference, Anaheim, California, USA, June 11-15, 1990.
3. J. L. Hennessy, D. A. Patterson, "Computer Architecture: A Quantitative Approach," Morgan Kaufmann, 1990.
4. D. D. Clark, V. Jancobson, J. Romkey, H. Salwen, "An Analysis of TCP Processing Overhead," *IEEE Communications Magazine*, June 1989, pp 23-29.
5. J. M. Smith, G. Q. Maguire Jr., "Measured Response Times for Page-Sized Fetches on a Network," *ACM SIGARCH Computer Architecture News*, Volume 17, No. 5, September 1989, pp 71-77.
6. P. Druschel, M. B. Abbott, M. A. Pagles, L. L. Peterson, "Network Subsystem Design," *IEEE Network Magazine*, Volume 7, No.4.
7. V. Jacobson, "Tutorial Notes from SIGCOMM '90," Philadelphia, USA, September 1990.
8. G. Watson, D. Banks, C. Calamvokis, C. Dalton, A. Edwards, J. Lumley, "Afterburner: Architectural support for high performance protocols," *IEEE Network Magazine*, Volume 7, No.4.
9. P. Druschel, L. L. Peterson, B. S. Davie, "Experiences with a High-Speed Network Adaptor: A Software Perspective," *Proceedings of ACM SIGCOMM 1994*, London, Sep. 1994, pp 2-13
10. C. B. S. Traw and J. M. Smith, "Hardware/Software Organization of a High-Performance ATM Host Interfase," *IEEE Journal on Selected Areas in Communications*, February 1993, Volume 11, No.2

Session III: Resource Management ant Quality of Service
Chair: Aurel Lazar, Columbia University

The papers in this session focused on resource management and quality of service related primarily to video delivery. Two full papers were presented followed by three adjunct papers. A discussion on "middleware" led by Aurel dominated the round-table period.

The first paper by Eleftheriadis and Anastassiou dealt with traffic shaping of compressed video streams for a variety of compression standards. The technique, dubbed "dynamic rate shaping," is applicable to MPEG, JPEG, and H.261 formats of compressed video. Essentially, a simple mechanism (algorithms) was proposed that considers a bandwidth constraint to generate a modified bitstream from a compressed video source.

The second paper by Campbell, Hutchison, and Aurrecoechea introduced a concept of "dynamic QOS management." A number of abstract entities were described that mitigate the heterogeneity of multimedia applications, networks, and terminals. These include "QOS adaptors," "QOS filters," and "QOS groups." These entities along with a proposed adaptive network service mechanism are used to achieve scalable video flows.

The remaining adjunct papers spanned a variety of topics. The first, by Venkatesh and Little considered "service aggregation" as a means to economize network bandwidth by combining video multicasts based on a dynamic batching mechanism. The authors claimed that this mechanism is most appropriate for busy periods – when the density of access is highest the likelyhood of savings via aggregation is also highest. The second adjunct paper, by Kawachiya, Ogata, Nishio, and Tokuda described a QOS control mechanism designed to manage interactive behavior in the context of the RT-Mach operating system. The third paper by Scheier and Davis presented a resource management model based on "benefit functions." In this model the system attempts to maximize a set of benefit functions associated with an application by adjusting various processing, communications, and storage resources.

Meeting Arbitrary QoS Constraints Using Dynamic Rate Shaping of Coded Digital Video

Alexandros Eleftheriadis and Dimitris Anastassiou

Department of Electrical Engineering
and Center for Telecommunications Research
Columbia University, New York, NY 10027, USA
{eleft,anastas}@ctr.columbia.edu

Abstract. We introduce the concept of *Dynamic Rate Shaping*, a technique to adapt the rate of compressed video bitstreams (MPEG-1, MPEG-2, H.261, as well as JPEG) to dynamically varying rate (and delay) constraints. The approach provides an interface (or filter) between the encoder and the network, with which the encoder's output can be perfectly matched to the network's quality of service characteristics. Since the presented algorithms do not require interaction with the encoder, they are fully applicable to precoded, stored video (as in, for example, video-on-demand systems). By providing decoupling of the encoder and the network, universal interoperability can be achieved. A set of low-complexity algorithms for dynamic rate shaping is presented, and both optimal and extremely fast designs are discussed. The latter are simple enough to allow software-based implementation. Experimental results are provided using actual MPEG-2 bitstreams.

1 Introduction

In applications of digital video communications there are many cases where control of the bit rate of video is needed, even after encoding has already taken place. One example is video-on-demand services, in which transmission of precoded material may occur over a wide variety of channels; multiresolution coding with too many layers would be undesirable, due to the loss in coding efficiency. Another example is transmission of real-time or precoded video material over channels with limited or no quality of service guarantees (e.g. CSMA/CD LANs). Although techniques have been developed to employ rate control for live sources based on network feedback [4, 6], no solution is currently available for prerecorded material. Similarly, consider a variable bit rate (VBR) video source that is fed to an ATM virtual circuit: due to the difficulties in modeling VBR video traffic, the traffic characterization used for admission control and policing will not necessarily match that of the source. Instead of dropping vital information at the source or in internal network nodes, an operation that would manipulate the bitstream so that it complies with what the network can deliver would be an extremely useful proactive measure against resource exhaustion.

Another environment that could potentially benefit from such post-encoding rate control operation would be multipoint communication with mobile hosts:

since the mobile link is typically of much lower bandwidth than wired ones, by reducing the video rate at the base-to-mobile link, wired participants would still be able to utilize the full bandwidth available to them without being compromised by the presence of wired ones. The same argument holds for heterogeneous (at least in terms of bandwidth) internetworks.

Finally, an environment that continuously grows in importance is that of general purpose computers. Due to the variety of network transport mechanisms that can be employed and the potential use of video for non-communication applications, it is most likely that general-purpose (transport-independent) video codecs will be used. It is desirable, then, to provide a mechanism that can gracefully interface the codec with the particular transport facilities used, if any.

In all the above cases, the common theme is the need to manipulate the coded bitstream so that it complies with the bandwidth availability of the underlying communication resources. In general, this manipulation is performed at the transmitting host, just above the transport layer, and interfaces the coded video bitstream with the transport service.

We refer to this rate manipulation operation as *Dynamic Rate Shaping* (DRS). The term dynamic refers to the possibility that rate constraints are time-varying, while shaping is used instead of rate control to: 1) differentiate with classical encoder rate control in which the variable rate of an entropy-coded bitstream is matched to a fixed channel rate, and 2) to more accurately capture the posterior (with respect to coding) nature of the operation. Note that DRS is quite different from traffic shaping (e.g. in DRS the traffic's average rate can change). Also, DRS can be used in new types of hybrid guaranteed/best-effort services, such as the ones described in [2].

In order for rate shaping to be viable it has to be implementable with reasonable complexity and yield acceptable visual quality. With respect to complexity, the straightforward approach of decoding the video bitstream and recoding it at the target rate would be obviously unacceptable; the delay incurred would also be an important deterrent. Hence algorithms of complexity less than that of a cascaded decoder and encoder will be sought. In terms of quality, it should be noted that recoding does not necessarily yield optimal conversion; in fact, since an optimal encoder (in an operational rate-distortion sense) is impractical due to its complexity, recoding can only serve as an indicator of an acceptable quality range. As will be shown, regular recoding can be quite lacking in terms of quality, with DRS providing significantly superior results.

We present a set of algorithms that solve the problem of dynamic rate shaping for—possibly motion-compensated—block-based transform coders, including MPEG-1, MPEG-2, H.261, and JPEG. After formulating the DRS problem in an operational rate-distortion context, we derive both optimal and fast approximate algorithm. The latter are shown to perform within 0.5 dB of the optimal ones (a typically non-perceptible difference), hence providing a very good tradeoff between algorithmic complexity and visual quality. The complexity of the optimal algorithm is shown to be less than that of an encoder, while for the fast approximations it is shown to be significantly less than that of a decoder's. While the approach is applicable to any motion-compensated block-based transform codec, the MPEG-2 [1] draft international standard is used for all simulation results presented.

The structure of the paper is as follows. In Section 2 we formulate the problems of general and constrained dynamic rate shaping. In Section 3 we discuss optimal and fast approximate algorithms for constrained rate shaping of intra-coded pictures. In Section 4 we generalize the approach to tackle the mixed-mode (I, P, and B) coding case. Finally, in Section ?? we present some concluding remarks.

2   Dynamic Rate Shaping

We define rate shaping as an operation which, given an input video bitstream and a set of rate constraints, produces a video bitstream that complies with these constraints. For our purposes, both bitstreams are assumed to meet the same syntax specification, and we also assume that a—possibly motion-compensated—block-based transform coding scheme is used. This includes both MPEG-1 and MPEG-2, as well as H.261 and so-called "motion" JPEG. If the rate constraints are allowed to vary with time, the operation will be called dynamic rate shaping. Throughout the paper we assume that MPEG-2 is used as the video coding syntax. For the benefit of the non-expert reader, in the following section we briefly review MPEG's main characteristics; an overview can be found in [7], while the actual standard is detailed in [1].

2.1   MPEG-2 Overview

The algorithmic foundation of MPEG is motion-compensated, block-based transform coding (H.261 falls in the same category). Each picture (either frame or field for interlaced sources) is decomposed into a hierarchical structure consisting of blocks, macroblocks, and slices (see Fig. 1). A block is an 8×8 array of pixels, and is the unit for transform coding. A macroblock is an array of 2×2 luminance blocks (the YUV format is used), together with the corresponding blocks of the chrominance components (an additional 2 to 8 blocks depending on the chroma format used). Macroblocks are the units of motion compensation and quantizer selection, as discussed below. A horizontal strip of macroblocks forms a slice, which is the unit for bitstream resynchronization (several recursively computed quantities are reset at the beginning of a slice).

Each block is transformed using the 2-D Discrete Cosine Transform (DCT), and is subsequently quantized. Quantization is the sole source of quality loss in MPEG, and of course a major source of compression efficiency. The quantized coefficients are converted to a one-dimensional string using a zig-zag pattern (Fig. 1) and then run-length encoded. Run-length codes jointly encode the number of consecutive zero DCT coefficients as well as the value of the next non-zero coefficient. The motivation behind this approach is that typical pictures contain

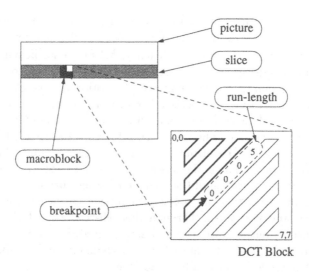

Fig. 1. MPEG picture structure and DCT coefficient zig-zag scanning pattern.

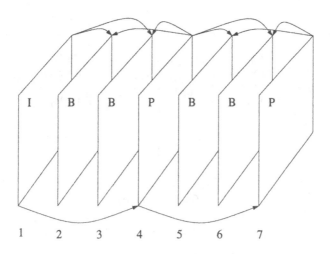

Fig. 2. MPEG sequence structure and motion-compensated prediction reference pictures.

large sequences of zeros in the zig-zag pattern after quantization, and hence run-length coding can very efficiently represent them.

There are three types of pictures in a video sequence: I, P, and B. I or intra pictures are individually coded, and are fully self-contained. P pictures are predicted from the previous I or P picture, while B (or bidirectional) pictures are interpolated from the closest past and future I or P pictures. Fig. 2 shows a typical pattern, including the pictures used as prediction references. Prediction is motion-compensated: the encoder finds the best match of each macroblock in the past or future picture, within a prespecified range. The displacement(s), or motion vector(s), is (are) sent as side information to the decoder.

In order to increase the coding efficiency, MPEG relies heavily on entropy coding. Huffman codes (variable length codewords) are used to represent the various bitstream quantities (run-length codes, motion vectors, etc.). As a result, the output of an MPEG encoder is inherently a variable rate bitstream: the ratio of bits per pixel varies from one block to the next. In order to construct a constant bit rate bitstream (when needed), rate control is used. This is achieved by connecting a buffer to the output of the encoder, that is emptied at a constant rate (the channel rate). The buffer's occupancy is fed back to the encoder, and is used to control the selection of the quantizer for the current macroblock. High buffer occupancy leads to more coarsely quantized coefficients, and hence less bits per block, and vice versa. Through this self-regulation technique one can achieve a constant output rate; clever design is needed in order to avoid buffer overflows and underflows (if required by the channel), and to allocate bits so that the best possible image quality is achieved.

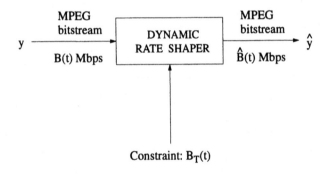

Fig. 3. Operation of a dynamic rate shaper.

2.2 DRS Problem Definition

The rate shaping operation is depicted in Fig. 3. Note that no communication path exists between the rate shaper and the source of the input bitstream, which ensures that no access to the encoder is necessary. Of particular interest is the source of the rate constraints $B_T(t)$. In the simplest of cases, $B_T(t)$ may be just a constant and known a priori, e.g. the bandwidth of a circuit-switched connection. It is also possible that $B_T(t)$ has a well (a priori) known statistical characterization, e.g. a policing function. Finally, another alternative is that $B_T(t)$ is generated by the network over which the output bitstream is transmitted; this could be potentially provided by the network management layer, or may be the result of end-to-end bandwidth availability estimates (as in [4, 6]). The objective of a rate shaping algorithm is to minimize the conversion distortion, i.e.:

$$\min_{\hat{B}(t) \leq B_T(t)} \{\|y - \hat{y}\|\} \tag{1}$$

Note that no assumption is made on the rate properties of the input bitstream, which can indeed by arbitrary. The attainable rate variation $(\hat{B}/B)$ is in practice limited, and depends primarily on the number of B pictures of the bitstream and the original rate $B(t)$.

Assuming that MPEG-2 (or, more generally, a motion-compensated block-based transform coding technique) is used to generate the input bitstream and decode the output one, there are two fundamental ways to reduce the rate: 1) modifying the quantized transform coefficients by employing coarser quantization, and 2) eliminating transform coefficients. In general, both schemes can be used to perform rate shaping; requantization, however, leads to recoding-like algorithms which are not amenable to fast implementation and, as we will see, do not perform as well as selective-transmission ones. Consequently, in the rest of this paper we only consider selective-transmission based algorithms, and more specifically we address the particular case of truncation (a set of DCT coefficients at the end of each block is eliminated). This approach will be referred to as *constrained* dynamic rate shaping.

The number of DCT run-length codes within each block which will be kept will be called the *breakpoint* (Fig. 1). Assuming use of MPEG, and to avoid certain syntax complications [1], we require that at least one DCT coefficient will remain in each block. Consequently, breakpoint values will range from 1 to 64.

3 Rate Shaping of Intra-Coded Pictures

In intra-picture rate shaping, there is no temporal dependence between pictures. Consequently, the shaping error will simply consist of the DCT coefficients that are dropped. It can then be shown that the DRS problem can be expressed as follows:

$$\min_{\hat{B}(t) \leq B_T(t)} \{\|y - \hat{y}\|\} \iff \min_{\sum_{i=1}^{N} R_i(B_i) \leq B_T(t)} \left\{ \sum_{i=1}^{N} D_i(b_i) \right\} \tag{2}$$

with

$$D_i(b_i) \equiv \sum_{k \geq b_i} [E^i(k)]^2 \tag{3}$$

---

[1] These include recoding the coded block patterns, and reexecuting DC prediction loops.

where $b_i \in \{1, \ldots, 64\}$ is the breakpoint value for block i (run-length codes from b_i and up will be eliminated), N is the number of blocks considered, $E^i(k)$ is the value of the DCT coefficient of the k-th run in the i-th block, and $R_i(b_i)$ denotes the rate required for coding block i using a breakpoint value of b_i.

This constrained minimization problem can be converted to an unconstrained one using Lagrange multipliers: instead of minimizing $\sum_i D_i(b_i)$ given $\sum_i R_i(b_i)$, we minimize:

$$\min \left\{ \sum_{i=1}^{N} D_i(b_i) + \lambda \sum_{i=1}^{N} R_i(b_i) \right\} \tag{4}$$

Note that the two problems are not equivalent; for some value of λ, however, which our algorithm will have to find, their solutions become identical [8].

The unconstrained minimization problem can be solved using an iterative bisection algorithm (on λ), which at each step k separately minimizes $D_i(b_i) + \lambda R_i(b_i)$ for each block. A similar algorithmic approach but in a different context has been used in [3, 5, 8]. A short description of the complete algorithm is as follows. We denote by $R_i^*(\lambda)$ and $D_i^*(\lambda)$ the optimal rate and distortion respectively for block i for that particular λ (i.e. they minimize $D_i + \lambda R_i$). We also denote by $b_i^*(\lambda)$ the breakpoint value that achieves this optimum.

Lagrangian Optimization Algorithm

Step 1: Initialization
Set $\lambda_l = 0$ and $\lambda_u = \infty$. If the inequality:

$$\sum_{i=1}^{N} R_i^*(\lambda_u) \leq R_{\text{budget}} \leq \sum_{i=1}^{N} R_i^*(\lambda_l) \tag{5}$$

holds as an equality for either side, an exact solution has been found. If the above does not hold at all, then the problem is infeasible (this can happen if the target rate $\hat{B}$ is too small). Otherwise go to Step 2. Note that these two initial λ's correspond to the minimum and maximum possible breakpoint values (the former minimizes distortion, while the latter minimizes the rate).

Step 2: Bisection and Pruning
Compute:

$$\lambda_{\text{next}} := \left| \frac{\sum_{i=1}^{N} [D_i^*(\lambda_u) - D_i^*(\lambda_l)]}{\sum_{i=1}^{N} [R_i^*(\lambda_u) - R_i^*(\lambda_l)]} \right| \tag{6}$$

and find $R_i^*(\lambda_{\text{next}})$ and $D_i^*(\lambda_{\text{next}})$ such that $b_i^*(\lambda_u) \leq b_i^*(\lambda_{\text{next}}) \leq b_i^*(\lambda_l)$.

Step 3: Convergence Test
If

$$\sum_{i=1}^{N} R_i^*(\lambda_{\text{next}}) = \sum_{i=1}^{N} R_i^*(\lambda_u) \quad \text{or} \quad \sum_{i=1}^{N} R_i^*(\lambda_{\text{next}}) = \sum_{i=1}^{N} R_i^*(\lambda_l) \tag{7}$$

then stop; the solution is $b_i^*(\lambda_u)$, $i = 1, \ldots, N$. If

$$\sum_{i=1}^{N} R_i^*(\lambda_{\text{next}}) > R_{\text{budget}} \tag{8}$$

then $\lambda_l := \lambda_{\text{next}}$, else $\lambda_u := \lambda_{\text{next}}$.

The bisection algorithm operates on the convex hull of the $R(D)$ curve of each slice. Consequently, points which lie above that, and hence are not $R(D)$ optimal, are not considered by the algorithm. One can easily verify that actual $R(D)$ curves from real sequences are to a significant degree convex (i.e. only a few points are above the convex hull), particularly for P and B pictures. In some cases, if the $R(D)$ curve of a slice is sufficiently misbehaved, the bisection algorithm can be set off track, with a resulting underutilization of the target bit budget. In order to mitigate this effect, and also to speed up operation, each iteration considers a continuously shrinking interval of possible breakpoint values ("pruning"). This will result in convergence of the algorithm to a much smaller set of non-convex points. The computational overhead of the algorithm is small, and convergence is achieved within 8–10 iterations.

The collection of necessary data in (2) requires only parsing of the bitstream up to inverse quantization of the DCT coefficients. Since this represents a small fraction of the complete decoding process, the algorithm has complexity less than that of a decoder. The window N in which the algorithm operates is a design parameter. Since rate shaping is performed on top of encoding (although not necessarily at the same time), it is desirable to minimize the additional delay introduced by the extra processing step. A plausible selection is then a single picture (frame or field). The target bit budget R_{budget} of each picture can be set to: $R_{\text{budget}} = (B_T/B)R - R_o$, where R is the size (in bits) of the currently processed picture, and R_o is the number of bits spent for coding components of the bitstream that are not subject to rate shaping. R is immediately available after the complete picture has been parsed. Allocated bits that are left over from one picture are carried over to the subsequent picture.

Since a full resolution picture (704×480) may contain up to 15,840 blocks (for a 4:4:4 format), the processing required within each iteration in order to find the breakpoint value that minimizes $D_i(b_i) + \lambda R_i(b_i)$ can be significant. Consequently, it is worth examining *clustering* approaches, in which a common breakpoint value is selected for a set of macroblocks. We refer to such algorithms as $C(n)$, where n is the number of sequential macroblocks contained in each cluster. An additional benefit of clustering is that the distortion can be defined on only the luminance part of the signal, hence greatly simplifying the implementation. Clustering, of course, will degrade performance; for example, the $C(44)$ algorithm reduces the quality by about 2 dB, but at a substantial decrease in complexity.

4 Mixed-Mode Rate Shaping

When all types of picture coding types are used (I, P, and B) the problem is significantly more complex. The decoding process for the original and the rate shaped signal can be described by $P_i = \mathcal{M}_i(P_{i-1}) + e_i$ and $\hat{P}_i = \mathcal{M}_i(\hat{P}_{i-1}) + \hat{e}_i$, where P_i denotes the i-th decoded picture (in coding order), $\hat{P}_i$ denotes the rate shaped decoded picture, $\mathcal{M}_i(\cdot)$ denotes the motion compensation operator for picture i, and e_i and $\hat{e}_i$ denote the coded original and rate shaped prediction errors respectively. The first picture is assumed to be intra-coded, and hence $P_0 = e_0$ and $\hat{P}_0 = \hat{e}_0$. Although, for simplicity, a single reference picture is shown above for motion compensation, the expression can be trivially extended to cover the general case (which includes B-pictures).

We can then rewrite (1) as:

$$\min_{\sum_{i=1}^N R_i(b_i) \leq B_T} \left\| \sum_{p=1}^M \mathcal{M}_i(P_{i-1}) - \mathcal{M}_i(\hat{P}_{i-1}) + e_i - \hat{e}_i \right\| \tag{9}$$

where M is the number of pictures over which optimization takes place. Note that in general $\mathcal{M}_i(P_{i-1}) - \mathcal{M}_i(\hat{P}_{i-1}) \neq \mathcal{M}_i(P_{i-1} - \hat{P}_{i-1})$, i.e. motion compensation is a non-linear operation, because it involves integer arithmetic with truncation away from zero.

From (9) we observe that, in contrast with the intra-only case, optimization involves the accumulated error $a_i \equiv \mathcal{M}_i(P_{i-1}) - \mathcal{M}_i(\hat{P}_{i-1})$. Furthermore, due to the error accumulation process, rate shaping decisions made for a given picture will have an effect in the quality and partitioning decisions of subsequent pictures. As a result, an optimal algorithm for (9) would have to examine a complete group of pictures (I-to-I), since breakpoint decisions at the initial I-picture may affect even the last B or P picture. Not only the computational overhead would be extremely high, but the delay would be unacceptable as well.

An attractive alternative algorithm is one that solves (9) on a picture basis, and where only the error accumulated from past pictures is taken into account; this algorithm will be referred to as *causally optimal*. Note that in order to accurately compute a_i, two prediction loops have to be maintained (one for a decoder that receives the complete signal, and one for a decoder that receives only partition 0). This is because of the nonlinearity of motion compensation, which involves integer arithmetic with truncation away from zero. With the penalty of some lack in arithmetic accuracy, these two loops can be collapsed together.

The causally optimal problem can be formulated as follows:

$$\min_{\sum_{i=1}^N R_i(b_i) \leq B_T} \left\{ \sum_{i=1}^N \hat{D}_i(b_i) \right\} \tag{10}$$

with

$$\hat{D}_i(b_i) \equiv \sum_k A^i(k)^2 + \sum_{k \geq b_i} 2A^i(\mathcal{I}(k))E^i(k) + E^i(k)^2 \tag{11}$$

where N is such that a complete picture is covered, $A^i(k)$ is the k-th DCT coefficient (in zig-zag scan order) of the of the i-th block of the accumulated error a_i, and $\mathcal{I}(\cdot)$ maps run/length positions from the prediction error $E^i(\cdot)$ to actual zig-zag scan positions. This minimization problem can be solved using the Lagrangian multiplier approach of Section 3, with this new definition for the distortion D.

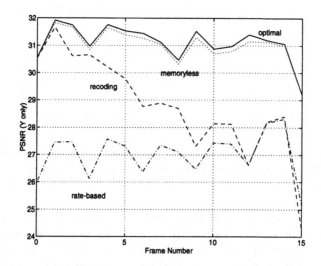

Fig. 4. Results of various rate shaping algorithms on the "Mobile" sequence, MPEG-2 coded at 4 Mbps and rate shaped at 3.2 Mbps.

An important issue in mixed-mode coding is the target bit budget that will be set for each picture. In a typical situation, I and P picture DCT coding requires a significant number of bits, while B picture sizes are dominated by header and motion vector coding bits. Consequently, B pictures provide much less flexibility for data partitioning. In order to accommodate this behavior, I and P pictures are assigned proportional bit budgets as in Section 3; for B pictures the same is done, except when the resulting bit budget is negative, in which case it is set to 0. The negative budget, however, is accounted for, so that the bits spent for the B picture are subtracted from the budget of the immediately following picture. Note that an optimal bit allocation for each picture would be a direct by-product of the optimal (non-causal) algorithm.

The complexity is solving 10 is significant, and can be shown to be between that of a decoder and an encoder. In order to examine the benefit of error accumulation tracking, one can apply the intra-only algorithm of Section 3 to the mixed-mode case, since the only difference is the accumulated error term a_i. Surprisingly, the results of this *memoryless* mixed-mode partitioning algorithm are almost identical. Fig. 4 shows the relevant PSNR values for the "Mobile" sequence; the difference is in general less than 0.1 dB and the curves can hardly be

99

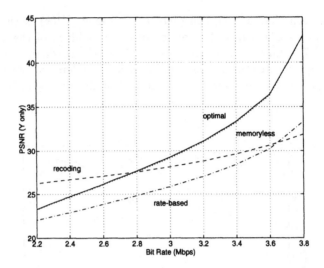

Fig. 5. Results of various rate shaping algorithms on the "Mobile" sequence, MPEG-2 coded at 4 Mbps and rate shaped at various different target bitrates.

distinguished. It turns out that this holds for a wide range of bit rates (Fig. 5), although the difference increases slightly to 0.2-0.3 dB. This is a very important result, as it implies that we can dispense completely with the error accumulation calculation and its associated computational complexity, for a minimal cost in performance: the quality degradation between the causally optimal and memoryless algorithms will be perceptually insignificant, across the spectrum of cluster sizes and partition rates.

For comparison purposes, we also examine the performance of a purely rate-based optimization algorithm. Breakpoint selection here is performed proportionally to the number of bits used to originally code each block. Fig. 4 depicts the results obtained on the "Mobile" sequence, coded at 4 Mbps and rate shaped at 3.2 Mbps, while Fig. 5 shows average PSNR values for a wide spectrum of rates. Fixed input and output rates have been selected here for simplicity; similar results can be obtained for more complex rate characteristics. All algorithms (except from recoding) are based on $C(1)$ clustering; i.e. breakpoint selection is performed on a macroblock basis. It is important to note that regular recoding gives inferior results to both the optimal and memoryless algorithms for a wide range of rates, while the latter two can hardly be distinguished.

5 Concluding Remarks

The concept of Dynamic Rate Shaping was introduced as an adaptation mechanism between coded video rate characteristics and transport service capabilities, and analyzed in an operational rate-distortion context. For the case of constrained DRS, an optimal algorithm based on Lagrangian multipliers was derived for intra-only coding. For the mixed-mode case (I, P, and B pictures) the optimal algorithm was shown to possess significantly high complexity and delay, and a causally optimal algorithm was introduced. It was then shown that a memoryless version of the algorithm performs almost identically, hence significantly simplifying the implementation complexity with no compromise in terms of quality. It was also shown that this DRS approach can outperform regular recoding for a wide range of rates. Due to its relative simplicity, the algorithm (particularly clustered versions, e.g. C(4)) can be implemented in software and operate in real-time on high-end general purpose CPUs.

References

1. Generic Coding of Moving Pictures and Associated Audio (MPEG-2). ITU-T Draft Recommendation H.262, ISO/IEC 13818-2 Draft International Standard, 1994.
2. A. Campbell. A Dynamic QoS Management Scheme for Adaptive Hierarchically Coded Flows. In *Proceedings of the 5th International Workshop on Network and Operating System Support for Digital Audio and Video (NOSSDAV-95)*, April 1995.
3. A. Eleftheriadis and D. Anastassiou. Optimal Data Partitioning of MPEG-2 Coded Video. In *Proceedings of the 1st IEEE International Conference on Image Processing*, pages I.273–I.277, August 1993.
4. A. Eleftheriadis, S. Pejhan, and D. Anastassiou. Architecture and Algorithms of the Xphone Multimedia Communication System. *ACM/Springer Verlag Multimedia Systems Journal*, 2(2):89–100, August 1994.
5. K. Ramchandran and M. Vetterli. Rate-distortion optimal fast thresholding with complete JPEG/MPEG decoder compatibility. In *Proceedings of the Picture Coding Symposium '93*, March 1993.
6. H. Kanakia, P. P. Mishra, and A. Reibman. An Adaptive Congestion Control Scheme for Real-Time Packet Video Transport. In *Proceedings of the ACM SIG-COMM '94 Conference*, pages 20–31, September 1993.
7. Didier LeGall. MPEG: A Video Compression Standard for Multimedia Applications. *Communications of the ACM*, 34(4):46–58, April 1991.
8. Y. Shoham and A. Gersho. Efficient bit allocation for an arbitrary set of quantizers. *IEEE Transactions on Acoustics, Speech, and Signal Processing*, 36(9):1445–1453, 1988.

Dynamic QoS Management for Scalable Video Flows

Andrew Campbell* and David Hutchison
Department of Computing,
Lancaster University,
Lancaster LA1 4YR, U.K.
mpg@comp.lancs.ac.uk

Cristina Aurrecoechea
Center for Telecommunications Research
Columbia University
New York, NY 10027-6699.
cris@ctr.columbia.edu

Abstract. We introduce the concept of *Dynamic QoS Management (DQM)* for control and management of hierarchically coded flows operating in heterogeneous multimedia networking environments. The motivation that underpins our scheme is to bridge the heterogenity gap that exists between applications, end-systems and networks. *QoS adaptors, QoS filters* and *QoS groups* are key *scalable objects* used in resolving quality of service capability mismatch. QoS filters manipulate hierarchically coded flows as they progress through the communications system, QoS adaptors scale flows at the end-systems based on the flow's measured performance and user supplied *QoS scaling policy*, and QoS groups provide baseline quality of service for multicast communications. The focus of the work is driven by a) the special features of scalable video flows - in particular MPEG2, b) the needs of both scalable and single-layer video for transmission over multimedia networks such as ATM. A novel *adaptive network service* is proposed for the transmission of multi-layer coded flows that offers "hard" guarantees to the base layer, and "fairness" guarantees to the enhancement layers based on a new bandwidth allocation technique called *Weighted Fair Sharing (WFS)*.

1. Introduction

The interplay between hierarchically coded flows [1], end-to-end communication support [2] and receiver-oriented [3] Quality of Service (QoS) requirements is an interesting and active area of research [4] [5] [6]. The basic technique used by coders (e.g., MPEG1, MPEG2 and H261) for compression of audio-visual flows is to remove redundant information in the signal. Using creative design techniques that take into account the perceptual capabilities of the human aural and visual system, it is possible to eliminate substantial parts of the signal with little or no perceived loss of information.

Both end-systems and networks impact continuous media communications through degradation in the delivered QoS (i.e., late frames, momentary loss of bandwidth, or highly variable delay jitter). Many audio and video applications exhibit robustness in adapting to fluctuations in the quality of service offered by the network and end-system. By trading off temporal and spatial quality to available bandwidth [7] [8], or manipulating the playout time of continuous media in response to variation in delay [9] [10], the video signal can be kept meaningful at the playout device with minimal perceptual distortion. The perceptible quality of service presented at the receiver is therefore a complex of quality of service management functions that includes source coding, filtering, communications support and QoS adaptation.

In this paper we present a *Dynamic QoS Management (DQM)* scheme and an *adaptive network service* which have been specifically designed to cater for the needs of both single and multi-layer coded video flows. We first motivate our approach by discussing some of the relevant end-to-end QoS challenges in transporting digital video over multimedia networks. We then present an API for scalable flows, followed by a detailed description of our adaptive service and dynamic QoS management scheme. DQM is in part built on existing techniques in the literature [1] [4] [5] [7] [9] [13] in provinding end-to-end QoS management [2] of digital video flows [15] [7].

---

*Visiting Scholar at the Center for Telecommunications Research, Columbia University.

2. Motivation

Heterogenity issues are present in applications, end-systems and networks. The range of audio and video QoS requirements is likely to be very diverse and the capability of applications, end-systems and networks to handle continuous media is likely to be quite diverse too. For example multimedia conferencing may only require low resolution video but high resolution sound. Considering the end-system only, heterogeneity is present in: CPUs, I/O devices, storage capabilities, compression support, communication support, network interfaces, etc. - all place fundamental limits on the capability of end-systems to consume and generate digital video. End-systems are likely to be connected to a wide variety of networks which not only have differing bandwidth capabilities but also varying access delay, jitter and loss characteristics. A key challenge is resolving this potential quality of service mismatch. We suggest that QoS scalability is central in bridging this heterogenity gap [5]. To meet this challenge we propose a DQM scheme that accommodates differing application, end-system and network QoS needs.

Another challenge is the transmission of variable bit rate video over multimedia networks. In order to derive algorithms for supporting variable bit rate network transmission (e.g., admission control, resource reservation and packet scheduling) of digital video, significant effort has been expended to obtain statistical models for video traffic [11]. The problem is extremely complex, since the rate is intimately related to both the coding scheme and the actual source material through the use of entropy coding: video sequences that deviate from the "norm" will require more bits than the average, and may exhibit highly variable behaviour.

As a result, models tend to be quite complex for variable bit rate video, and there is currently no known universally acceptable one. The drawback of inadequate modeling is that it can result in either loss of information (by underestimating the traffic behaviour) or to wasteful use of network resources (through overestimation) or reliance on constant bit rate "circuits". Some general observations have been made regarding coded digital video [7]: (i) burstiness is heavily dependent on the content of the image being coded and the coding algorithm used; (ii) source generation rates are highly sensitive to scene and background changes; and (iii) highly correlated source traffic is potentially persistent over very long periods. All this makes modeling video in a general sense extremely difficult and complex. Because modeling video sources is so difficult, and constant bit rate channels so inefficient in exploiting statistical multiplexing we focus our attention in this paper on an alternative approach: an adaptive channel, which supports QoS adaptation through the semantics of scalable video flows [5] [12] and resource fairness [12] [14] as part of the DQM scheme.

3. Scalable Video Flows

MPEG2 [15] provides for the simultaneous representation of a video signal at various different levels of quality, through the use of multiple independent bitstreams or sub-signals. This is achieved through the use of pyramidal, or hierarchical coding: one first constructs a coarse or base representation of the signal, and then produces successive enhancements. The latter assume that the base representation is available, and only encode the incremental changes that have to be performed to improve the quality. There are four different scalability modes: spatial, SNR, temporal, and data partitioning.

Although MPEG's scalability features are useful in resolving heterogeneity problems described above [5], and are useful in numerous applications, their use in continually QoS-varying channels is problematic. This is because they only allow the representation of the signal at a number of discrete quality points (temporal or spatial resolution, or spatial quality). These points are typically significantly apart, and transitions between the two are perceptually significant. Table 1 [16] shows an example of hybrid scalability with spatial (E1) and SNR (E2) enhancement layers.

layer name	profile	symbol	frame size	bit rate	subjective QoS
base layer	main	BL	304x112	0.32 Mbps	VHS
enhancement 1 layer	spatial	E1	608x224	0.83 Mbps	super VHS
enhancement 2 layer	SNR	E2	608x224	1.85 Mbps	laser disc

Table 1: MPEG-2 hybrid scalable bitstream using spatial and SNR scalability (24 fps)[16]

Consider for example a channel that temporarily sustains rate variability for a period of a few seconds. Switching to a lower quality point (by discarding the enhancement layer(s)) for such a brief interval will essentially create a "flash" that is very annoying to viewers (we call this *discrete adaptation*); this type of degradation would be rather noticable in the case of the spatial enhancement described in Table 1. An additional issue is that, as soon as compression parameters are established, it is impossible to modify them later on (after compression is completed). Hence scalability modes can be used for well-defined, simple channels that vary slowly. Since the variety of different access mechanism to multimedia information makes it very difficult to select a priori a set of universally interoperable coding parameter, it is necessary to provide mechanisms that allow the representation of the "signal at a continuum of qualities and rates" (we call this *continuous adaptation*) [5], so that scalable channels can be accommodated. This is possible through the use of dynamic rate shaping filters [8] and the provision of adaptive network services - providing a QoS continuum for fully scalable flows. The adaptive service uses explicit feedback from network resource management to dynamically shape the video source based on the available network resources. Some benefits of an adaptive scheme are non-reliance on video modeling techniques and statistical QoS specification and specific support for the semantics of scalable video flows e.g., MPEG scalable profiles. Dynamic rate shaping filters manipulate the rate of MPEG-coded video, matching it to the available bandwidth (indicated by the adaptive service) while minimising the distortion observed by the receiver.

4. Application Programming Interface for Scalable Flows

4.1 Scalable Objects

QoS adaptors, QoS filters and QoS groups are key scalable objects in dynamic QoS management. These objects are used to resolve quality of service capability mismatches in the end-systems and network and provide communication support for single and scalable video flows. QoS adaptation relates to the monitoring (using *flow monitors*) and adjustment (using QoS adaptors) of flows at the edge of the network to ensure that the user and provider quality of service is maintained. In this role QoS adaptors are seen as quality of service arbiters between the user and network. QoS adaptors scale flows at the end-systems based on a user supplied QoS scaling policy (see section 4.2) and the measured performance of on-going flows. In contrast to adapting flows at the end-systems, QoS filters manipulate hierarchically coded flows [1] [6] at the end-systems and as they progress through communications systems. In dynamic QoS management we refer to *scaling* [5] [12] as an "umbrella" term to cover the combination of QoS adaptation in end-systems, and QoS filtering [4] [2] in end-systems and the network. The QoS scaling policy is central to DQM and is the driver of QoS adaptation and QoS filtering mechanisms for end-to-end QoS management.

We describe three styles of QoS filters in dynamic QoS management:(i) *shaping filters*, which manipulate coded video and audio by exploiting the structural composition of flows to match network, end-system or application QoS capability. Shaping filters are generally situated at the edge of the network; (ii) *selection filters*, which are used for sub-signals source selection and media dropping are of low complexity and low computational intensity.

Selection filters are designed to operate in the network and are located at switches; and (iii) *temporal filters*, which manipulate the timing characteristics of media to meet delay bound QoS are also low in complexity and trivial computationally. Temporal filters are generally placed at receivers or sinks of continuous media were jitter compensation or orchestration of multiple related media [2] is required.

The first and third types of QoS filters are predominantly located in the edges of the network. Shaping filters utilise knowledge of the coding details of the flow they are processing, and require non-trivial computational power. Selection filters, on the other hand, perform simple packet filtering and hence can be located in internal network nodes. In some cases, shaping filters can be located in special network nodes, either as a bearer service, or as part of special environments such as mobile communication links. As an example, rate shaping filters placed at base stations can be useful for multi-point communication [1] with both mobile and wired hosts. Through the use of rate shaping, wired users can utilise the full bandwidth at their disposal, without compromising quality to that attainable to the least capable link of the session. A distributed object-based facility (e.g. CORBA [22]) can be particularly effective in providing the foundation for the incorporation of filters throughout the networking infrastructure (see section 6.) [12].

Before receivers or senders bind [17] media source and sink devices, media protocols and scalable objects to form end-to-end connections they must first join a QoS group [18]. A flow is represented by a QoS group in our adaptive (CORBA-based) environment. Group management announces QoS group capability in terms of its quality of service capability. The concept of a QoS group is used to associate a baseline quality of service capability to a particular flow. All sub-signal of a multi-resolution stream can be mapped into a single flow and multicast to multiple receivers [1]. Each receiver can select to take the complete signal advertised by the QoS group or a partial signal based on resource availability. Alternatively each sub-signal can be associated with a distinct QoS group. In this case receivers "tune" into different QoS groups (using signal selection) to build up the overall signal. Both methods are supported in DQM. Receivers and senders interact with QoS groups to determine what the baseline service is, and tailor their capability to consume the signal by selecting filter styles and specifying the degree of adaptability sustainable (viz. discrete, continuous).

4.2 QoS Specification

In [2] we formalised the end-to-end QoS requirements of the user and the potential degree of service commitment of the provider in a service contract. In this work, we focus on the extensions to the flow specification, QoS commitment and QoS scaling clauses required to accommodate the special needs of adaptive multi-layer flows over multimedia networks. Multi-layered flows are characterised by three sub-signals in the flow specification: a base layer (BL), and up to two enhancement layers (E1 and E2, respectively). Each layer is represented by a frame size, bit rate and subjective or perceptive quality of service as illustrated in Table 1. Based on these characteristics the MPEG2 coder [16] [8] determines approximate bit rate for each sub-layer. In the case of MPEG-2's hybrid scalability, BL would represent the main profile bit rate requirement (e.g., 0.32 Mbps) for basic quality, E1 would represent the spatial scalability mode bit rate requirement (e.g., 0.83 Mbps) for enhancement, and finally E2 would represent the SNR scalability mode bit rate requirement (e.g., 1.85 Mbps) for further enhancement. For full details of deriving these bit rates. The remaining flow specification performance parameters for jitter, delay and loss are assumed to be common across the all sub-signals. We use the term *sub-signal* to represent a single layer of a multi-layer video flow; and the term *flow* as a non-assured simplex uni-media stream, comprising of one source and potentially many receivers; flows always have end-to-end QoS associated with them [2].

The scaling policy characterises the degree of adaptation that the flow can tolerate and still achieve meaningful QoS. The scaling policy has been extended to capture the special needs of multi-layer flows, and includes adaptation modes, QoS filter styles, and user level notifications options for bandwidth, delay, jitter and loss QoS signals. Two types of adaptive mode are supported [5]: continuous mode, for applications that can exploit any availability of bandwidth above the base layer; and discrete mode that is suitable for applications which can only accept discrete improvement in bandwidth based on a full enhancement (viz. E1, E2). The adaptive modes option covers both highly adaptive (e.g., MPEG2 using dynamic rate shaping) and coarsely adaptive (e.g., MPEG2 scalable profiles).

```
typedef struct {                        typedef    struct {
        gid             flow_id;                adaptMode       adaptation;
        commit          commitment;             filterStyle     filtering;
        mediaType       media;                  events          adaptEvents;
        bitRate         BL;                     actions         newQoS;
        bitRate         E1;                     signal          bandwidth;
        bitRate         E2;                     signal          loss;
        int             delay;                  signal          delay;
        int             loss;                   signal          jitter;
        int             jitter;         } QoSscalingPolicy;
} flowSpec;

typedef enum {MPEG1, MPEG2, H261, JPEG} mediaType;
typedef enum {drs,sbr,sub_signal,hierarch,hybrid,sync,orch} filterStyle;
typedef enum {besteffort, adaptive, deterministic} commit;
typedef enum {continuous, discrete} adaptMode;
```

The QoS scaling policy provides user-selectable QoS adaptation and QoS filtering. QoS filters are broadly divided into source-based (viz., drs-filter and sbr-filter - see section 6.1), network-based (viz., sub_signal-filter, hierarch-filter, hybrid-filter - see section 6.3), and receiver-based (viz., sync-filter, orch-filter - see section 6.2) filters. While receivers select filter styles to match their capability to consume media at the receiver, senders select filter styles to shape flows in response to the availability of network resources such as bandwidth and delay. Receivers and senders can select periodic performance notifications including available bandwidth, measured delay, jitter and losses for an on-going flows. The QoS signal field in the scaling policy allows the user to specify the interval over which a QoS parameter is to be monitored and the user informed. Both single and multiple quality of service signals can be selected depending on the applications needs. For full details on the service contract see [2]. In addition, the QoS commitment clause has been extended to offer an adaptive network service that specifically caters for the needs of scalable audio and video flows.

5. Adaptive Network Service for Multi-layer Flows

The adaptive service provides "hard" guarantees to the base layer (BL) of a multi-layer flow and *Weighted Fair Share (WFS)* to each of the enhancement layers (E1 and E2). To achieve this, the base layer undergoes a full end-to-end admission control test [19]. On the other hand, enhancement layers are admitted without any such test but must compete for *residual bandwidth* among all other adaptive flows. Enhancement layers are rate controlled based on explicit feed back about the current state of the on-going flow and the availability of residual bandwidth.

5.1 Service Goals and Requirements
Both end-system and network communication resources are partitioned between the deterministic and adaptive service commitment classes. This is achieved by creating and maintaining "firewall" capacity regions for each class. Resources reserved for each class, but not currently in use can be borrowed by the best effort service class on condition of pre-emption [19]. The adaptive service capacity region (called the available capacity region and denoted by B_{avail}) is further sub-divided into two regions: (i) guaranteed capacity region (B_{guar}), which is used to guarantee all base rate layer flow requirements; (ii) and residual

capacity region (B_{resid}), which is used to accommodate all enhancement rates were competing flows share the residual bandwidth.

Three goals motivate our adaptive service design: First, to admit as many base layer (BL) sub-signals as possible. As more base layers are admitted the guaranteed capacity region B_{guar} grows to meet the hard guarantees for all base signals. In contrast, the residual capacity region B_{resid} shrinks as enhancement layers compete for diminishing residual bandwidth resources. The following invariants must be maintained at each end system and switch:

$$B_{avail} = B_{guar} + B_{resid} \text{, and } \sum_{i=1}^{N} BL_{(i)} \leq B_{avail} \tag{1}$$

Second, to share [13][14] the residual capacity B_{resid} among competing enhancement sub-signals based on a flow specific *weighted factor (W_{fact})*, which allocates residual bandwidth in proportion to the range in bandwidth requested that in turn is related to the range of perceptual QoS acceptable to the user. In DQM, residual resources are allocated based on the range of bandwidth requirements specified by the users (i.e., BL.. BL+E1+E2 is the range of bandwidth required e.g., from 0.32 Mbps to 3 Mbps for the hybrid scalable MPEG2 flow in Table 1). As a result, as resources become available each flow experiences the same "percentage increase" in the perceptible QoS, we call this weighted fair share. W_{fact} characterises the notion of WFS (see (2)) and is calculated for each flow as the ratio of a flow's perceptual QoS range to the sum of all perceptual QoS ranges.

$$W_{fact(i)} = (BL_i + E1_i + E2_i) / \sum_{j=1}^{N} (BL_j + E1_j + E2_j) \tag{2}$$

All residual resources B_{resid} are allocated in proportion to $W_{fact(i)}$ metric. Using this factor we calculate the proportion of residual bandwidth allocated to a flow to be $B_{wfs(i)} = W_{fact(i)} B_{resid}$ and the proportion of the available bandwidth allocated to be $B_{flow(i)} = B_{wfs(i)} + BL_{(i)}$. We describe this aggregate as the flow bandwidth (B_{flow}).

Third, to adapt flows both discretely and continuously based the adaptation mode. In the discrete mode no residual bandwidth is allocated by the WFS mechanism unless a complete enhancement can be accommodated (i.e., $B_{wfs(i)}$ = E1(i) | E1(i)+E2(i) e.g., 0.83 Mbps or 2.68 Mbps from Table 1). While in continuous mode any increment of residual bandwidth $B_{wfs(i)}$ can be utilised (i.e., $0 < \text{Bwfs(i)} \leq E1(i) + E2(i)$ e.g., from 0 to 2.68 Mbps from Table 1). Adaptive applications can be considered to be either coarsely (e.g., MPEG-2 scalable profiles) or highly adaptive (e.g., scalable MPEG2 using a dynamic rate shaping). By selecting continuous adaptation highly adaptive applications can take advantage of any availability in bandwidth to enhance QoS. While coarsely adaptive applications are more suited to the discrete mode were only E1 and E2 sub-signals can be accommodated, nothing more nothing less. In addition, WFS always accommodates the full E1 signal before attempting to deliver the E2.

5.2 Rate Base Flow Control

We build on the rate-based flow control mechanism described in [2] were the transport protocol at the receiver measures the bandwidth, delay, jitter and loss over an interval which we call an "era". An era is currently defined as simply the reciprocal of the frame rate in the flow specification (e.g., for a frame rate of 24 frames per second as shown in Table 1 the interval era is approx. 42 ms.). The receiver-side transport protocol periodically inform the sender-side about the currently available bandwidth, and measured delay, loss and jitter. This rate control information is used by the source or virtual source (see later) as the rate over the next interval. The reported rate is temporally correlated with the on-going flow. An important result in [7] shows that variable rate encoders can track quality of service variations as long as the QoS feed back is within four frame times or less. This feed-back is used by the dynamic rate shaping filter and network based filters to control the data generation of the video or the selection of the signal respectively. In the case of dynamic rate shaping the rate is adjusted while keeping the perceptual quality of the video flow meaningful to the user.

Based on the concept of eras, control messages (see [2] for format and semantics) are forwarded from the receiver-side transport protocol to either virtual source or the source-side transport using reverse path forwarding. We use the term virtual source to represent a network switch that modifies the source flow via filtering. A core-switch [20] [18] were flows are filtered is always considered to be a virtual source for one or more receivers. The WFS mechanism updates the advertised rate as the control messages traverse the switch on the reserve path to the source or virtual source. Therefore any switch can adjust the flow's advertised rate before the source or virtual source receives the rate based control message. The source-side transport hands the measured delay and aggregate bandwidth off (B_{flow}) to the dynamic rate shaping filter.

DQM maintains *flow state* at each end-system and switch that a flow traverses. Flow state is updated by the WFS algorithm and the rate-based flow control mechanism. Flow state maintained in the network constitutes: (i) capacity (viz. B_{avail}, B_{guar}, B_{resid}); (ii) policy (viz. filterStyle, adaptMode); (iii) flowSpec (viz. BL, E1, E2) ; and (iv) wfsShare (B_{flow}, B_{wfs}, W_{fact}). The end-systems holds an expanded share turple for measured delay, loss and jitter metrics. An admission control test is conducted at each end-system and switch on route to the core for base layer signal. This test simply determines whether there is sufficient bandwidth available to guarantee the base layer BL given the current network load:

$$\sum_{j=1}^{N} BL_{(j)} \leq B_{avail} \qquad (3)$$

If the admission control test is successful, WFS determines the additional percentage of the residual bandwidth made available B_{wfs} to meet any enhancement requirements in the flowSpec:

$$B_{wfs(i)} = W_{fact(i)}.(B_{avail} - \sum_{j=1}^{N} BL_{(j)}) \cdot \qquad (4)$$

The WFS rate computation mechanism can causes new B_{wfs} rates to be computed for all adaptive enhancement signals that traverse the output link of a switch; switches are typically non-blocking which means the critical resource are the output links, however, our scheme can be generalised to other switch architecture [19].

6. Dynamic QoS Management

Dynamic QoS management, illustrated in Figure 1, is broadly divided into three "middleware" domains (which are represented as "slices" in the diagram) for end-to-end dynamic QoS management: (i) *sender-oriented DQM*, senders select source filters (i.e. drs, sbr filters) and adaptation modes, and setup flow specifications for video and audio communications. The sender-side transport protocol provides periodic bandwidth and delay assessments to the dynamic rate shaping filter which regulates the source flow. Senders creates QoS groups which announce the quality of service of the flow to receivers via QoS group management [18]; (ii) *network-oriented DQM*, provides the adaptive service to receivers and senders by guaranteeing the base signal and provides weighted fair share using a novel rate base flow control mechanism to switch in discrete or partial enhancements. Network level QoS filters (i.e., sub-signal, hierarch and hybrid-filters) are instantiated based on the user selection, and propagated in the network under the control of filter management[21]; and (iii) *receiver-oriented DQM*, receivers join QoS groups and select the portion of the signal which matches their QoS capability. Receiver selected filters propagate in the network for source and signal selection. In addition, receiver-based QoS filters (i.e., sync-filter and orch-filter) are instantiated by default unless otherwise directed. These filters are used to smooth and synchronise multiple media. The receiver-side transport provides essential bandwidth management for enhancement announcements; delay-jitter and late packet management trading off timeliness against loss.

Based on the receiver supplied scaling policy, QoS adaptors can take remedial actions to scale flows, inform the user of a QoS indication and degradation, fine tune resources and initiate complete end-to-end QoS renegotiation based on a new flowSpec [2]. The QoS scaling policy also allows the user to modify existing QoS filters; and based on this policy, filter management [21] installs new filters at optimal points in the media path.

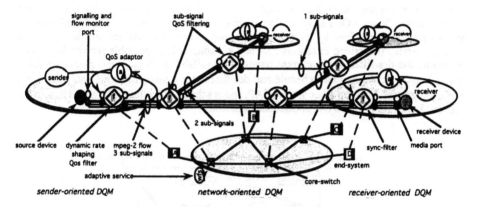

Fig.1: Dynamic QoS Management

Components of a distributed adaptive environment consist of a number of algorithms for QoS group management, flow management, filter management (we neglect to illustrate the interaction of these components with senders and receivers in Figure 1 for reasons clarify) and dynamic QoS management. Each element provides a set of interfaces and methods to manage flows in multimedia networks. Communication between interfaces is based on CORBA running over AAL5/ATM in our distributed environment at Columbia [17] [18] Figure 1 illustrates how adaptive receivers (at nodes B, C and D) and senders (node A) are built on top of multimedia networks which consist of Fore Systems ASX200 ATM switches. The middleware includes the sender, network and receiver-oriented DQM infrastructure and represents the system software components lying in the region between the switching and transmission firmware and specific multimedia applications. CORBA [22] runs on the end-systems and in the ATM switches, providing a seamless object oriented environment where filters, adaptors, QoS group manager, flow monitors and flow managers can propagate [4] [21] throughout the communication system base. In DQM each sub-signal (i.e. base and enhancement layers) can be carried as sub-signal multiplexed onto a single flow, or independently by distinct flows. DQM can handle either case, and leaves it up to the receivers and senders to determine which approach is more suitable.

In Figure 1 a sender at end-system A creates a flow by instantiating a QoS group which announce the characteristics of the flow and its adaptation mode i.e., for MPEG-2 in Table 1 (viz. layer, frame size, bit rate, subjective quality) for BL, E1 and E2 respectively. Receivers join the QoS group. In the example scenario shown in Figure 1 three end-systems join the QoS group created by sender A and "tune" into different parts of the multi-layer signal. The example shows B taking BL the main profile (which constitutes a bandwidth of 0.32 Mbps for VHS perceptual QoS), C taking BL and E1 (which constitutes an aggregate bandwidth of 1.15 Mbps for super VHS perceptual QoS), and D taking the complete signal BL+E1+E2 (which constitutes an aggregate bandwidth of 3 Mbps for laser disc perceptual QoS). In this example the complete signal is multiplexed onto a single flow, therefore, sub-signal selection filters are propagated by filter management [21]. Receive, senders, or any third party or filter management can select, instantiated and modify source, network and receiver-based QoS filters.

6.1 Sender-oriented DQM

A sender-oriented end system architecture illustrated in Figure 2 shows the functions of the sender-side transport that support dynamic QoS management and the interface to a dynamic rate sharing filters. Currently senders can select from two types of shaping filter at the source: drs and sbr. Both of these QoS filters adapt the signal to meet the available bandwidth by keeping the signal meaningful at the receiver or core. The sender-side transport mechanisms includes a QoS adaptor, flow monitor and media scheduler. Bandwidth updates are synchronously received by the flow monitor mechanism from the network as part of the adaptive service (described in section 5). The QoS adaptor is responsible for synchronously informing the drs-filter of the current bandwidth availability (B_{flow}) and measured delay (D_{flow}), and calculating new schedule and deadliness for transport service data units [19]. Media progresses from drs-filter at the TSAP, and is scheduled by the media scheduler to the network at the NSAP based on the calculated deadlines.

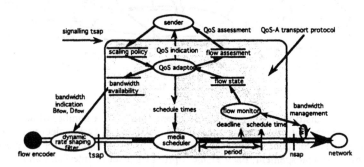

Fig. 2.: Sender-side Transport QoS Mechanisms

The QoS adaptor is responsible for informing the sender of the state of the on-going QoS based on options selected in the QoS scaling policy. As in the receiver side, senders can request periodic updates of bandwidth, delay, loss and jitter. Alternatively, senders can select the QoS monitoring selection [2] to receive periodic updates of all QoS parameters as part of the QoS maintenance operation. Senders, therefore, have the option to discretely select specific QoS parameters, or a set, or all QoS parameters as in the case of QoS assessments [2]. Informing the application of the current state of the resources associated with a specific flow is key in implementing adaptive application in end-systems. In this case the sender is simply used to managed the flow by receiving updates and interacting with the QoS adaptor to adjust the flow e.g., change adaptation mode from continuous to discrete, request more bandwidth for BL, E1 and E2, or change the characteristics of the source filter, etc..

Dynamic rate shaping of compressed digital video [8] (as shown in Figure 2) is a technique to adapt the rate of compressed video bitstreams (MPEG1, MPEG2, H261, as well as JPEG) to dynamically varying rate (and delay) constraints. The approach provides an interface (or filter) between the encoder and the network, with which the encoder's output can be perfectly matched to the network's quality of service characteristics. Although a number of techniques have been developed for the control of live source (which call source bit rate filters) [7] [8] they cannot be used for the transmission of pre-compressed material (e.g., in on-demand video systems). Dynamic rate shaping filters do not require interaction with the encoder and hence are fully applicable to both live and stored video applications. The drs-filter operate directly in the compressed domain of the video signal, manipulating the bitstream so that rate reduction can be effected.

6.2 Receiver-oriented DQM

Receiver-oriented adaptation can be broken down into a number of receiver-side transport functions: (i) delay-jitter management, which calculates flow playout points based on the actual measured delay-jitter from the network; (ii) late-frame management, which monitors late arrivals in relation to the loss metric and the current playout times and takes appropriate action to trade of timeliness and loss; and (iii) bandwidth management, which receives bandwidth indications in the control message portion of the TSDU and adapts the receiver appropriately. In essence the transport protocol "controls" the progress of the media while the receiver "monitors and adapts" to the flow based on the flow specification and the scaling policy

QoS adaptors, which are resident at senders and receivers, are transport-based QoS adaptation managers that arbitrate between the receiver specified QoS and the monitored QoS of the on-going flow. When the transport is in monitoring mode [2] the flow monitor uses an absolute timing method to determine frame receptions times based on timestamps [9] [10]. The flow monitor, as shown in Figure 3, updates the flow state to include these measured reception times statistics. Based on these flow statistics, the sync-filter derives new playout times which are used by the media schedule to adjust the playout point of the flows to the decoding delivery device.

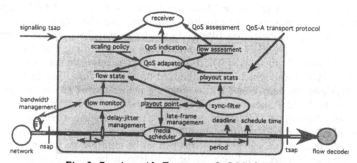

Fig. 3: Receiver-side Transport QoS Mechanisms

Packets that arrive after their expected playout points are discarded by the media scheduler and the late-packet metrics in the playout statistics are updated. The media scheduler simply discards late packets which have missed their schedule time. The media scheduler is based on a split-level scheduler architecture [19] which provides hard deadline guarantees to base layer flows via admission control, and best effort deadlines to the enhancements. Some remedial action may be taken by the QoS adaptor should the loss metric exceed the loss parameter in the flow specification. If the QoS adaptor determines that too many packet losses have occurred over an era, it pushes out the playout time to counter act the late state of packets from the network. Similarly, if loss remains well within the prescribed ranges then the QoS adaptor will automatically and incrementally "pull in" the playout time until loss is detected; see [2] for full details.

Another important receiver-side transport function is bandwidth management. The adaptive service built on the notion of WFS, periodically informs the receiver that more bandwidth is available or announces that the flow is being throttled back. Bandwidth management only covers the enhancement signals of multi-resolution flows. The baseline is not included since resources are guaranteed to the baseline and shared only amongst the enhancements. The announcement of available bandwidth on a flow allows the receiver to take either a full or partial enhancement layer. This depends on whether the flow is in continuous or discrete adaptation mode.

In scalable MPEG2 coding, sources (or virtual sources) produce a base layer signal and up to two enhancement signals, packetize them, and then transmit multiple flows over the network towards the core-switch [18]. The network inevitably introduces some variation in delay of the delivered flows. The receiver depacketizes the flow and then attempts to faithfully play back the complete or partial layers to the decoder. This is accomplished in part by buffering the incoming flow to remove the network-induced jitter and then playing the signal back at some fixed delay offset from the original departure; the term playback point [9] [10] refers to this point in time, which is offset from the original departure time by this fixed delay. The transport protocol utilises sync-filters object for delay-jitter management by calculating playout times of on-going flows based on the user supplied jitter parameter in the flow specification. Sync-filters can also operate on multiple related audio and video flows to provide low-level orchestration management (via the orch-filter).

6.3 Network-oriented DQM

Filter management [4] [21] includes filter placement algorithms which selects the optimum position on a core-based tree [20] to locate filters. Filter placement criteria is based on the current flow topology and the QoS specified by the receiver. As illustrated in Figure 1, QoS filters can be placed at any switch on the media path to meet the needs of receivers. DQM supports a QoS-based multicast scheme where senders and receivers can independently join QoS groups and connect to a core (which is addressed as a core-switch and core-id) [18]. Receivers and senders are said to be "decoupled" at cores. Currently DQM supports three selection filters at the network. These are low complexity and computationally simple filters for selecting sub-signals. Selection filters do not transform the structure of the internal stream i.e. have no knowledge of the format of the encoded flow above differentiating between BL, E1 and E2 sub-signals: (i) *sub-signal filters*, manipulate base and enhancement layers of multi-layer video which are multiplexed on a single flow. The definition of sub-signals is kept general here. Since a flow may be comprised of an anchor and scalable extensions or the I and P pictures of MPEG2's simple profile, or the individual hybrid scalable profile. Sub-signal filters are installed in switches when a receiver joins an on-going session; (ii) *hierarchical-filters*, manipulate base and enhancement layers which are transmitted and received on independent flows in a non multiplexed fashion. In functional terms sub-signal and hierarchical filters can be considered to be equivalent in some cases. In sub-signal filtering one flow characterises the complete signal and in hierarchical-filtering a set of flows characterise the complete signal; and (iii) *hybrid-filters*, combine the benefits of sub-signal and hierarchical filtering techniques to meet the needs for complex sub-signal selection. For example hierarchical filter allows the BL, E1 and E2 to be carried over distinct flows, and the user can accordingly tune into each sub-signal. As an example, the base and enhancement layers of the hybrid scalable MPEG2 flow are each in turn made up of I,P and B pictures at each layer i.e., BL(I,P,B), E1(I,P,B) and E2(I,P,B). Using hybrid-filters the receiver can join the BL QoS group for the main profile and E1 QoS group for the spatial enhancement and then select sub-signals within each profile as needs be (e.g., the I and P pictures of the BL or E1 flows).

7. Conclusion

We have introduced a scheme for the dynamic management of multi-layer flows in heterogeneous multimedia networking environments. Dynamic QoS management (DQM) manipulates and adapts hierarchically coded flows at the end-systems and in the network using a set of scalable objects. The approach is based on three basic concepts: weighted fair share (WFS) service for adaptive flows, the scalable profiles of the MPEG2 standard that can provide discrete adaptation, and dynamic rate shaping algorithms for compressed digital video that provide continuous adaptation. At the present time DQM his being implemented at Lancaster University. The experimental infrastructure at Lancaster is based on 80486 machines running a multimedia enhanced Chorus mirco-kernel [19] using programmable Olivetti Research Limited 4x4 ATM switches. At Columbia we currently using CORBA [17] to propagate selection filters in the network using ASX200 switches. In addition to the implementation we are conducting an extensive simulation study into the feasibility of the adaptive network service for large scale use, and investigating the feasibility of extending the adaptive service concept into the micro-kernel itself [19] for end-to-end QoS support. The results of this phase of the work will be the subject of a forthcoming paper.

8. References

1. Shacham, N, "Multipoint Communication by Hierarchically Encoded Data", *Proc. IEEE INFOCOM'92*, Florence, Italy, Vol.3, pp. 2107-2114, May 1992.
2. Campbell, A., Coulson, G. and Hutchison, D., "A Quality of Service Architecture", *ACM Computer Communications Review*, April 1994.
3. Zhang, L., et. al. "RSVP Functional Specification", Working Draft, draft-ietf-rsvp-spec-03.ps, 1995.
4. Pasquale, G., Polyzos, E., Anderson, E., and V. Kompella, "Fitter Propagation in Dissemination Trees: Trading Off Bandwidth and Processing in Continuos Media Networks", *Proc. Forth International Workshop on Network and Operating System Support for Digital Audio and Video*, Lancaster, November, 1993.
5. Delgrossi, L., Halstrinck, C., Henhmann, D.B, Herrtwich R.G, Krone, J., Sandvoss, C., and C. Vogt, "Media Scaling for Audio-visual Communication with the Heidelberg Transport System", *Proc ACM Multimedia'93* Anaheim, USA, August 1993.
6. Hoffman, D., Speer, M. and G. Fernando, "Network Support for Dynamically Scaled Multimedia Data Streams", *Fourth International Workshop on Network and Operating System Support for Digital Audio and Video*, Lancaster, November, 1993.
7. Kanakia, H., Mishra, P., and A. Reibman, "An Adaptive Congestion Control Scheme for Real Time Packet Video Transport", *Proc. ACM SIGCOMM '93*, San Francisco, USA, October 1993.
8. Eleftheriadis, A., and D. Anastassiou, "Meeting Arbitrary QoS Constraints Using Dynamic Rate Shaping of Code Digital Video", *Fifth International Workshop on Network and Operating System Support for Digital Audio and Video*, April 1995.
9. Jeffay K., Stone, D.L., Talley T. and F.D. Smith, "Adaptive, Best Effort Delivery of Digital Audio and Video Across Packet-Switched Networks", *Proc. Third International Workshop on Network and Operating System Support for Digital Audio and Video*, San Diego, November 1992.
10. Shenker, S., Clark, D., and L. Zhang, "A Scheduling Service Model and a Scheduling Architecture for an Integrated Service Packet Network", Working Draft available via anonymous ftp from parcftp.xerox.com: /transient/service-model.ps.Z, September 1993.
11. Lazar, A. A., Pacifici, G. and D. Pendarakis, "Modeling Video Source for Real Time Scheduling", Multimedia Systems, 1994.
12. Kappner, T. and L. Wolf, "Media Scaling in Distributed Multimedia Object Service, *2nd International Workshop on Advanced Teleservices and High Speed Communication Architectures*, Heidelberg, Germany, September 1994.
13. Steenstrup, M., "Fair Share for Resource Allocation", pre-print, December 1992.
14. Tokuda, H., Tobe, Y., Chou, S.T.C. and Moura, J.M.F., "Continuous Media Communication with Dynamic QOS Control Using ARTS with an FDDI Network", *Proc. ACM SIGCOMM '92*, Baltimore, August 1992.
15. H.262 "Information Technology - Generic Coding of Moving Pictures and Associated Audio", Committee Draft, ISO/IEC 13818-2, International Standards Organisation, UK, March 1994.
16. Paek, S., Bocheck, P., and Chang S.-F., "Scalable MPEG-2 Video Servers with Heterogeneous QoS on Parallel Disk Arrays", *Fifth International Workshop on Network and Operating System Support for Digital Audio and Video*, April, 1995.
17. Lazar, A. A., Bhonsle S., Lim, K.S., "A Binding Architecture for Multimedia Networks", Proceedings of COST-237 Conference on Multimedia Transport and Teleservices, Vienna, Austria, November, 1994
18. Aurrecoechea, C., Campbell, A., Hauw, L. and Hisaya Hadama, "A Model for Multicast for the Binding Architecture", Technical Report, Center for Telecommunications Research, Columbia University, 1995.
19. Coulson, G., Campbell, A and P. Robin, "Design of a QoS Controlled ATM Based Communication System in Chorus", *IEEE Journal of Selected Areas in Communications (JSAC)*, Special Issue on ATM LANs: Implementation and Experiences with Emerging Technology, 1995 (to appear)
20. Ballardie, T., Francis, P. and Jon Crowcroft, "Core Based Tree (CBT) An Architecture for Scalable Inter-Domain Multicast Routing", Proc. ACM SIGCOMM '93, San Francisco, October 1993.
21. Yeadon, N., Garcia, F., Campbell, A and D. Hutchison, "QoS Adaptation and Flow Filtering in ATM Networks", *2nd International Workshop on Advanced Teleservices and High Speed Communication Architectures*, Heidelberg, Germany, 28th September 1994.
22. OMG, "The Common Object Request Broker: Architecture & Specification, Rev 1.3., December 1993.

Dynamic Service Aggregation for Efficient Use of Resources in Interactive Video Delivery

D. Venkatesh and T.D.C. Little

Multimedia Communications Laboratory
Department of Electrical, Computer and Systems Engineering
Boston University, Boston, Massachusetts 02215, USA
{*dinesha,tdcl*}@bu.edu

Abstract. To support future interactive information delivery services there is a need to balance individual interactivity with the desire to maximize the number of supported sessions. Currently, few techniques have demonstrated the ability to renegotiate and scale service parameters per session in progress as required to adapt to differing terminal equipment characteristics and network congestion. This paper addresses this problem through the definition of decomposable service groups that permit aggregation of interactivity, terminal characteristics, and levels of service scaling. The proposed approach applies the characteristics of end applications and data storage requirements to the design of a data scaling mechanism.

1 Introduction

Evolving information delivery applications including video-on-demand (VOD), distance learning, and information browsing are becoming the dominant bandwidth consumers on the Internet and are expected to be so on future CATV and PSTN (public switched telephone networks). There is a trend among service providers towards supporting mixed bidirectional services. To support such services, broadcast technologies (e.g., CATV) must be modified support individual interaction by data recipients. Point-to-point technologies (e.g., Internet, PSTN) must be adapted to support multipoint data distribution. Fig. 1 illustrates such a spectrum of possible services for interactive video delivery. Case (a) requires a high-bandwidth outbound video stream from a data server and a low bandwidth interactive return signal. Case (b) is the multipoint scenario without interaction. Case (c) is fully interactive wherein each client requires a point-to-point session. This final case consumes the most system resources but is typical of true video-on-demand (T-VOD) services.

We propose a mechanism that effectively extends the number of viable sessions that a system can support. This mechanism is called *dynamic service aggregation*. In dynamic service aggregation, service scaling based on the level of interactivity is supported by providing a number of service groups, each permitting a different level of interactivity. Inter-group scaling involves shifting the user between different groups based on the level of interactivity demanded and the

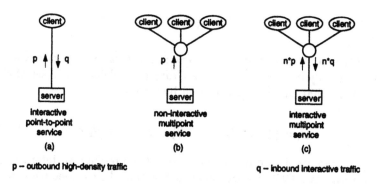

Fig. 1. Interactive Point-to-Point vs. Broadcast Services

availability of network resources. Sessions can be *promoted* by moving them to a group with a higher level of interactivity, or *aggregated* (demoted) by clustering them with similar sessions.

Consider the following distance learning scenario to illustrate the proposed mechanism: An instructor begins a lecture at 1:00PM. Due to limited server I/O bandwidth and network connection service, access to the course and course database is restricted to a window of opportunity during peak hours (e.g., midday). As the course is recorded on the fly, students can join a *service group* for the live multicast or can join late, forming a new group skewed by 10 min. Students who join late can "catch up" by starting interactive point-to-point sessions and browsing the recorded content and moving through it at a quicker pace. Ultimately they *aggregate* their interactive sessions by joining the live service group. When the instructor presents a reference to the previous class, some students may decide to access the video recorded from the previous class. This group can be either aggregated into a single session or spawned out as individual point-to-point connections, depending upon the availability of network resources. Near (in time) sessions are demoted by aggregation into service groups or a subset of the point-to-point sessions are provided with substandard service. A similar scenario exists for entertainment and information (news) video delivery, but with a much larger user population and potential for scaling gains.

The aforementioned scenario benefits from service scaling within and between service groups. The dynamic service aggregation is a greedy approach in that it attempts to reclaim network and server resources from interactive sessions by aggregating them with related non-interactive service groups when they become passive. The proposed scheme assumes clustering (in time) of user requests for common information items as is typical in large-scale video delivery scenarios. This assumption is most valid when it is most useful; as the clustering of requests will most likely occur during periods of high system utilization (e.g., when a new movie or newscast is released). The remainder of this paper describes the dynamic service aggregation protocol in more detail.

2 Dynamic Service Aggregation

Service Group Definition: *Service Groups* allow us to aggregate sessions with similar service (QOS) needs. A *Service Group G_i* is defined as a set of client-to-server sessions that can be characterized by a tuple

$$G_i = (T_j, I_l, S_k) \qquad T_j \in T, I_l \in I, S_k \in S,$$

where T_j represents a terminal-device class, I_l represents an interaction class, and S_k represents a QOS service class; each within their respective superclasses (i.e., T, I, S). I characterizes the delivery of a particular stream of information (e.g., the delivery of an instance of a video recording). The existence of identical tuples indicates the presence of nontrivial service groups (non-unitary) and the gains yielded via aggregation. Masking of terms permits aggregation of service groups across the masked attribute. This masking facilitates an appropriate group decomposition by the scaling mechanism for various services. The number of service groups at a given time is determined by the cardinality of the set of G_i (with masked terms dropped), or $|\cup G_i|$.

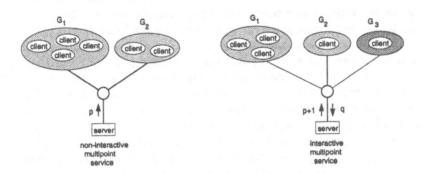

Fig. 2. Service Group Promotion

A service group with more than one element cannot be a T-VOD (interactive) session. A service group of size one represents the presence of a point-to-point interactive session. For broadcast services, users are initially assigned to a single service group based on their terminal and QOS requirements. When a user decides to shift from one mode of operation to another (e.g., broadcast to interactive), the system accommodates the switch by creating a new service group. The tuple describing the new service group differs by the I_l term. This example is illustrated in Fig 2.

Criteria for Service Promotion or Aggregation: Service promotion and aggregation is intended to provide interactive services to virtually all customers while simultaneously supporting a large customer population and yielding improved system utilization. However, this requires that the system carefully manage the distribution of resources. The scheme proposed in this paper attempts to reclaim unused interactive sessions (*passive* sessions) by aggregation. To do this we define the criteria for promoting or demoting sessions to service groups or the consolidation of service group as follows:

A passive session is defined as a session in which the user receives a data stream but has not interacted for some time period Δ. As a first criterion, we propose to aggregate passive connections that have a temporal locality within some duration ϵ. An appropriate value of ϵ is not known at this time; however, we expect this value to be in the range of seconds to minutes, depending on the constraints of the system resources and the number of supported clients. For example, existing PPV systems use values of order 30 minutes for ϵ. Clearly, skewed session groups cannot be merged arbitrarily for temporal locality within an ϵ as this can cause abrupt changes in the data stream and loss of continuity. However, the potential gains by using this approach are significant and are justified because they can be returned to the customer.

The criterion for promotion is the initiation of interaction by an existing client. The system can then try to accommodate this new interaction by the establishment of a dedicated point-to-point session. If appropriate, the newly defined service group can be immediately aggregated with an equivalent service group. In addition, if a client desires improved session quality, a session can be transferred to a different service group for a higher cost. This is achieved by manipulation of the S_k term. Finally, service demotion (aggregation) can be applied by the system to to reduce congestion or server loading.

3 Summary

We described a scheme to efficiently support multipoint information delivery applications by providing levels of constrained interaction and quality of service (QOS), and a means to switch among them. These levels are designed to allow flexibility for clients to adapt to interactive or non-interactive service at various levels of service quality, thereby permitting the system to accommodate the largest possible user population without sacrificing interactive functions.

References

1. Eleftheriadis, A., et al., "Multicast Group Address Management and Connection Control for Multi-Party Applications," Submitted for publication to the *IEEE/ACM Trans. on Networking*, 1994.
2. C. Szyperski and G. Ventre. "Efficient Group Communication with Guaranteed Quality of Service," *Proc. 4th IEEE Workshop on Future Trends in Distributed Computing Systems*, Lisboa, Portugal, September 1993.
3. Vonderweidt, G. et al., "A Multipoint Communication Service for Interactive Applications," *IEEE Trans. on Communications*, Vol. 39, No. 12, 1991, pp. 1875-1885.

Evaluation of QOS-Control Servers on Real-Time Mach*

Kiyokuni Kawachiya[1], Masanobu Ogata[2], Nobuhiko Nishio[3], Hideyuki Tokuda[3]

[1] IBM Research, Tokyo Research Laboratory, <kawatiya@trl.ibm.co.jp>
[2] Power Mobile Systems, IBM Japan, Ltd.
[3] Faculty of Environmental Information, Keio University

Abstract. In an interactive multimedia environment that handles multiple sessions dynamically, a mechanism to control QOS among sessions is very important. As such a mechanism, the QOS-Control Server has been developed on RT-Mach. This paper gives the results of several experiments with this server, and describes the extensions of RT-Mach.

1 Introduction

In the Keio-MMP (MultiMedia Platform) project, we are extending Real-Time Mach 3.0 (RT-Mach) [1] and constructing servers for multimedia processing on our extension [2, 3]. One goal of our project is to incorporate the concept of Quality of Service (QOS), and to manage system resources over multiple continuous-media sessions on the basis of this concept. For such support, there should be some framework for QOS management at the system-software level. We adopted a QOS Manager-based scheme [4], and developed an experimental QOS-Control Server. This paper gives the results of several experiments with this server, and describes the extensions of RT-Mach needed for efficient QOS control.

There have been several studies of QOS-control architecture. The QoS-A by Lancaster University [5] tries to provide an integrated and coherent framework for QOS control. The IBM European Networking Center has proposed a media-scaling architecture with its transport system, HeiTS [6]. Most of these research projects focus on the QOS control in individual sessions over a network, while this paper focuses on dynamic QOS control among multiple sessions in a system.

2 A QOS-Control Server on RT-Mach

In RT-Mach, continuous-media processing programs can be written by using the system's periodic real-time thread, which processes a media data unit, such as a frame of video data, on every invocation. In this paper, such threads will be called "CM-Threads." Deadline misses of the thread can be reported through a deadline port. Using these features, we developed an experimental QOS-Control Server shown in Fig. 1(a). When a CM-Thread is started, it registers its "QOS

---

* This research is conducted under the Open Fundamental Software Technology Project of Information-technology Promotion Agency, Japan (IPA).

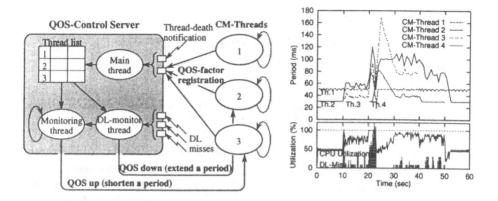

Fig. 1. Experimental QOS-Control Server (a), and the result of QOS control (b)

factor," which describes the characteristics of the session. In accordance with the QOS factors, the server changes the periods of the CM-Threads. To judge the system load, the server monitors the deadline ports of the CM-Threads.

First experiment was carried out with this server using four dummy CM-Threads.[4] Thread 1 represents a session whose period (QOS) is fixed to 50 msec. Thread 2 allows a change in the QOS, but requests 100 msec period in the worst case. Threads 3 and 4 are high-priority sessions started during thread 2. Figure 1(b) shows the actual period of each thread and system status. In this result, QOS control is partially achieved, but there are two major problems: first, the period of each thread jumps up and down before settling, as shown in the section between 20 sec and 30 sec; and second, it vibrates even after the jump is settled.

3 OS Support for Efficient QOS Control

The main reason for the problems is that the OS support is insufficient for efficient QOS control. For more efficient QOS control, we made several extensions to RT-Mach and the QOS-Control Server.

3.1 Extending the Real-Time Thread Model

The largest problem in the experiment is the jump in the period. We found that the problem is caused by the "CATCH UP" semantics of the periodic thread. Figure 2 shows the invocation timing and the actual execution of a periodic real-time thread during overload (hatched area) in RT-Mach. The behavior of the CATCH UP mode is shown in Fig. 2(a). In this mode, the invocation timing is decided in advance and is not changed. If a processing unit is not finished before the next invocation time, the "debt" is transferred to the subsequent invocations.

---

[4] IBM ThinkPad 755C (9545-L, IntelDX4-75MHz) with RT-Mach MK83g was used.

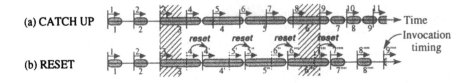

Fig. 2. Behavior of periodic real-time threads during overload

So, even after the overload, the deadlines continue to be missed until the thread catches up its original timing. This causes the jump in the experiment.

In continuous-media processing with QOS control, the settlement of transient overload is more important than the exact invocation timing. Therefore, several new semantics are added to RT-Mach, including a RESET mode, shown in Fig. 2(b). In this mode, the invocation timing is "reset" if a processing unit is not finished before the next invocation. By using the RESET mode, we can create a thread suitable for continuous-media processing. This thread works as a periodic thread if the system load is light, and in best-effort mode in a (transient) overload situation that needs QOS control.

3.2 QOS Control Based on CPU Reservation

By using the RESET mode, the jump-up problem is solved, but there still remains the second "vibration" problem. In the experimental server, it is impossible to avoid deadline misses. CPU utilization at times reaches 100%, and the real-time scheduler in RT-Mach cannot schedule CM-Threads properly. To solve the problem, tighter cooperation between the server and OS is necessary. For this purpose, RT-Mach's CPU reservation mechanism [7] can be used. This mechanism provides a new abstraction named "reserve." Every thread in the system is associated with a reserve, and can gain preferential use of the CPU through it.

Figure 3(a) shows the structure of the new QOS-Control Server based on CPU reservation. Instead of changing the period of CM-Threads directly, the new server "issues" a reserve. The CPU-resource assignment to these reserves is calculated in accordance with the QOS factors. Each CM-Thread adjusts its own QOS (period) to meet the restriction imposed by its reserve. The CPU-time information in the reserve can be used as a hint in making this adjustment. Second experiment was carried out with this new QOS-Control Server. The RESET mode was used for the four dummy CM-Threads. As shown in Fig. 3(b), the behavior of CM-Threads becomes very stable. CPU utilization is also stable at 80%–90%, and the number of deadline misses is almost zero.

In accordance with these experiments, we are now designing a new QOS-control model based on "QOS-Ticket" [8]. In this QOS-Ticket model, QOS control is achieved through cooperation between a QOS Manager and each continuous-media session. The QOS-Ticket, which represents the resource reservation for each session, mediates these two activities. The new QOS-Control Server based on CPU reservation can be considered as a prototype of this model.

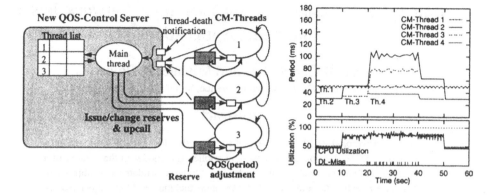

Fig. 3. New QOS-Control Server (a), and the result of QOS control (b)

4 Conclusion

We have described several QOS-control experiments with QOS-Control Servers on RT-Mach. Through these experiments, we found that appropriate OS support is important for effective QOS control. For example, the thread-model extension makes it possible to create a thread suitable for continuous-media processing, and the CPU-reservation mechanism gives more efficient QOS control. Based on these experiments, we are now designing a "QOS-Ticket" model as a new QOS-control scheme.

References

1. H. Tokuda et al.: "Real-Time Mach: Towards a Predictable Real-Time System," *Proc. USENIX Mach Workshop*, pp. 73–82 (1990).
2. K. Kawachiya et al.: "Extending Real-Time Mach for Continuous Media Applications," *Collected Abstracts 4th NOSSDAV*, pp. 55–58 (1993).
3. N. Nishio et al.: "Conductor-Performer: A Middle Ware Architecture for Continuous Media Applications," *Proc. 1st Intl. Workshop on Real-Time Computing Systems and Applications*, pp. 122–131 (1994).
4. H. Tokuda and T. Kitayama: "Dynamic QOS Control based on Real-Time Threads," *Proc. 4th NOSSDAV*, pp. 113–122 (1993).
5. A. Campbell et al.: "A Multimedia Enhanced Transport Service in a Quality of Service Architecture," *Proc. 4th NOSSDAV*, pp. 123–136 (1993).
6. L. Delgrossi et al.: "Media Scaling for Audiovisual Communication with the Heidelberg Transport System," *Proc. ACM Multimedia '93*, pp. 99–104 (1993).
7. C. W. Mercer et al.: "Processor Capacity Reserves: Operating System Support for Multimedia Applications," *Proc. Intl. Conf. on Multimedia Computing and Systems*, pp. 90–99 (1994).
8. K. Kawachiya et al.: "QOS Control of Continuous Media: Architecture and System Support," *IBM Research Report, RT0108*, IBM (1995).

System-Level Resource Management for Network-Based Multimedia Applications[*]

Louis C. Schreier and Michael B. Davis

SRI International, 333 Ravenswood Avenue, Menlo Park, California 94025

Abstract

SRI International (SRI) has developed a model for system-level resource management in distributed systems, and applied this model in the context of a multimedia conferencing application. The model considers user objectives, resource constraints, and adaptable execution techniques. User objectives are specified by means of benefit functions. We have implemented a prototype of a distributed multimedia display application that demonstrates key aspects of the model, including adaptation to a changing execution environment.

1. Introduction

Multimedia applications, especially distributed ones, require large amounts of processing, communication, and storage resources. Current operating system and resource management technologies attempt to provide the maximum set of system resources requested by each application, whether or not the application actually benefits from the full use of those resources.

SRI International (SRI) has developed a system resource management (SRM) model that allows users to express their preferences for media quality by associating *benefit functions* with performance attributes. In our model, the underlying execution system adjusts the amount of processing, communication, and storage resources provided to an application so as to maximize the set of benefit functions that characterize the application. We have developed a demonstration prototype that uses commercial technologies and implements a meta-level execution system on top of operating-system and communication services. In our prototype, we parameterized the benefits a user derives from different frame rates, display window sizes, and compression quality factors. As the underlying resources become more or less available, or as the user changes the benefit functions, the underlying execution system integrates the benefit functions and adjusts the resource usage pattern to maximize the user's benefit.

2. Benefit Model

The users of a distributed system have requirements and preferences regarding the resources that should be made available for accomplishing various tasks. For example, in a multimedia conferencing application, the recipient of an audio and video stream has preferences regarding how the information will be communicated and presented (e.g., the audio quality, the frame rate, the image quality, and the degree of audio/video synchronization). Each quality-of-service preference, or *objective*, can be quantified

---

[*]This research was supported by Rome Laboratory under Contract F30602-91-C-0099.

122

by being expressed as a *benefit function* that relates the benefit accrued to the level of service obtained. This abstraction is similar to the time-value function used in the Alpha operating system [1], in which the value of a computation is related to the time at which it is completed. We extend and generalize the Alpha abstraction to allow the specification of arbitrary objectives, not just timelines.

Figure 1 shows two sample benefit functions for multimedia streams. In Figure 1(a), the benefit increases as the frame rate increases, up to a plateau after which the user perceives no improvement. In Figure 1(b), the benefit decreases as the time difference between the corresponding audio and video streams increases.

By quantifying the level of service for a given objective and assigning relative benefits to various levels, we can construct a benefit function for any objective we wish to define. A resource manager can use benefit functions to compare the relative benefits of different objectives, or of different levels of a single objective, without needing to understand the semantics of particular objectives.

3. Execution Model

Based on the objectives expressed by users, and on the availability of system resources, tradeoffs must be made and appropriate execution techniques must be selected. For example, using lower frame rates and lower video resolutions may free up CPU and communication resources to provide higher-quality audio. Using additional memory and disk buffers may improve audio and video synchronization, while increasing delays.

Resource management decisions are made at two levels, as shown conceptually in Figure 2. Decisions involving medium- to long-range tradeoffs among activities and their objectives are made by a high-level decision maker. The high-level decision maker considers the user objective functions, resource constraints, characteristics of candidate techniques, and system status information to choose (1) the activities (e.g., multimedia conferences or periodic tasks) to execute; (2) the nominal amount of resources to devote to each activity; and (3) the techniques and parameters to use when executing these activities, such that the objectives can be met to the optimal degree consistent with satisfying the resource constraints.

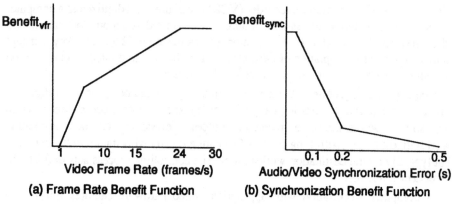

(a) Frame Rate Benefit Function   (b) Synchronization Benefit Function

Figure 1. Sample Benefit Functions for Multimedia

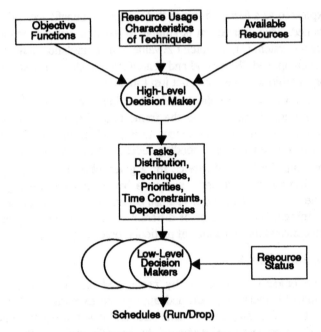

Figure 2. Decision-Making Concept

Real-time scheduling decisions among competing tasks are made by low-level schedulers for each resource. Each low-level scheduler uses status information about its resource, as well as process control abstractions passed down from the high-level decision makers, to make local decisions. While low-level resource scheduling is decentralized, integrated control (through shared resource status information and the consistent interpretation of process control abstractions) is used to ensure that the schedulers complement each other's decisions.

4.   Proof-of-Concept Implementation

We implemented a simple remote video presentation application in which video from a video camera or video cassette recorder (VCR) is captured and digitized at a computer workstation, transferred across a local area network to a destination workstation, and displayed on the monitor of the destination workstation [2,3]. The key concept demonstrated is the adaptation of the distributed application to limited communication resources, according to preferences specified by the user.

The logical architecture of the demonstration implementation is shown in Figure 3. The implementation consists logically of three parts: a sending process (executing on the source workstation); a receiving process (executing on the destination workstation); and a controlling process (executing on any workstation in the network, but typically on the destination workstation). The controlling process acts as the high-level decision maker.

A computer workstation with appropriate video hardware captures full-motion video from a video camera or VCR, digitizes the video frames, and compresses them,

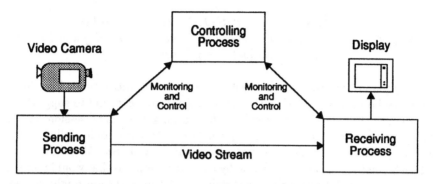

Figure 3. Logical Architecture of SRM Multimedia Demonstration

using the Joint Photographic Experts Group (JPEG) image compression algorithm. The stream of digitized video frames is sent via a local-area network to a destination workstation, using standard communication protocols. The destination workstation reads the digital video stream from the local-area network, uncompresses the frames, and displays them in full motion on its color monitor. By means of a graphical user interface on the destination workstation, the user can connect to the source workstation, start and stop the video playback process, and exit the program. The user can also specify benefit functions that express his or her preferences regarding frame rate, frame size, and Q factor (the latter controls the lossiness of the compression and therefore the quality of the images). The controlling process monitors the amount of video data transferred, and uses a simple heuristic technique to determine the combination of frame rate, frame size, and Q factor that produces the highest total benefit under the current resource constraints. The controlling process controls the video capture, compression, and transfer process accordingly.

The implementation is currently in the prototype stage, but preliminary results show that the system is able to adapt to available resources, according to the preferences expressed by the user. If additional funding becomes available, we plan to further develop and formalize the benefit and execution models, develop distributed algorithms for making distributed control decisions, and extend the demonstration application to support multiple sending and receiving processes.

References

1. J.D. Northcutt and R.K. Clark: *The Alpha Operating System: Programming Model*, Archons Project Technical Report 88021, Department of Computer Science, Carnegie Mellon University, February 1988.

2. M.B. Davis, A. Downing, and T. Lawrence: Adaptable System Resource Management for Soft Real-time Systems, *Symposium on Command and Control Research and Decision Aids*, Monterey, California, June 1994.

3. M.B. Davis: *System Resource Management for Distributed Real-Time Systems*, Final Technical Report, ITAD-2655-FR-95-060, SRI International, Menlo Park, California, 1995.

Session IV: A NOSSDAV Retrospective

Chair: Domenico Ferrari, University of California, Berkeley and Daniel Swinehart, Xerox PARC

This session had two related objectives: to evaluate the nature of the NOSS-DAV workshop process itself, with the goal of improving it, and to suggest technical themes that should be stressed in future workshops. The session had two corresponding parts: each panelist spoke briefly to each topic, followed by a constructive discussion. The first part dealt with how NOSSDAV might evolve?

Dan Swinehart opened the session by floating a proposal that would represent a radical departure from earlier workshops: that the workshop might choose a subject area, and attempt to provide structure to that area, producing perhaps a work product that would provide a bridge between the prototypes that are produced in the research laboratory and the products that reach the market. This type of workshop in the past has produced architectures such as the UIMS model for user interfaces. The workshop would, as a result, include less opportunity to share specific research results or discuss a wider range of topics.

Henning Schulzrinne observed that the successes in the marketplace of the technologies that NOSSDAV addresses has changed the context in which its future should be planned. It must be decided whether to continue to use the prototype hardware and software platforms on which the research has been done, or transition to the commercial platforms on which multimedia systems are being deployed. However NOSSDAV changes, it should remain a venue whose participants share a common language, and should remain a venue for folklore. Although the focused field is dissipating with the emergence of many other conferences that cover the same topics, we need to maintain NOSSDAV as an attractive enough venue that the leading-edge ideas appear here first.

Ralf Steinmetz also observed that while NOSSDAV was a unique event in 1989, there are now many conferences with similar themes. However, the quality level of this workshop remains high. It has not been absorbed by any society or organization and thus can set its own agenda. There is little emphasis on video presentations or demonstrations, leaving time and energy for paper presentations and discussions. The number of participants should be kept low, to encourage interactivity. Ralf would like to see more controversial topics, since they are the ones that engage the audience. On the other hand, he recommends that each workshop include a tutorial presentation on a chosen topic, since none of us is expert on all of the components that make up our systems.

Hide Tokuda echoed the value of maintaining NOSSDAV as a limited-attendance workshop, held alternately at differing sites throughout the world, encouraging all attendees to share research results and discuss burning issues. He suggested that we find a way to attract user interface experts, application writers, and tool builders to the workshop, in order to help inform the operating systems and networking communities about their requirements. He favored the use of video and live demonstration to support points that are being made in presentations, since many of the claims are subjective. In addition, he encouraged the development of common tools permitting the research community to share experimental results.

Domenico Ferrari expressed his delight that NOSSDAV has evolved into such a strong venue, based on the work of the program chairs and committees that have succeeded him since he inaugurated the workshop in 1989. He reminded us that the format, date, size, etc., have been experimented with over the years, each time generally improving the quality of the result. He expressed the widely-held sentiment that the existing objectives of the workshop, to share results and folklore and to address vital issues, are sufficiently important that changes should be evolutionary, and that those seeking more revolutionary approaches should be encouraged to make their own workshops.

In the discussion that followed, there seemed to be considerable (although never total) consensus about the primary qualities that participants find valuable. Rather than recount the discussion, presented here is a summary interpretation of some of these positions:

- Full-length presentations of papers are valuable. Quantitative reports on research results, and detailed reports on work in progress, are more valuable than architectural specifications or taxonomies. No clear consensus emerged about the number of such papers to accept, but some of the other interests would seem to require that this number be reduced.
- In the interests of discussing controversial topics, wild ideas, and outrageous positions, while retaining some sort of structure and content, very short position papers should be explicitly solicited, perhaps some of them invited, in order to seed vigorous discussions. (There is a danger that imposed topics could fail due to lack of true interest by participants.) The format (separate sessions or mixed activities in single sessions) was not extensively discussed. This year's short papers tended to be those that were rejected as long papers, and as a result often the presentations were attempts to squeeze full talks into ten minutes.
- In any given year, a couple of topics tend to be hot. One or two should be identified and treated with particular attention. Possible examples: QOS across heterogeneous networks, or the ATM-meets-Internet topic proposed later. Opinions differ about whether each workshop should have an overall theme.
- One long-term desire has been to design sessions that will produce involved discussion. It would be nice if there were a way to sustain discussions that are going particularly well. This could only be done at the cost of sacrifices to schedule contributed by other sessions. No good approach to achieving this flexibility stood out.
- Separate sessions to discuss outrageous ideas, evaluate claims of "best in class," or support birds of a feather discussions might be useful, but they have their costs in the context of an already full schedule.
- Output from the conference should be limited to proceedings of papers and panels.
- Demonstrations and videos might be useful in order to augment the points being made by presenters, but should not require effort sufficient to distract

from the major goals. They are not considered crucial to the success of the event.

– It would be useful to solicit participation from implementors operating at higher levels in the "food chain," but only if they come prepared to contribute constructively to the core topics of the workshop, by expressing requirements and preferred approaches, not to focus on their own specialties.

Additional comments and positions included:

The Web-based publication approach of this year's NOSSDAV conference is very powerful. Many use NOSSDAV as one of the primary resources for learning about topics falling within its charter. Both long papers and short ones can effectively serve this purpose by including extensive dynamic (URL) references. There was considerable sentiment for working on ways to share research artifacts, and to permit researchers to validate each other's work. This could include the creation of a laboratory at NOSSDAV conferences, where participants could explore these issues with each other, or simply a commitment to discussing the standards and platforms that we might jointly try to attain, so that ideas and artifacts can be shared. Although the use of multimedia technology in the demonstration context was discussed, its use as a tool in support of the collaborative process of workshops such as this was not. We probably do not yet believe that these technologies are mature enough to be used as are overhead projectors, video cameras, and perhaps even laptops connected to LCD panels. Perhaps this is so, but the possibility of bringing our technology along to help with the process should be evaluated. If our technology is too distracting for us ourselves to use, its long-term utility is called into question.

Some other possibilities considered were perhaps NOSSDAV sessions should be broadcast on the MBone. Perhaps audio/video capture tools more capable than analog recorders should be employed. Perhaps in alternate years, NOSSDAV should be a distributed workshop.

The second part of this session was concerned with what themes and technologies NOSSDAV should be addressing? This closing segment of the meeting was much briefer.

Dan put in a pitch for increasing the focus on control issues, such as signaling, conference management, or connection management. This year's session on signaling raised considerable controversy, and was quite interesting. As the basic technology is mastered, these facilities, which provide the application interfaces to the higher levels, will take on increased importance.

Henning urged us to transfer our focus from the individual components, many of which are now being standardized, to a focus on further integrating these components, and increasing their performance.

Ralf believes that the pendulum has swung too far towards networking issues, and that we have given proportionately less attention to operating system features, particularly the implications on applications of feature choices within operating systems. Of particular concern is that the bulk of products are based on commercial OSs, whereas the bulk of our experiments are based on either experimental or increasingly-deprecated ones. Attention needs to be given as to how to bridge this gap.

Hide reminded us that most of our work has been based on workstations hard-wired to networks. We need to pay more attention to mobile, wireless configurations. In addition, we need to learn much more about how to harness the incredible power of myriad networked systems, including supercomputers and very high performance networks, to improve the sophistication and power of multimedia processing.

Domenico suggested that a particular area would benefit from the attention of the NOSSDAV community. Fundamentalists within the Internet community and the ATM community have created a rift that prevents the two groups contributing to each others' efforts. If, as seems likely, the future of the global information infrastructure will be heavily influenced by both forces, whereas neither is likely to dominate, at least for the next few decades, any convergence of these cultures would be valuable. NOSSDAV includes participants from each culture who seem to have a more ecumenical outlook, and may be able to assist with this convergence.

In the ensuing discussion, this latter topic was taken up briefly. One contribution the Internet culture could make would be to stress the value of simple approaches over more complex ones. This is particularly important, because of all of the simple devices that will be connected to tomorrow's networks.

However, there was also a concern that this issue is so big that a focus on it would result in the disappearance of audio and video issues from our plate; there is further danger that fundamentalist elements would be attracted to the conference. However, these issues could certainly be the topic of one session.

There was an enumeration of topics missing from this year's workshop, including papers on the MBone, IP issues, transport protocols, and hardware network interfaces. Domenico points out, however, that we cannot accept what is not submitted. Nor, of course, can we address everything.

Should there be more emphasis on influencing commercial products and activities? Should we declare victory on the audio/video front and expand our vision (and of necessity, the title of the workshop!) to new areas such as virtual reality?

Session V: Audio and Video Systems
Chair: Raj Yavatkar, University of Kentucky

This session focused on a variety of topics that span from scalable video encoding and distributed flow-controlled video delivery to audio packet loss on the internet and industrial uses of multimedia.

The first paper, by Chaddha, Wall, and Schmidt, presented a software-only video delivery system. The system is comprised of a new scalable video compression technique, a delivery subsystem, and a playout mechanism. This exciting approach trades off the use of system resources for a range of delivered video spatial and temporal resolutions.

The second paper, by Cen, Pu, Staehli, Cowan, and Walpole, described a distributed MPEG video and audio player. This system provides the necessary flow control and synchronization to facilitate client-server-based delivery of real-time audio and video across the Internet. A video taped demonstration illustrated the improvement in stream quality achieved by the implemented system over a point-to-point Internet connection of more than 25 hops.

The third paper, by Bolot, Crepin, and Garcia, considered a related Internet application: the delivery of packet audio. The paper investigated the effects of packet losses and consecutive packet losses. Both analytic and observational studies indicate that except in heavy loading scenarios, few consecutive losses occur, suggesting the viability of using forward-error-correction schemes to accommodate packet losses.

The remaining two adjunct papers covered industrial audio/video applications and the use of optimistic resource use for real-time streams. The paper by Lauer et al. covered industrial applications the require audio and video. The paper by Fall, Pasquale, and McCanne described the vic video conferencing application and the implications of not using a real-time resource management mechanism.

An End to End Software Only Scalable Video Delivery System

Navin Chaddha[+], Gerard A. Wall[*] and Brian Schmidt[+]

[+]Computer Systems Laboratory,
Stanford University, CA- 94305.

[*]Sun Microsystems Laboratory,
Mountain View, CA- 94043.

Abstract

Precompressed video delivery systems commonly operate at fixed data rates. However, variations in the availability of network bandwidth and processor cycles are common in dynamic general purpose computing environments. Variability arises from the outright lack of resources (e.g. network bandwidth and cpu cycles), contention for available resources due to congestion, or a user's unwillingness to allocate needed resources to the task. Users of a scalable video delivery system have greater flexibility and therefore, the system can more effectively deliver video in the presence of system resource scarcity. This paper describes an end-to-end system combining a new scalable video compression algorithm, video delivery software, a software video decoder, and a market-based mechanism for the resolution of conflicts in providing video to the user.

1. Introduction

Sun Microsystems Laboratories and Stanford University are building a number of applications and services which require video storage, processing, and transmission as a component. Among the services are a video library and an interactive lecture distribution system. A hierarchical video storage system is being built at Sun Microsystems Laboratories which will use a combination of magnetic disk, CDROM, and digital tape to store a year of television news broadcasts and accompanying annotations. Using text, speech, and image search engines being developed at Sun Microsystems Laboratories, a user will be able to browse the material for relevant news segments which the user may then select for full review. The video storage server migrates the full resolution, full frame rate news stories based on their age and access history from disk to CDROM to tape, leaving lower resolution versions behind to support the browsing operation. If a news segment becomes more popular or important, the higher resolution can then be retrieved and stored at a more accessible portion of the storage hierarchy. We present the design of such a system here.

This paper presents an end-to-end scalable video delivery system for situations in which the encoder operates independently of the decoder's capabilities and requirements. It produces an embedded bit-stream from which different streams at different spatial and temporal resolutions can be easily extracted. Bandwidth scalability with a dynamic range of a few Kbps to several Mbps is provided. The embedded bit-stream produced is prioritized with bits arranged in order of visual importance. The algorithm also allows easy joint-source channel coding on heterogenous networks. The subjective quality of compressed images improves significantly by the use of perceptual distortion measures.

A typical application of scalable compression is multicast over heterogenous networks consisting of ATM, Ethernet, ISDN, and wireless networks having differing bandwidth capabilities, and hosting decoders with various spatial and temporal resolutions, etc. Scalable compression is also important in image browsing, multimedia applications, transcoding to different formats, and embedded television standards. In addition, it can be used to overcome congestion due to contention for network bandwidth, CPU cycles etc., in the dynamic environment of general purpose computing systems.

Most existing compression systems do not have the desired properties of scalable compression. Compression standards like MPEG-2 offer scalability to a limited extent and lack the significant range in bandwidth. There is a significant body of work relating to video servers, most of this research has focussed on scheduling policies for on-demand situations, admission control, and RAID issues. However, there has been very little work on end-to-end software only scalable video delivery systems.

Our work differs in that it provides an end to end software only solution. The overall system combines the scalable compression algorithm, a multiple-user video storage system, disk management, network transport, video delivery software, decoder and synchronization mechanisms. It also provides a market-based mechanism for the resolution of conflicts in providing an end-to-end scalable video delivery service to the user. The service is divided into three groups of components: preprocessing, media server, and media player.

This paper is organized as follows. Section 2 gives the problem statement. Section 3 describes the technical approach. Section 4 presents the scalable video delivery system. Section 5 describes the performance results, and we conclude in Section 6.

2. Problem Statement

The aim of this work is to provide scalable video delivery over a wide range of different networks (ATM, ISDN, ethernet). The target decoder system should be able to define the spatial resolutions (i.e. 160x120, 320x240, 640x480 pixels) and temporal resolution (1 to 30 frames per seconds). Bandwidth scalability, with a dynamic range of the video data from 10 kbps to 10 Mbps, is also a requirement. The video encoding should output an embedded stream from which different streams at different resolutions (both spatial and temporal) and different data rates can be extracted depending on the decoder capabilities and requirements.

The software-based video decoder should be able to operate using minimal CPU resources on a range of systems. Inside the network, it must be possible to easily scale the embedded video stream to fit into a lower bandwidth link or to adapt to congestion. In addition, there should be error resilience in the decoder algorithm to allow for communication errors, such as bit errors or cell loss. The end-to-end system also requires support for audio-video synchronization and a scalable, multiple-user video storage system. Finally, there should be a simple mechanism to transform the user's selection of a delivery bandwidth to choose the most appropriate point in the spatial resolution, temporal resolution, data-rate and quality space.

3. Technical Approach

To meet the goal of a low cost, scalable video delivery system, a new video compression algorithm has been developed. Other standard compression algorithms were rejected as inappropriate. For example, MPEG-2 lacks the dynamic range of bandwidth, is costly to implement in software and uses variable length codes which require additional error correction support. Our scalable compression algorithm produces an embedded bit stream that can easily be rescaled by dropping less important bits from the video stream. Then a low cost, software-based decoder of the scalable video stream has been developed which only performs table lookups and additions to decode a frame of video. We have implemented a disk server which uses careful layout and scheduling to support multiple users of prerecorded video streams. The disk server utilizes the embedded stream of video to scale to the appropriate network bandwidth. Finally, the system utilizes an existing media synchronization framework and an electronic market based mechanism to provide a complete solution for end-to-end video delivery.

The following subsections present the different parts of the system. Section 3.1 describes the encoding and decoding algorithms. Section 3.2 describes the rate scalability algorithm. Section 3.3 describes the decoder architecture. Section 3.4 presents the disk server. Section 3.5 describes the network layer. Section 3.6 discusses the audio sub-system and section 3.7 describes audio-video synchronization. Section 3.8 gives the costing structure.

3.1. Description of algorithm

The video coding algorithm is based on a Laplacian pyramid decomposition [1] (see Figure 1). The original 640x480 image is decimated (filtered and sub-sampled) to 320x240 and 160x120 pixels for encoding. The base 160x120 is compressed and then decompressed. The resulting decompressed image is upsampled and subtracted from the 320x240 pixel image to give an error image. The error image is compressed and transmitted. The 160x120 decompressed image is also upsampled to 640x480 pixels. Then it is subtracted from the original 640x480 image to give an error image which is compressed and transmitted. Thus the encoding stage consists of three image resolutions. The base layer transmitted has the compressed data for 160x120 pixels image. The enhancement layer has the error data for the 320x240 and 640x480 images.

The decoder can support up to three spatial resolutions i.e. 160x120, 320x240 and 640x480 (see Figure 2). It can further support any frame rate as the frames are coded independently. To decode a 160x120 image the decoder just decompresses the 160x120 image. To get 320x240 or 640x480 image the decoder first decompresses the base layer (i.e. 160x120) image and then upsamples it to the correct spatial resolution. The next step is to decompress the error data in the enhancement layer and add it to the upsampled base image.

3.2. Rate or Bandwidth Scalability

In order to achieve bandwidth scalability with an embedded bit stream we use vector quantization [2] as our quantization scheme. Embedded coding is essential in achieving many of the above goals. Vector quantization (across transform bands) is critical in achieving the remaining goals. Both embedded coding and vector quantization can be performed by tree-structured vector quantization (TSVQ). TSVQ is a successive approximation version of vector quantization (VQ) [2]. In ordinary VQ, the codewords lie in an unstructured codebook, and each input vector is mapped to the minimum distortion codeword. This induces a partition of the input space into Voronoi encoding regions. In TSVQ, on the other hand, the codewords are arranged in a tree structure, and each input vector is successively mapped (from the root node) to the minimum distortion child node. This induces a hierarchical partition, or refinement of the input space as the depth of the tree increases. Because of this successive refinement, an input vector mapping to a leaf node can be represented with high precision by the path map from the root to the leaf, or with lower precision by any prefix of the path. Thus TSVQ produces an embedded encoding of the data. If the depth of the tree is R and the vector dimension is k, then bit rates $0/k, 1/k, \ldots\ldots, R/k$ can all be achieved. To achieve further compression the index-planes can be run-length coded followed by entropy coding. Algorithms for designing TSVQs and its variants have been studied extensively. For a survey, see [2].

Instead of using the mean squared error as our distortion measure, we use subjectively meaningful distortion measures in the design and operation of our TSVQ. For this purpose we transform the vector using Discrete Cosine Transform (DCT), and then apply the following input-weighted squared error to the transform coefficients: (1)

$$d_T(y, \hat{y}) = \sum_{j=1}^{K} w_j (y_j - \hat{y}_j)^2$$

133

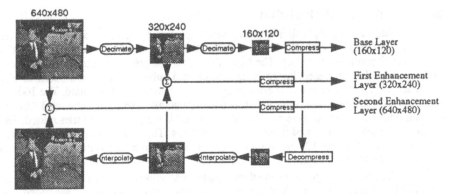

Figure 1. Block Diagram of the Laplacian Pyramid Encoding Algorithm

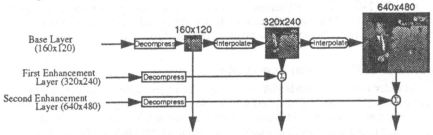

Figure 2. Block Diagram of the Laplacian Pyramid Decoding Algorithm

Here, y_j and $\hat{y}_j$ are the components of the transformed vector y and the corresponding reproduction vector $\hat{y}$, and w_j is a component of the weight vector depending in general on y. That is, the distortion is the weighted sum of squared differences between the coefficients of the original transformed vector and the corresponding reproduced vector.

The weights reflect human visual sensitivity to quantization errors in different transform coefficients, or bands. The weights are input-dependent to model masking effects. When used in the perceptual distortion measure for vector quantization, the weights control an effective stepsize, or bit allocation, for each band. When the transform coefficients are vector quantized with respect to a weighted squared error distortion measure, the weights $w_1, ..., w_K$ play a role corresponding to the stepsizes in the scalar quantization case. By incorporating the perceptual model into the VQ distortion measure, rather than into a stepsize or bit allocation algorithm, the weights can vary with the input vector while the decoder can still operate without the encoder transmitting any side information about the weights.

In the first stage of the compression encoder (Figure 1) an image is transformed using DCT. The second stage of the encoder forms a vector of the transformed block. Next the DCT coefficients are vector quantized using a TSVQ designed with a perceptually meaningful distortion measure. The encoder sends the indices as an embedded stream with different index planes. The first index plane contains the index for the rate $1/k$ TSVQ codebook. The second index plane contains the additional index which along with the first index plane gives the index for the rate $2/k$ TSVQ codebook. The remaining index planes similarly have part of the indices for $3/k, 4/k, ..., R/k$ TSVQ codebooks respectively. The advantage of this encoding of the indices is that it produces an embedded prioritized bitstream. Thus rate or bandwidth scalability is easily achieved by dropping index planes from the embedded bit-stream. The decoder can use the remaining embedded stream to index a TSVQ codebook of the corresponding rate.

Frame-rate scalability can be easily achieved by dropping frames as there is no inter-frame compression in the algorithm right now. The algorithm further provides a perceptually prioritized bit-stream because of the embedding property of TSVQ. There is currently no motion estimation or conditional replenishment in the system. For future work these schemes will be incorporated in the system.

3.3. Decoder Architecture

The decoder of our video system is very simple. The decoder uses the indices from the embedded bit-stream to lookup from a codebook which is designed to use the processor cache efficiently. The process used for decoding the video stream consists of loading the codebooks into the processor cache and performing lookups from it. The base layer is obtained by performing lookups while the enhancement layers are obtained by performing lookups of the base and error images followed by addition. All operations of the decoder are performed beforehand i.e. by preprocessing.

The TSVQ decoder codebook has the inverse DCT performed on the codewords of encoder codebook. Thus at the decoder there is no need for performing inverse block transforms. Color conversion i.e. YUV to RGB conversion is also performed as a pre-processing step by storing the corresponding color converted codebook. To display video on a limited color palette display we color quantize the resulting codewords of the decoder codebook using the color quantization algorithm proposed by Chaddha et al [3]. This is achieved by forming a RGB or YUV color vector from the codewords of the codebook and color quantizing them to the required alphabet size. Thus the same embedded index stream can be used for displaying images on different alphabet decoders which have the appropriate codebooks with the correct alphabet size. (1-bit to 24-bit color)

3.4. Disk Layout

The disk layout consists of laying the video as two streams: base layer and enhancement layer streams. For our system we have not stored the error signal for the 640x480 resolution, since fairly good quality video was provided by bilinear interpolation of the 320x240 resolution images.

The base layer data is stored as a separate stream on the disk subsystem from the enhancement layer data. This allows the system to admit more users if fewer users choose to receive the enhancement layer data. The base layer data is stored with the following hierarchy:

1. Frames: Data for each frame is stored together. Each frame has a set of index planes corresponding to different number of bits used for the lookup.

2. Scalable Stream: The compressed stream consists of lookup indices with different number of bits depending on the bandwidth and quality requirement. The lookup indices for each frame are stored as groups of index planes pre-formatted with application level headers for network transmission. The 4 most significant bits of the lookup indices are stored together as the first section of the frame block. Then 4 additional 1-bit planes of lookup are stored in sequence as separate sections of the frame block to provide lookup indices with 4, 5, 6, 7, 8 bits respectively. The different lookup indices provide data streams with different bandwidth requirements. The server fetches the base signal frame block from the disk, transmits the selected sections on the network leaving the repacking of the bit planes into lookup indices to the receiving application.

The error data is placed similarly as another data stream. The lookup indices are stored as the most significant 2 bits of the lookup indices in the first section for each frame block. Then again the second 2 bits of the lookup indices as the second section. Then the 4 additional 1-bit sections of lookup indices are stored to provide lookup indices with 2, 4, 5, 6, 7, 8 bits respectively.

The video server uses RAID-like techniques [4] to stripe each (data stream) across several drives. The design allows for recovery from failure of any single disk without diminishing the capacity of the server. Because of the RAID approach, there is no restriction on the number of active users of a given title, as long as they can be accommodated within the servers's total bandwidth. That is, the usage can range from all active users receiving the same title at different offsets to all receiving different streams.

The streams of base and enhancement layer data are striped in fixed size units across the set of drives in the RAID group with parity placed on an additional drive. The selection of the parity drive is fixed since data updates are extremely rare compared to the number of times the streams are read. The current striping policy keeps all of the lookup indices for an individual frame together on one disk; while this costs some loss of storage capacity due to fragmentation, this policy allows for ease of positioning when a user is single stepping or fast forwarding their display. Use of parity on the stripe level allows for quick recovery after a drive failure at the cost of using substantially more buffer space to hold the full xor recovery data set.

3.5. Network Layer

The video server utilizes the planar bit stream format directly as the basis of the packet stream in the network layer. The embedded stream bits plus the application packet header are read from the disk and transmitted on the network in exactly the same format. For example, the base video layer has the four most significant bits of the lookup indices stored together so those bits are transmitted as one 2440 byte packet and each additional index bit plane of the less significant bits is transmitted as a separate 640 byte packet. The header contains a frame sequence number, nominal frame rate, size, a virtual time stamp, and a bit plane type specifier sufficient to make each packet an identifiable stand-alone unit. The server uses the self identifying header to extract the each bit plane group packet from the striped frame data retrieved from the disk subsystem.

The server also uses the sequence and rate information in the header as the means to pace the network transmission and disk read requests. The server uses a feedback loop to measure the processing and delivery time costs of the disk reads and queuing the network packets for transmission. The server then uses these measures to schedule the next disk read and packet transmission activities to match the video stream's frame rate (i.e. at X milliseconds in the future start transmitting the next frame of video). The server can moderate the transmission rate based on slow down/speed up feedback from the decoder.

The video decoder is responsible for the reassembly of the lookup indices from the packets received from the network. In the event of the loss of one of the less significant index bit plane packets, the decoder uses the more significant bits to construct a shorter lookup table index yielding a lower quality but still recognizable image.

The use of separately identified packets containing index bit planes makes it possible for networks to easily scale the video as a side effect of dropping less important packets. In networks providing QOS qualifiers such as ATM, multiple circuits can be used to indicate the order in which packets should be dropped (i.e. the least significant bit plane packets first). In an IP router environment, packet filters can be constructed to appropriately discard less important packets. For prioritized networks the base layer will be sent on the high priority channel while the enhancement layer will be sent on the low priority channel. In order to provide error resiliency the use of a fixed-rate coding scheme with some added redundancy, allows robustness in the face of packet loss.

The server supports two usage scenarios:

1. **Point-to-Point demand**: In this case each destination system decoder presents its specific requirements to the server. The server then sends the selected elements of the embedded stream across the network to the destination. A separate network stream per destination allows the user to have VCR style functionality such as play/stop/rewind fast forward/fast

reverse. If congestion occurs on the network, then the routers and switches can drop packets from the embedded stream to give a lesser number of lookup bits.

2. **Multicast:** In this case the server puts out the entire embedded stream for the different resolutions and rates onto the network as a set of trees. The server has no idea about the decoders at the destinations. There may be one to eleven trees depending on the granularity of traffic control desired. The primary traffic management is performed during the construction of the unicast trees, by not adding branches of the trees carrying the less important bit streams to the lower bandwidth networks. The network in this case takes care of bandwidth mismatches by not forwarding packets to the networks which are not subscribed to a particular tree. Switches and routers can still react to temporary congestion by dropping packets from the embedded stream to deliver fewer bits of lookup.

3.6. Audio Subsystem

The delivery system treats the audio track as a separate stream which is stored on disk and transmitted across the network as a separate entity. The audio format supports multiple data formats from 8 KHz telephony quality (8 bit mu-law) to 48 KHz stereo quality (2 channel, 16 bit linear samples) audio. Most of the video clips on the current system have 8 KHz telephony audio since the intent is to be able to distribute the material over medium to low bandwidth networks. The server has the capability to store separate high and low quality audio tracks and to transmit the audio track selected by the user. Since the audio transits the network on a separate circuit, the audio can easily be given a higher QOS than the video streams. Rather than load the networks more with duplicate audio packets such as [8], we ramp the audio down to silence when packets are lost or overly delayed.

3.7. Audio/Video Synchronization

Since audio and video are delivered via independent mechanisms to the decoding system, the two streams must be synchronized for final presentation to the user. At the decoder, the receiving threads communicate through the use of a shared memory region, into which the sequence information of the current audio and video display units are written. Since the human perceptual system is more sensitive to audio dropouts and audio is difficult to temporally reprocess, the decoder uses the audio codec as the master clock for synchronization purposes. As the streams progress, the decoder threads post the current data items' sequence information onto the "blackboard", and the slave threads (such as the video decoder) use the posted sequence information of the audio stream to determine when their data element should be displayed. The slave threads then delay until the appropriate time if the slave is early (more than 80 milliseconds ahead of the audio). If the slave data is too late (more than 20 milliseconds behind the audio), then it is discarded on the assumption that continuing to process late data will delay more timely data. The video decoder can optionally measure the deviation from the desired data delay rate and send speed up and slow down indications back to the video server. This process synchronizes streams whose elements arrive in a timely fashion and does not allow a slow stream to impede the progress of the other streams.

3.8. Costing Structure

In the event of scarcity of resources, some global prioritization of user requests must take place, or overload collapse is likely. This system utilizes payment for services and resources as the means of defining the overall value of each resource allocation decision. Given these values, a total ordering of the user requests can be made and the less important requests can be dropped. The user specifies what he or she is willing to pay for a given service; this proposed payment along with the required resources (network and disk bandwidth) are submitted to an electronic market which uses micro-economic models to decide what amount of bandwidth resource is available to the user [5]. For that particular bandwidth a table is indexed to find the best possible combination of spatial resolution, frame rate and data rate (number of bits of lookup to be used) to give the best quality of decompressed video. This table is built using a subjective distortion measure [6]. The user also has the option of specifying the spatial resolution, frame rate and bandwidth directly.

4. Scalable Video System

The overall system combines the compression algorithm, disk management, network transport, decoder and synchronization mechanisms to provide an end to end scalable video delivery service. The service is divided into three groups of components: preprocessing, media server, and media player.

The preprocessing components are audio capture, video capture, video compression, and a data stripping tool. The video is captured and digitized using single step VCR devices. Then each frame is compressed off-line (non-real time) using the encoding algorithm. Currently, it takes about one second on a Sparc 20 Workstation to compress a frame of video data and the single step VCR devices can step at a one frame per second rate so capture and compression can be overlapped. The audio data is captured as a single pass over the tape. The audio and video time stamps and sequence numbers are aligned by the data striping tool as the video is stored to facilitate later media synchronization. The audio and video data are striped onto the disks with a user-selected stripe size. Currently, all of the video data on the server uses a 48 kilobyte stripe size since 48 kilobytes per disk transfer provides good utilization at peak load with approximately 50% of the disk bandwidth delivering data to the media server components.

The media server components include a session control agent, the audio transmission agent, and the video transmission agent. The user connects to the session control agent on the server system and arranges to pay for the video service and network bandwidth. The user can specify the cost he/she is willing to pay and an appropriately scaled stream will be provided by the server. The session control agent then sets up the network delivery connections and starts the video and audio transmission agents. The session control agent is the single point of entry for control operations from the consumers remote control, the network management system, and the electronic market. The audio and video transmission agents read the media data from the striped disks and pace the transmission of the data onto the network. The video transmission agent scales the embedded bit-stream in real-time by transmitting only the bit planes needed to reconstruct the selected resolution at the decoder. For example, a 320x240 stream with 8 bits of base, 4 bits of enhancement signal at 15 frames per second will transmit every other frame of video data with all 5 packets for each frame of the base and only two packets containing the four most significant bits of the enhancement layer resulting in 864 kilobits of network utilization. The server sends the video and audio either for a point-to-point situation or a multicast situation.

The media player components are the software based video decoder, the audio receiver, and a user interface agent. The decoder receives the data from the network and decodes it using lookup tables and places the results onto the frame buffer. The decoder can run on any modern microprocessor without the CPU loading significantly. The audio receiver loops reading data from the network and queuing up the data for output to the speaker. In the event of audio packet loss, the audio receiver will ramp the audio level down to silence level and then back up to the nominal audio level of the next successfully received audio packet. The system performs media synchronization [7] to align the audio and video streams at the destination. End to end feedback is used in the on demand case to control the flow. In the multicast case, the destinations are slaved to the flow from the server with no feedback. The user interface agent serves as the control connection to the session agent on the media server passing flow control feedback as well as the user's start/stop controls. The user can specify the cost he or she is willing to pay and an appropriate stream will be provided by the system.Figure 3 shows the block diagram of the system. The entire scalable system makes collaborative video over hetrogeneous networks possible without any special purpose hardware support.

5. Performance Results

A prototype of the system described in this paper has been implemented at Sun Microsystems Labs. The video data rate varies from 19.2 kbps to 2 Mbps depending on the spatial and temporal requirement of the decoder and the network bandwidth available. The PSNR varies between 31.63 dB to 37.5 dB. Table 1 gives the results for the decoding of a 160x120 resolution video on a Sparc Station 20. It can be seen from Table 1 that the time required to get the highest quality stream (8-bit index) at 160x120 resolution is 2.45 ms per frame (sum of lookup and packing time). This corresponds to a potential frame rate of 400 frames/sec. Similarly Table 2 gives the results for the decoding of a 320x240 resolution video on a Sparc Station 20. It can be seen from Table 2 that the time to required to get the highest quality stream (8-bit base index and 8-bit first enhancement layer index) at 320x240 resolution is 7.76 ms per frame (sum of lookup and packing time). This corresponds to a potential frame rate of 130 frames/sec. Table 3 gives the results for the decoding of a 640x480 resolution video again on a Sparc Station 20. It can be seen from Table 3 that the time to required to get the highest quality stream (8-bit base and 8-bit enhancement layer) at 640x480 resolution is 24.62 ms per frame (sum of lookup and packing time). This corresponds to a potential frame rate of 40 frames/sec.

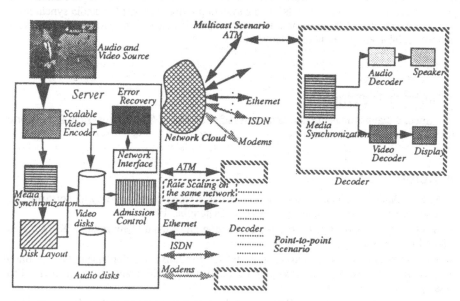

Figure 3. Block Diagram of the Scalable Video Delivery System

Table 4 shows the results for each individual disk for 160x120 resolution video. It can be seen from the Table that to get the highest quality stream (8-bit base) at 160x120 takes 5.60 ms of CPU time and an average CPU load of 2% on a Sparc 20 workstation. The average disk access time per frame is 16ms. Similarly Table 5 shows the results for each individual disk for 320x240 resolution video. It can be seen from the Table that to get the highest quality stream (8-bit base and 8-bit enhancement layer) at 320x240 takes 12.73 ms of CPU time and an average CPU load of 7% on a Sparc 20 workstation. The average disk access time per frame is 18ms.

6. Conclusions

In this paper we have presented a low cost, end-to-end scalable video delivery system combining a new scalable video compression algorithm, video delivery software, multiple-user video storage system, a software video decoder, and a market-based mechanism for the resolution of conflicts for shared resources which occur in providing streams of video to a community of users. In contrast with existing schemes, this approach provides clients with the ability to trade off video quality for system resources, permitting a much higher degree of overall value to be delivered with a given configuration of hardware.

The video encoding process creates an embedded video stream from which different streams at different resolutions (both spatial and temporal), and different rates, can be extracted depending on the capabilities and requirements of the decoders. In this system, the decoding subsystem defines the spatial and temporal resolutions of its displayed video stream (i.e., either 160x120, 320x240, or 640x480 pixels per frame, and from 1 to 30 frames per second). The various video quality specifications result in communications bandwidth scalability with a dynamic range from 10 Kbps to 10 Mbps. A low cost, software-based decoder of the scalable video stream has been developed which primarily uses table lookups and additions to decode frames of video. A disk-based video server has also been implemented which makes use of careful layout and scheduling to support multiple clients of the prerecorded video streams. In addition, the system provides support for media synchronization and makes use of an electronic-market-based mechanism to provide a complete solution for scalable end-to-end video delivery.

7. Acknowledgments

Special thanks to Duane Northcutt and James Hanko of Sun Microsystem Laboratories for many fruitful discussions.

8. References

1. N. Chaddha, "An efficient algorithm for scalable video compression with software only decode," Technical Report Sun Microsystems, September 1994.

2. A. Gersho and R.M. Gray, Vector Quantization and Signal Compression, Kluwer Academic Press, 1992.

3. N. Chaddha, et al. "Fast Vector Quantization Algorithms for Color Palette Design Based on Human Vision Perception," accepted for publication IEEE Transactions on Image Processing.

4. F. Tobagi, et al., "Streaming RAID- A disk array management system for video files," Proc. ACM Multimedia 1993.

5. M. Miller, "Extending markets inward," Bionomics Conference, San Francisco, Oct. 1994.

6. N. Chaddha and T.H.Y. Meng, "Psycho-visual based distortion measures for image and video compression", Proc. of Asilomar Conference on Signals, Systems and Computers, Nov. 1993.

7. J.D. Northcutt and E.M. Kuerner, "System Support for Time-Critical applications," Proc. NOSSDAV' 91, Germany, pp. 242-254.

8. K. Jeffay, et al. "Adaptive, Best-Effort Delivery of Digital Audio and Video Across Packet-Switched Networks," Proc. NOSSDAV' 92.

Table 1. Results for 160x120 resolution (Decoder)

No. of Bits of Lookup	PSNR (dB.)	Bandwidth as a function of frame rate (N) Kbps	CPU time per frame (ms)	Packing time per frame (ms)
4	31.63dB.	19.2 N	1.24 ms	0 ms
5	32.50 dB.	24 N	1.32 ms	0.52 ms
6	34 dB.	28.8 N	1.26 ms	0.80 ms
7	35.8 dB.	33.6 N	1.10 ms	1.09 ms
8	37.2 dB	38.4 N	1.18 ms	1.27 ms

Table 2. Results for 320x240 resolution (8 bit-lookup base)

No. of Bits of Lookup	PSNR (dB.)	Bandwidth as a function of frame rate (N) Kbps	CPU time per frame (ms)	Packing time per frame (ms)
2	33.72 dB.	48 N	6.01 ms	0.385 ms
4	35.0 dB.	52.8 N	6.04 ms	0.645 ms
5	35.65 dB.	62.4 N	6.05 ms	0.92 ms
6	36.26 dB.	67.2 N	6.08 ms	1.20 ms
7	36.9 dB.	72 N	6.04 ms	1.48 ms
8	37.5 dB.	76.8 N	6.09 ms	1.67 ms

Table 3. Results for 640x480 with 320x240 interpolated

No. of Bits of Lookup	PSNR (dB.)	Bandwidth as a function of frame rate (N) Kbps	CPU time per frame (ms)	Packing time per frame (ms)
2	33.2 dB	48 N	22.8 ms	0.385 ms
4	34 dB	52.8 N	22.87 ms	0.645 ms
5	34.34 dB	62.4 N	23.14 ms	0.92 ms
6	34.71 dB	67.2 N	22.93 ms	1.20 ms
7	35.07 dB	72 N	22.90 ms	1.48 ms
8	35.34 dB	76.8 N	22.95 ms	1.67 ms

Table 4. Results for 160x120 at the disk server

No. of Bits of Lookup	Bandwidth as a function of frame rate (N) Kbps	CPU time per frame (ms)	Seek-time (ms)	Avg. CPU Load
4	19.2 N	2.84 ms	16 ms	1%
5	24 N	3.67 ms	16 ms	1%
6	28.8 N	4.48 ms	14 ms	2%
7	33.6 N	4.92 ms	14 ms	2%
8	38.4 N	5.60 ms	16 ms	2%

Table 5. Results for 320x240 at the disk server

No. of Bits of Lookup	Bandwidth as a function of frame rate (N) Kbps	CPU time per frame (ms)	Seek-time (ms)	Avg. CPU Load
2	48 N	10.47 ms	18 ms	6%
4	52.8 N	11.02 ms	16 ms	6%
5	62.4 N	11.55 ms	18 ms	6%
6	67.2 N	12.29 ms	20 ms	7%
7	72 N	12.55 ms	20 ms	7%
8	76.8 N	12.73 ms	18 ms	7%

A Distributed Real-Time MPEG Video Audio Player *

Shanwei Cen, Calton Pu, Richard Staehli,
Crispin Cowan and Jonathan Walpole

Department of Computer Science and Engineering
Oregon Graduate Institute of Science and Technology
Portland, Oregon, USA
{*scen, calton, staehli, crispin, walpole*} *@cse.ogi.edu*

Abstract. This paper presents the design, implementation and experimental analysis of a distributed, real-time MPEG video and audio player. The player is designed for use across the Internet, a shared environment with variable traffic and with great diversity in network bandwidth and host processing speed. We use a novel toolkit approach to build software feedback mechanisms for client/server synchronization, dynamic Quality-of-Service control, and system adaptiveness. Our experimental results show that the feedback mechanisms are effective, and that the player performs very well in the Internet environment.

1 Introduction

Modern workstation and network technology has made software-only solutions for real-time playback of compressed continuous video and audio feasible, even across the Internet. The Internet environment is characterised by the lack of a common clock, wide-spread resource sharing, dynamic workload, and great diversity in host processing speed and network bandwidth. To meet the strict timing requirements of distributed multimedia presentation in the face of such characteristics requires new approaches to client/server synchronization, Quality-of-Service (QoS) control and system adaptiveness.

One approach to client/server synchronization is to use an external mechanism, such as the Network Time Protocol (NTP) [4], to build the illusion of a common clock. However, since such protocols are not ubiquitous, and are rarely engaged between geographically separate sites, it is currently necessary for distributed real-time applications to implement their own mechanisms for maintaining client/server synchronization. Similarly, it has been shown that QoS guarantees can be provided with admission control and resource reservation. However, such approaches are not possible in the current Internet environment, and are still far from being supported in commercial operating systems.

---

* This project is supported in part by grants from ARPA and the National Science Foundation, and donations from Tektronix, Hewlett-Packard and the Portland Trail Blazers.

This paper explores the use of *software feedback* [5, 6] for client/server synchronization, dynamic QoS control and system adaptiveness in the Internet environment. Software feedback mechanisms already exist in many forms, such as the flow control mechanism used in TCP [2], the clock synchronization mechanism used in NTP [4], and Rowe's video stream frame rate control mechanism [8]. However, most existing approaches are implemented in an ad-hoc manner, and are usually hard-coded for a particular application. Consequently, they suffer from arbitrary structure, hard-to-predict behavior, and wasted effort due to repeated design and implementation of logically similar components. We are developing a toolkit-based approach [6] in order to overcome these drawbacks.

To study the effectiveness of software feedback mechanisms for client/server synchronization, dynamic QoS control and system adaptiveness, and to investigate the toolkit approach, we have constructed a distributed real-time MPEG video and audio player. The player consists of a client and audio and video servers which can be distributed across the Internet. It supports variable play speed and random positioning as well as common VCR functions. The salient features of the player include: (a) real-time, synchronized playback of MPEG video and audio streams, (b) user specification of desired presentation quality, (c) QoS adaptation to variations in the environment, and (d) a toolkit approach to building software feedback mechanisms.

This paper presents the design, implementation and experimental analysis of the player and the software feedback mechanisms. Section 2 describes the overall system architecture. Section 3 discusses the software feedback mechanisms used in the player. Section 4 outlines the implementation. Section 5 presents performance results. Section 6 outlines related work. Finally, Section 7 discusses future work and concludes the paper.

2 System Architecture

Figure 1 shows the architecture of the player. The player has five components: a video server (VS), an audio server (AS), a client, and video and audio output devices. VS manages video streams. AS manages audio streams. The client is composed of a video decoder and a controller which controls playback of both video audio streams and provides a user-interface. The client, VS and AS reside on different hosts, communicating via network. Video and audio output devices reside on the same host or high speed local area network as the client.

A program for the player is a video and audio stream pair: <video-host:video-file-path, audio-host:audio-file-path>, where a video stream is a sequence of frames, and an audio stream is a sequence of samples. These two streams are recorded strictly synchronously. We refer to a contiguous subsequence of audio samples corresponding a video frame as an *audio block*. Therefore, there is a one-to-one correspondence between video frames and audio blocks.

During playback of a program, VS and AS retrieve the video and audio streams from their storage and send them to the client at a specified speed. The

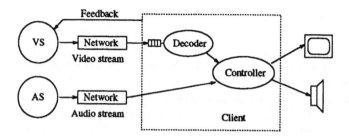

Fig. 1. Architecture of the player

client buffers the streams to remove network jitter, decodes video frames, resamples audio, and plays them to the video and audio output devices respectively.

Programs can be played back at variable speed. *Play speed* is specified in terms of frames-per-second (fps). The player plays a program in real-time by mapping its logical time (defined by sequence numbers for each frame/block) into system time (real time, in seconds) on the client's host machine. Suppose the system time at which frame(i) is displayed is T_i, and the current play speed is P fps, then the time at which frame($i + 1$) is played is $T_{i+1} = T_i + \frac{1}{P}$. VS and AS also map the program's logical time into their own system time during the retrieval of the media streams. Synchronization between audio and video streams is maintained at the client by playing audio blocks and displaying video frames with the same sequence number at the same time.

If any stage of the video pipeline, from VS through the network and client buffer to the decoder, does not have sufficient resource to support the current QoS specification it can decide independently to drop frames. The controller of the client also drops late frames (frames which arrive after their display time). A similar approach is implemented for the audio pipeline.

One metric to measure the actual QoS level of the player is its video *display frame rate*. The display frame rate is the number of frames-per-second displayed by the client. Display frame rate should not be confused with play speed, which is also specified in frames-per-second. A valid display frame rate is always equal to or lower than the current play speed. For example, Suppose in a playback, the play speed is P fps, and the display frame rate is F fps ($0 \leq F \leq P$), then $\frac{P-F}{P} * 100\%$ of all frames are dropped by the player.

The maximum actual QoS level supported by a pipeline is referred to as its *effective bandwidth*. In a dynamic system, the effective bandwidth changes with the current system load level. Since our player adapts to changes in effective bandwidth, it can be classified as taking a *best effort* approach to maintaining QoS. However, the player's interface allows users to specify desired QoS levels for video and audio playback. This approach allows users to trade presentation quality for reduced resource consumption, which is useful in a shared environment with limited and diverse resources.

User QoS specification is currently restricted to a single dimension, a desired display frame rate. Future versions of the player will support QoS specifications in several other dimensions [11]. The player tries to yield a display frame rate up to the user-specified frame rate. To comply with the user-specified frame rate, the player drops excessive frames at the source of the pipeline, i.e., VS does not retrieve them from storage. VS also spaces the dropped frames evenly throughout the video stream.

We assume that the video and audio devices are very close to the client and hence delay from the client to the output devices can be ignored. We also assume that the mapping from logical time to client system time is precise. In practice, these assumptions are reasonable, especially if the client controller runs with real-time priority. However, a number of other serious problems still remain to be solved. These problems include client/server clock drift, insufficient effective bandwidth to meet the user-specified QoS, and stalls and skips in the pipeline. The next section introduces the basic concepts behind software feedback and shows how it can be used to solve these problems.

3 Software Feedback for Synchronization & QoS Control

Software feedback is a technique that uses feedback mechanisms similar to hardware feedback such as phase-lock loops in control systems [1, 5]. A feedback mechanism monitors the output or internal state of the system under control, compares it to the goal specification, and feeds the difference back to adjust the behavior of the system itself. One beneficial property of feedback mechanisms is that they can control complex systems even when they have only partial knowledge of the system's internal structure. This property suggests that they could be useful in controlling systems, such as our player, that must operate in highly complex and unpredictable environment, such as the Internet.

3.1 A Toolkit Approach to Software Feedback

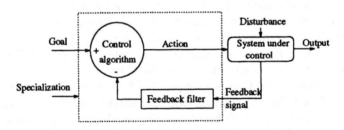

Fig. 2. Software feedback system structure

The structure of a software feedback mechanism is shown in Fig. 2. The mechanism has two basic components: a feedback filter and a control algorithm. The output or internal state of the system under control is measured to get a feedback signal. This signal is then input to the filter to eliminate transient noise.

The control algorithm compares the output of the feedback filter against a goal specification, and takes action to adjust the system under control to keep its behavior within the specification.

A software feedback toolkit includes a set of basic filters and control algorithms, building blocks that are well specified and understood. Filters and control algorithms for a specific feedback mechanism can then be composed from these building blocks. The filters and control algorithms can also be specialized by changing parameter values or modifying structures. In a large feedback system, this specialization might be the result of actions taken by other feedback mechanisms. Hence, the toolkit enables the construction of a potentially large network of interacting feedback mechanisms.

The set of basic filters can include low-pass filters, differential filters, integration filters etc. Consider an input sequence $input[i]$ $(i \geq 0)$. The output sequence $lowpass[i](i \geq 0)$ of the low-pass filter described by Massalin [5], with a parameter R $(0 \leq R \leq 1.0)$, is defined as:

$$lowpass[0] = input[0]$$
$$lowpass[i] = (1.0 - R) * lowpass[i - 1] + R * input[i] \qquad \text{where } i > 0$$

Here the output of the low-pass filter is actually the weighted sum of recent inputs with an aging factor. The construction of filters and control algorithms is the subject of ongoing research, and will appear in future work.

3.2 Software Feedback for Client/Server Synchronization

VS works ahead of the client to mask the video pipeline delay, and a buffer at the client side removes network delay jitter. The remaining client/server synchronization problems are: (a) the server and client system clocks may not be running at exactly the same rate, causing the client and server logical clocks to drift apart and the client buffer to eventually overflow or become empty, (b) the VS logical clock may skip or stall causing a permanent drop or rise in the fill level of the client buffer, and (c) the work-ahead time of VS may be unnecessarily large, reducing player responsiveness and consuming more client buffer space than necessary. We propose a software feedback mechanism which solves these synchronization problems and adapts the player to its dynamic environment.

The synchronization feedback mechanism is implemented in the client, as shown in Fig. 3. It measures the current client time, T_c, and the server time, T_s, as observed at the client, and computes the raw server work ahead time, $T_{rswa} = T_s - T_c$. T_{rswa} is input to a low-pass filter, F_1, to eliminate high frequency jitter and get the server work ahead time, T_{swa}. The control algorithm then compares T_{swa} with the target server work ahead time, T_{tswa}, and takes action accordingly.

T_{twsa} in turn is determined by the current network delay jitter level. The jitter of the measured current server work ahead time, $|T_{rswa} - T_{swa}|$, is fed to another low-pass filter, F_2, to get the network delay jitter, J_{net}. J_{net} is then used

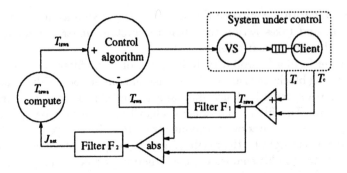

Fig. 3. Structure of the synchronization feedback mechanism

Event	Feedback Action
T_{swa} too low $\quad T_{swa} < \frac{1}{2}T_{tswa}$	Speed up C_s rate or skip C_s
T_{swa} too high $\quad T_{swa} > \frac{3}{2}T_{tswa}$	Slow down C_s rate or stall C_s
T_{tswa} too low $T_{tswa} < \frac{1}{4}K * J_{net}$	Double T_{tswa}
T_{tswa} too high $T_{tswa} > K * J_{net}$	Halve T_{tswa}

Table 1. Functionality of the synchronization feedback mechanism

to compute T_{tswa}. We get a composite jitter level filter by composing the basic low-pass filters F_1 and F_2.

Table 1 describes the functionality of the synchronization feedback mechanism. C_s refers to the VS clock, and $K > 0$ is a constant. Whenever the control algorithm detects that T_{swa} has deviated too far from T_{tswa}, it adjusts the VS clock rate or skips or stalls it for a certain amount of time, to bring T_{swa} back to T_{tswa}. The decision to adjust the rate or stall/skip the VS clock is based on the rate of deviation. Each time the VS clock is adjusted, the mechanism backs off for a certain amount of time (which is a function of T_{tswa}) to let the effect of the adjustment propagate back to the feedback signal input. T_{tswa} is re-specialized exponentially according to the current network delay jitter level J_{net}. T_{tswa}, filter parameters, back-off time, etc. are also re-specialized upon play speed change.

3.3 Software Feedback for QoS control

The user may specify a desired presentation quality. However, the specified QoS could be greater than the effective bandwidth of the video pipeline. In this case, the pipeline will be overloaded, bottle-neck stages will drop frames randomly, and resources such as server/client processing power and network bandwidth are wasted processing or transmitting the frames that will never be displayed. Further more, the QoS yielded by an overloaded pipeline is usually worse than that yielded by a fully-loaded one. Rather than relying solely on intermediate pipeline stages to control congestion by dropping frames at random, we feed back the QoS observed at the client to VS and allow VS to drop frames intelligently at the source of the pipeline.

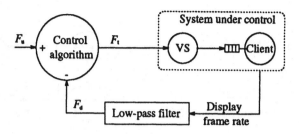

Fig. 4. Structure of the QoS control feedback mechanism

Event		Feedback Action
Pipeline over-loaded	$F_d < F_t - T_h$	$F_t = F_t - \Delta$
Pipeline under-loaded $F_d > F_t - T_l$ and $F_d < F_u$		$F_t = Min(F_t + \Delta, F_d)$

Table 2. Functionality of the QoS control feedback mechanism

The QoS control feedback mechanism is also implemented in the client, as shown in Fig. 4. Initially, the target frame rate, F_t, at which VS sends frames is set to the user-specified frame rate, F_u. The feedback mechanism monitors the display frame rate at the client and uses a low-pass filter to remove transient noise. The filtered display frame rate, F_d, is then compared against F_u and the existing F_t by the control algorithm. If the pipeline is found to be under- or over-loaded, a new F_t value is computed and fed back to VS.

The control algorithm adjusts F_t linearly. The functionality of the feedback mechanism is described in Table 2. T_l, T_h, and Δ are three parameters: low and high thresholds and adjust step, where $T_l > 0$, $T_h > 0$, $\Delta > 0$ and $T_h - T_l > \Delta$. These parameters, as well as the back-off time after a feedback action, are re-specialized upon play speed change. The back-off time is also adapted to T_{swa} measured in the synchronization feedback mechanism.

4 Implementation

The player is written in C, using code modified from the Berkeley MPEG decoder [7], and a Motif interface based on a modified version from the University of Minnesota. The streams supported by the player are MPEG-1 video and 8-bit $8K$ sample rate μ-law audio. The software is publicly available [3].

Figure 5 shows the structure of the player. VS and AS run as daemons on their respective hosts. The client is a set of collaborating processes which communicate via shared memory, semaphores, pipes and signals. The video and audio output devices are X Window and AudioFile [10] processes respectively.

The client sends control messages to AS and retrieves the audio stream through a TCP channel. Synchronization between the client and AS is maintained by the TCP flow control mechanism. We assume that the TCP channel has enough bandwidth to support the user-specified audio playback quality.

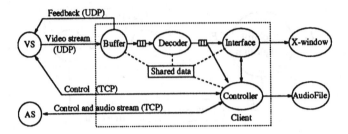

Fig. 5. Process oriented structure of the player

VS sends video frames to the client via UDP, chopping big frames into pieces to comply with UDP packet size limit. The client buffer process reassembles the frames before passing them to the decoder process. To accommodate the Motif programming interface, a separate process from the controller is used to drive the user interface and the display of video frames. VS, AS and the client controller processes run at real-time priority. Logical play time is mapped into system time via the UNIX interval timer.

5 Experiment Results

Several experiments were conducted to evaluate the performance of the player and to study the effectiveness of the feedback mechanisms. We used short clips of action video and audio from basketball games for the experiments. The AS, VS and client processes were run on various architectures (Sun SPARC, HP 9000, and i486). We also tested the player over the Internet with the client at OGI and the servers 28 hops away at Georgia Tech.

In all experiments, our player maintained good audio/video synchronization at the specified play speed. When AS is within our department, even when lots of video frames were dropped due to bandwidth limitations or system overload, audio quality remained high. In the experiments discussed below, the following default configuration was used except when noted otherwise:

- *Servers (VS, AS)*: HP 9000/755 file server.
- *Client*: HP 9000/712.
- *Network*: 10Mb/s Ethernet, server and client on the same subnet.
- *Video stream*: A basketball game clip, frame size 256x192, 9259 frames encoded at 30 fps (about 5 min.), average MPEG frame 2.37KBytes, picture group pattern IBBPBBPBBPBB.

We have defined display frame rate in Sect. 2 as a QoS measurement. However, the display frame rate alone is not sufficient for measuring QoS. Consider two playbacks of the same video stream at the same play speed and display frame rate. If one drops frames more evenly than the other, the former playback will be smoother than the latter. We need a metric to quantify this smoothness aspect of QoS.

One smoothness measure is the deviation of *presentation jitter* [11] from the desired value of zero. Using our assumption that the mapping of logical time (frame number) into system time is precise, and that the delay from the client to the video output can be ignored, we measure the presentation jitter in terms of logical display time.

Consider a video stream of frame sequence $(f_0, f_1, \ldots f_n)$ and a playback displaying a subsequence of these frames: $(f_{i_0}, f_{i_1}, \ldots f_{i_m})$. At each logical display time i ($i \geq 0$ and $i \leq n$), we calculate the logical time error, $e_i = i - i_k$ between the expected frame f_i and the actually displayed frame f_{i_k}, where $i_k \leq i$ and $i_{k+1} > i$, producing the error sequence $E : (e_0, e_1, \ldots e_n)$.

Smoothness S of a playback is the deviation of the sequence E from the perfect playback, which drops no frames and has an error sequence of all zeros. Thus S is defined as:

$$S = \sqrt{\frac{\sum_{e \in E} e^2}{n}}$$

This definition of S is independent of play speed. A lower value of S indicates a smoother playback. S equal to zero denotes perfect playback.

To evaluate the performance of the player and the QoS feedback mechanism, we played the default video stream at various play speeds, at the maximum user-specified frame rate, and synchronization feedback on. Two sets of experiments were done, one with QoS feedback on, and the other with it off. To evaluate the overhead of the player, we also ran the basic Berkeley MPEG decoder, from which our decoder was derived, on the same client host with the same stream. The basic decoder simply plays as fast as possible, without dropping frames. Figure 6(a) shows the frame rate sent by VS and the display frame rate for each of these experiments, and the basic decoder's display frame rate. Comparing the display frame rate curve of our player with QoS feedback on against that of the basic decoder shows that the overhead of our player is 5–20%.

When play speed exceeds 20 fps, the client processor becomes the bottle-neck, and the player consistently yields a higher display frame rate with QoS feedback than without. The rate of frame-drops is simply the difference between sent and displayed frame rates. The frame-drop rate is also consistently lower with QoS feedback, wasting fewer resources. With QoS feedback at any play speed, less then 10% of frames are dropped, while without it, the player drops up to 66% of the frames sent by VS.

Figure 6(b) shows the smoothness measurement S of the two sets of experiments. We see that when the video pipeline is overloaded the player also consistently yields smoother playback with QoS feedback.

These experiments show that QoS feedback is effective when the client processor becomes the bottle-neck in the video pipeline. This is also true when the network is the bottle-neck. To demonstrate this, we conducted two sets of experiments similar to the ones above, but with VS on a remote Sun SPARC workstation at Georgia Tech. From Fig. 7(a), we see that the Internet bandwidth limits display frame rate to about 15 fps. With QoS feedback, most of the time,

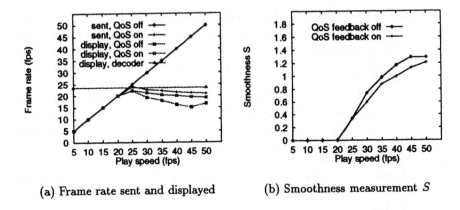

(a) Frame rate sent and displayed   (b) Smoothness measurement S

Fig. 6. Comparison with QoS feedback on/off, and with a basic MPEG decoder

we get almost the same display frame rate, but without QoS feedback, up to 83% of the frames sent by VS are dropped, wasting Internet bandwidth. The QoS feedback reduces the frame drop rate to a level of less than 30%. While the QoS feedback does not significantly impact the display frame rate, Fig. 7(b) shows that it does result in smoother playback.

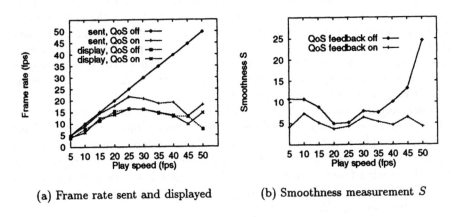

(a) Frame rate sent and displayed   (b) Smoothness measurement S

Fig. 7. Comparison with QoS feedback on/off, with congested network

The system clocks on our server and client workstations are precise and already well synchronized. To demonstrate the effectiveness of the synchronization feedback, we purposely changed the logical to system time mapping on VS to make its logical clock drift from the client's at a rate of about -0.2%. We played the default video stream at a play speed of 30 fps twice, once with synchronization feedback on and once with it off.

Figure 8 shows the server work ahead time, T_{swa}, as measured in the client, against logical play time for the two experiments. In the absence of synchronization feedback, T_{swa} declines gradually from the startup level to zero, at which point the player stalls because all frames arrive too late. Synchronization feedback detects and compensates for the drift, and keeps T_{swa} at a stable level, despite clock drift and clock skip/stall problems. As discussed in Sect.3.2, the synchronization feedback can also

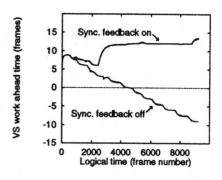

Fig. 8. Synchronization feedback effect

adapt target server work ahead time to network delay and delay jitter. In experiments with the default configuration, T_{tswa} was kept at a level where VS worked ahead of the client by about 0.3 seconds. In other experiments with VS on a host at Georgia Tech and the client on our default host, if the Internet was congested VS could work ahead of the client by about 1 second.

6 Related Work

The Berkeley Continuous Media Player [8, 9] has had the most significant influence on the design and implementation of our player. The Berkeley player and ours use the same MPEG decoder. The Berkeley player uses an ad-hoc software feedback mechanism to adjust the frame rate sent by its server. We follow a toolkit approach, and our feedback mechanism is more efficient and more adaptive to play speed and environmental changes than that used in the Berkeley player as shown by comparing Fig. 6 to similar figures in [9]. However, the Berkeley player relies on NTP [4] for client/server synchronization, while our feedback approach to synchronization is built into the player and does not need external synchronization. Thus our player is more robust and adaptive in Internet environments. Finally, our player supports user-specified QoS.

The idea of software feedback was identified in the Synthesis operating system project [5]. Massalin and Pu demonstrated that software feedback can be used in process scheduling to adapt quickly to system changes. Pu and Fuhrer [6] proposed a toolkit approach to software feedback. Our work furthers the idea of a toolkit approach to software feedback by applying it in our player to solve real-world problems of client/server synchronization, dynamic QoS control and system adaptiveness.

7   Discussion and Future Work

The design, implementation and evaluation of a distributed real-time MPEG video and audio player has been presented. We also discussed a toolkit approach to building software feedback mechanisms for client/server synchronization, dynamic QoS control and system adaptiveness. Our experimental results demonstrate that these feedback mechanisms are effective. With these mechanisms, our player can adapt its QoS to variations in processor speed, network bandwidth and system workload. It can also adapt to variations in network delay and delay jitter, and can compensate for client/server clock drift. These mechanisms make our player robust and allow it to perform well across the Internet.

Our experiences with building feedback mechanisms in the player suggests that the toolkit approach is useful. It leads to a better understanding of system behavior, clearer system structure and design and code reuse. Future research will further refine and evaluate the feedback mechanisms for the player, and further explore the idea of a software feedback toolkit. We will apply this toolkit approach to real-time scheduling, another important consideration for multimedia applications. We also plan to extend our player to incorporate user specification of QoS along more dimensions including spatial and temporal resolution, color quantization, and synchronization accuracy.

References

1. William L. Brogan. Modern Control Theory. Quantum Publishers, Inc. 1974.
2. Lawrence S. Brakmo et. al. TCP vegas: New Techniques for Congestion Detection and Avoidance. Proc. SIGCOMM'94 Symposium, pages 24-35. August 1994.
3. Shanwei Cen. A Distributed Real-Time MPEG Video Audio Player. Software available via anonymous FTP from ftp://ftp.cse.ogi.edu/pub/dsrg/Player, or via WWW from http://cse.ogi.edu/DISC/projects/synthetix/Player/.
4. D. L. Mills. Network Time Protocol (Version 3) Specification, Implementation and Analysis. DARPA Network Working Group Report RFC-1305. University of Delaware, March 1992.
5. H. Massalin and C. Pu. Fine-Grain Adaptive Scheduling Using Feedback. Computing System, 3(1):139-173, Winter 1990.
6. Calton Pu and Robert M. Fuhrer. Feedback-Based Scheduling: a Toolbox Approach. Fourth Workshop on Workstation Operating Systems. Oct. 14-15, 1993.
7. Ketan Patel et. al. Performance of a Software MPEG Video Decoder. ACM multimedia'93, Anaheim, California. August 1993.
8. Lawrence A. Rowe and Brian C. Smith. A Continuous Media Player. Proc. 3rd NOSSDAV. San Diego, California. November 1992.
9. Lawrence A. Rowe et. al. MPEG Video in Software: Representation, Transmission and Playback. Symp. on Elec. Imaging Sci. & Tech., San Jose, CA, February 1994.
10. Thomas M. Levergood et. al. AudioFile: a Network-Transparent System for Distributed Audio Applications. Proc. the USENIX Summer Conference, June, 1993.
11. Richard Staehli, Jonathan Walpole and David Maier. Quality of Service Specifications for Multimedia Presentations. To appear in Multimedia Systems. August, 1995.

Analysis of Audio Packet Loss in the Internet

Jean-Chrysostome Bolot   Hugues Crépin   Andres Vega Garcia

INRIA
B. P. 93
06902 Sophia-Antipolis Cedex
France
bolot@sophia.inria.fr

Abstract. We consider the problem of distributing audio data over networks such as the Internet that do not provide support for real-time applications. Experiments with such networks indicate that audio quality is mediocre in large part because of excessive audio packet losses. In this paper, we show using measurements over the Internet as well as analytic modeling that the number of consecutively lost audio packets is small unless the network load is very high. This indicates that open loop error control mechanisms based on forward error correction would be adequate to reconstruct most lost audio packets.

1 Introduction

We consider the problem of distributing real-time data, and specifically audio data, over networks such as the Internet that do not provide guaranteed resources such as bandwidth or guaranteed performance measures such as maximum delay or maximum loss rate. Two approaches have emerged to support real-time applications over these networks.

One approach is to extend current protocols and switch scheduling disciplines to provide the desired performance guarantees. This approach requires that admission control, policing, reservation, and/or sophisticated scheduling mechanisms be implemented in the network. The design, analysis, and evaluation of such mechanisms is an active research area [11]. Another approach is to adapt applications to the service provided by the network. One way to do this is to control the rate at which packets are sent over a connection, the objective being to limit this rate to the capacity of the connection. In FIFO networks such as the Internet, this capacity changes with time because the number of connections routed through each switch varies and because sources do not send data at a constant rate. The control mechanism must be somehow informed of such changes. One way is for sources of packets to receive feedback about the state of the network. Feedback control mechanisms have been used in the Internet to control sources of non real time traffic (e.g. the window control mechanism in TCP). Recently, they have been advocated and used to control video [10, 4] and audio [19] traffic as well.

Such control mechanisms help reduce packet losses, but they do not prevent them entirely. In fact, the experience accumulated over the Internet indicates that audio packet losses are in large part responsible for the mediocre quality of many audio transmissions over the network.

In this paper, we characterize the packet loss process of audio streams sent over the Internet. We use measurements (in Section 2) as well as analytic modeling (in Section 3). The analytical results tie in well with the measurements. Our main result is that the number of consecutively lost audio packets is small except when the Internet load is high. This suggests that open loop error control mechanisms based on forward error correction would be adequate to reconstruct most lost audio packets. We briefly describe (in Section 4) one such mechanism and report on preliminary evaluations of audio quality obtained with this mechanism.

2 Measurements

We have measured the loss process of audio packets using the audio tool of IVS (INRIA Videoconference System). IVS [18] is a software system combining a H.261 video codec and a number of audio codecs (PCM, DPCM, ADPCM, and LPC codecs). In all the experiments described in this paper, we used the PCM (Pulse Coded Modulation) coder. Each audio packet sent by this coder includes 320 voice samples, or 40 ms of speech. Therefore, voice packets are sent periodically every 40 ms during talkspurts.

We have measured the audio loss process over a number of connections, i.e. of source-destination pairs. Because of lack of space, we focus on one specific connection between INRIA Sophia Antipolis in southern France and University College London (UCL) in the UK. This connection is heavily loaded during daytime. We have examined it both in unicast and multicast mode. In unicast mode, audio packets are sent from a source at INRIA to a destination at UCL using the standard protocol stack of the Internet, i.e. IP/UDP/RTP. In multicast mode, audio packets are sent between the same source destination pair as in unicast mode, but they are sent over the MBone (i.e. the virtual network running on top of the IP layer which provides a multicasting facility in the Internet).

Each audio packet includes a sequence number to detect packet losses. For convenience of presentation, we introduce a boolean variable l_n which is set to 1 if packet n is lost, and 0 otherwise. We record for every packet, i.e. every n, the value of l_n. Many different measures can be used to characterize the loss process of audio packets. The obvious measure is the average loss, or unconditional loss probability, which is the expected value of l_n. We denote $ulp = E[l_n]$. However, ulp does not characterize the burstiness of the loss process, or equivalently the correlation between successive packet losses. One way to capture such correlation is to consider the conditional probability that a packet is lost given that the previous packet was lost. We denote $clp = P[l_{n+1} = 1 | l_n = 1]$. A related measure is the expected number of consecutively lost packets, or packet loss gap [6], which we denote by plg. If the sequence of d_n is stationary and ergodic, then [1] $plg = 1/(1 - clp)$.

156

Unicast mode

Figure 1 shows the evolutions of the number of consecutively lost packets as a function of n measured at 8:00 am and at 4:00 pm. As expected, the total number

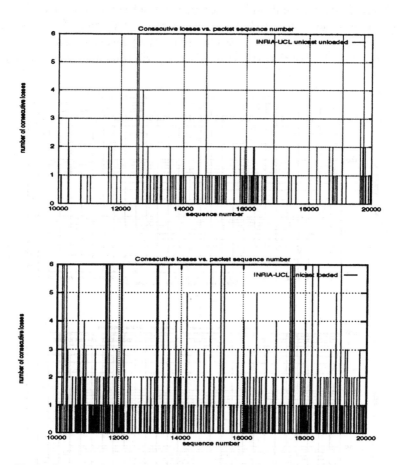

Fig. 1. Evolutions of the number of consecutively lost packets at 8:00 am (top) and 4:00 pm (bottom)

of losses is higher at 4:00 pm, i.e. when the network load is higher. In the top graph, we observe that most losses are isolated except for "almost periodic" loss periods when the number of consecutive losses exceeds 6 (in fact, this number can exceed 100). These loss periods occur around packet number 12500, 14700, 16900, and 19000. The interval between periods is thus approximately 40 ms × 2200 ≈ 88 s. Therefore, it seems likely that these losses would be triggered by the periodic overload caused at routers by the synchronization of IGRP routing

update messages every 90 seconds[1] [8]. The observations we make for the top
graph are still valid for the bottom graph, i.e. when the network load is high. In
particular, it appears that the average number of consecutively lost packets is
small.

This observation is confirmed by looking at the frequency distribution of the
number of consecutive losses. Figure 2 shows the distributions (i.e. the number
of occurrences of n consecutive losses for different n) corresponding to the traces
in Figure 1. We observe that the slope of the distribution decreases linearly near

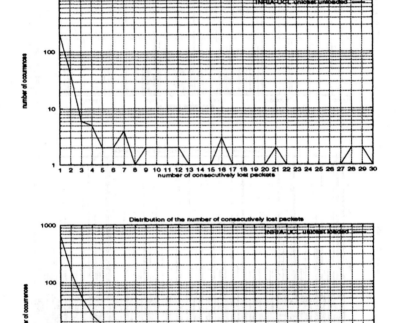

Fig. 2. Frequency distribution of the number of consecutive lost packets at 8:00
am (top) and 4:00 pm (bottom)

the origin. Since the figures are drawn on a log scale, this indicates that the
probability distribution decreases geometrically fast away from the origin.

---

[1] This synchronization problem has very recently been eliminated on the French
backbone.

We have examined the loss process of audio packets over connections other than the INRIA-UCL connection. In all cases, we have found that the frequency distribution of the number of consecutively lost packets is similar to that described above. To illustrate this, we next present the evolutions and the frequency distribution of the number of consecutively lost packets measured over a connection between INRIA and the University of Maryland. The measurements were taken at 3:00 pm local time (9:00 am EST) when we expect the transatlantic link between France and the US to be reasonably loaded.

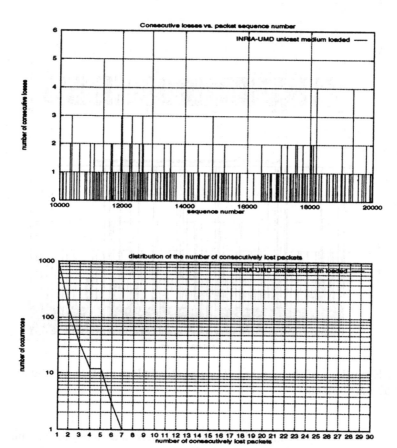

Fig. 3. Evolutions (top) and frequency distribution (bottom) of the number of consecutive lost packets measured over the INRIA-UMD connection

Multicast connections

The results obtained for multicast connections are essentially the same as those obtained for the unicast connections. Figure 4 shows the evolutions of the number of consecutively lost packets between INRIA and UCL as a function of n in multicast mode at 8:00 am and at 4:00 pm.

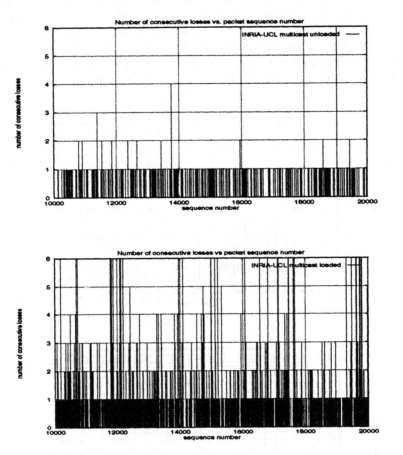

Fig. 4. Evolutions of the number of consecutively lost packets at 8:00 am (top) and 4:00 pm (bottom)

The observations we made in Figure 1, namely that most losses appear to be isolated[2], are still valid in Figure 4. These observations are confirmed by the shapes of the frequency distributions of the number of consecutive losses.

---

[2] Interestingly, the "almost periodic" loss periods we observed earlier have disappeared. This is because the path followed by the audio packets on the MBone between a source and a destination has little to do with the path that would be taken by packets between the same source and the same destination using the standard IP routing. Furthermore, much of the queueing in the MBone is done at the gateways running *mrouted* daemons. Many such gateways are workstations which are therefore not affected by phenomena such as the routing update synchronization visible in "standard" IP routers.

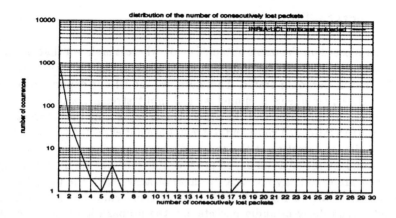

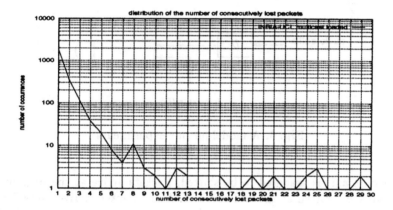

Fig. 5. Distribution of the number of consecutive lost packets at 8:00 am (top) and 4:00 pm (bottom)

In summary, the results presented in this section indicate that the number of consecutively lost packets is small especially when the network load is low or moderate. This is in agreement with previous experimental results obtained with non-audio UDP packets over many different connections in the Internet [3].

Note, however, that we have not defined what is meant by "low" or "moderate" load above. This is because it is essentially impossible for us to control the load of the network. We controlled it in a simple (but obviously very rough) way by modifying the time at which experiments were carried out.

In the next section, we present a model that captures the impact of the Internet traffic on a flow of audio packets sent from a source to a destination. The model can be solved analytically in part, and it provides a mathematical basis for the conclusions above. Furthermore, it can be used to evaluate the impact of the network load on the audio packet loss process in a more flexible way than can be done with experiments.

3 A Discrete-Time Model

The model is based on the result obtained in [3], where it is shown that the impact of the Internet traffic on a periodic stream of packets can be approximated by that of a batch Bernoulli traffic. Therefore, we model our experiments with a simple single-server queueing model with 2 input streams, where one stream represents the audio traffic and the other stream represents the Internet traffic. We note that PCM-coded voice audio streams are not expected to be continuous because of silence detection at the coder. We have considered models where the audio stream is modeled as an on/off process. However, the results regarding the loss process are essentially identical to those obtained with the periodic model. Our model is shown in Figure 6. The delay D represents the fixed part of the total end to end delay of audio packets, i.e. the propagation and transmission delays.

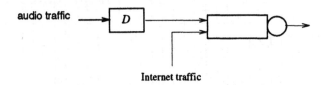

Fig. 6. A model for our experiments

The time axis is assumed to be slotted. Packets arrive at the beginning of a slot and are serviced at the end of a slot. Audio packets arrive every T slots, and Internet packets arrive every slot. Packet sizes are expressed in multiple of a base size equal to P bytes which corresponds to a service time equal to one slot. For convenience, we refer to this base size unit also as a slot. Audio packets have a fixed size of A slots (i.e. $A \times P$ bytes). In practice, a slot is equal to 32 bytes, and hence $A = 10$. Internet packets have independent and identically distributed sizes drawn from general distribution. Specifically, we denote by b_i the probability that the size of the Internet packet is $i \times P$ bytes. In [3], it is shown how measures of end to end delays of audio packets can be used to find the value of b_i. Our measures of end to end delays indicate, not surprisingly, that the Internet packet size distribution is a multimodal distribution. In our model, we take the size of Internet packets to be equal to either 1 slot (this models 32-byte Telnet packets), or a multiple of 16 slots (this models 512-byte FTP and SMTP packets). We assume that the buffer can hold $K > A$ slots.

Throughout the rest of the paper, we assume that an audio packet arrives as the last packet during a slot. Note that if the audio packet arrives first, it is always admitted. Thus, we obtain the $D + D^X/D/1/K$ model shown in Figure 7.

Many models similar to that in Figure 7 have been studied assuming an infinite buffer size. The finite buffer case has been considered in [13]. In this

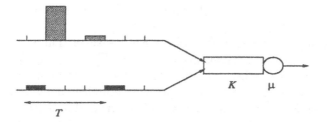

Fig. 7. The $D + D^X/D/1/K$ model

paper, we use an approach based on state transition matrices similar to that used in [16]. The state of the system is defined as the workload (expressed in terms of slots) before the arrival of packet(s) in a slot. Thus the state ranges over $[0...K-1]$. The $K \times K$ transition matrix for the Internet stream assuming no audio arrival is

$$Q = \begin{bmatrix} b_0 + b_1 \ b_2 \ ... \ b_{K-1} & 1 - \sum_{i=0}^{K-1} b_i \\ b_0 & b_1 \ ... \ b_{K-1} & 1 - \sum_{i=0}^{K-1} b_i \\ 0 & b_0 \ ... \ b_{K-1} & 1 - \sum_{i=0}^{K-2} b_i \\ & \ddots & \vdots \\ 0 & 0 \ ... \ b_0 & 1 - b_0 \end{bmatrix}$$

The $K \times K$ transition matrix assuming an audio arrival is

$$Q' = \begin{bmatrix} 0 \ 0 ... \ b_0 \ b_1 \ ... \ b_{K-A-1} & 1 - \sum_{i=0}^{K-A-1} b_i \\ 0 \ 0 ... 0 \ b_0 \ ... \ b_{K-A-2} & 1 - \sum_{i=0}^{K-A-2} b_i \\ 0 \ 0 ... 0 \ 0 \ ... \ b_{K-A-3} & 1 - \sum_{i=0}^{K-A-3} b_i \\ \ddots \qquad ... & \vdots \\ 0 \ 0 ... \qquad ... \ 0 & 1 \end{bmatrix}$$

Note that if only $x < A$ slots are available when an audio packet arrives, then all x slots are filled with whatever fraction of the audio packet can fit in. Thus, the audio packet is not entirely discarded.

The transition matrix between two audio arrivals is $P = Q'Q^{T-1}$. The steady state probability vector π seen by the first bit in a slot with an audio arrival is the solution of $\pi = \pi P$. The distribution of the state ξ seen by an audio packet is thus $\xi_i = \sum_{k=0}^{i} \pi_k b_{i-k}$

We can now derive various performance measures. The unconditional loss probability for audio packets is given by $ulp = \sum_{i=K-A+1}^{K} \xi_i$. To compute the conditional loss probability clp, we note that the state of the system after an audio packet loss is always $K - 1$. Thus clp is obtained as the sum of the $A - 1$ rightmost elements on the bottom row of the transition matrix $Q^{T-1}R$ where R is the matrix describing the transition caused by the arrivals preceding an audio packet. We do not write R for lack of space, but it is easy see that it is almost identical to Q. The average number of consecutively lost packets is then $plg = 1/(1 - clp)$.

The Internet load , i.e. the traffic intensity of the Internet stream, is given by expected value of b_i. Figure 8 shows the variations of plg as a function of the Internet load, computed from the model above. We observe that plg stays

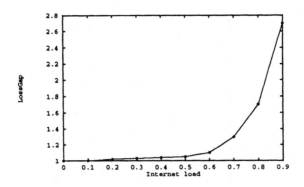

Fig. 8. Variations of plg as a function of Internet load

close to 1 unless the load generated by the Internet traffic exceeds 0.8. This is confirmation that we should expect the average number of consecutive losses to be small except when the load in the network Not surprisingly, our results tie in well with others in [16] obtained with a similar model which indicate that losses for a periodic stream (e.g. an audio stream) are isolated as long as the periodic stream uses less than 10% of the server capacity. They are also in agreement with other results in the literature [14, 16, 3].

Interestingly, packet losses are generally thought to be "bursty". However, it is important to consider carefully the hypotheses made regarding the traffic model [5]. Furthermore, many analytic studies consider the aggregate loss process at a node, i.e. the loss process from all input streams. In the model above, we evaluate the loss process of the audio stream *only*.

4 Packet Loss Recovery

An error control mechanism is required if the number of lost audio packets is higher than that tolerated by the listener at the destination. Typical mechanisms fall in one of two classes. Automatic Repeat Request (ARQ) mechanisms are closed-loop mechanisms based on the retransmission of the packets that were not received at the destination. Forward Error Correction (FEC) mechanisms are open-loop mechanisms based on the transmission of redundant information along with the original information so that (at least some of) the lost original data can be recovered from the redundant information. ARQ mechanisms are not acceptable for live audio applications such as audioconferencing over the Internet because they dramatically increase end to end latency. Furthermore, they are not well suited to multicast environments such as the MBone.

FEC is an attractive alternative to ARQ for providing reliability without increasing latency. This is particularly important for applications with real time constraints over high speed networks (e.g. [17, 2]). However, the potential of FEC mechanisms to recover from losses depends crucially on the characteristics of the packet loss process in the network. Clearly, FEC mechanisms are more effective when lost packets are dispersed throughout the stream of packets sent from a source to a destination. Our results above then indicate that FEC is particularly well suited for live audio applications over the Internet.

The simplest way to add redundancy to an audio packet is to add no redundancy at all. Indeed, it is possible to recover at the destination from packet losses without any redundant information. For example, a lost packet can be replaced by silence or by noise. A better way is to reconstruct it by duplicating the previous packet (assuming this packet was actually received) [9].

A large variety of more elaborate FEC mechanisms have been proposed in the literature. Many such mechanisms involve exclusive-OR operations, the idea being to send every nth packet a redundant packet obtained by exclusive-ORing the other n packets [17]. This mechanism can recover from a single loss in a n packet message. It is a very simple mechanism, but it increases the send rate of the source by a factor of $1/n$, and it adds latency since n packets have to be received before the lost packet can be reconstructed.

Within the MICE project (a European project devoted to multimedia research), we have developed a novel mechanism for loss recovery [12]. Consider for example the case when audio is sent using PCM encoding. In our mechanism, packet n includes in addition to its encoded PCM samples, a highly compressed version of packet $n-1$. This redundant information would typically be obtained using linear predictive coding (LPC) [15] of packet $n-1$. Clearly, this mechanism can recover from isolated losses. It can also recover from two consecutive losses. One way of doing this is to combine it with packet repetition. Another way is to use as redundant information in packet n a LPC version of packet $n-2$.

The impact of this mechanism on the quality of the audio delivered over the Internet is being carefully evaluated by our MICE colleagues at UCL. They have obtained results which show that audio quality as measured by intelligibility is much improved (the details of the study are in [7]) even when a relatively low quality LPC coder is used to obtain the redundant information. These results suggest that audio tools for the Internet should include FEC mechanisms, and they provide added motivation to continue our work on the design of efficient uneven error recovery schemes.

References

1. F. Baccelli, P. Brémaud, *Palm Probabilities and Stationary Queues*, Lecture Notes in Statistics, vol. 41, Springer, Heidelberg, 1987.
2. E. W. Biersack, "Performance evaluation of FEC in ATM networks", *Proc. ACM Sigcomm '92*, pp. 248-257, Baltimore, MD, Aug. 1992.
3. J-C. Bolot, "End-to-end packet delay and loss behavior in the Internet", *Proc. ACM Sigcomm '93*, San Fransisco, CA, pp. 189-199, Aug. 1993.
4. J-C. Bolot, T. Turletti, "A rate control scheme for packet video in the Internet", *Proc. IEEE Infocom '94*, Toronto, Canada, pp. 1216-1223, June 1994.
5. I. Cidon, A. Khamisy, M. Sidi, "Analysis of packet loss processes in high-speed networks", *IEEE Trans. Info. Theory*, vol. 39, no. 1, pp. 98-108, Jan. 1993.
6. J. Ferrandiz, A. Lazar, "Monitoring the packet gap of real-time packet traffic", *Queueing Systems*, vol. 12, pp. 231-242, Dec. 1992.
7. V. Hardman et al., "Reliable audio for use over the Internet", to appear in *Proc. INET '95*, Hawaii, June 1995.
8. V. Jacobson, S. Floyd, "The synchronization of periodic routing messages", *Proc. ACM Sigcomm '93*, San Fransisco, CA, pp. 33-44, Sept. 1993.
9. N. Jayant, "Effects of packet losses in waveform-coded speech", *IEEE Trans. Comm.*, vol. COM-29, pp. 101-109, Feb. 1981.
10. K. Jeffay, D. L. Stone, T. Talley, F. D. Smith, "Adaptive, best-effort delivery of digital audio and video across packet-switched networks", *Proc. NOSSDAV '92*, San Diego, CA, Nov. 1992.
11. J. Kurose, "Open issues and challenges in providing QoS guarantees in high-speed networks", *Computer Comm. Review*, vol. 23, no. 1, pp. 6-15, 1993.
12. The MICE home page is found at URL http://www.cs.ucl.ac.uk/mice.
13. M. Murata, Y. Oie, T. Suda, "Analysis of a discrete-time single-server queue with bursty inputs for traffic control in ATM networks", *IEEE JSAC*, vol. 8, no. 3, pp. 447-458, April 1990.
14. I. Norros, J. Virtamo, "Who loses cells in the case of burst scale congestion", *Proc. ITC 13*, Copenhagen, pp. 829-833, June 1991.
15. L. R. Rabiner, R. W. Schafer, *Digital Processing of Speech Signals*, Prentice Hall, 1978.
16. H. Schulzrinne, J. Kurose, D. Towsley, "Loss correlation for queues with bursty input streams", *Proc. IEEE ICC '92*, Chicago, IL, pp. 219-224, 1992.
17. N. Shacham, P. McKenney, "Packet recovery in high-speed networks using coding and buffer management", *Proc. IEEE Infocom '90*, San Fransisco, CA, pp. 124-131, May 1990.
18. T. Turletti, "A H.261 software codec for videoconferencing over the Internet", INRIA Research Report 1834, January 1993.
19. N. Yin, M. G. Hluchyj, "A dynamic rate control mechanism for source coded traffic in a fast packet network", *IEEE JSAC*, vol. 9, no. 7, pp. 1003-1012, Sept. 1991

Digital Audio and Video in Industrial Systems

Hugh C. Lauer,[*] Chia Shen,[*] Randy Osborne,[*] John Howard,[*] Qin Zheng[*]
Mitsubishi Electric Research Labs, Cambridge, Massachusetts

Morikazu Takegaki,[†] Hiromitsu Shimakawa,[†] Ichiro Mizunuma[†]
Mitsubishi Electric Corporation, Amagasaki, Japan

Introduction

In industrial environments such as power plants, automated factories, sewage treatment facilities, railways, etc., digital audio and video play at least three important roles:–

- *On-line documentation and training.* Pre-stored video in documentation databases is typically viewed interactively, both during routine operation and during emergency situations.
- *Monitoring and surveillance.* Video cameras posted around plants allow operators to keep track of security and proper operation and to provide a visual record for subsequent auditing and analysis.
- *Sensors for plant control.* Video and image processing are being used increasingly in the automated operation of the plant itself — for example, in equipment to measure speeds, count objects, search for production flaws, detect wear of machinery, etc.

In these kinds of settings, it is often desirable to integrate many different functions into the same network — for example, functions or applications with hard real-time requirements, continuous media such as audio and video, functions requiring rapid response, and traditional applications using traditional data protocols such as TCP/IP. At first glance, this may not seem too difficult if one simply dedicates a portion of total network bandwidth to the traffic with hard real-time requirements, then a portion of the remainder to audio and video, etc.

However, bandwidth is only one of the resources and problems that must be considered in a complete network system. Because of the widely different communication requirements of these functions, the demands of their traffic characteristics, flow control, constraints, and performance criteria are typically more challenging than they would be in typical local area or office networks with workstations, PCs, client and server machines, etc.

In this position paper, we discuss a number of issues regarding industrial networks, digital audio and video in those networks, and implications on current research directions. These are considered in the context of ATM (Asynchronous Transfer Mode) networks having speeds ranging from 100 megabits/second to one gigabit/second.

---

*. Address: Mitsubishi Electric Research Labs, 201 Broadway, Cambridge, MA 02139
†. Address: Industrial and Electronic Systems Laboratory, Mitsubishi Electric Corporation, 1-1, Tsukaguchi-Honmachi 8-Chome, Amagasaki, Hyogo, 661, JAPAN

Resource Allocation

Resources in an ATM network include:–
- Bandwidth.
- Buffer space in switches and end systems.
- Priority levels.
- Redundant paths for fault tolerance.

In traditional LANs, resources are typically allocated on demand and shared "fairly" among competing users and/or applications. In industrial environments, resources for critical connections — e.g., hard real-time and some audio and video — are allocated in advance. There are many theoretical solutions to aspects of this problem, especially for allocating bandwidth and buffer space in order to ensure bounded delay, given *a priori* knowledge of the characteristics of the traffic on each critical connection [2, 6]. ATM networks are particularly attractive for implementing such solutions because connections can be controlled to enforce those traffic characteristics.

One kind of resource receives very little attention in traditional LANs, namely redundant paths for fault tolerance. At least two approaches are possible, both of which require assigning primary and alternate paths at the time a connection is created:–
1. When a fault occurs, reconfigure the tables of the switches in the network to re-route each affected connection from its primary to its alternate path. The problem is that re-configuring an ATM switch is time-consuming in today's technology and compounds the problems of fault recovery rather than solving them.
2. At each source, multicast the data stream over both the primary and alternate paths at all times. At each destination, maintain cell counters to detect the forward progress of each branch and to select one. This has the advantage that the alternate paths are continuously exercised and that no reconfiguration is required in any switch at the time of a fault.

Note that in emergency situations, a lot of video streams are likely to be open at one time, imposing extreme demands on the network.

A ripe area for research is to investigate how these theoretical approaches to resource allocation apply in practice, especially in industrial environments at ATM speeds. The biggest gap between theory and practice lies in the assumptions — assumptions that are usually drawn from experience with less demanding networks.

Switching, Scheduling, and Priorities

It is inevitable in a network integrating many different kinds of applications with widely varying requirements that cell-by-cell scheduling is required. Two open questions are
1. how many priority levels are required in practical networks, and
2. whether static or dynamic priorities are required.

In the past, static priority scheduling algorithms such as Rate Monotonic have been preferred because of their closed form solutions to certain classes of problems. Dynamic priority algorithms such as Earliest Deadline First are more general but have been shunned because it was assumed that they are too hard to implement, especially at ATM speeds. In fact, both require the same basic function in the scheduling fabric of the switch, namely the ability to make an n-way comparison among a set of queues during every cell cycle to determine the queue position or dispatching order, where n is the number of possible priority levels. The question of complexity then reduces to how many priority levels are required in a practical environment and how to implement a fast enough comparator for that many levels. Fortunately, silicon implementations that support a separate priority for every cell in a queue are beginning to emerge [1, 3].

However, there has been very little research on the larger question of how many priority levels are needed in a practical network in a demanding environment, especially with hard real-time connections and a lot of audio and video. There is also scant evidence that vendors are addressing this question seriously. Therefore, it is likely that we will see a long period of evolution of ATM networks, increasingly more sophisticated and probably with growing numbers of priority levels.

End System Interface Requirements

By contrast, network interfaces in end systems — workstations, servers, and "non-intelligent" devices such as video cameras — are getting a lot of attention by vendors and others. One key problem is the performance of higher level protocols — that is, how to handle volumes of data quickly enough. It is now widely recognized that it is absolutely necessary to avoid copying of data between levels of the protocol stack and to avoid interrupting the host processor for each packet.

Less widely recognized is that the network interface device has to perform many of the functions of a switch. On the transmission side, its inputs are the applications and its single output is the physical link to the ATM network. In real time networks and in environments with a lot of audio and video, this interface must support multiple priority levels and be capable of cell-by-cell scheduling, using the same kinds of algorithms as are required in the network switches.

As with switches, the number of priority levels needed in network interfaces in a practical network is still an open question.

Traffic Characteristics and Flow Control

Traffic in most computer networks is extremely bursty and has been characterized as self-similar [5], but in industrial environments it is worse. For example, in a typical system, distributed real-time processes maintain a consistent model of the state of the plant through distributed, reflective, shared memory. This is a special block of memory replicated in each node and kept consistent by low level processes that periodically transmit updates from each node to all others. These updates occur at intervals of one-half millisecond or less and involve a few kilobytes or so. The result is a timely copy of the distributed state of the plant operation to every process.

These update messages are the highest priority communications in the network. They represent bursts that consume the entire bandwidth for frequent, non-trivial amounts of time. Although they are predictable, they are not constant bit rate connections and cannot be converted to constant bit rate connections by traffic shaping.

Lower in priority than the distributed shared memory are the video streams. Uncompressed video streams are fairly easy to schedule because they require constant bit rate connections. The only apparent complication is jitter due to interference by higher priority connections, something that can be avoided with enough buffering in end systems. Compressed video streams are more interesting. For example, compression algorithms such as MPEG generate streams with bandwidth variations of a factor of ten from frame to frame. This has two effects:– it makes resource allocation more difficult, particularly when planning for emergency situations, and it makes flow control of lower priority connections more challenging. Note that lossy video is rarely acceptable in the industrial environment, and therefore methods that throw away video frames during periods of network congestion are not applicable.

It is natural to want to use surplus capacity of the industrial network for more traditional data traffic that does not have real-time constraints. In ATM parlance, this is called *ABR* (Available Bit Rate) traffic. In general, users of ABR applications want to be able to request all of the uncommitted capacity of the network at any time, on demand, without prior reservation, and subject only to fair sharing with the other ABR connections. The network, of course, must ensure that this traffic does not get in the way of real-time or audio and video traffic.

Flow control for this purpose has been the topic of extensive research and discussion at the ATM Forum. Although the ATM Forum recently voted to adopt a rate-based approach to flow control, the debate is far from over. In particular, it is already apparent that this will not work very well in the industrial environment because of the worse-than-bursty nature of traffic. The distributed shared memory updating processes and the variable bandwidth of compressed video create transients in the "available" bandwidth that are much shorter than the response times of rate-based flow control algorithms. This is considered in more detail in [4].

References

1. H. Jonathan Chao, Necdet Uzun, "A VLSI Sequencer Chip for ATM Traffic Shaper and Queue Manager," *IEEE Journal of Solid-State Circuit*, Vol. 27, No. 11, Nov. 1992.

2. D. Ferrari and D. Verma, "Real-Time Communication in a Packet-Switching Network," *Proc. Second International Workshop on Protocols for High-Speed Networks*, Palo Alto, November 1990.

3. H. Lauer, A. Ghosh, and C. Shen, "A General Purpose Queue Architecture for an ATM Switch," *Proc. of First Annual Conference on Telecommunications R&D in Massachusetts*, Massachusetts Telecommunications Council, University of Lowell, October 25, 1994, Vol. 6, pp 17-22.

4. H. Lauer, "On the Duality of Rate-based and Credit-based Flow Control," *Technical Report* TR95-03, Mitsubishi Electric Research Labs, Cambridge, MA, January 1995. (Submitted for publication.)

5. W. Leland, M. S. Taqqu, W. Willinger, and D. V. Wilson, "On the Self-Similar Nature of Ethernet Traffic," *IEEE/ACM Transactions on Networking*, volume 2, number 1, February, 1994.

6. Q. Zheng, K. Shin, and C. Shen, "Real-time Communication in ATM Networks," *19th Annual Local Computer Network Conference*, Minneapolis, MN, October 2-5, 1994.

Workstation Video Playback Performance with Competitive Process Load

Kevin Fall[1], Joseph Pasquale[1] and Steven McCanne[2]

[1] University of California, San Diego, CA 92093–0114, USA
[2] Lawrence Berkeley Laboratory, Berkeley, CA 94720, USA

Abstract. While many researchers believe that multimedia applications are best managed with hard, real-time scheduling mechanisms, models based on application-level adaptation with relaxed scheduling constraints are gaining acceptance. We analyze an existing video conferencing application that was designed without explicit support for CPU resource management, and propose modifications to its architecture to support CPU load adaptation. We show that this display jitter can be significantly reduced by gracefully adapting the application's load requirements to match the available CPU resources.

1   Introduction

Improving playback continuity of continuous media applications is generally accomplished by employing reservation-based CPU scheduling, or by shedding load when resources are in short supply. To alleviate the user from preselecting resource requirements, some systems rely on *adaptive resource management* (ARM) [1, 2]. In ARM, applications self-adapt over time in order to match their resource demands to the system's resource availability. Although ARM was originally proposed for real-time systems, it can also improve system performance on non-real-time scheduled systems.

We define multiple processes executing to accomplish a common task *cooperating processes*. Unrelated (interfering) processes are called *competitive processes*. Generally, the traditional scheduler (the UNIX scheduler in our case) provides poor playback continuity to processes unable to modulate their resource utilization whether they are cooperative or competitive. Even when real-time kernel support is available, specifying the parameters needed to ensure cooperative processes are scheduled at appropriate times is difficult [3].

When competitive processes are present, an application may fail to deliver its media stream at a sufficiently fast rate or at a sufficiently regular rate to maintain playback continuity. In this overloaded state, applications can resort to *load shedding* to reduce their CPU resource requirements. It has been suggested that load shedding may be combined with application-implemented adaptive control to provide good continuous media performance without the need for user-specified resource requirements [4].

2 The *vic* Video Conferencing Application

To investigate the effect of competitive process load on the operation of a continuous media application, we instrumented the UCB/LBL video conferencing application, *vic* [5]. Packets containing encoded video arrive from the network and are reassembled into encoding-specific framing units, which are decoded by a software or hardware codec. The decoded frames are then rendered and displayed.

The configuration under study consists of the three processes. The `vic` process executes in tandem with a video device server (`jvdriver`) and the X server. The platform under test was a DEC Alpha 3000/M500 running under DEC OSF/1 v. 1.3. DEC's "JVideo" hardware codec, managed by the `jvdriver` process, performs Motion-JPEG decompression at a target rate of 30 frames per second. The JVideo hardware decompresses, scales, and dithers each frame. Compressed and uncompressed frames are both maintained in shared memory buffers to reduce memory-to-memory copies.

To isolate the CPU scheduling effects from network induced jitter, we used an early version of `vic` which allowed compressed frames to be played back from local memory. A periodic timer, driven off wall clock time, schedules frames to be decompressed every 33ms. When `vic` gets behind, it attempts to catch up by running faster than 30Hz. If it gets too far behind (200ms), it catches up by resetting the frame clock, resulting in a burst of lost frames and a visible discontinuity in the playback video.

Our data was collected by instrumenting `vic` to log a timestamp each time the X server finished displaying a frame. From these absolute frame times, we compute the inter-frame display times (IDTs). The variance of IDT samples represents the irregularity or *jitter* of frame buffer display updates and provides a quantitative measure of playback continuity. We used a 16.8MByte Motion-JPEG trace file that was read into memory at start up. The file fit entirely within physical memory and required no subsequent disk access.

3 An Adaptive Architecture

For smooth media playback, the IDTs should remain nearly constant; that is, the IDT sample variance should be close to zero. Not surprisingly, we found the IDT variance to be strongly correlated to the level of compute-bound competitive load. As more processes compete for the CPU, the likelihood that `vic` gets to run when its frame timer expires becomes lower. Moreover, when it does run, it further increases the IDT variance (and hence display update jitter) by trying to catch up as fast as possible.

We enhanced the application with a *load monitoring agent*, which determines when CPU resources become scarce and induces the application to shed load. Within `vic`, load shedding could occur by rendering frames at a rate below the source rate. A stateful decoder might still need to decode every frame that arrives, but not every frame need be dithered and displayed (which often accounts for the majority of the computation). Alternatively, parameters to

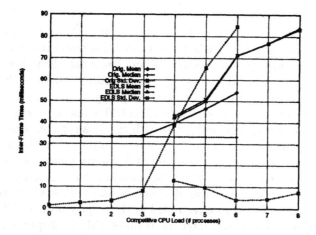

Fig. 1. Comparison of Drop-on-Overload and EDLS

a compute-scalable decoder might be altered (for example, by employing arithmetic approximations for faster decoding at lower quality). Later, when resources become plentiful, load can be increased.

We constructed a simple control algorithm to demonstrate the viability of our approach. In Motion-JPEG, compressed frames are independent of each other, so we can very simply adjust our induced load by dropping some number of frames at the input (i.e. before they are decompressed). For example, M out of N spaced frames ($M < N$) can be dropped uniformly to gracefully degrade the playback performance and reduce load.

We call this approach *early discard load shedding* (EDLS) because it discards frames deterministically at the input, instead of relying implicitly on input buffer overflows to shed load. We term the latter method *drop-on-overload*, because load is shed well *after* the system is heavily saturated.

4 Results

Figure 1 shows various statistics as a function of multiprocessing load. A load of n indicates that n compute-bound processes are competing for CPU time with vic. The graph indicates results for both the drop-on-overload, as well as EDLS. Statistics include the mean, median, and standard deviation of IDT. All values are observed results from our experiments.

We define the *saturation point* to be the point at which the standard deviation exceeds the median IDT. This point occurs at a CPU load of approximately 4. Below the saturation point, the playback application functions well enough to provide qualitatively continuous video, but exhibits observable discontinuities at or above this point.

The curves to the left of the saturation point depict the operation of vic under drop-on-overload. The three additional curves to the right of the saturation point depict the same statistics computed for vic using EDLS. With drop-on-overload, the standard deviation and mean of the IDT grows with increasing process load. When EDLS is used, the IDT deviation remains low and relatively flat as compared with its mean and median. The small deviation with EDLS results in improved qualitative video playback continuity beyond the saturation point as compared with the drop-on-overload policy.

As can be seen from the graph, the median IDT remains constant across load for the drop-on-overload case and grows with the mean for the EDLS case. The median predicts the most common IDT more accurately than the mean for high variance. For drop-on-overload, the standard deviation grows noticeably beyond load level 3, but decreases with increasing median in the EDLS case. This effect is due to the way EDLS performs decimation based on load. Increasing load causes a reduction in frame rate requested at the display process. The reduction in frame rate gives rise to longer inter-frame times with less dispersion, explaining the similar curves for mean and median in the EDLS case.

5 Conclusion

In this paper, we explored the effects of the traditional Unix scheduler on an application that requires periodic execution to display continuous media. We proposed a generic framework, based on the existing software architecture in vic, for CPU load adaptation. By considering a special case of the general architecture, namely EDLS of Motion-JPEG frames using IDT sample variance, we demonstrated the viability of the approach.

We defined a *saturation point* with respect to competitive process load and showed that beyond this point, playback performance under the drop-on-overload policy suffers dramatically. By using the IDT sample variance to detect saturation, EDLS reacts to overload and adjusts the playback rate to gracefully degrade performance in the presence of competitive load.

References

1. M. Jones, "Adaptive Real-Time Resource Management Supporting Modular Composition of Digital Multimedia Services," *Proc. 4th Intl. Workshop on Network and OS Support for Digital Audio and Video*, 1993.
2. J. D. Northcutt and E. M. Kuerner, "System Support for Time-Critical Media Applications," *Sun Microsystems Internal Research Notes*, no. SMLI-92-0077, 1990.
3. J. Nieh, J. Hanko, D. Northcutt, and G. Wall, "SVR4 UNIX Scheduler Unacceptable for Multimedia Applications," *Proc. 4th Intl. Workshop on Network and OS Support for Digital Audio and Video*, 1993.
4. C. Compton and D. Tennenhouse, "Collaborative Load Shedding for Media-Based Applications," *International Conference on Multimedia Computing and Systems*, May 1994.
5. S. McCanne and V. Jacobson, *VIC: Video Conference*. U.C. Berkeley and Lawrence Berkeley Laboratory. Software available via ftp://ftp.ee.lbl.gov/conferencing/vic.

When can we unplug the radio and telephone?

Henning Schulzrinne

GMD Fokus
Berlin, Germany
hgs@fokus.gmd.de

Abstract. Despite high-performance workstations, special-purpose communication devices like telephones and radio still dominate. Reasons include inadequate system and network support, both in terms of performance and the ability to write applications without specialized signal processing knowledge. The interaction of applications with the network will depend largely on the future tariff structures rather than protocol issues.

This paper briefly summarizes some open issues that stand in the way of having a true convergence of computers and audio/video communications. Most of these problems are actually engineering, rather than research, issues.

1 Audio

The availability of graphical user interface toolkits has significantly accelerated computer deployment and new applications. The same reasoning has led to a number of efforts to build the equivalent of Xlib for audio. Experience in porting the NeVoT audio tool to different platforms has unfortunately shown that the easiest to work with are those sticking most closely to the traditional Unix file model, allowing integration into the X event handler mechanism or simple blocking read/write. Some toolkits force the use of timers to continuously read audio, causing overhead and synchronization problems.

An improved architecture for an audio server distinguishes a real-time path, where local and remote audio applications communicate via a non-flow-controlled, unreliable network association (like RTP over UDP) instead of TCP, from a path used to simply download audio clips for later play. A control path would be used to set the local audio encodings, initiate playback of audio clips and carry events such as audio activity indication or VU meter values.

Other desirable changes for audio support include:

- interfaces with independent input/output and setable DMA sizes, possibly even built-in echo cancellation;
- standard system libraries for DSP tasks like AGC, rate conversion, silence detection;
- CPUs with efficient support for DSP operations (fast multiply-adds);
- predictable delays and timestamps so that input and output audio samples can be correlated in time;

2   Video

Most current systems force a copy of 24-bit uncompressed video across the system bus to the display adapter. It should be possible to integrate MPEG decoders or at least YUV-to-RGB converters and dithering into video display systems. For smooth motion, asynchronous framegrabbers must be replaced by interfaces that signal the availability of new video frames or at least include timing information with the digitized image. Operating systems must support bounds on the process scheduling jitter, so that the period between invocations never exceeds the buffering depth of the video adapter.

3   Network Support

Standard local area networks like Ethernet or token ring can serve audio and video reasonably well, particulary in their switched versions. However, multicast should enjoy the same learning-bridge filtering as unicast.

In wide-area networks, support for some form of resource reservation (with the attendant charging mechanisms) or very low network load is necessary for acceptable media quality. Despite claims, ATM still falls short in this regard. The current ATM UNI signaling requires adding each user individually to a point-to-multipoint connection, which is cumbersome and scales poorly; future versions may allow receiver-initiated joins.

With the appropriate financial inducement, many users would be willing to reduce network usage during periods of congestion. Current networks provide only crude information (packet loss) on network loading; further work is needed to determine whether ABR-like feedback mechanisms are useful, particularly in the case of multicast. Also, multicast combined with the increasing range of network speeds calls for scalable media codings, with RSVP-style filters or RTP-style translators at low-speed network access points. Advance scheduling, desirable for important applications, changes the reservation model in that newly arriving reservations might be given a time-limited rather than open-ended commitment.

The actual use of reservations will largely depend on the tariff model. For example, peak-rate reservations avoids the difficulty of characterizing VBR video and may be attractive if there is a rebate for unused bandwidth.

It is not yet clear whether *near-real-time* applications like video-on-demand or distance learning are best served by TCP-like protocols, with the danger of starving the receiver but increased network utilization and guaranteed reliability, or some hybrid protocols which offer some retransmission capability and some rate flexibility. The use of packet FEC in real networks bears further scrutiny.

Virtual reality combines the stringent delay requirements of interactive multimedia (to achieve rapid response to user actions) with the high quality requirements of video-on-demand.

Session VI: Scheduling and Synchronization
Chair: Chuck Kalmanek, AT&T Bell Laboratories

In the first talk of the session, Kurt Rothermel presented a paper on "An Adaptive Stream Synchronization Protocol (ASP)." ASP can be used to synchronize the playout of temporally related streams at multiple nodes. ASP assumes that nodes have synchronized clocks. The basic idea is that each data unit of a stream has a timestamp and data units with the same timestamp are played out at the same time. If network delays or QOS requirements change, ASP provides a mechanism for adapting the playout rates. ASP supports a number of different synchronization policies and uses the notion of a master stream to control the advance of slave streams.

ASP consists of several protocols. The buffer control protocol at the master adapts the playout rate to keep the buffer delay within a target area. A master/slave synchronization protocol propagates changes in the playout rate to slaves. A master switching protocol allows the current master to be switched, say if a slave is close to underflow or overflow because of changing network delays. Kurt presented simulations using delay data from the Internet. Depending on the buffer delay chosen, one can achieve different probabilities of data loss due to late arrival. Henning Schulzrinne asked whether widely varying network conditions in a large community could cause "thrashing" between masters. Kurt indicated that this is a possibility, although in simulations the scheme performs well.

In the second talk, Brian Schmidt described "A Method and Apparatus for Measuring Media Synchronization" which can provide a quantitative measure of the synchronization quality of different media players. Brian's measurements used a controlled audio and video input sequence: the audio stream consisted of occasional clicks; the video stream consisted of alternating frames of black and a white square in a black field. The measurement system compares the playout times of the original sequence and that produced by a media player. The precision and accuracy of the clock in the measurement system is calibrated using a GPS receiver. The results compared the ideal and actual playout times and considered the skew (offset), drift, and jitter. For example, there is often jitter because the player does not know when the data will actually be displayed.

Jason Nieh presented a paper entitled "Integrated Processor Scheduling for Multimedia." The work integrates real-time multimedia applications with conventional applications in a workstation. Since many applications cannot be assigned meaningful deadlines, the scheduler also allows the specification of a desired minimum computation rate. In order to cope with overload, processes are assigned a priority and a share. Under overload, lower priority work is shed. Within a priority, both conventional and real-time tasks are allocated their fair share of system resources. In response to a question about lottery scheduling, Jason pointed out that lottery scheduling provides fairness, but doesn't consider deadlines.

Andreas Mauthe presented a paper entitled "Scheduling and Admission Testing for Jitter Constrained Periodic Threads." The paper describes admission tests for periodic real-time threads which guarantee that a scheduler can honor all of the deadlines, even when the deadlines are sooner than the end of the current period. Kevin Jeffay said that the work is similar to work done at the University of Texas.

The last paper was presented by K. Lakshman who described "A CPU Scheduling Algorithm for Continuous Media Applications." Lakshman noted that the resources needed by multimedia applications are often not known in advance. His work is based on the premise that multimedia applications are designed to adapt their resource requirements. A rate-based CPU scheduler can provide feedback to applications based on current load and the measurements of the resources used by the application.

Julio Escobar concluded the session with an invited talk about intermedia synchronization in distributed multimedia systems. For most applications, it is now clear that real-time OS support is not needed for intermedia synchronization over a network. Human perception can tolerate skews of 50-100 ms, while typical OS code can easily achieve synchronization on the order of 10 ms. With a few exceptions (e.g., stereo streams) we are reaching the limits of what is useful in intermedia synchronization. Synchronization is mostly relevant in wide area networks. The Internet has a typical standard deviation of delay of 100 ms, although even this is not noticed when using 5 frame per second video. Both the requirements and network performance will change as higher frame rates are supported and as QOS support on the Internet becomes more common.

Julio observed that inter-stream synchronization is fairly inexpensive. What is lacking is an understanding of the right architecture for synchronization services, including scheduling, intra- and inter-stream synchronization. Looking forward, Julio believes that the next set of challenges in synchronization will come from the distributed processing world where the requirements are both more stringent than those of multimedia and less understood.

An Adaptive Stream Synchronization Protocol

Kurt Rothermel, Tobias Helbig

University of Stuttgart
Institute of Parallel and Distributed High-Performance Systems (IPVR)
Breitwiesenstraße 20-22, D-70565 Stuttgart, Germany
{rothermel,helbig}@informatik.uni-stuttgart.de

Abstract. Protocols for synchronizing data streams should be highly adaptive with regard to both changing network conditions as well as to individual user needs. The Adaptive Synchronization Protocol we are going to describe in this paper supports any type of distribution of the stream group to be synchronized. It incorporates buffer level control mechanisms allowing an immediate reaction on overflow or underflow situations. Moreover, the proposed mechanism is flexible enough to support a variety of synchronization policies and allows to switch them dynamically during presentation. Since control messages are only exchanged when the network conditions actually change, the message overhead of the protocol is very low.

1 Introduction

In multimedia systems, synchronization plays an important role at several levels of abstraction. At the data stream level, synchronization relationships are defined among temporally related streams, such as a lip-sync relationship between an audio and a video stream. To ensure the synchronous play-out of temporally related streams, appropriate stream synchronization protocols are required.

Solutions to the problem of data stream synchronization seem to be quite obvious, especially if clocks are synchronized. Nevertheless, designing an efficient synchronization protocol that is highly adaptive with regard to both changing network conditions and changing user needs is a challenging task. If the network cannot guarantee bounds on delay and jitter, or a low end-to-end delay is of importance, the protocol should operate on the basis of the current network conditions rather than some worst case assumptions, and should be able to automatically adapt itself to changing conditions. Moreover, the protocol should be flexible enough to support various synchronization policies, such as 'minimal end-to-end delay' or 'best quality'. This kind of flexibility is important as different applications may have totally different needs in terms of quality of service. In a teleconferencing system, for example, a low end-to-end delay is of paramount importance, while a degraded video quality may be tolerated. In contrast, in a surveillance application, one might accept a higher delay rather than a poor video quality.

Protocols for synchronizing data streams can be classified into those assuming the existence of synchronized clocks and those making no such assumption. The Adaptive Synchronization Protocol (ASP), we are going to propose in this paper, belongs to the first class and has the following characteristics:
- ASP supports any distribution of streams to be synchronized, i.e. sources and sinks may reside on different nodes. Streams may be point-to-point or point-to-multipoint.
- ASP incorporates local buffer control mechanisms. They enable immediate reactions on changing network conditions. A stream's play-out rate is adapted when the stream becomes critical, i.e. when it runs the risk of a buffer underflow or overflow. If several streams become critical at the same time, each stream immediately may initiate adaptions independently from others to improve the intrastream synchronization quality.

- ASP performs rate adaptions only if they are actually required, i.e. only when a stream becomes critical. Due to this fact, the overhead for exchanging control messages is almost zero if the streams' average network delay and jitter are rather stable.
- ASP supports the notion of a master stream, which controls the advance of the other streams, called slaves. The roles can be changed dynamically during the presentation.
- ASP is a powerful and flexible mechanism that forms the base for various synchronization policies. A policy is determined by setting a set of parameters and assigning the master role appropriately. For a chosen policy ASP can be tuned to achieve the desired trade-off between end-to-end delay and intrastream synchronization quality. This tuning and even the applied policy can be changed during the presentation.

The remainder of this paper is structured as follows. After a discussion of related work in the next section, the basic assumptions and concepts of ASP are introduced in Sec. 3. Then, Sec. 4 presents ASP by describing its protocol elements for start-up, buffer control, master/slave synchronization and master switching. We show in Sec. 5 how synchronization policies can be efficiently realized on top of the proposed synchronization mechanism, and provide some simulation results illustrating the performance of ASP in Sec. 6. Finally, we conclude with a brief summary.

2 Related Work

The approaches to stream synchronization proposed in literature differ in the stream configurations supported. Some of the proposals require all sinks of the synchronization group to reside on the same node (e.g., Multimedia Presentation Manager [5], ACME system [2]). Others assume the existence of a centralized server, which stores and distributes data streams. The scheme proposed by Rangan et al. [10], [11] plays back stored data streams from a server. Sinks are required to periodically send feedback messages to the server, which uses these messages to estimated the temporal state of the individual streams. Since clocks are not assumed to be synchronized, the quality of these estimations depends on the jitter of feed-back messages, which is assumed to be bounded. A similar approach has been described in [1], which requires no bounded jitter but estimates the difference between clocks by means of probe messages.

Both the Flow Synchronization Protocol [4] and the Lancaster Orchestration Service [3] assume synchronized clocks and support configurations with distributed sinks and sources. However, neither of the two protocols allows a sink to react immediately when its stream becomes critical. Moreover, the former protocol does not support the notion of a master stream, which excludes a number of synchronization policies. Finally, both schemes do not provide buffer level control concepts at their service interfaces, which makes the specification of policies more complicated than for ASP.

Some buffer level control schemes have been proposed also. The scheme described in [7] aims at intrastream synchronization only. In [6], stream quality is defined in terms of the rate of data loss due to buffer underflow. A local mechanism is proposed that allows either to minimize the stream's end-to-end delay or to optimize its quality.

3 Basic Concepts and Assumptions

The set of streams, which are to be played out in a synchronized fashion is called *synchronization group* (or sync group for short). ASP distinguishes between two kinds of streams, the so-called *master* and *slave streams*. Each sync group comprises a single master stream and one or more slave streams. While the rate of the master stream can be individually controlled, the ones of the slave streams are adapted according to the progress of the master stream. The master and slave role can be switched dynamically.

For each sync group there exists a single synchronization server and several *clients*, two for each stream. The server is a software entity that maintains state information and performs control operations concerning the entire sync group. In particular, it controls the start-up procedure and the switching of the master role. Moreover, it is this entity that enforces the synchronization policy chosen by the user. The server communicates with the clients, which are software entities controlling individual streams. Each stream has a pair of clients, a sink client and a source client, which are able to start, stop, slow-down or speed-up the stream. Depending on the type of stream it is controlling, a sink client either acts as a *master* or *slave*. To achieve interstream synchronization, the master communicates with its slaves according to a synchronization protocol.

ASP supports arbitrarily distributed configurations: A sync group's sources may reside on different sites, and the same holds for the sinks. The location of the server may be chosen freely, e.g., it may be located on the node that hosts the most sink clients.

We will assume that control messages are communicated reliably and that the system clocks of the nodes participating in a sync group are approximately synchronized to within ε of each other, i.e. no clock value differs from any other by more than ε. Well-established protocols, such as NTP [8], achieve clock synchronization with ε in the lower milliseconds range.

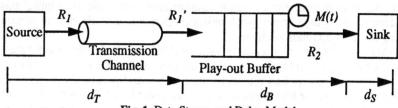

Fig. 1. Data Stream and Delay Model

The basic principle of interstream synchronization adopted by ASP and various other protocols based on the notion of global time (e.g., [4]) is very simple: Each data unit of a stream is associated with a timestamp, which defines its media time. To achieve synchronous presentations of streams, the streams' media time must be mapped to global time, such that data units with the same timestamp will be played out at the same (global) time. Similarly, the sources exploit the existence of synchronized clocks: data units with the same timestamp are sent at the same (global) time. Different transmission delays that may exist between different streams are equalized by buffering data units appropriately at the sink sites.

Our model of stream transmission and buffering is depicted in Fig. 1. The data units of a stream are produced by a source with a *nominal rate R_1* and are transmitted to one or more sinks via an unidirectional transmission channel. The transmission channel introduces a certain delay and jitter, resulting in a *modified arrival rate R_1'*. At the sink's site, data units are buffered in a play-out buffer, from which they are released with a *release rate R_2*. The release rate, which determines how fast the stream's presentation advances, is directly controlled by ASP to manipulate the fill state of the play-out buffer and to ensure synchrony.

On its way from generation to play-out, a data unit is delayed at several stages. It takes a data unit a *transmission delay d_T* until it arrives in the buffer at the sink's site. This includes all the times for generation, packetization, network transmission and transfer into the buffer. In the buffer, a data unit is delayed by a *buffer delay d_B* before it is delivered to the sink device. In the sink, a data unit may experience a *play-out delay d_S* before it is actually presented.

The *media time M(t)* specifies the stream's temporal state of play-out. It is derived from the timestamp *TS* of the data unit which is the next to be read out from the play-out buffer and the actual *play-out delay d_S* of the sink: $M(t) = TS - d_S$. However, the granularity of media time were too coarse would it simply be based on timestamps. Due to this fact, media time is interpolated between timestamps of data units to achieve a finer granularity

4　The Adaptive Synchronization Protocol

ASP can be separated into four rather independent subprotocols. After a brief overview, the start-up protocol, buffer control protocol, master/slave synchronization protocol, and master switching protocol are described in detail. It is important to point out, that this section concentrates on mechanisms, while possible policies exploiting these mechanisms will be discussed in the next section.

4.1　Overview

The *start-up protocol* initiates the processing of the sinks and sources in a given sync group. In particular, it ensures that the sources synchronously start the transmission and the sinks synchronously start the presentation. Start-up is coordinated by the server, which derives start-up times from estimated transmission times, selects an initial master stream depending on the chosen synchronization policy and sends control messages containing the start-up times to clients.

The *buffer control protocol* is a purely local mechanism, which keeps the fill state of the master stream's play-out buffer in a given target area. The determination of the target area depends on the applied synchronization policy and thus is not subject to this mechanism. Whenever the fill state moves out of the given target area, the buffer control protocol regulates the progress of the master stream by manipulating release rate R_2 accordingly.

The *master/slave synchronization protocol* ensures interstream synchronization by adjusting the progress of slave streams to the advance of the master stream. Processing of this protocol only involves a sync group's sink clients, one of them acting as master and the other ones acting as slaves. Whenever the master changes release rate R_2, it computes for some future point in time, say t, the master's media time $M(t)$, taking into account the modified value of R_2. Then, $M(t)$ and t are propagated in a control message to all slaves. When a slave receives such a control message, it locally adjusts R_2 in a way that its stream will reach $M(t)$ at time t. Obviously, this protocol ensures that all streams are in sync again at time t, within the margins of the accuracy provided by clock synchronization. Notice that this protocol does not involve the server and is only initiated when the buffer situation or - in other words - the network conditions have changed.

The *master switching protocol* allows to switch the master role from one stream to another at any point in time. The protocol involves the server and the sink clients, whereas the server is the only instance that may grant the master role. Switching the master role may become necessary when the user changes its synchronization policy or some slave stream enters a critical state, i.e. runs the risk of having a buffer underflow or overflow. A nice property of this protocol is that a critical slave can react immediately by becoming a so-called tentative master, which is allowed to adjust R_2 accordingly. The protocol takes care of the fact that there may be a master and several tentative masters at the same point in time and makes sure that the sync group eventually ends up with a single master.

4.2 Start-up Protocol

Our start-up procedure is very similar to that described in [4]. The server initializes the synchronous start-up of a sync group's data streams by sending *Start* messages to each sink and source client. Each *Start* message contains besides other information a start-up time. All source clients receive the same start-up time, at which they are supposed to start transmitting data units. Similarly, all sink clients receives the same start-up time, which tells them when to start the play-out process.

Starting clients simultaneously requires the *Start* messages to arrive early enough. The start-up time t_0 of sources is derived from the current time t_{now}, the message transmission delay d_m experienced by *Start* messages, and processing delays d_{proc} at the server site: $t_0 = t_{now} + d_m + d_{proc}$. Start-up of sinks is delayed by an additional time to allow the data units to arrive at the sinks' locations and to preload buffers. This delay, called expected delay d_{exp}, is computed from average delays $d_{ave,i}$ of the sync group's streams and the buffer delay $d_{pre,i}$ caused by preloading: $d_{exp} = max (d_{ave,i} + d_{pre,i})$, where $d_{pre,i}$ primarily depends on stream i's jitter characteristic. We assume some infrastructure component that provides access to the needed jitter and delay parameters.

A *Start* message sent to a source client (at least) contains start time t_0 and the nominal rate R_1. *Start* received by a sink encompasses the start time $t_0 + d_{exp}$, the release rate R_2 = R_1 and a flag assigning the initial role (i.e. master or slave). Furthermore, it includes some initial parameters concerning the play-out buffer: the low water mark, high water mark and - in case of the master stream - the initial target area (see below).

Each client starts stream transmission or play-out at the received start-up time. Therefore, the start-up asynchrony is bounded by the inaccuracy of clock synchronization provided *Start* messages arrive in time. However, even if some *Start* messages are too late, ASP is able to immediately resynchronize the 'late' streams.

4.3 Buffer Control Protocol

Before describing the protocol, we will take a closer look at the play-out buffer. The parameter $d_B(t)$ denotes the *smoothed buffer delay* at current time t. The buffer delay at a given point in time is determined by the amount of buffered data. In order to filter out short-term fluctuations caused by jitter, some smoothing function is to be applied. ASP does not require a distinct smoothing function. Some examples are the geometric weighting smoothing function [9]: $d_B(t_i) = \alpha\, d_B(t_{i-1}) + (1-\alpha)\, ActBufferDelay(t)$, or the Finite Impulse Response Filter as used in [7].

For each play-out buffer a *low water mark (LWM)* and *high water mark (HWM)* is defined. When $d_B(t)$ falls under *LWM* or exceeds *HWM*, there is the risk of underflow or overflow, respectively. Therefore, we will call the buffer areas below *LWM* and above *HWM* the *critical buffer regions*. As will be seen below, ASP takes immediate corrective measures when $d_B(t)$ moves into either one of the critical buffer regions. Note that the quality of intrastream synchronization is primarily determined by the *LWM* and *HWM* values (for details see Sec. 5).

The buffer control protocol is executed locally at the sink site of the master stream. Its only purpose is to keep $d_B(t)$ of the master stream in a so-called *target area*, which is defined by an *upper target boundary (UTB)* and a *lower target boundary (LTB)*. Clearly, the target area must not overlap with a critical buffer region. The location and width of the target area is primarily determined by the chosen synchronization policy. For example, to minimize the overall delay the target should be close to *LWM*.

The buffer delay $d_B(t)$ may float freely between the lower and upper target boundary without triggering any rate adaptions. Changing transmission delays (or a modification of the target area requested by the server) may cause $d_B(t)$ to move out of the target area. When this happens, the master enters a so-called *adaption phase*, whose purpose is to move $d_B(t)$ back into the target area.

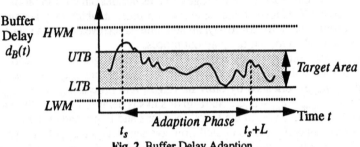

Fig. 2. Buffer Delay Adaption

At the beginning of the adaption phase, release rate R_2 is modified accordingly. The adapted release rate is $R_2 + R_{corr}$, where $R_{corr} = (d_B(t) - (LTB + (UTB-LTB)/2)) / L$. Length L of the adaption phase determines how aggressively the algorithm reacts. At the end of the adaption phase, it is checked whether or not $d_B(t)$ is within the target area. If it is in the target area, R_2 is set back to its previous value, the nominal rate R_1. Otherwise, the master immediately enters a new adaption phase.

In order to keep the slave streams in sync, each adaption of the master stream has to be propagated to the slave streams. This is achieved by the protocol described next.

4.4 Master/Slave Synchronization Protocol

The master/slave synchronization protocol ensures that the slave streams are played out in sync with the master stream. This protocol is initialized whenever the master (or a tentative master as will be seen in the next section) modifies its release rate. Protocol processing involves all sink clients, each of which acts either as master or slave.

Whenever it enters an adaption phase, the master performs the following operations. First, it computes the so-called target media time for this adaption phase, which is defined to be the media time the master stream will reach at the end of this phase. Assume that the adaption phase starts at real-time t_s and is of length L. Then the target media time is $M(t_s+L) = M(t_s) + L \cdot (R_2 + R_{corr})$. Subsequently, the master propagates an *Adapt* message to each slave in the sync group. This message includes the following information: end time $t_e = t_s+L$ of the adaption phase, target media time $M(t_e)$ at the end of the adaption phase, and a structured timestamp for ordering competing *Adapt* messages (see next section).

When a slave receives an *Adapt* message, it immediately enters the adaption phase by modifying its release rate R_2 according to the received target media time (see Fig. 3). The modified release rate is $R_2 = (M(t_e)-M(t_a)) / (t_e - t_a)$, where t_a denotes the time at which the slave received *Adapt*. At time t_e (i.e. at the end of the adaption phase), R_2 is set back to its previous value, the nominal stream rate. Obviously, this protocol ensures that at the end of each adaption phase all streams in the sync group reach the same target media time at the same point in real-time. Between two adaption phases, streams stay in sync as their nominal release rates are derived from global time.

As with all synchronization schemes based on the notion of global time, skew among sinks is introduced by the inaccuracy of synchronized clocks, which is assumed to be bounded by ε. In our protocol, an additional source of skew is the adaption of release rates at different points in time. The worst case skew S_{max} during the adaption phase of the master depends on transfer time d_m of the *Adapt* message and master stream's correction rate R_{corr}: $S_{max} = d_m \cdot |R_{corr}| + \varepsilon$. Between adaption phases, the skew is bounded by ε.

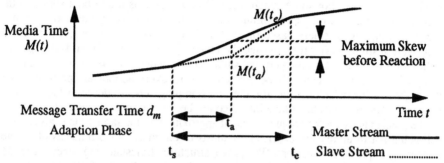

Fig. 3. Master/Slave Synchronization

4.5 Master Switching Protocol

We distinguish between two types of master switching. The first type of switching, called *policy-initiated*, is performed whenever (a change in) the synchronization policy requires a new assignment of the master role. In this case, the server, which enforces the policy, performs the switching just by sending a *GrantMaster* message to the new master and a *QuitMaster* message to the old master. *GrantMaster* specifies the target buffer area of the new master, which is determined by the server depending on the chosen policy. With this simple protocol it may happen that for a short period of time there exist two masters, which both propagate *Adapt* messages. Our protocol prevents inconsistencies by performing *Adapt* requests in timestamp order (see below).

The second type of switching is *recovery-initiated*. The slave initiates recovery when its stream becomes critical. A stream is called critical if its current buffer delay is in a critical region and (locally) no rate adaption improving the situation is in progress. An appealing property of our protocol is that a slave can immediately initiate recovery when its stream becomes critical: First, the slave makes a transition to a so-called tentative master (or t-master for short) and informs the server by sending an *IamT-Master* message. Then - without waiting on any response - it enters the adaption phase to move its buffer delay out of the critical region by adapting R_2 accordingly. In order to keep the other streams in sync, it propagates an *Adapt* request to all other sink clients, including the master. At the end of the adaption phase, a t-master falls back in the slave role. Should the stream still be critical by this time, then the recovery procedure is initiated once more.

Obviously, our protocol allows multiple instances to propagate *Adapt* concurrently, which may cause inconsistencies leading to the loss of synchronization if no care is taken. As already pointed out above, policy-initiated switching may cause the new master to send *Adapt* messages while the old master is still in place. Moreover, at the same point in time, there may exist any number of t-masters propagating *Adapt* requests concurrently. It should be clear that stream synchronization can be ensured only if *Adapt* messages are performed in the same order at each client. This requirement can be fulfilled by including a timestamp in *Adapt* requests and performing these requests in timestamp order at the client sites. The latter means that a client accepts an *Adapt* request only if it is younger than all other requests received before. Older requests are just discarded.

However, performing requests in some timestamp order is not sufficient. Assume, for example, that the master and some t-master propagate *Adapt* requests at approximately the same time, and the former requests an increase of the release rate, while the latter requests a decrease. For some synchronization policies, this might be a very common situation (see for example the minimum delay policy described in the next section). If the timestamps were solely based on system time and the master would perform the propagation slightly after the t-master, then the t-master's request would be wiped out, although it is the reaction on a critical situation and hence is more important. The stability of the algorithm can only be guaranteed if recovery actions are performed with the highest priority.[1] Consequently, the timestamping scheme defining the execution order of *Adapt* requests must take into account the 'importance' of requests.

The precedence of *Adapt* requests sent at approximately the same time is given by the following list in increasing order: (1) requests of old masters (2) requests of the new master (3) requests of t-masters. We apply a structured timestamping scheme to reflect this precedence of requests. In this scheme, a timestamp has the following structure: $<E_R.E_M.T>$, where E_R denotes a *recovery epoch*, E_M designates a *master epoch*, and T is the *real-time* when the message tagged with this timestamp was sent. A new recovery epoch is entered when a slave performs recovery, while a new master epoch is entered whenever a new master is selected. As will be seen below, entering a new recovery epoch requires a new master to be selected.

Each control message contains a structured timestamp, which is generated before the message is sent on the basis of two local epoch counters and the local (synchronized) clock. The server and the clients keep track of the current recovery and master epoch by locally maintaining two epoch counters. Whenever they accept a message whose timestamp contains an epoch value greater than the one recorded locally, the corresponding counter is set to the received epoch value. Moreover, a client increments its local recovery epoch counter when it performs recovery, i.e. the *IamT-Master* message sent to the server already reflects the new recovery period. The server increments its master epoch counter when it selects a new master, i.e. the *GrantMaster* message already indicates the new master epoch.

Adapt requests are accepted only in strict timestamp order. Should a client receive two requests with the same timestamps, total ordering is achieved by ordering these two request according to the requestors' unique identifiers included in the messages. As a slave performing recovery enters a new recovery epoch, all *Adapt* request generated by some master in the previous recovery epoch are wiped out. Similarly, selecting a new master enters a new master epoch, and by this wipes out all *Adapt* request from former masters. When a master receives an *Adapt* request indicating a younger master or recovery epoch, it can learn from this message that there exists a new master or a t-master performing recovery, respectively. In both cases, it immediately gives up the master role and becomes a slave.

As already mentioned above, a critical slave sends an *IamT-Master* message when it becomes a t-master. When the server receives such a message indicating a new recovery epoch, it must select a new master. Which stream becomes the new master, primarily depends on the synchronization policy chosen. For example, the originator of the *IamT-Master* message establishing a new recovery epoch may be granted the master role. All other messages of this type belonging to the same recovery epoch are just discarded upon arrival (see Fig. 4).

---

1. We assume that at no point in time there exist two t-masters that try to adapt the release rate in contradicting directions, i.e. one tries to increase the rate while the other tries to decrease it. This is achieved by dimensioning the play-out buffer appropriately.

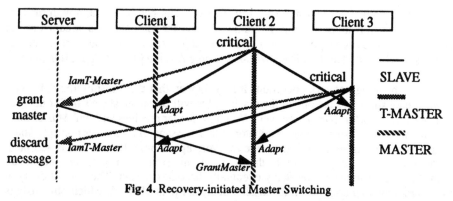

Fig. 4. Recovery-initiated Master Switching

The worst case skew S_{max} among sinks can be observed when master and a t-master decide to adapt their release rates in opposite directions at approximately the same time. S_{max} can be shown to be $d_m \cdot (|R_{corr, master}| + |R_{corr, t-master}|) + \varepsilon$, where d_m denotes the transmission delay of *Adapt* messages.

5 Synchronization Policies

ASP has many parameters for tuning the protocol to the characteristics of the underlying system as well as to the quality of service expected by the given application. A discussion of all these parameters would go far beyond the scope of this paper. Therefore, we will focus on the most important parameters, in particular those influencing the synchronization policy: the low and high water mark, the width of the target area and its placement in the play-out buffer, as well as the rules for granting the master role.

The intrastream synchronization quality in terms of data loss due to underflow or overflow is primarily influenced by the *LWM* and *HWM* values. A good rule of thumb for the width of the critical regions defined by these two parameters is $j/2$ for each, where j denotes the jitter of the corresponding data stream. Increasing *LWM* also increases the quality as the probability of underflow is reduced. On the other hand, this modification may also increase the overall delay, which might be critical for the given application. ASP allows to modify *LWM* and *HWM* values while the presentation is in progress. For example, it is conceivable that a user interactively adjusts the stream quality during play-out. Alternatively, an internal mechanism similar to the one described in [6] may monitor the data loss rate and adjusts the water marks as needed.

The width of the target buffer area determines the aggressiveness of the buffer control algorithm. The minimum width of this area depends on the smoothing function applied to determine $d_B(t)$. The larger the width of the target area, the less adaptions of the release rate are required. Rather constant release rates require almost no communication overhead for adapting slaves. On the other hand, with a large target area there is only limited control over the actual buffer delay. If, for example, the actual buffer delay has to be kept as close as possible to the *LWM* to minimize the overall delay, a small target area is the better choice.

The location of the target area in the buffer together with the way how the master role is granted are the major policy parameters of ASP. This will be illustrated by the minimum delay policy.

The goal of the *minimum delay policy* is to achieve the minimum overall delay for a given intrastream synchronization quality. To reach this goal the stream with the currently longest transmission delay is granted the master role, and this stream's buffer delay is kept as close as possible to *LWM*. The target area for the master is located as follows: *LTB = LWM* and *UTB = LWM* + Δ, where Δ is the jitter of $d_B(t)$ after smoothing.

Due to changing network conditions it may happen that the transmission delay of a slave stream surpasses the one of the master. This will cause the slave's buffer delay to fall below its *LWM* triggering recovery. When the server receives an *IamT-Master* message it grants the master role the originator of this message. If it receives multiple *IamT-Master* messages originated in the same recovery epoch only the first one is accepted, all the other ones are discarded. In the long run, this strategy ensures that the stream with the longest transmission delay eventually becomes master. The overall delay at time *t* amounts to the longest transmission delay at *t* plus *LWM*+Δ, which obviously is the minimal overall delay that can be achieved at *t*.

The possibility of dynamically tuning *LWM* makes this policy very powerful. By increasing the *LWM* value the quality but also the overall delay is increased. Conversely, the quality and delay is decreased if *LWM* is decreased. Consequently, by tuning *LWM* the user may (interactively) determine the appropriate trade-off between delay and intrastream synchronization quality.

Not only individual parameters but the entire policy can be changed during presentation. When changing the policy, the server may require knowledge about the state of the play-out buffers (e.g., current buffer delay, *LWM*, *HWM*). For that purpose, the ASP provides services for requesting buffer state information from clients.

In our opinion, the minimum delay policy described above is the most important one in practice. However, other policies such as "best quality" are conceivable as well.

6 Simulation Results

The section presents some simulation results showing the behavior of ASP's buffer control protocol and discusses results regarding the skew among streams.

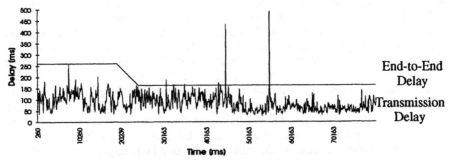

Fig. 5. Transmission and End-to-End Delay

The simulation of the buffer control protocol is based on delay data measured on the Internet. Incoming data units have an average transmission delay between 50 and 200 ms with some peeks up to 500 ms (Fig. 5). The data units are buffered in the play-out buffer of the master stream. Its target area is first set to LTB=100 ms and UTB=200 ms (Fig. 6). The buffer delay is smoothed by the geometric weighting smoothing function with α set to 0.9. The buffering leads to a constant release rate R_2 (Fig. 7), which equals the nominal rate R_1. There is no data loss due to late arrival (Fig. 8).

188

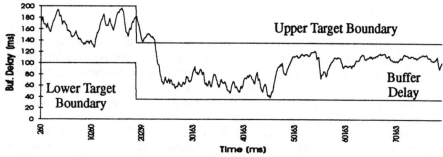

Fig. 6. Buffer Level of Master Stream

As mentioned before, ASP supports the adaption of target levels even when a presentation is in progress. By moving the target area to LTB=35 ms and UTB=135 ms, the overall delay of the played out data units can be reduced by approx. 80 ms (Fig. 6). However, the quality of the stream is degraded as the loss rate of data units discarded due to late arrivals increases (approx. 2.5% lost data units). The adaption is performed in a single adaption phase causing only one *Adapt* message for each slave stream.

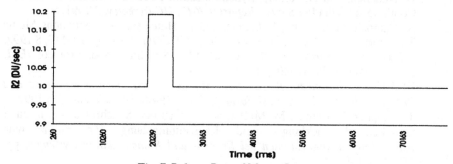

Fig. 7. Release Rate of Master Stream

Our simulations have shown that rate correction R_{corr} is less than 3%. If we assume the delay for control messages to be less than 500 ms, the skew is bounded by 15 ms + ε during an adaption phase (see Sec. 4.4). While the master switching protocol is in progress, the skew bound increases to 30 ms + ε (see Sec. 4.5). Note that during the normal operation (i.e. no master switching and no adaption phase) the skew is bounded by ε, the maximum inaccuracy of clocks.

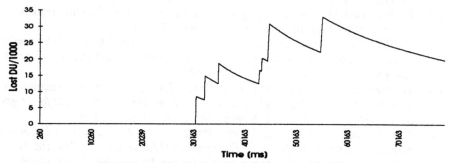

Fig. 8. Losses Due to Late Arrival (Data Units / 1000)

7 Summary

ASP achieves interstream synchronization in distributed environments. It adapts to changing network conditions and allows to tune the quality of data streams to application requirements by supporting a wide range of synchronization policies. Stream quality is improved by reacting on critical situations immediately. Furthermore, by limiting reactions to critical situations, a considerably low message overhead is achieved. The simulation results show good performance even if the underlying communication system does not guarantee quality of service.

The design of ASP was conducted in the context of the *CINEMA* project [12], [13]. *CINEMA* is a system platform for developing distributed multimedia applications. We are currently integrating ASP into the *CINEMA* system. Future work will be to verify our simulation results in the context of various applications.

References

[1] N. Agarwal and S. Son. Synchronization of Distributed Multimedia Data in an Application-Specific Manner. *Proc. ACM Multimedia '94*, pp. 141–148, 10 1994.

[2] D. Anderson and G. Homsy. Synchronization Policies and Mechanisms in a Continuous Media I/O Server. *Report 91/617, UC Berkeley*, 2 1991.

[3] A. Campell, G. Coulson, F. Garcia, and D. Hutchison. A Continuous Media Transport and Orchestration Service. *Proc. SIGCOMM '92*, pp. 99–110, 8 1992.

[4] J. Escobar, C. Partridge, and D. Deutsch. Flow Synchronization Protocol. *IEEE Transactions on Networking*, 1994.

[5] IBM Corp. *Multimedia Presentation Manager Programming Reference and Programming Guide 1.0, IBM Form: S41G-2919-00, S41G-2920-00*, 3 1992.

[6] T. Käppner, F. Henkel, M. Müller, and A. Schröer. Synchronisation in einer verteilten Entwicklungs- und Laufzeitumgebung für multimediale Anwendungen. *Innovationen bei Rechen- und Kommunikationssystemen*, pp. 157–164, 1994.

[7] D. Köhler and H. Müller. Multimedia Playout Synchronization Using Buffer Level Control. *Intl. Workshop on Advanced Teleservices and High-Speed Communication Architectures, Heidelberg, Germany*, 9 1994.

[8] D. Mills. On the Accuracy and Stability of Clocks Synchronized by the Network Time Protocol in the Internet System. *Computer Communications Review*, pp. 65–75, 1990.

[9] Postel. Transmission Control Protocol, DARPA Internet Program, Protocol Specification. *RFC 793*, 9 1981.

[10] S. Ramanathan and V. Rangan. Continuous Media Synchronization in Distributed Multimedia Systems. *NOSSDAV '92*, 11 1992.

[11] V. Rangan, S. Ramanathan, and T. Käppner. Performance of Inter-media Synchronization in Distributed and Heterogeneous Multimedia Systems. *Computer Networks and ISDN Systems*, 1993.

[12] K. Rothermel, I. Barth, and T. Helbig. CINEMA - An Architecture for Distributed Multimedia Applications. In *Architecture and Protocols for High-Speed Networks*, p. 253–271. Kluwer Academic Publishers, 1994.

[13] K. Rothermel and T. Helbig. Clock Hierarchies: An Abstraction for Grouping and Controlling Media Streams. *To appear in IEEE Journal on Selected Areas in Communications - Synchronization Issues in Multimedia Communications*, 1996.

A Method and Apparatus for Measuring Media Synchronization

Brian K. Schmidt[†], J. Duane Northcutt[‡], and Monica S. Lam[†]

[†]*Computer Systems Laboratory, Stanford University, Stanford, CA 94305*
[‡]*Sun Microsystems Laboratories, 2550 Garcia Avenue, Mountain View, CA 94043*

Media synchronization is widely regarded as a fundamental problem in the field of multimedia. While much work has been conducted in this area, and many different solutions have been proposed, no method for obtaining a repeatable, objective measure of synchronization performance exists. Thus, there has been no means for determining the effectiveness of potential media synchronization solutions. In this paper we present an experimental methodology for quantitatively measuring the performance of different media synchronization schemes. We describe a complete (hardware and software) test environment for measuring audio/video synchronization quality of various media players, and we also present empirical performance measurements of an example media player. The results show that external observation is necessary for accurate assessments of synchronization performance. This test and evaluation methodology is applicable to other media delivery systems and can serve as the first step in isolating and quantifying the effects of individual components of a media delivery system.

1   Introduction

Multimedia refers to the use of one or more types of *media data* — data designed to be consumed by humans, such as text, graphics, audio, and video. These data typically possess timeliness requirements with respect to their presentation. For example, digital audio samples may be required to be displayed at a uniform rate of 48KHz. The media synchronization problem is to assure the correct temporal alignment of such time-critical activities relative to a physical clock.

Although there is a relatively large body of research describing various solutions to the synchronization problem, no metrics have been defined to measure the performance and efficacy of this work. Effectiveness assessments have been largely subjective in nature, thus making comparisons between different approaches quite difficult. To determine the degree to which media synchronization is achieved, a means for obtaining a repeatable, objective measure of (externally visible) system performance must exist. We present such a scheme below.

1.1   Background

To help characterize the media synchronization problem we present the following terminology. A *media element* is a single unit of a multimedia data type, such as a video frame, or audio sample. A *media stream* (or stream) is a series of media elements. Common examples of streams include video clips and audio sound bites. A time-ordered collection of media streams is termed a *media sequence* (or sequence). A good example of a sequence is a music album, i.e. a set of audio streams (songs). Given these definitions we decompose the media synchronization problem space into three classes: event-based, stream-based, and element-based.

Event-based synchronization refers to synchronization activities performed in response to external events such as user input, whereas *stream-based* and *element-*

based synchronization refer to activities which attempt to control the timely interactions between related media data. The units of synchronization for stream-based and element-based synchronization are media streams and media elements respectively. The interactions between synchronization units may be within the same sequence (intra-sequence), across different sequences (inter-sequence), within the same stream (intra-stream), or across different streams (inter-stream).

Several methods have been proposed to address all or part of the media synchronization problem. One common approach for dealing with the case of inter-stream element-based synchronization (e.g. managing lip sync in movie clips) is to interleave the associated media streams. However, this scheme suffers from a number of different shortcomings — including the coupling of failure modes resulting from packet loss during transmission, and the inability to prioritize the data streams or handle them in a manner appropriate to their data type ([7], [8], [10]). An approach which attempts to address all types of element-based synchronization is to assign each media element a timestamp that represents the time at which it must be displayed ([1], [4]). While this scheme has the benefit of simplicity, it does not take into account the variations between the different physical clocks involved in actual systems (i.e. system, frame buffer, and audio codec clocks). Some approaches designed to provide general support for media synchronization in distributed settings are based on the use of synchronized system clocks ([5], [14]), while others employ centralized synchronization servers ([13], [15]). Work has also been done in other areas, such as operating systems ([3], [11], [12]) and network protocols ([6], [9], [18]), to provide support for media synchronization. These approaches have vastly different properties and address different aspects of the problem. Without a means for quantitatively measuring their performance, it is difficult to accurately and objectively determine what impact these schemes have on the achieved quality of media synchronization.

1.2 System Overview

This paper presents a methodology for quantitatively measuring the performance of media delivery systems. Below, we present an overview of a complete framework for measuring synchronization quality. In Section 2 we outline our experimental methodology, and Section 3 describes the implementation of our framework. Section 4 presents some experimental results, and we conclude in Section 5.

A generalized media delivery system is capable of capturing, manipulating, and presenting synchronized media data. Evaluating the performance of such a system requires a repeatable procedure for presenting the system with a stimulus and quantitatively measuring its output relative to an ideal response. To meet this goal we have developed a complete synchronization test environment as depicted in Figure 1. The environment is comprised of three components: the media delivery system being tested, a stimulus production system, and a measurement system. The components execute on separate machines in order to avoid interference effects.

The stimulus production system must generate a controlled stimulus and present it as input to the system under test. This stimulus must be a well-defined media sequence that requires synchronization, and it must be produced in a reliable, accurate, and repeatable manner. In practice, a media delivery system typically receives its input either from a storage system (as in a movie player) or from a live analog source (as in a teleconferencing application). To simulate typical use, the stimulus production system must be able to generate a sequence for both situations.

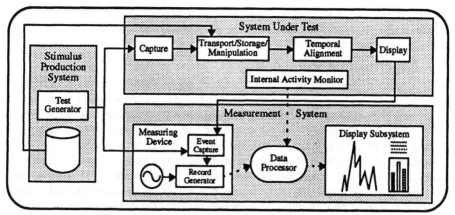

Figure 1. Schematic view of a synchronization test environment.

A stored sequence can be generated once and recorded in a file (in a format suitable for input by the system under test). All timing information of the media elements within the sequence can then be recovered by simply examining the properties of the stored data. If, however, live data are to be used, it is necessary to produce the sequence using a test sequence generator — a specialized media delivery system. The test generator must be able to display the defined sequence in a repeatable fashion and with a small error bound. In addition, the accuracy of the generated sequence must exceed the acquisition and synchronization accuracy of the system under test. Although the sequence generated by this method may be highly accurate, it is still not perfect. So, the output from the test generator is not only sent to the media capture device(s) of the system under test, but it is also sent to the measurement system (described below), which then characterizes the actual sequence timing for later comparison with the output from the system being tested.

Once the sequence is input to the test system, it may be stored, manipulated, transmitted across a network, etc. When the system is ready to display the sequence, it will analyze the synchronization requirements, attempt to temporally align the media elements to their ideal presentation times, and then finally display them. The system under test might also record information regarding its activity and pass it to the measurement system (described below). This information can then be correlated with the measured output of the system to establish causal relationships between externally- and internally-observed system behavior.

The measurement system contains three components: a measuring device, a data processor, and a display subsystem. The measuring device is responsible for collecting the output of both the test generator and the system under test. It then analyzes these data, looking for particular *media events*. A media event corresponds to the display of one or more semantically meaningful media elements, e.g. an audible click, a certain type of video frame, etc. For each media event that it receives, the measuring device generates an *event record* (or record). Records consist of a timestamp and an identifying tag. All generated records are output to the data processor, which is responsible for analyzing the data from the measuring device and compiling statistics on the timing of events. These statistics are then passed to the display subsystem, which presents graphical and tabular summaries of media synchronization quality for the system being tested. The measurement system provides an indication of the end-to-end synchronization performance of the system under test, and it can be used to isolate and quantify the effects of individual system components.

2 Experimental Methodology

Since displaying synchronized audio and video is such a common activity in practice, we have chosen to measure element-based intra-stream audio, intra-stream video, and inter-stream audio/video synchronization as the initial test cases. We use a timestamp-based audio/video test generator and a timestamp-based movie player as two sample media delivery systems. However, since we make no *a priori* assumption on the manner in which the problem is attacked, any system capable of displaying audio and video can be measured. We will conduct experiments with other media delivery systems in the future, and we also plan to measure other forms of synchronization performance. This section presents the design issues of the input sequence as well as the types of synchronization measurements that can be made.

2.1 Designing a Media Sequence for Controlled Input

To provide reliable measurements, the media sequence which is used as a controlled input must be well-defined so that all timing information is known *a priori*. Thus, given that the ideal display time of each media event is known, and since the actual display time is measurable, it is possible to detect any deviations. The sequence must also be defined in such a manner that the measurement system can reliably quantify these timing differences. For example, typical quartz oscillators have a frequency offset from ideal which is on the order of 100 parts per million (ppm). Without some method of compensation, this error accumulates over time and will result in media elements being displayed increasingly farther from their ideal presentation times. This effect is usually termed *drift*. Since this type of error becomes noticeable (to a human) only very slowly, the test sequence must be sufficiently long-running to allow the potential error to accumulate to an appreciable level. Also, the event inter-arrival times must be varied in order to avoid resonance effects with any other clocks in the system. For instance, if the scheduler executes every 10ms, a media delivery system displaying a stream with a period of 30ms between element presentation times may appear to have better (or worse) performance than the same system displaying a stream with a 33ms period.

For our initial experiments with simple audio/video synchronization, we defined the following sequence to satisfy the above requirements. To simplify matters, monaural audio is used, and the video is comprised of only two different frames: a solid black frame, and a black frame with a white square in the center. Two types of media events are recognized by the measuring device: video events, and audio events. A *video event* occurs whenever the type of video frame being displayed is changed, and an *audio event* occurs when a click sound is played. The sequence is defined so that audio and video events should occur simultaneously. This limits the granularity of synchronization to a video frame time. Clearly, this is the smallest meaningful unit for intra-stream video and inter-stream audio/video synchronization, but intra-stream audio synchronization could be measured at a finer granularity. While this is possible, it adds unneeded complexity since measuring the rate at which audio samples are output from the system can be much more easily achieved by monitoring the output voltage levels of the audio codec (a technique supported by the system we have implemented).

The test sequence runs for at least two hours — a sufficient length to allow drift to accumulate to a noticeable level. The sequence displays video at rates of 30Hz, 29.97Hz, 29Hz, and then cycles down to 1Hz with a step size of 1Hz. For each rate, the ratio of the duty cycles of white-square frames to black frames is varied as follows: 1:1 (one white-square frame, then one black frame), 1:2, 1:3, 1:5, 1:7. A pseudo-random sequence of frame types is also displayed for each rate. The sequence is defined in this way to avoid any possible resonance effects with clocks in the system. This pattern is repeated until the time limit for the test is reached.

2.2 Performance Measurements

The above measurement environment is defined in such a way that for each media event ε, the following values are available: the generation time $\tau_G(\varepsilon)$, the ideal display time $\tau_I(\varepsilon)$, and the actual display time $\tau_A(\varepsilon)$. Based on these values, we define six quantitative performance measurements. The *end-to-end latency* of a media event is defined as $\lambda_\varepsilon = \tau_A(\varepsilon) - \tau_G(\varepsilon)$. *Absolute asynchrony* represents the deviation of a particular media event from its ideal display time and is given by $\delta_\varepsilon = \tau_A(\varepsilon) - \tau_I(\varepsilon)$. *Relative asynchrony* is given by $\pi_{\varepsilon_i, \varepsilon_j} = \tau_A(\varepsilon_i) - \tau_A(\varepsilon_j)$, where ε_i and ε_j denote events from streams i and j respectively. It corresponds to the relative display time of nominally simultaneous events from different streams.

With these measures we can derive additional quantities for *skew*, *drift*, and *jitter*. Intuitively, given two sets of values over time (e.g. actual and ideal presentation times of media elements from a given stream), skew refers to a constant offset between pairs of values, drift denotes the amount by which the difference between value pairs changes over time, and jitter is characterized by the instantaneous variations in these values when skew and drift effects have been removed. These quantities can be computed for both absolute and relative asynchrony through simple statistical analysis techniques. For example, given a series of media events $\varepsilon_1, \varepsilon_2, ..., \varepsilon_N$ and the corresponding series of absolute asynchronies $\delta_{\varepsilon_1}, \delta_{\varepsilon_2}, ..., \delta_{\varepsilon_N}$, for each event ε_i we can plot absolute asynchrony (δ_{ε_i}) vs. ideal display time ($\tau_I(\varepsilon_i)$) on a graph and use a curve interpolation technique (e.g. linear least squares) to fit a straight line through these points. Then, the skew is given by the intercept of this line on the absolute asynchrony axis, the drift corresponds to the slope, and the dispersion about the line gives an indication of the amount of jitter. We can also plot a series of relative asynchrony values ($\pi_{\varepsilon_i, \varepsilon_j}$) against a series of actual display time values ($\tau_A(\varepsilon_i)$) and perform a similar analysis to yield skew, drift and jitter figures for stream j relative to stream i.

For our audio/video experiment, analyzing the statistical distributions of the absolute asynchronies for either type of stream provides an indication of intra-stream synchronization quality, while the distribution of relative asynchronies describes the effectiveness of inter-stream synchronization. The relative importance of each of the above measures is application- and media-dependent. For example, low latency is extremely important for interactive applications, and drift is only a concern for long-running sequences. Also, the level at which jitter becomes noticeable depends on the media type (e.g., tolerable video jitter is large compared to tolerable audio jitter). Further, the extent to which asynchronies can be tolerated by a viewer is dependent upon human perceptual limits as well as personal taste. Steinmetz and Engler conducted user studies in [17], and they report several figures of merit for quantifying tolerable asynchrony limits. This type of information must be taken into account when judging the merits of any media delivery system.

3   System Design

Utilizing the above experimental methodology, we implemented a complete test environment for measuring the synchronization performance of arbitrary media delivery systems. As an initial exercise of the capabilities of this system, our test generator and a locally developed media player were used as test cases for measurement. In this section we describe the implementations of our example media player, test sequence generator, and measurement system.

3.1   Media Player Implementation

The chosen test case media player was developed at Sun Microsystems Laboratories. It is a timestamp-based system capable of playing synchronized audio, video, and text streams. Media data are displayed at a single site, but may originate from arbitrary sources, including network connections and local capture devices. Each media stream flows under the direction of an independent thread of control. At the receiver, these threads communicate through a shared memory region, and use time stamps to synchronize the display of their media elements.

Since humans are more sensitive to intra-stream audio asynchronies (i.e. audio delays and drop-outs) than to asynchronies involving the video or text, the clock from the audio codec is used as a master reference to which all threads attempt to synchronize the display of their media elements. The thread controlling the audio stream free-runs, and the other "slave" threads use the information it posts into the shared memory region to determine when to display their elements. If a slave thread is ready to display its element early, then it delays until the appropriate time; but if it is late (>20ms behind audio), it discards its current element on the assumption that continued processing will cause further delays later in the stream.

The player uses the following data format. Video frames are captured at 320x240 pixel resolution and stored using JPEG compression. The audio data are standard 8-bit μ-law monaural samples. The average decompression and display time for the black and white-square frames was measured to be about 33.5ms on a Sun SparcStation 20, and the maximum data rate required is 7.8KB/s for audio and 60.4KB/s for video. Given these values, the media player should be able to sustain the necessary display rates without encountering frequent overload conditions.

In addition, the environment we used to conduct our experiments provides a lightweight event tracing facility. Applications can make calls to tracing routines in order to log the time (relative to the system clock) that some internal event occurred. These tracing routines are very low-cost (a few microseconds). Thus, when used judiciously, they do not significantly perturb an application's normal behavior. By inserting tracepoints into the system under test, it is possible to correlate tracing information to the measured output data so that causal relationships between system activity and noted asynchronies can be determined.

3.2   Test Generator Implementation

We implemented a test generator capable of producing the audio/video sequence defined in Section 2.1. The test generator is an application which executes in the real-time scheduling class at the highest priority on a dedicated machine. It utilizes a simple peripheral I/O device to generate an NTSC composite video signal. This device can store two video frames and allows the user to select which frame is displayed. We use this feature to avoid moving data through the system so that the generator is not limited by any bandwidth constraints. When started, the test generator downloads the pixels for the black and white-square frames into these buffers, and then enters a control loop, waiting for the presentation times of the media events. It displays video events by sending a command to the video encoder telling it which frame to display, and it displays audio events by sending two digital audio samples to the machine's standard audio output device. These samples have the maximum allowable difference in amplitude and thus create an audible click.

This produces highly accurate results since the high priority level of the process and lack of other system activity ensure that deadlines can be met. Also, since each set of media events requires only a few bytes of data to be moved, there are sufficient resources to ensure no overload exists. Further, we avoid any issues that normally arise when multiple clock domains are involved, i.e. the system, audio codec, and NTSC encoder clocks. This is because the audio/video data/commands are delivered to their respective devices under the control of the system clock and asynchronously with respect the audio codec and NTSC encoder clocks. While many implementations of test generators are possible, this choice represents a balanced trade-off between flexibility and performance.

3.3 Measurement System Implementation

The measurement system must be capable of measuring the media output from both the test generator and the system under test, and it must tag and timestamp any events that it detects and then pass them on for processing and display. To accomplish these goals we built a general-purpose, timestamp-generating I/O device called CHAOS (Chronological Hardware Activity Observation System). CHAOS consists of a set of input ports and a counter driven by the system clock. When a signal is detected on a port, a tag identifying the port is generated and attached to the current value of the counter. This timestamp record is then made available for processing. Since this device merely responds to signals at input ports, it is completely generic in its ability to log the times of external events. Thus, the actual display time of any type of media event can be accurately detected and used to measure synchronization quality for any of the classes mentioned in Section 1.1. In particular, we use the event records generated by CHAOS to compute the synchronization quality metrics presented above in order to obtain an accurate, quantitative measure of how well a given media delivery system performs.

For our initial experiments we utilized three inputs. The first comes from a microphone which acts as a transducer to gather audio data. When an audible click registers, a pulse is generated on an input port, causing CHAOS to create an *audio event record*. We use a photo-diode-based transducer to detect the white-square video frame and then send a pulse to a second input port. CHAOS generates a *video event record* for each frame time that the white square is displayed. The final input comes from a Global Positioning System (GPS) receiver and generates *time correction event records*, which are used to improve timestamp accuracy.

One of the most important aspects of the measuring device is the accuracy and precision of its clock, which must surpass that of the clocks used by the system under test. A precision time reference such as an atomic clock would provide an excellent timer for the device, but this is generally not practical due to the high cost and special handling requirements associated with such a device. Furthermore, the exceedingly high resolution of an atomic clock is unnecessary for measuring media synchronization, where the smallest meaningful units tend to be in the microsecond range (e.g. for stereo audio synchronization [17]). A much better approach is to use the standard quartz oscillator found in modern computers as the time base, but also have CHAOS tag and timestamp the input from a highly reliable chronometer.

An inexpensive GPS receiver can provide a precise 1Hz signal with short term error on the order of 10 parts per billion (ppb) and long term error on the order of 1 part per trillion (ppt) [2]. Given the nominal frequency of the system clock, the correct number of ticks between time correction events is known (e.g. for a 25MHz oscillator, the difference between consecutive time correction event records should be 25 million ticks). The measured value represents the true oscillator frequency and can be used to convert timestamps to real time. This frequency changes so slowly that it is sufficient to measure it once at the beginning of an experiment, and a mean computed over 60 seconds is adequate for obtaining a figure that accurately represents the true value [19]. For example, using an atomic-clock-based frequency counter, we measured the actual frequency of a 25MHz oscillator to be 25,001,109Hz. Using the GPS receiver we calibrated the same clock over a one minute interval and arrived at a frequency of 25,001,117Hz. This indicates that the clock is fast by a perceived amount of around 44μs/s.

4   Experimental Results

Using the test sequence, test generator, media player and measurement system described above, we conducted six experiments to obtain an initial assessment of the quantitative effects of some of the causes of asynchrony in modern systems. In the first five experiments we measured the test sequence generator under various conditions. Initially, the generator was run as a process in the real-time scheduling class on a stand-alone Sun SparcStation 20. No peripheral devices (except for the local disk) were attached, and no other processes (except standard system processes) were running. The output was generated using the standard speaker device and the NTSC video encoder. In the second experiment we attached the machine to the local network and repeated the test. In the next experiment we moved the test generator process into the time-sharing scheduling class, and in the fourth experiment we introduced additional load/processes by performing the test with the window system running. In the fifth experiment we rendered the video directly to the frame buffer. For each of these tests the sequence was played out of non-paged memory so that no disk effects are observed. In the final experiment we measured the performance of the media player. We used the same machine and executed the player in the time-sharing class. The same sequence was used, but the player read the data from a local disk in the format described in Section 3.1. For each experiment the system under test maintained internal state regarding the times at which it considered media elements to have been displayed (or discarded due to missed deadlines), and external measurements were made with the CHAOS device.

4.1   Internal Measurements

During each experiment the system under test gathered internal statistics by querying the system clock after the display of each media event and recording those timestamps. This is done for several reasons. First, such measures were the only indication of synchronization performance in the past, and are thus useful for comparison. Next, it provides an indication of how well the test system believes it is performing, and finally, it helps to isolate causes of poor synchronization. In the future we plan to utilize the tracing facility described in Section 3.1 to acquire more detailed information. The results of our experiments are summarized in Table 1.

Internal Measurements of Synchronization Performance											
Type	SUT	Dest	Sched Class	Net	Win	Skew (μsecs)	Drift (μsecs/sec)	Jitter (μsecs)			Losses (%)
								Min	Max	Std Dev.	
A	TG	TV	RT			-61	0.0003	-20	610	17	0.004
A	TG	TV	RT	✔		-63	0.0012	-25	670	28	0.007
A	TG	TV	TS	✔		-46	0.0057	-54	61245	536	0.6
A	TG	TV	TS	✔	✔	-37	0.0015	-33	67266	471	0.8
A	TG	FB	TS	✔	✔	-16	0.000061	-49	64920	706	0.9
A	MP	FB	TS	✔	✔	0	0	0	0	0	0
V	TG	TV	RT			13	-0.00011	-13	597	22	0.002
V	TG	TV	RT	✔		14	0.00062	-19	754	37	0.003
V	TG	TV	TS	✔		27	0.006	-57	61252	536	0.6
V	TG	TV	TS	✔	✔	35	0.0016	-36	67273	471	0.8
V	TG	FB	TS	✔	✔	3342	-0.011	-586	250136	1583	0.9
V	MP	FB	TS	✔	✔	-109329	51	-360736	464338	136877	0.9
AV	TG	TV	RT			62	0.00014	-5	11	2	0.004
AV	TG	TV	RT	✔		63	0.00019	-5	274	3	0.007
AV	TG	TV	TS	✔		74	0.00031	-15	496	10	0.6
AV	TG	TV	TS	✔	✔	72	0.00014	-14	293	4	0.8
AV	TG	FB	TS	✔	✔	3674	-0.016	-180	249852	1689	0.9
AV	MP	FB	TS	✔	✔	-106879	51	-361860	341950	137159	0.9

KEY:
SUT - system under test   A - intra-stream audio synchronization   RT - real-time scheduling class
TG - test sequence generator   V - intra-stream video synchronization   TS - time-share scheduling class
MP - SML media player   AV - inter-stream synchronization of
                                    video relative to audio
TV - video displayed on television   Net - machine connected to network
FB - video displayed on frame buffer   Win - window system running

Table 1. Synchronization performance as reported by the application displaying the test media sequence. Skew, drift, and jitter are the quantities described in Section 2.2, and losses refers to the percentage of media elements which were not displayed due to missed deadlines.

It can be seen from this table that in general the players performed very well. Measured skew is insignificant in the first four experiments, and drift is negligible in the first five. Except for the media player, jitter values are within reason, and in all cases few elements were discarded since sufficient resources were available. There are, however, some interesting observations that can be made.

First, note that the media player reports that it displayed the audio data with perfect synchrony. This is because it uses the audio codec clock as a master reference and assumes that the display of audio events cannot deviate from it, i.e. it does not generate timestamps corresponding to when the audio clicks are actually played. This also helps explain the reason for the non-negligible drift values it reports for the intra-stream video and inter-stream audio/video synchronization. Since the internal time stamps for the video events are generated by querying the system clock when the audio codec clock reports that display is complete, this drift reflects the fact that the system clock is about 51μs/s slow relative to the audio clock. This drift is an artifact of the way in which internal timestamps were generated, and hence the media player itself perceives no such drift.

Next, note that even in the best case, intra-stream audio jitter is high relative to the needs of stereo synchronization ([17]). This suggests that separate control of related audio streams is not feasible with this type of approach. In addition, all intra-stream measurements show dramatic increases in the amount of observed jitter when the system under test is placed in the time-sharing class, indicating that lack of appropriate scheduling support can adversely affect synchronization quality.

Finally, there is a dramatic drop in intra-stream video and inter-stream audio/ video synchronization quality in experiment five, in which the test generator displayed video on the frame buffer. This is because the test generator was originally designed to use only the NTSC encoder to produce video, and so the expected time to display a video frame is hard-coded into the application. Thus, when a display path of differing length is encountered, it cannot adjust appropriately. This emphasizes the need for adaptive display algorithms which scale automatically to account for varying display lengths.

4.2 External Measurements

In addition, to the internal measures reported above, we used the CHAOS device to gather performance information for each experiment. These data represent what is actually observed by viewers. The results are summarized in Table 2, from which several interesting observations can be made.

External Measurements of Synchronization Performance											
Type	SUT	Dest	Sched Class	Net	Win	Skew (μsecs)	Drift (μsecs/sec)	Jitter (μsecs)			Losses (%)
								Min	Max	Std Dev.	
A	TG	TV	RT			—	101	-70	587	30	0.004
A	TG	TV	RT	✓		—	101	-139	730	51	0.007
A	TG	TV	TS	✓		—	102	-61	867	35	0.6
A	TG	TV	TS	✓	✓	—	101	-106	728	53	0.8
A	TG	FB	TS	✓	✓	—	101	-50	723	22	0.9
A	MP	FB	TS	✓	✓	—	150	-348425	231271	125036	0
V	TG	TV	RT			—	100	-17645	17749	9586	0.002
V	TG	TV	RT	✓		—	101	-17423	16771	9624	0.003
V	TG	TV	TS	✓		—	101	-17153	62690	9690	0.6
V	TG	TV	TS	✓	✓	—	101	-17348	66388	9610	0.8
V	TG	FB	TS	✓	✓	—	190	-247842	1027000000	426948	0.9
V	MP	FB	TS	✓	✓	—	150	-364994	337882	136359	0.9
AV	TG	TV	RT			26095	-0.36	-17584	17812	9587	0.004
AV	TG	TV	RT	✓		25114	0.094	-17309	16667	9620	0.007
AV	TG	TV	TS	✓		25616	-0.15	-17127	62552	9689	0.6
AV	TG	TV	TS	✓	✓	24411	0.17	-17117	66326	9606	0.8
AV	TG	FB	TS	✓	✓	-138529	92	-247917	1027000000	4302378	0.9
AV	MP	FB	TS	✓	✓	-28377	-2.0	-55798	278188	26680	0.9

Table 2. Synchronization performance as measured with the CHAOS device. See Table 1 for a description of the symbols used in this chart.

First, note that no intra-stream skew numbers are reported. This is due to the fact that the actual starting time of the experiment cannot be determined with certainty, i.e. externally, we can only determine when the first event is displayed, not when the system under test began to display it. Inter-stream skew, on the other hand, is internally measured as being relatively small (except for the media player) but is observed as being substantially larger. In fact, the value for the experiment in which the test generator displayed video on the frame buffer falls within a range that would be easily noticed by a human observer ([17]). These differences between internal and external measures can be attributed to the fact that the system under test has no means for determining how long it takes for a media element to appear as output. Instead, it only knows when the element was last under its control, and there can clearly be a substantial time difference between those two events.

Next, since the tested systems control the display time of media elements using a single time base (either the system clock or the audio clock) and since no external reference is utilized, the internally measured values for drift were negligible (except as noted above). However, most of the external measurements exhibit a significant amount of drift. For example, in the first four experiments the test generator references only the system clock to produce its output. Hence, the measured intra-stream drift values in these cases indicate that the system clock is about 100μs/s slow relative to real-time. Additional measurements of the system clock accuracy confirmed that this was indeed the case. Similarly, the other observed drift values indicate differences between other pairs of clocks (e.g. audio clock vs. real-time, frame buffer clock vs. real-time). In addition, the intra-stream video and inter-stream audio/video drift values reported internally by the media player in the last experiment do not correspond to the externally measured values. This is because the internally reported drift is due to differences between the audio and system clocks, whereas the external drift is due to differences between the audio clock and real-time. Drift can result whenever multiple time references are used, and these observations make it clear that without an external reference, a media delivery system has no means to characterize it and will operate under the false notion that it is correctly displaying media elements.

Other interesting features can be observed by comparing the internal and external values for jitter. Most significantly, it is clear from the tables that externally observed jitter is substantially worse than jitter reported by the systems under test. In addition, when the test system is moved into the time-sharing class in the third experiment, the external measurements do not reflect the drop in jitter quality that was reported internally. This can most easily be understood by examining intra-stream video synchronization for the first four experiments, which display video using the NTSC encoder. In these cases the dispersion of the jitter is around 9.6ms about the mean. The NTSC encoder outputs video frames with a period of about 16.7ms. When a toggle command arrives at the encoder, it will be deferred until the next period. Since the period is so large relative to the internally observed jitter values, it will effectively mask the large drop in jitter quality when the time-sharing class is utilized. The lack of discontinuities in the other experimental data can be attributed to similar effects. This is significant since it suggests that accounting for the clock rates of the output devices is more important over a long interval than scheduling decisions.

5   Conclusions

This work provides a means of determining the actual effectiveness of arbitrary media synchronization schemes. First, several forms of media synchronization were defined, and then a methodology was presented for measuring the degree of synchronization which is achieved both within and among streams of media elements. The defined approach was validated by implementing a complete test environment for measuring the audio/video synchronization performance of media delivery systems. The measurements match the expected performance of the tested systems extremely well, and thus give us confidence in our experimental design. In addition, the results clearly indicate that internal assessments of synchronization performance are insufficient. Accurate appraisals of the quality of media synchronization cannot be achieved without an external reference.

In the future we will use this methodology and test environment to evaluate different mechanisms for media synchronization, as well as the effects that changes in the system have on the provided synchronization quality. Furthermore, this tool forms the foundation for an effort to identify and quantify the various components of media players that are the major contributors of display time variation.

Acknowledgements

We would like to thank David Lee who developed the internal logic of the CHAOS board, Marc Schneider who helped construct the test setup, and Jim Hanko and Jerry Wall for many insightful discussions. This work is supported in part by Sun Laboratories, an NSF Young Investigator Award, and an NSF Fellowship.

References

1. D. P. Anderson and G. Homsy, "A Continuous Media I/O Server and Its Synchronization Mechanism," *IEEE Computer*, 24(10), October 1991, pp. 51–57.

2. Bancomm, *bc700VME GPS Satellite Receiver Operation and Technical Manual*, October 1991.

3. D. C. A. Bulterman and R. van Liere, "Multimedia Synchronization and UNIX," in *LNCS*, 614, R. Herrtwich (Ed.), Springer-Verlag, 1992.

4. J. A. Boucher, Z. Yaar, E. J. Rubin, J. D. Palmer, and T. D. C. Little, "Design and Performance of a Multi-Stream MPEG-I System Layer Encoder/Player," in *IS&T/SPIE Symposium on Electronic Imaging Science & Technology*, San Jose, CA, February 1995.

5. J. Escobar, C. Partridge, and D. Deutsch, "Flow Synchronization Protocol," *IEEE/ACM Transactions on Networking*, 2(2), April 1994, pp. 111–121.

6. D. Ferrari, "Design and Applications of a Delay Jitter Control Scheme for Packet-Switching Internetworks," *Computer Communications*, 15(6), July/August 1992, pp. 367–373.

7. K. Jeffay, D. L. Stone, and F. D. Smith, "Kernel Support for Live Digital Audio and Video," in *Computer Communications*, 15(6), July/August 1992, pp. 388–395.

8. P. Leydekkers and B. Teunissen, "Synchronization of Multimedia Data Streams in Open Distributed Systems," in *LNCS*, 614, R. Herrtwich (Ed.), Springer-Verlag, 1992, pp. 94–104.

9. T. D. C. Little and F. Kao, "An Intermedia Skew Control System for Multimedia Data Presentation," in *LNCS*, 712, V. Rangan (Ed.), Springer-Verlag, 1993.

10. C. Nicolaou, "An Architecture for Real-Time Multimedia Communication Systems," *IEEE JSAC*, 8(3), April 1990, pp. 391–400.

11. J. Nieh, J. Hanko, J. D. Northcutt, and G. Wall, "SVR4 UNIX Scheduler Unacceptable for Multimedia Applications," in *LNCS*, 846, D. Shepherd, et. al. (Eds.), Springer-Verlag, 1994.

12. J. D. Northcutt and E. M. Kuerner, "System Support for Time-Critical Applications," *Computer Communications*, 16(10), Oct. 1993, pp. 619–636.

13. S. Ramanathan and P. V. Rangan, "Adaptive Feedback Techniques for Synchronized Multimedia Retrieval over Integrated Networks," *IEEE/ACM Transactions on Networking*, 1(1), February 1993.

14. L. A. Rowe and B. C. Smith, "A Continuous Media Player," in *LNCS*, 712, V. Rangan (Ed.), Springer-Verlag, 1993.

15. S. H. Son and N. Agarwal, "Synchronization of Temporal Constructs in Distributed Multimedia Systems with Controlled Accuracy," *International Conference on Multimedia Computing and Systems*, May 1994, pp. 550–555.

16. R. Steinmetz, "Synchronization Properties in Multimedia Systems," *IEEE JSAC*, 8(3), April 1990, pp. 401–412.

17. R. Steinmetz and C. Engler, "Human Perception of Media Synchronization," *Technical Report 43.9310*, IBM European Networking Center, Heidelberg.

18. D. L. Stone and K. Jeffay, "An Empirical Study of Delay Jitter Management Policies," To appear in *Multimedia Systems*.

19. D. B. Sullivan, D. W. Allan, D. A. Howe and F. L. Walls, "Characterization of Clocks and Oscillators," *NIST Technical Note 1337*, March 1990.

Integrated Processor Scheduling for Multimedia

Jason Nieh and Monica S. Lam

Computer Systems Laboratory
Stanford University
Stanford, CA 94305
{nieh, lam}@cs.stanford.edu

The advent of multimedia ushers forth a growing class of applications that must manipulate digital audio and video within well-defined timeliness requirements. Existing processor schedulers are inadequate in supporting these requirements. They fail to allow the integration of these continuous media computations with conventional interactive and batch activities. We have created a new scheduler that provides integrated processor scheduling for all classes of computational activities. Our solution achieves optimal performance when all timeliness requirements can be satisfied, and provides graceful degradation when the system is overloaded. Though unique in the degree to which it allows users control over the dynamic sharing of processing resources, the scheduler does not impose any draconian demands on the user to provide information he does not have or does not choose to specify.

1 Introduction

Applications that manipulate digital audio and video represent a new class of computations executed by workstation users. This new class of computations is known as *continuous media*. Continuous media activities are characteristic of applications that manipulate sampled digital media, such as television or teleconferencing. These activities must process and transport media samples within well-defined timeliness requirements. Their integration into the workstation environment requires that the operating system manage resources to meet their time constraints, while at the same time supporting the interactive and batch activities found in conventional applications today. As continuous media activities alone can consume the resources of an entire machine, the operating system must manage resources effectively not just when the system is underloaded, but more importantly, when the system is overloaded. (When all time constraints can be satisfied, the system is said to be underloaded, otherwise it is overloaded.) In particular, as processor cycles are often the most oversubscribed resource, effective processor scheduling is of paramount importance.

Anticipating that processor scheduling based on traditional timesharing would not be suitable for the support of multimedia applications, attempts have been made to adapt real-time schedulers [6][8][12] to support the timeliness requirements of multimedia applications [4][9]. To allow the co-existence of continuous media, interactive, and batch activities, they rely on artificial rate or deadline parameters to force-fit interactive and batch activities into an unsuitable real-time model. The result is that conventional applications are unable to share resources properly without hand-tuning artificial rates and deadlines through trial-and-error for each mix of activities. When the system is overloaded, the drawbacks of these schemes are even more egregious. At best, they load shed by relying on unique user-specified importances for all activities, and ignore the common case when many activities are of unspecified and indistinguishable importance from one another. At worst, they rely on first-come-first-serve admission control and deliver low utilization, while compelling users to hand-tune their specifications through trial-and-error to fit within their static reserve abstractions.

Because of the difficulty of scheduling conventional interactive and batch activities together with real-time continuous media activities, proposed solutions with actual implementations have predominantly been static two-level schemes [1][3][5]. By allowing multiple policies on top of a base-level mechanism [7], they attempt to avoid the integration problem by supporting separate conventional and real-time scheduling policies. Their drawback is that no matter how sophisticated the layered scheduling policies or how general the base-level mechanism may be [13], scheduling among computations in different policies is limited by the premature loss of information in the static mapping to the base-level mechanism. In particular, none of these schemes can account for timeliness requirements among activities in separate policies. At best, the static isolation of real-time continuous media activities limits the utilization of the system and artificially constrains the range of behavior the system can provide. At worst, such hybrid schemes lead to experimentally demonstrated unacceptable behavior, allowing runaway real-time activities to cause basic system services to lock up, and the user to lose control over the machine [10]. All of these schemes lack the desired degree of control for the user, and lack the ability to provide integrated support and effective overload management for multimedia applications.

2 An Overview of our Scheduler

We have created a new processor scheduler that provides integrated support and effective overload management for all classes of computational activities, whether real-time or conventional, such as those found in multimedia applications. When used to schedule real-time applications, our unified scheduler has the desirable behavior of a typical real-time scheduler: it delivers optimal performance by satisfying the specified deadlines whenever possible. When used to schedule conventional applications, our scheduler has the desirable behavior of a conventional scheduler: it provides good system responsiveness for interactive activities with steady forward progress for batch activities. More importantly, not only does our unified scheduler handle each type of activity effectively, it also handles the combination of both types of tasks seamlessly, without requiring any user parameters.

To support both real-time and conventional tasks, the key problem that must be addressed is how to allocate processing resources in overload. Our solution to this problem is based on fairness. All tasks are given a fair allocation of the processor. Real-time tasks are given their fair allocation first and executed in earliest-deadline-order to meet their deadlines. Any task that cannot meet its deadline within its allocation of processor time is notified that it will miss its deadline and is shed by the scheduler. After the real-time tasks have run, conventional tasks are given the remaining time to run using a round-robin discipline. Since the real-time tasks receive no more than their fair allocation of the processor, conventional tasks are assured that the remaining time enables them to run for their fair allocation of processor time as well.

Unlike previous real-time approaches which confuse the notions of urgency and importance, our scheduler does not give real-time tasks priority over conventional tasks simply because they have well-defined deadlines. Among tasks of unspecified and indistinguishable importance, all tasks should have equal rights to the processor. A more urgent real-time task should run earlier, but it should not run for more than its fair share of the processor to the starvation of conventional tasks; conventional tasks are expected to make reasonable forward progress as well. Unlike timesharing or static two-level schemes, the scheduler actively seeks to meet the deadlines of real-time tasks by giving them their fair allocation before the conventional tasks. Our combination of fairness-based allocation with deadline-aware scheduling provides a consistent default policy for sharing processor resources among all classes of computations.

As different users may have different preferences as to how processing resources should be shared for a given mix of applications, the scheduler provides simple controls to allow users to bias the processor allocation away from fairness in accordance with user preferences. The controls are used for two kinds of sharing policies: a traditional priority-based policy where important tasks, which can be either real-time or conventional jobs, can monopolize the resources, and a weighted-share policy where different types of activities can obtain a portion of the machine in proportion to their weighting. By incorporating user preferences when the user chooses to specify the information, the system can bias the allocation of resources to maximize the value it delivers to the user. The scheduler is unique in the degree to which it allows users control over the dynamic sharing of processing resources, and yet does not impose any draconian demands on the user to provide information he does not have or does not choose to specify.

Due to space constraints, the details of our scheduling algorithm and performance measurements based on our scheduler implementation in the Solaris operating system [2] are not presented here; they can be found in [11].

3 Conclusions

This paper introduces a novel solution to the difficult problem of scheduling multimedia applications, which have a mix of activities that have very different expected performance characteristics and resource requirements. Our solution handles mixes of conventional interactive and batch activities and real-time continuous media activities in a unified and tightly integrated manner, even when the system is overloaded. Unlike previous approaches, it does not rely on hand-tuning artificial rate or deadline parameters for conventional activities, it does not require specifying importances for all activities, nor does it limit system behavior or utilization as in static two-level schemes. Instead, our scheduler provides all activities with their fair allocation of resources toward satisfying their time constraints without the need for any user parameters. As different users may have different preferences for the behavior of a mix of applications, simple controls are provided that allow the user a high degree of predictable control over the dynamic sharing of processing resources.

4 Acknowledgments

We thank J. Duane Northcutt and James G. Hanko for many enlightening discussions. This work was supported in part by an NSF Young Investigator Award and Sun Microsystems Laboratories.

5 References

1. AT&T: UNIX System V Release 4 Internals Student Guide, Vol. I, Unit 2.4.2., AT&T, 1990.

2. J. R. Eykholt, S. R. Kleiman, S. Barton, R. Faulkner, et. al.: *Beyond Multiprocessing...Multithreading the SunOS Kernel*, USENIX Summer 1992, San Antonio, Texas.

3. D. B. Golub: *Operating System Support for Coexistence of Real-Time and Conventional Scheduling*, Technical Report CMU-CS-94-212, School of Computer Science, Carnegie Mellon University, November 1994.

4. J. G. Hanko, E. M. Kuerner, J. D. Northcutt, G. A. Wall: *Workstation Support for Time-Critical Applications*, Proceedings of the Second International Workshop on Network and Operating Systems Support for Digital Audio and Video, November 1991.

5. J. G. Hanko: *A New Framework for Processor Scheduling in UNIX*, Abstract talk from the Fourth International Workshop on Network and Operating Systems Support for Digital Audio and Video, November 1993.

6. J. P. Lehoczky, L. Sha, J. K. Strosnider: *Enhanced Aperiodic Responsiveness in Hard Real-Time Environments*, Proceedings of the IEEE Real-Time Systems Symposium, December 1987.

7. R. Levin, E. Cohen, W. Corwin, F. Pollack, W. Wulf: *Policy/Mechanism Separation in Hydra*, Proceedings Fifth Symposium on Operating Systems Principles, ACM, November, 1975.

8. C. D. Locke: *Best-Effort Decision Making for Real-Time Scheduling*, Ph.D. Thesis, Department of Computer Science, Carnegie Mellon University, May, 1986.

9. C. W. Mercer, S. Savage, H. Tokuda: *Processor Capacity Reserves: Operating System Support for Multimedia Applications*, Proceedings of the IEEE International Conference on Multimedia Computing and Systems, May 1994.

10. J. Nieh, J. G. Hanko, J. D. Northcutt, G. A. Wall: *SVR4 UNIX Scheduler Unacceptable for Multimedia Applications*, Proceedings of the Fourth International Workshop on Network and Operating Systems Support for Digital Audio and Video, November 1993.

11. J. Nieh, M. S. Lam, J. G. Hanko, J. D. Northcutt: *Integrated Processor Scheduling in Support of Multimedia Applications*, submitted for publication.

12. S. Ramos-Thuel, J. P. Lehoczky, *On-Line Scheduling of Hard Deadline Aperiodic Tasks in Fixed-Priority Systems*, Proceedings of the IEEE Real-Time Systems Symposium, December 1993.

13. M. Ruschitzka, R. S. Fabry: *A Unified Approach to Scheduling*, Communications of the ACM, July 1977.

Scheduling and Admission Testing for Jitter Constrained Periodic Threads

Andreas Mauthe and Geoff Coulson

Computing Department,
Lancaster University,
Lancaster LA1 4YR, UK
e.mail: [andreas, geoff]@comp.lancs.ac.uk

1 Introduction

In this short paper, we address the issue of real-time CPU scheduling in operating systems. Our approach is to design new admission tests for periodic real-time threads which guarantee that a run time scheduler, say an earliest deadline first (EDF) or a fixed priority scheduler, will be able to honour all specified deadlines *where the specified deadlines may be earlier than the end of the current period*. We refer to threads whose deadlines and periods may differ as *jitter constrained threads* because they exhibit less jitter (i.e. variation in periodicity) than conventional periodic threads. In the extreme case, where the deadline is specified to be identical to the execution time, a jitter constrained thread executes perfectly isochronously. Jitter constrained threads are particularly appropriate for high quality continuous media applications such as video and animation playouts as the display jitter of high quality video or animation can be reduced to an arbitrary degree without relying on a hardware clocked display device.

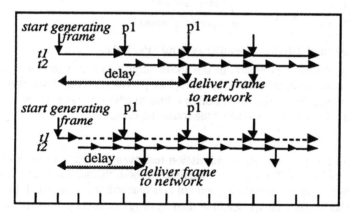

Fig. 1. Reducing delay with jitter constrained threads

The provision of jitter constrained threads also helps end-systems to honour delay and jitter-related QoS parameters. To see how delay and buffering requirements are affected, consider an application that sends large video frames over a network using a rate based transport protocol. This scenario may be realised as a periodic thread t_1 which executes application code to generate video frames, and another periodic thread t_2 which performs fragmentation and rate control. With conventional real-time periodic threads, the delay incurred by this two thread system would be the sum of the period of t_1 plus three times the period of t_2 (assuming three packets per frame as illustrated in figure 1). However, if we are able to specify an earlier deadline for t_1, the delay (and hence buffering requirement) can be significantly reduced. The top part of figure 1 shows the timing of the scenario in the normal case. In the bottom part of figure 1, t_1 is a jitter constrained thread which completes the generation of a frame within one time unit of the start of a frame period. It can be seen that significant delay reductions are achieved.

The scheduling work introduced in this paper is part of a broader resource management framework carried out within SUMO, a collaborative project involving Lancaster University and CNET, France Telecom [1]. The aim of this project is the design and implementation of a Chorus microkernel based operating system infrastructure for supporting distributed multimedia applications.

2 Admission Testing of Jitter Constrained Threads

Our scheduling approach is principally based on the dynamic *earliest deadline first* (EDF) algorithm [2]. The algorithm can be simply expressed as follows:

> *Every time a thread becomes runnable, or a periodic thread invocation finishes, select the runnable thread with the earliest deadline to run next.*

EDF is an attractive policy as it is an optimal, dynamic algorithm, i.e. it is *guaranteed* to find a valid schedule (i.e. one that honours the deadlines of all threads) *if such a schedule exists* [3]. In addition, it fully utilises the CPU resource. For periodic threads with deadlines equal to periods a simple admission test exists: it only has to be checked if the processor utilisation of all threads is less or equal than 100%. More formally, the admission test is expressed as follows [2]:

$$\sum_{i=1}^{\#t} e_i \Big/ p_i \leq 1 \qquad \begin{array}{l} e_i = execution\,time \\ p_i = period\,of\,thread\,i \end{array}$$

2.1 Extension Utilising Deadlines and Periods

A straightforward extension of the above admission test is to consider explicit deadlines smaller than the period, i.e. to replace p_i with d_i in the above formula. The problem with this test is that it will often refuse to admit thread sets for which EDF could find a valid schedule. Consider the following thread set:

$$t_1 : p = 3, d = 1, e = 1$$
$$t_2 : p = 5, d = 4, e = 2$$

This set will not pass the above admission test even though a valid schedule can easily be found that will honour the deadlines of both threads: in figure 2, it can be seen that every time the scheduling time of t_1 is reached, it is scheduled immediately because either it has a closer deadline than t_2, or t_2 has already finished processing when t_1 becomes ready.

We can use the above example to extract the following general insight:

> *A candidate thread can be accepted if, in the period length of each of its invocations, there is sufficient spare resource to schedule the required number of invocations of all other threads with an earlier or equal deadline, even when the scheduling times of all threads concerned coincide.*

Relating this to figure 2, we can see that, in a system currently supporting only t_1, it should also be possible to support t_2. This is because in each instance of t_2 it is possible to fit the required number of invocations of t_1 (i.e. 2 invocations of 1 time unit each) plus the per-period invocation execution time of t_2 itself (i.e. 2 time units) within the deadline of t_2 (i.e. 4 time units).

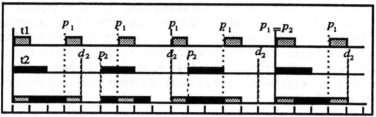

Fig. 2: Deadline scheduling of jitter constrained threads

This argument is more formally captured in the following admission test:

$$\forall c \ in \ \left\langle c_{\min}, \ ..., \ c_{\max} \right\rangle \ \left(\sum_{j=1}^{k} etime(j, \ d_c) + \sum_{i=1}^{l} e_i \right) \Big/ d_c \leq 1$$

$$where \ etime(j, \ t) = e_j \left\lfloor t/p_j \right\rfloor + \begin{cases} e_j, & if \ t \geq p_j \left\lfloor t/p_j \right\rfloor + d_j \\ \dfrac{e_j}{d_j}(t - p_j \left\lfloor t/p_j \right\rfloor), & otherwise \end{cases}$$

In the above, the inequality is applied iteratively over an ordered sequence of *deadline equivalence classes* and must hold for all these classes. Each deadline equivalence class c contains all threads in the system that have a deadline d_c, and the sequence of classes as a whole is ordered smallest deadline first to largest deadline last.

The function $etime(j, t)$ gives the maximum processing time required by a thread j in some time span t. Given this definition of $etime$, it can be seen that the first term in the numerator of the top equation sums the required execution times of some number of threads within the period d_c. In fact, the summation ranges over $(1..k)$ which is defined to contain all threads in deadline classes *lower* in the ordered sequence than the current class c. The second term, ranging over $(1..l)$, sums the execution time required by all threads in the current deadline class c within the interval d_c. The numerator as a whole thus evaluates to the total CPU time required, in the worst case, in the time interval d_c by all threads with a deadline $\leq d_c$.

2.2 Extension Utilising Predictable Scheduling Times

A limitation of the above test is that it pessimistically assumes that all threads can become ready at the same time. Where it can be demonstrated that this cannot occur, a further degree of freedom in admission testing is possible. For example, due to the implicit timing relationship between threads t_1 and t_2 in figure 1, it is only possible for their invocations to coincide at certain fixed instants. This is so because the scheduling times of invocations of t_2 are always located at a fixed offset from the deadlines of invocations of t_2.

One situation where it is possible to assume fixed timing relationships is in the context of so called *harmonic sets*. A harmonic set [4] is a thread set in which the constituent threads can be ordered such that the period of each thread divides its successor; e.g. 3 divides 6 divides 12. Harmonic sets can, in principle, be recognised *automatically* by the infrastructure without requiring the user to explicitly specify scheduling time relationships. The special case of harmonic sets containing multiple threads with the same period is likely to be quite common as applications frequently open multiple instances of a given connection time (e.g. multiple video connections). In the revised admission test (shown below) we recognise harmonic sets with pre-defined timing relationships as described above; the test is a relatively straightforward extension of our first test:

$$\forall c \ \ in \ \left\langle c_{min}, \ ..., \ c_{max} \right\rangle \ \left(\sum_{j=1}^{k} etime(j, \ d_c) + \sum_{i=1}^{l} e_i + \sum_{H=1}^{\#H} E_H \right) \Big/ d_c \leq 1$$

The differences are, first, that the original two terms now only consider those threads that are *not* placed in a harmonic set, and, second, that a new term is added to express the maximum required processing time of any harmonic sets in the thread set. The expression E_H represents the maximum processing time requirement over any interval d_c for the subset of threads in a harmonic set H whose deadlines are $\leq d_c$.

Due to lack of space we are not able to present the derivation and the full formula for E_H. Basically, we use an iterative function over scheduling times and deadlines to determine the required maximum processing time.

3 Summary and Conclusions

In conclusion, we have briefly presented admission tests that ensure that a run time EDF algorithm will be able to maintain the required semantics of jitter constrained threads. The second test involves more admission time overhead, but is able to admit a wider range of candidate thread sets. In the full version of this paper [5], the tests are derived fully and proofs are given. In addition, the (minimal) necessary adaptations to the run time scheduler are discussed. We also generalise our tests to accommodate fixed priority scheduling schemes.

References

1 Coulson, G., Campbell, A., Robin, P., Blair, G. S., Papathomas, M. and D. Shepherd, "The Design of a QoS Controlled ATM Based Communications System in Chorus", *To be published in IEEE JSAC, Special Issue on ATM Local Area Networks*, 1994.

2 Liu, C. L. and Layland, J. W., "Scheduling Algorithms for Multiprogramming in a Hard Real-time Environment", *Journal of the Association for Computing Machinery*, Vol. 20, No. 1, pp 46-61, February 1973.

3 Mauthe, A., Schultz, W. and Steinmetz, R., "Inside the Heidelberg Multimedia Operating System Support: Real-Time Processing of Continuous Media in OS/2", Technical Report No. 43.9214, IBM European Networking Center, Tiergartenstrasse 8, D-6900 Heidelberg 1, 1992.

4 Kuo, T.-W. and Mok, A. K., "Load Adjustment in Adaptive Real-Time Systems", *Proc. 12th IEEE Real Time System Symposium*, 1991.

5 Mauthe, A and G. Coulson, "Scheduling and Admission Testing for Jitter Constrained Periodic Threads", Internal Report MPG-95-04, Distributed Multimedia Research Group, Department of Computing, Lancaster University, Lancaster LA1 4YR, UK, January 1995.

A CPU Scheduling Algorithm for Continuous Media Applications*

Raj Yavatkar and K. Lakshman**

Department of Computer Science
University of Kentucky, Lexington, KY

Abstract. We provide an overview of a CPU management algorithm called RAP (Rate-based Adjustable Priority Scheduling) that provides *predictable* service and dynamic QOS control in the presence of varying compute times, arrival and departure of processes, and CPU overloads. A significant feature of RAP includes an application-level QOS manager that implements policies for graceful adaptation in the face of CPU overload.

1 Introduction

We are currently investigating operating system (OS) mechanisms and policies for managing end-system resources (such as CPU, network interface, memory, and bus bandwidth) so that an OS can provide *predictable service* to multimedia (MM) applications. In this paper, we provide an overview of a CPU management algorithm called RAP (Rate-based Adjustable Priority Scheduling). Our design goal is similar to the objectives of the dynamic QOS control schemes proposed earlier [1, 3, 4]. However, our aim is to provide dynamic QOS control and predictable service in the presence of varying compute times, arrival and departure of processes, and CPU overloads.

The design of RAP is based on the following assumptions. First, RAP does *not* assume a priori knowledge of compute times needed by MM applications. In particular, we have observed that the resource requirements of an MM application usually vary a lot during an application's lifetime. For example, the traces of execution times needed by the Berkeley MPEG player show that the amount of execution time needed to play back a single frame varies a lot within a GOP (Group of Pictures) and even the average execution time needed over a GOP shows considerable variations as a result of changes in scene or video contents. Second, RAP assumes that MM applications can tolerate occasional delays in execution and, therefore, does not try to schedule processes to meet their deadlines on per execution basis. Instead, RAP only ensures that each process will execute at an average rate within an acceptable range specified by the process. Third, RAP assumes that MM applications are adaptive in nature and

---

* This research was supported in part by the National Science Foundation Grant No. NCR-9111323 and Grant no. STI-9108764.
** Supported by the Center for Computational Sciences, University of Kentucky.

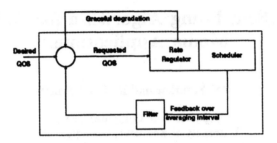

Fig. 1. The figure shows an abstract representation of the RAP algorithm.

can gracefully adapt to resource overloads by modifying their behavior to reduce their resource requirements. Examples of such adaptations include dynamically reducing spatial or temporal resolution in the case of a video application, selectively playing back portions of a hierarchically encoded video, and adjusting the audio sampling rate without compromising the ability to deliver consistently good playback quality.

2 Rate-based Adjustable Priority Scheduling

The RAP algorithm is based (figure 1) on the Phase-Locked-Loop (PLL) principle and consists of two components: a rate-based CPU scheduler which ensures that MM applications are serviced at a steady rate, and an application-level QOS manager which provides adaptive QOS management. The CPU scheduling algorithm is based on a service discipline called *Rate Controlled Static Priority* (RCSP) introduced in [5] for real-time packet scheduling. RAP borrows the ideas on admission control and scheduling from RCSP and extends them to the problem of CPU scheduling for providing predictable service to multimedia applications. In the following, we briefly outline a typical scenario for an application using RAP and describe the functions of each of the components that make up RAP (more details can be found in [2]).

- At the beginning, an application specifies a desired *average* rate of execution (e.g., 20 times a second) and an averaging interval over which the rate of execution is to be measured.
- RAP's admission control algorithm must first decide whether to accept a new process. RAP maintains an estimate of the average computing time needed by each admitted process. Based on these estimates, RAP's admission control algorithm calculates the available capacity for the new process, determines whether the new process can be accepted, and if so, allocates the new process a computing time based on the remaining available capacity.
- The new process is assigned a priority based on its requested rate and is inserted in a priority-based queue for execution.
- RAP schedules admitted processes using a *rate regulator* and a priority-based scheduler. The rate regulator ensures that a process with an accepted rate R

of execution does not execute more than R times a second and the scheduler ensures that a process roughly executes once every $T = \frac{1}{R}$ time interval.

- After the application starts executing, the average computing time it needs, and its rate of execution are monitored over the averaging interval. At the end of the averaging interval for a process, the RAP scheduler provides feedback to the application-level QOS manager about the observed rate of progress.

- The QOS manager compares the observed rate against previously requested rate and reacts either by reducing the process's computing time per execution or by asking for a reduced rate of execution.

- In addition, the RAP scheduler also provides feedback to application-level QOS managers when CPU capacity is over-utilized (under-utilized) and the scheduler wants each process to reduce (or increase) its individual demand by a fraction proportional to the process's current share of CPU capacity.

3 Preliminary Results

We have evaluated the performance of RAP using a trace-driven simulator that uses traces of execution times needed by the Berkeley MPEG player on a Sun Sparc-20. The experiments involved two classes of applications, namely, a CBR (Constant Bit Rate) class corresponding to audio or music player and a VBR (Variable Bit Rate) class corresponding to a compressed video player. CBR applications need almost constant amount of compute time per execution whereas computing times needed by VBR applications vary over time. In the following, we present results of a sample experiment designed to demonstrate the effectiveness of admission control and rate adaptation algorithms.

- Figure 2A shows an overload condition with admission control turned off. Without admission control, the overload causes missed deadlines and wide rate fluctuations for the processes.

- Figure 2B shows the effect of introducing admission control test in the previous case. Due to admission control, the CBR process that arrives at the 3 second mark is refused service. The VBR process that requests execution rate of 50 is admitted and allocated a maximum compute time of only 1 ms based on the available capacity. However, the VBR application needs more CPU and experiences significant rate fluctuations.

- Figure 2C shows the result of adding application level rate adaptation to case B. Based on the observed rate jitter, the QOS manager for the VBR application chooses to reduce its desired rate to 30 times/second. However, due to the limited available capacity, the admission control still accepts it with maximum compute time of only 1 ms and the VBR application still sees rate fluctuations. Its QOS manager then further reduces its rate and eventually stabilizes at 20 executions per second.

- Figure 2D shows the result of graceful degradation when the scheduler asks processes to reduce their share of CPU capacity. Admission of both *cbr_100_3* and the VBR application would cause overload and, therefore, the scheduler

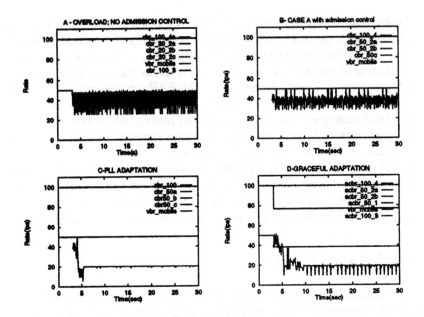

Fig. 2. Plots show average rates of execution for a combination of processes in different cases. The notation used is as follows: class_rate_compute-time; i.e., cbr_100_3 means a CBR applications running 100 times a second with an average compute time of 3 ms. VBR_mobile is based on a MPEG stream with varying compute times.

asks all processes to reduce their rates before admitting new processes. In the case of CBR applications, the rate reduction is sufficient to execute them at a steady rate, but the VBR application needs a lot more processor capacity and does not stabilize. In that case, the VBR application's QOS manager observes the rate jitter and reduces its own rate further until the jitter is within its acceptable range.

References

1. Andrew Campbell, Geoff Coulson, and David Hutchison. A multimedia enhanced transport service in a quality of service architecture. In *4th International NOSSDAV Workshop*, pages 124–137, 1993.
2. K. Lakshman and Raj Yavatkar. Adaptive CPU Management for Multimedia Applications. Technical report, University of Kentucky - Dept. of Computer Science, March 1995.
3. K.K. Ramakrishnan and et.al. Operating system support for a video-on-demand file service. In *4th International NOSSDAV Workshop*, pages 216–227, 1993.
4. Hide Tokuda and Takuro Kitayama. Dynamic QOS Control based on Real-Time threads. In *4th International NOSSDAV Workshop*, pages 114–123, 1993.
5. Hui Zhang and Domenico Ferrari. Rate-controlled static priority queueing. In *Proc. IEEE Infocom '93*, May 1993.

Session VII: Multicasting
Chair: Jim Kurose, University of Massachusetts at Amherst

The topic of Session VII was multicasting. Following the four paper presentations, a lively discussion ensued for forty five minutes, covering a wide range of multicasting issues. The following issues were discussed by the workshop participants:

- What are the proper service models for multicasting? This topic generated the most discussion of all by far. It was noted that there are many dimensions along which a multicast service model must be characterized:
- Connectivity. What are the pros and cons of the Internet model of "full-mesh connectivity" in which any multicast group member can communicate with any other, versus a sender-oriented ATM-like model in which one sender can send to many receivers but receivers can not communicate amongst themselves within the same multicast connection. The majority of discussants argued in favor of the full-mesh model, but it was noted that there are applications when the one-to-many model may be more appropriate.
- Reliability. Should the multicast service model provide for full reliability of data among receivers, no data reliability among receivers (as is the case in IP multicast), or something in between? Several discussants argued for making the reliability service model as simple as possible, and allowing applications to provide application-specific error control.

  The need to support heterogeneous receivers (e.g., with different reliability requirements) was also discussed. Here, the argument was forcefully made to free the sender from having to know the reliability requirements (or indeed, even the identities) of the individual receivers. An alternate model might provide, for example, facilities which would allow a receiver to request a retransmission from a sender. In this case, the sender's interface to the receivers is simple (it simply retransmits when requested), and the decision as to what degree of reliability is required is left up to each of the individual receivers.
- Group membership. The pros and cons of having group membership tightly controlled (e.g., by a multicast session moderator) versus an open group membership policy (e.g., anyone who wants to join a multicast group can do so) were discussed. It was noted that a strong notion of group membership required a significant amount of state be maintained at the end systems, and required protocols for moderating/resolving group membership – a potential drawback. On the other hand, some multicast sessions may want to restrict group membership for privacy reasons.

  The issue of whether an application might itself use a large number of multicast groups (e.g., as in distributed interactive simulation (DIS)) or would instead use a relatively small number of multicast groups (e.g., as in today's Internet teleconferencing tools) was also discussed. Are different service models required for these two very different ways in which applications use multicast groups?

– Other issues. The work in the distributed systems community on reliable, atomic, causal multicast was cited as a service model that was significantly more complex than the relatively simple service models being discussed in the networking community. It was noted, however, that this stronger multicast service model could itself be implemented on top of a simpler underlying multicast service (again, raising the question of what level of service should be provided by the network, and what should be in the realm of the application programmer).

The use of transactional multicast was also cited as an example of an additional service model.

In the end, a majority of the discussants (certainly the most vocal ones!) argued in favor of having the network provide a simple multicast service model and allowing applications to provided richer multicast functionality (whether it be reliability, group membership, or connectivity).

An interesting analogy was made to manufacturing, where the desire to gain economies of scale results in homogeneous goods (e.g., a mass produced product) being manufactured/provided cheaply. Individualized goods (e.g., a hand-tailored product), on the other hand, are expensive. Is the move towards receiver-initiated multicast a move towards hand-tailored (and hence expensive) services? RSVP and hierarchical multicast were cited as examples where the work in hand-tailoring a service is done (and hence the complexity is incurred) primarily at the receiver.

Dynamic Configuration of Conferencing Applications using Pattern-Matching Multicast

Henning Schulzrinne

GMD Fokus
Berlin, Germany
hgs@fokus.gmd.de

Abstract. Multimedia conferencing systems are usually large, complex software systems. We describe a local control architecture and communication protocols that allow to tie together media agents, controllers and auxiliary applications such as media recorders and management proxies into a single conference application. Unlike other systems, control of a single conference can be shared between several controllers. Each media can be handled by one or more independent media agents. Parts of the system have been implemented using an IP-multicast-based audio conferencing tool (NeVoT). The communicating applications disseminate state and control information through a replicator. The replicator mainly limits distribution of messages based on expressed interest of other applications, thus implementing an application-level, receiver-driven local multicast. It also automatically starts applications as needed. The same functionality was also implemented IP multicast restricted to the local host.

1 Introduction

The problem domain of multimedia conferencing can be roughly divided into three separate areas: the transport of data, the management of conferences and the local control and marshalling of components and resources. While there are numerous proposals for the first two areas, relatively little has been said about the third. Here, we define components as the individual applications that are brought into a conference by participants as well as those applications that are responsible for controlling these and the overall conference. There are probably two reasons of why this particular issue has received relatively little attention in the past. First, many conferencing applications are monolithic, often written by a single group, with a single application that at most would spawn some helper applications. Secondly, every such suite of applications had its own set of protocols, so that there was little opportunity to replace, say, one video agent by another.

The set of media agents[1] built by a diverse set of research groups for use

---

[1] We generally follow the terminology of [1], where media agents are defined as "a software entity that handles media-specific functions such as encoding, compression and transport packetization that are used by conferences. Media in a conference might include audio, video, graphics and text".

on the Internet multicast backbone (MBONE) [2, 3] depart from this approach. Here, each media is typically handled by a distinct media agent, with control delegated to an external conference controller [4]. This separation allows graceful evolution, local control, diversity and reuse of media agents. For example, the same video application might be used both within seminar-style, "loosely-controlled" conferences initiated from multicast or centralized directories as well as a "telephone-style", "tightly-controlled" invitation-based conference [5]. Examples of a multicast directory include sd [6]), while WWW is becoming popular for centralized session rendezvous [7, 8].

While the MBONE conference controllers allow the combination of different media agents, these controllers are of the "fire-and-forget" variety. The conference controller simply starts the media agent processes, passing parameters such as multicast address, port number or media encoding as command line arguments. Once a conference has been started, media agents are on their own, unaware of other local media agents within the same or other conferences and beyond reach of the conference controller. While it would be possible to add applications to an ongoing conference, this is not currently implemented in the MBONE tools.

For a number of applications, more elaborate control is desirable:

Controller(s) to media agent: A single conference may have multiple controllers, i.e., media agents may receive commands from multiple sources. In a typical scenario, there might be a basic conference controller that issues and answers invitations to join conferences, as well as manage conference parameters such as media encodings. (These might well change during a conference to accommodate new members or different interaction requirements.) In addition, a floor controller enables and disables individual media applications on the sending side or disables receiving from all but one session member. Both can be implemented independently, but the floor controller, for example, needs to know when conferences start and stop or members leave.

There may also be purely local controllers, e.g., a radio broadcast controller might automatically enable the audio media agent on the hour to tune in to the news.

It should also be possible to have both per-media activity indication, as is used by most of the existing MBONE tools, or a per-session joint activity indication across all media. A single activity display saves screen real-estate and allows easier determination of how a conferee is participating in a conference, but also may be less natural than associating the information directly with the object controlled by the conferee, e.g., a pointer or a video thumbnail. Using the architecture described here, it is relatively easy to use both approaches at the same time, simply by adding another controller that just tracks membership and activity information.

Media agents within the same conference: Media agents and other applications within a conference may also want to communicate. Examples include variations of video-follows-audio or highlighting-follows-audio as well as recording and playback applications. These recorders and playback devices could make use of speaker detection, so that only certain sources are recorded or that video is recorded only when a particular speaker is talking.

Applications across conferences: In some cases, auxiliary applications might wish to communicate across sessions. For example, a priority mechanism might automatically lower the volume or reduce the video image size of a less important conference when activity on another is detected.

All of these interactions are between applications run by a single user. Communications between users is considered the realm of a conference control protocol, with different requirements in terms of functionality, naming, security and reliability.

Most of these control functions could be explicitly coded into the media agents. However, many of these are also specialized and may only be useful in very limited circumstances. Rather than bloating already complicated media agents (even assuming that access to source code or a cooperative author exists), these tasks are often ideally suited for implementation by users or local administrators as small scripts in an interpreted language, such as Tcl [9].

The Tcl tool command language and the Unix shell share the same philosophy of composing larger applications from communicating components. While Tcl uses the **send** command to implement a remote procedure call, the Unix shell uses pipes to connect a linear sequence of independent tools. A related approach for constructing digital signal processing simulators was presented in [10]. The approach presented here is geared towards exchanging control information rather than data; it is point-to-multipoint rather than two-party and is based on an asynchronous communication model rather than the reply-response model. In all these properties, it differs from standard RPC[2].

2   Local Conference Control Architecture

Based on the descriptions and requirements presented above, we present a local application architecture particularly suited for "composing" multimedia conferencing applications from multiple, independently written components. These components generate and are controlled by event-driven messages that contain no specific destination, but are rather picked up by any other application that cares about that specific class of events.

The architecture is depicted in Fig. 1. We distinguish controllers and media agents. The former are conference control applications of various sorts, as indicated above, while examples of the latter also include shared applications, media recorders, and the like. The replicator simply forwards control messages to controllers and media agents that have expressed interest, without regard for content. The replicator is not aware of the distinction between controllers and media agents.

---

[2] [11, 12] discuss asynchronous RPC.

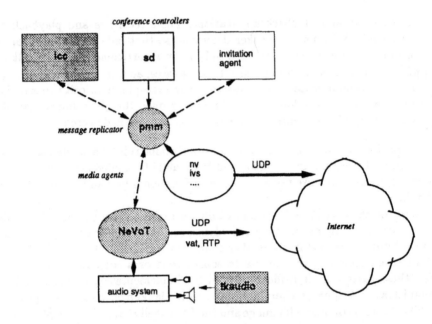

Fig. 1. Example multimedia conferencing control architecture

These control messages could be delivered through any Unix IPC mechanism (Unix sockets, TCP connections, UDP messages, RPC, pipes, stdin, ...) or specialized in-memory multicast support [13]. Three IPC methods have been implemented. In the first, a single message replicator process called pmm is used, listening for connections at a well-known TCP port. The second approach also uses a replicator process, but communicates using UDP datagrams. As described later, the replicator process can be told by each 'attached' process which messages it wants to receive, based on the message content. In the third approach, no replicator process is needed as applications send UDP datagram to an IP multicast address [14]. The reach of the multicast packets is restricted by setting their time-to-live value to zero[3]. Local multicast offers the advantage of dispensing with the replicator process and avoiding maintaining membership information in the replicator. It has the disadvantage that every message wakes up every process that subscribes to the local multicast address, even though each process may only care about a small subset of the messages. It is generally not possible to set up a set of multicast addresses or ports with the same filtering effect as the content-based filtering in the replicator since the interests of different listeners will have non-zero intersection. The relative run-time penalties of replicator vs. multicast will largely depend on the number of processes attached to the replicator or listening to the local multicast address.

The reason for choosing a network-based IPC rather than a Unix-domain socket or pipe is the easy N-to-1 connectivity, reaching if necessary beyond a

---

[3] To tie together applications on different hosts, a larger ttl value is needed.

single host. This allows the user to spread a single local session over several workstations, e.g., to harness additional processing power or special hardware resources.

A TCP-based message replicator has the advantage that it continues to work, if inefficiently, even if media agents are distributed over several hosts, while multicast and UDP-based replicators require additional reliability mechanisms to deal with packet loss. Since data rates are modest and losses are low in a local environment, a relatively simple reliable multicast protocol may be sufficient.

Currently, all conferences and all users on a workstation share a single replicator, however, a simple rendezvous mechanism (say, through a file at a well-known location created by pmm) could be used to restrict pmm to a single user. Maintaining a single message replicator per user eases the implementation of all communication modes listed earlier, including cross-conference. Similarly, a single well-known multicast address and port per user, as currently implemented, avoids rendezvous problems, particularly if there is no master application to track assignments. To reduce the number of processes needing to filter messages, per-conference or per-media multicast ports could be added. Some means of allocating a multicast address and UDP port must be found. This is more difficult if there is no single controlling entity.

The system presented here uses constants and information provided by the Real-Time Transport Protocol (RTP) [15] and the audio/video profile of that protocol [16]. In that protocol, each member of a session periodically announces itself by transmitting RTP control (RTCP) packets containing a globally unique *canonical name*, other "business-card" information and statistics about received sites. The canonical name is formatted like an Internet email address and meant to be the same for each user, across media and conferences. Note that the architecture does not depend on the use of RTP/RTCP or the particular form of the canonical name[4].

3 Protocol Operation

3.1 Message Format and Naming

In the following, we describe the basic operation of the "protocol" between conference components. All messages are sent as ASCII text and are formatted to be directly interpretable by a standard Tcl [9] interpreter.

Generally, messages are idempotent, so that the second request to join the same multicast group is simply ignored. This allows helper applications that are added later to an ongoing session to be initialized; the new application could simply send a query broadcast to all media agents, who would then respond with the necessary commands to join the ongoing sessions. Alternatively, the conference controller could distribute the information periodically.

---

[4] This is also the reason for not having controllers listening directly to the RTCP multicast address.

Each media session is named by a hierarchical descriptor containing identifiers for the conference, media and media instance, e.g., *C/audio/3* denotes the third audio session within conference C, where C is a locally unique name. Generally, each media session will have one media agent. It is assumed that one conference controller for a conference names the media sessions. A single application may implement several media agents, either for a single media type or several, but this is invisible to the protocol. Members of a media session are named by appending their RTP canonical name to the session name, e.g., *C/audio/3/hgs@ursa.fokus.gmd.de*. Messages are constructed to name the object, that is, a session or session member, followed by the operation to be applied to that object, followed by any parameters needed.

3.2 Basic Operation

Applications register or unregister for messages with the replicator by sending a wildcarded string prefixed by + or -, respectively. Currently, these strings follow Unix shell wildcard conventions, but could just as easily be treated as full regular expressions. For example, a video media handler might send + C/audio/* *active to the replicator if it wants to track talker activity.

First, the conference controller sends a message creating a "blank" media session: session C/audio/3 and waits for a created reply from the responsible media agent before proceeding. Auxiliary applications should not answer to avoid synchronization problems. If different media are to have different control ports to achieve reduced message processing load, the port number is conveyed as well.

The controller then proceeds to establish the parameters of the media session (in any order), shown here for audio:

```
C/audio/3 ttl 128
...
C/audio/3 transport RTP
C/audio/3 media PCMU 1 8000 0.02
C/audio/3 cname doe@foo.bar.com
```

The same commands are used to change parameters during the session. After the parameters have been set, the conference controller prods the media agent(s) to establish the actual network connection for this session: C/audio/3 open 224.2.0.1. For unicast or point-to-multipoint networks like ST-II or ATM, the open command can be repeated with different network addresses for the same session. If a network connection was successfully established, the responsible media agent answers with C/audio/3 opened 224.2.0.1. This message might also be used by other applications to create a record for that particular session.

A media agent rather than the controller introduces a new session member to the other local conference applications by sending a hello message, as in C/audio/3 hello hgs@ursa.fokus.gmd.de. Session members become known to media agents either through IP multicast or successful point-to-multipoint connection setup. Controllers can then send messages to the media agents to enable or disable sending and receiving, e.g., to achieve audio muting by a floor controller.

A number of other messages have been defined for the interaction of controllers and media agents. Media agents can be asked for statistics, either for an individual member or the whole media session. A media agent sends **alive** and **active** messages to inform others about changes in member status. To remove individual member or a whole media session, the controller sends a **close** command, which the media agent confirms with a **closed** message.

While asynchronicity and multicast simplify the remainder of the system, they tend to complicate error handling. Since commands are multicast, anonymous and asynchronous, there is no usually explicit success indication, but rather error notices received by all receivers of the original command. Indeed, since a command may be processed by several receivers, there may be several error messages generated. However, as evidenced by the **create/created** and **open/opened** pairs, success indication for *one* receiver is used to keep the controller from sending messages to the media agent before the agent is ready to receive them.

3.3 Starting up Media Agents

So far, we have silently assumed that media agents are created when necessary. This is reasonable for systems with a single controller and as long as a media agent handles either exactly one or all media sessions of a given type. (For audio, it may be advantageous to have only a single media agent for all sessions to allow easy mixing.) If more control is desired, e.g., to support multi-media agents, the replicator could check whether any application has registered for '*/media/* create' messages and invoke missing applications if not. In the multicast case, the controller would issue a **create** command, wait for the **created** response, timing out and starting a media agent if there were no takers.

4 Implementation

The gray elements shown in Fig. 1 have been implemented. A screen dump of the conference controller and media agent are shown in Fig. 2. A media agent for packet audio called NeVoT, shown in the lower left of Fig. 2, communicates with a session creator and activity indicator labeled icc. icc combines a session creator, shown active in the lower right, which becomes an activity indicator after starting up the media agents. Icc as an activity indicator for an MBONE conference is shown in the upper left. The activity indicator is rarely seen by the user, as icc is typically started from a session directory like sd, which supplies it with the necessary parameters.

Some initial helper applications have been implemented. A small applet listens to multicasts on the local network from the Active Badge [17] system. Whenever somebody enters or leaves the room, it changes the outgoing user

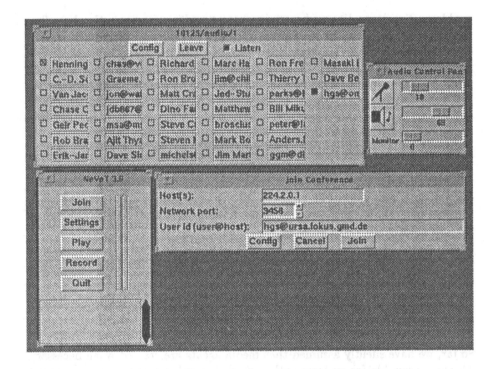

Fig. 2. Screen dump of NEVoT, icc and tkaudio

name indication to show the list of people gathered around the workstation for all active conferences.

Recently, stereo placement of session members was added to NEVoT. Instead of modifying the conference controller, another small application containing nothing but names and sliders was added. The application listens for **hello** messages and add sliders as new users joined the session. Moving the slider sends a message understood by the audio media agent that acoustically moves the speaker to the left or right, allowing the creation of a virtual conference table[5].

Another small application planned that is easy to implement within this framework is a talk timer, possibly sending commands destined for the floor controller. An SNMP management agent could gather statistics and control parameters, without the media agent having to be aware of the fact that it is now subject to yet another master.

Work on integrating a phone-style conference controller and video tools is in progress. Existing media agents require adding a small interface layer that translates the messages into application-specific actions. Adding a similar interface to a WWW browser would allow sharing of a single browser between applications and remote-controlled "slide shows".

---

[5] Automatic placement around a graphically displayed "table" would be easy enough to add, again without changing the main session controller or media agent.

5 Discussion and Open Issues

While the information passed between controllers and media agents is likely not to be as sensitive as the actual media data, there is still a need for additional security. Otherwise, any user with access to the host might enable the microphone for convenient eavesdropping. It is probably best to simply encrypt the messages after including a message digest, offering both privacy and message integrity. Since communication is between processes owned by a single user, keys can be handled through the file system, similar to the mechanism used by X11. Without encryption, discarding messages from other hosts offers some measure of protection.

The media agents presented so far are symmetric, that is, the agents running at all participants are functionally the same, even though they might differ in their actual implementation. This is generally true for audio and video agents as well as shared applications that are group-aware, e.g., shared drawing editors or whiteboards. However, for shared-X applications, the actual application is only running at one site, with remote displays at other sites. It requires further investigation to determine how well the presented inter-application communication model fits for that class of asymmetric applications.

While there is great flexibility in combining controllers and media agents, there has to be some coordination between controllers. For example, a session directory used to start a media session must start the conference controller containing activity indications as well.

Currently, a text-based protocol is being used as it simplifies debugging and allows direct use of tools like Tcl. Messages are sent on the order of once every few seconds, infrequent compared to the typical arrival rate of media packets, and thus the parsing costs are likely to be fairly small. Other considerations, like the necessity to escape various characters or carry extended character sets, might lead one to consider an XDR or ASN.1-based representation.

Applications beyond conferencing may well benefit from local multicast. For example, instead of repeatedly locking and then releasing a resource as quickly as possible in case some other process needs it, an application could simply hold the resource, waiting for a multicast message explicitly asking it to release it. This also allows to implement priorities, so that applications with lower priorities do not block those of higher priority. (This has been implemented in a different context for audio device access, as described below.)

For many applications, where currently signals are used, with their attendant problems due to asynchronous operation, local multicast would be preferable. Examples include notifying a number of processes of audio device changes (like speaker volume) or mail spool file changes.

Current IP multicast implementations can only designate whether packets are to be looped back to the sending *host* or not. There is no way for a process to disable receiving its own local multicast packets; rather, it has to filter by content or source port.

6 Related Work

The idea of subscribing to events is also found in [18], albeit for mediating access to shared hypermedia objects within a single system. A file-system event registration service called file-activity monitor (FAM) is offered within the Silicon Graphics Irix operating system. The CCCP approach to naming components is reflected in the message formats [19]. This approach could also be considered as a status-based system, as used for control networks [20]. However, the message replicator offers a selection mechanism beyond a predefined set of multicast addresses, somewhat similar to the receiver-directed filters are also central to the RSVP resource reservation protocol [21].

Independently, McCanne and Jacobson implemented an IPC mechanism based on local IP multicast that mediates access to the workstation audio device by several concurrently running **vat** audio tools through a per-host multicast address and port. Per-conference ports are used to implement video-follows-audio, enlarging the video window of the current talker in the **vic** video tool. The port is assigned by the session directory **sd**.

7 Conclusion

This paper has presented a local conference control architecture, allowing the composition of multimedia conferences in a modular, incremental and transparent fashion. Media agents and controllers can be designed independently, with a "narrow" interface between them, and can be combined with minimal manual configuration. Each component offers information, which is then selected by other components according to their needs. Applications that implement this scheme can be remote controlled during the whole lifetime of a session. The same application can appear as a GUI-less daemon, as part of a larger application (e.g., a WWW browser) or as an independent application, without affecting the remainder of the system. The media agents need not be aware of whether they are part of a "loosely controlled" or "tightly controlled" session, or indeed anything resembling a traditional multimedia conference.

This approach allows the construction of powerful collaboration tools with minimal mutual awareness. This multicast control greatly simplifies programming as all interested parties can track the global state, without explicit assistance from the party causing the change.

While the discussion has focused on managing conferencing applications, local multicast, possibly enhanced with filtering, offers a powerful tool for other application domains.

8 Acknowledgements

The stereo location tool was added by Thomas Becker.

References

1. T. J. Frivold and R. E. Lang, "Conference control glossary." based on presentation to MMUSIC working group at 27th IETF meeting, Amsterdam, Netherlands, July 1993.
2. S. Casner and S. Deering, "First IETF Internet audiocast," *ACM Computer Communication Review*, vol. 22, pp. 92–97, July 1992.
3. H. Eriksson, "MBONE: The multicast backbone," *Communications ACM*, vol. 37, pp. 54–60, Aug. 1994.
4. E. Schooler and S. L. Casner, "An architecture for multimedia connection management," *ACM Computer Communication Review*, vol. 22, pp. 73–74, Mar. 1992.
5. E. M. Schooler, "The connection control protocol: Specification (version 1.1)," technical report, USC/Information Sciences Institute, Marina del Ray, California, Jan. 1992.
6. V. Jacobson, "sd, the LBL session directory." Manual page, Nov. 1992.
7. T. J. Frivold, R. E. Lang, and M. W. Fong, "Extending WWW for synchronous collaboration," in *Proc. of the Second World Wide Web Conference '94: Mosaic and the Web*, (Chicago, Illinois), Oct. 1994.
8. J. Glicksman and V. Kumar, "A SHAREd collaborative environment for mechanical engineers," in *Proc. of Groupware'93*, pp. 335–447, 1993.
9. J. K. Ousterhout, *Tcl and the Tk Toolkit*. Reading, Massachusetts: Addison-Wesley, 1994.
10. H. Schulz-Rinne, "The DSP workbench: Modeling parallel architectures as concurrent processes," in *1986 IEEE International Conference on Acoustics, Speech and Signal Processing (ICASSP)*, (Tokyo, Japan), pp. 54.9.1 – 54.9.4, IEEE, Apr. 1986.
11. A. L. Ananda, B. H. Tay, and E. K. Koh, "A survey of asynchronous remote procedure calls," *ACM Operating Systems Review*, vol. 26, pp. 92–109, Apr. 1992.
12. E. Walker, P. Neves, and R. Floyd, "Asynchronous remote operation execution in distributed systems," in *Proc. 10th Intl. Conf. Distributed Computing Systems (ICDCS-10)*, (Paris, France), IEEE, May 1990.
13. B. Bhargava, E. Mafla, J. Riedl, and B. Sauder, "Implementation and measurements of an efficient communication facility for distributed database systems," Technical Report Purdue Technical Report CSD-TR-783, Department of Computer Science, Purdue University, West Lafayette, IN 47907-2004, June 1988.
14. S. E. Deering and D. R. Cheriton, "Multicast routing in datagram internetworks and extended LANs," *ACM Transactions on Computer Systems*, vol. 8, pp. 85–110, May 1990.
15. H. Schulzrinne, S. Casner, R. Frederick, and V. Jacobson, "RTP: A transport protocol for real-time applications." Internet draft (work-in-progress) *draft-ietf-avt-rtp-*.txt*, Nov. 1994.
16. H. Schulzrinne, "Sample profile and encodings for the use of RTP for audio and video conferences with minimal control," Internet Draft, GMD Fokus, May 1994. Work in progress.

17. R. Want, A. Hopper, V. Falcao, and J. Gibbons, "The active badge location system," *ACM Transactions on Information Systems*, vol. 10, pp. 91–102, Jan. 1992. also Olivetti Research Limited Technical Report ORL 92-1.
18. U. K. Wiil, "Using events as support for data sharing in collaborative work," in *International Workshop on CSCW*, (Berlin, Germany), pp. 162–176, Institute of Informatics and Computing Technique, Germany, Apr. 1991.
19. M. Handley and I. Wakeman, "CCCP: conference control channel protocol – a scalable base for building conference control applications." V1.4, Mar. 1994.
20. R. S. Raji, "Smart networks for control," *IEEE Spectrum*, vol. 31, pp. 49–55, June 1994.
21. L. Zhang, S. Deering, D. Estrin, S. Shenker, and D. Zappala, "Rsvp: a new resource ReSerVation protocol," *IEEE Network*, vol. 7, pp. 8–18, Sept. 1993.

WAVE: A New Multicast Routing Algorithm for Static and Dynamic Multicast Groups

Ernst Biersack, Jörg Nonnenmacher
Institut Eurécom,
2229 Route des Crêtes,
06904 Sophia-Antipolis — France
e-mail: erbi@eurecom.fr

Abstract. We present a new multicast algorithm called *WAVE* for establishing source-specific multicast trees. WAVE meets multiple quality of service requirements (constraints) such as delay, cost, and available bandwidth, simultaneously. Simulation results show that WAVE performs very good in terms of delay and cost for both, static and dynamic multicast groups, when compared to the best multicast algorithms known.

1 Introduction

Many new applications in the area of multimedia such as teleseminars or distribution of news require multipoint connections.These applications also typically have complex quality of service (QOS) requirements concerning delay, cost, and bandwidth needed that must be taken into account (as constraints) by the multicast (MC) algorithm. Existing MC algorithms are only able to consider one or two constraints.

1.1 Notation

Before discussing the MC algorithms, we need to introduce some notation [1].

A network is represented as a graph $N = (V_N, E_N)$, where V_N is the set of nodes and

$E_N \subset V_N \times V_N$ is the set of edges. The average number of edges that depart from a node is referred to as *outdegree*. Over the set of edges we define the two functions delay $Delay: E_N \to R^+ \backslash \{0\}$ and cost $Cost: E_N \to \{1\}$. The delay and the cost of a path are defined as the sum of the delay or cost of all the edges of the path.

The multicast receivers are referred to as *MC group*, and $Q \in V_N$ is the source of the MC group (we assume that there is a single source in a MC group.)

The *multicast tree* $MCT_M = (V_M, E_M)$ with $V_M \subset V_N$ and $E_M \subset V_N \times V_N \subset E_N$ is a directed, acyclic subgraph of N with Q as root that connects all nodes in the MC group.

The cost of MCT_M is defined as the sum over the cost of its edges:

$$Cost_M = \sum_{e \in E_M} Cost(e) = |E_M| \ .$$

1.2 Shortest Path First (SPF)

One of the simplest MC algorithms is the shortest path tree (SPT) [1]. The MC tree for the SPT consists of the shortest paths -- in terms of delay -- from the sender Q to all receivers in the MC group. The shortest paths are established using the existing unicast routing algorithm. When a new receiver R joins a MC group, the sender Q determines the shortest path from Q to R. If the beginning of this path from Q to a node A is already in the MC tree, the MC tree needs only be extended by the shortest path from A to R. See figure 1, where the path from Q to R_3 overlaps from Q to A with the existing MC tree.

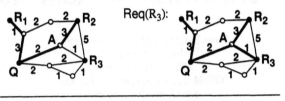

Figure 1: Shortest path tree.

While SPT minimizes the delay, it does not try to minimize the total cost of the MC tree.

1.3 Steiner Tree

Another class of MC algorithms solve the Steiner Tree problem, which consists of computing the tree with the minimum cost that connects a subset M of the nodes. Minimizing the total cost of the MC tree goes at the expense of the delays from the sender to the members in the MC tree. The delays are much higher than for SPT.

Computing the Steiner Tree is an NP-complete problem. However, there exist good heuristics that run in polynomial time. One of them, proposed by Kou, Markowsky, and Berman (KMB) [3] computes trees that have approximately 5% higher costs than the cost for the minimal Steiner Tree.

The KMB algorithm works as follows: (see figure 2)

- Starting from a graph G, a *complete* (every node is connected with every other node) graph G1 is constructed

- For G1, a minimal spanning tree T1 is constructed

- The edges in T1 are replaced by the shortest paths in G, which gives a subgraph G2.

- For G2, a minimal spanning tree T2 is constructed

- The branches in T2 that don't contain nodes that are members of the MC group are pruned.

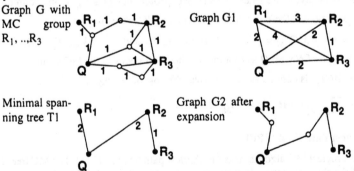

Figure 2: KMB algorithm.

1.4 WAVE

The basic principle of WAVE is very simple: When a node R wants to join a MC group, it sends a request Req to the source Q. Starting from Q, this request is propagated throughout the MC tree and answered (Rsp) by the nodes that received that request. A major advantage of WAVE is that complex QOS requirements can be taken into account since the path from the source Q to a new receiver is dynamically discovered. The Req and Rsp messages that are passed along the network can be used to dynamically collect and update information --such as delay, cost, or available bandwidth -- concerning the characteristics of the path. Each node that receives such a message can compare the QOS requested with the QOS characteristics of the path taken by this message. The message will only be forwarded if the path taken so far meets the QOS requirements. (In the following, we will for the sake of simplicity, only consider delay and cost as QOS requirements.) Each response received by R will have the form Rsp = ($n\_id,cost,delay$), where n_id denotes the node that generated the response and the other two entries denote the cost and delay of the connection from the source Q to R via node n_id.

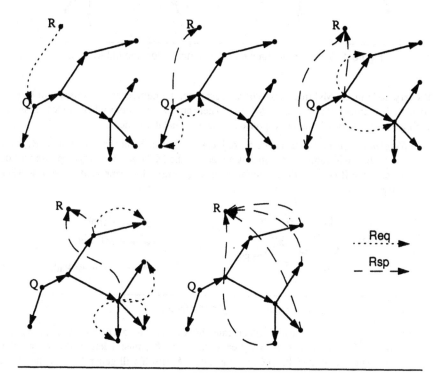

Figure 3: Requests and Responses in WAVE.

The basic steps to join a MC group are as follows (See figure 3 and figure 4):

- A new receiver R that wants to join the MC group contacts the source Q with a request Req.
- When the source or any other node in the MC tree receives a Req, it will send a reply Rsp to R along the shortest delay path.

- R will receive a set {Rsp} of responses from which it selects one Rsp = (*K,cost,delay*) (see below how). *R* then sends a connect to node *K* (*attachment node*) that generated this response.
- *K* will extend the MC tree from itself to *R* along the shortest path from *K* to *R*.

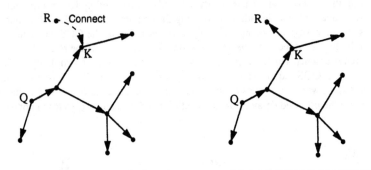

Figure 4: Selection of attachment node and extension of MC tree.

If every node in the MC tree generates are response, the number of responses will be proportional to the number of nodes in the MC tree. There are two situations where nodes can avoid producing a response or where the response is deleted by a later node.

- *Neighbor overlap*: When a node *K* produces a response, it checks if the link (K,K_s) over which *K* will send its response is already in the MC tree. If so, no response will be sent. It suffices that the neighbor node K_s generates/has generated a response. (See figure 5.)

Figure 5: Neighbor overlap.

- *Other overlap:* A response Rsp generated by *K* is sent along a path (K,K_1), ..., (K_l,K_m), where K_m is already in the MC tree. In this case, K_m must delete Rsp to ensure that the structure of the MC tree remains a tree. K_m itself will generate/has generated a response.

The results presented later in figure 11 indicate that suppressing responses whose path overlaps with the MC tree can reduce the number of responses by up 80%.

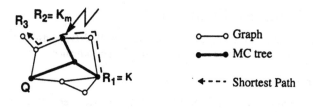

Figure 6: Other overlap.

In the following, we explain how the receiver selects the attachment node via which it will be connected to the MC tree.

Definitions

- $\mathfrak{R} \subset V_N$ defines the set of nodes in the MC tree from whom R has received a response.
- MCA denotes one of the three MC algorithms (WAVE, SPT, or KMB).
- $MCT_{MCA} = (V_{MCA}, E_{MCA})$ denotes the MC tree computed by MCA.
- The node $(K \in \mathfrak{R})$ via which R will be connected to the MC tree is called **attachment node**.
- $Delay_{MCA} (Q \text{-->} K)$ denotes the delay from Q to K along the path in the MC tree MCT_{MCA}.
- $Delay_{sp}(K \text{-->} R)$ denotes the delay along the shortest path from K to R.
- $Delay(Q \text{-->} K \text{-->} R)$ denotes the delay from Q via K to R and is defined as $Delay(Q \text{-->} K \text{-->} R) = Delay_{MCA} (Q \text{-->} K) + Delay_{sp}(K \text{-->} R)$.

Assumption

- The receiver R has received a set of responses
  $\{Rsp\} = \{(K, Delay(Q \text{-->} K \text{-->} R), Cost(K \text{-->} R), \text{where } K \in \mathfrak{R} \}$ from which he selects an attachment node $k \in \mathfrak{R}$.

Section of attachment node

- For each response $rsp \in \{Rsp\}$ with $rsp =(n\_id, delay, cost)$, the receiver computes a weighted cost $WC(n\_id) = w_c*(cost/max\_cost) + w_d*(delay/max\_delay)$,
  where $w_c \in [0, 1], w_d \in [0, 1]$ and max_cost and max_delay are the maximum cost and delay values over all responses $\{Rsp\}$ received.
- The receiver calculates for all responses $\{Rsp\}$ the weighted costs and selects the node $k \in \mathfrak{R}$ with the **minimal weighted cost**, i.e. $WC(k) \leq WC(K), \forall (K \in \mathfrak{R})$.

The choice of the weights w_c, w_d allows the receiver to trade-off cost versus delay:

- For $w_c \in (0, 1]$ and $w_d = 0$, the receiver chooses among all the shortest-delay paths from K to R the path with the minimal incremental cost.
- For $w_c = 0$ and $w_d \in (0, 1]$, the receiver ignores cost and chooses the path with the shortest delay between Q and R. In this case, WAVE yields the same MC tree as SPF.

2 Performance Evaluation

We used simulation to compare the performance of WAVE against SPT and KMB and to evaluate the impact of the choice of w_c, and w_d on the performance.

2.1 Performance Metrics

The MC tree MCT_{MCA} has a set $\aleph$, $\aleph \subset V_{MCA}$ of receivers. $\aleph$ denotes the set of the MC group members.

- Cost of the MC tree is $Cost_{MCA} = |E_{MCA}|$
- Average delay from the source Q to any receiver R is

$$AvgRecvDelay_{MCA} = \frac{1}{|\aleph|}\sum_{R \in \aleph} Delay_{MCA}\langle Q \to R \rangle$$

- Maximum delay from the source Q to any receiver R is

$$MaxRecvDelay_{MCA} = max_{R \in \aleph} \{Delay_{MCA}\langle Q \to R \rangle\}$$

In the following, we define several ratios that allows us to relate the performance of WAVE and SPT (for delay comparisons) and WAVE and KMB (for cost comparisons) and indicate the *inefficiency* of WAVE with respect to the MC algorithm available.

- Cost ratio $CostR = \dfrac{Cost_{MCA}}{Cost_{KMB}}$

- Mean delay ratio $AvgRecvDelayR = \dfrac{AvgRecvDelay_{MCA}}{AvgRecvDelay_{SPT}}$

- Maximum delay ratio $MaxRecvDelayR = \dfrac{MaxRecvDelay_{MCA}}{MaxRecvDelay_{SPT}}$

To evaluate the overhead reduction in WAVE due to neighbor overlap and other overlap, we compute the ratio between the nodes (*requested*) that received a Req and the number of Rsp that arrived at the receiver (*answered*).

2.2 Simulation Environment

For our simulation, we applied the MC algorithms to a set of random networks. To generate these networks we use an approach introduced first by Waxman and later slightly modified by Wei&Estrin [4,5]. A random network is constructed by randomly placing its n nodes on a cartesian grid. The coordinates of the nodes are expressed as integers. To determine whether nor not to connect a pair of nodes (u,v) by an edge we evaluate the edge probability function $P_k(u,v)$ that is defined as

$$P_k(u, v) = \beta \cdot exp\frac{-d(u, v)}{\alpha \cdot L}$$

where $d(u,v)$ is defined as the euclidean distance between (u,v), L is the maximum distance between any two nodes, α and β are parameters between $0 < \alpha, \beta \leq 1$. A large value for α increases the number of edges between nodes that are further apart, while a large value for β increases the outdegree. The delay of an edge is defined as $d(u,v)$.

then, the delay performance of WAVE is still much better than for KMB where the average delay is about twice as high as for SPT. The values for MaxRecvDelayR, which are not plotted, are very similar to the ones for AvgRecvDelayR.

We are not only interested in the average delays but also in the distribution of the delays as presented in figure 8. While the x-axis gives that absolute delay values, the y-axis gives the number of receivers that experience a certain delay value. We can use the delay distribution to determine how many percent of the requests to connect to the MCT would fail if the delay constraint demands that the delay must be below a certain value. We see that the delay distributions for WAVE approach the delay distribution for SPT as the value of delay weight increases relative to the value for the cost weight. The delay distribution for WAVE and SPT has a much narrower shape than for KMB. The delay distribution for KMB has a long tail with delay values up to 12000, while the delay values for WAVE are never higher than 6000 for $w_d > 0$.

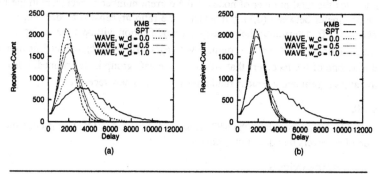

Figure 8: Delay histograms for (a) w_c=1 and (b) w_d=1
(200 nodes, outdegree = 3, MC group size = 40).

For w_d=1 and w_c < 1, the delay distributions for WAVE approximate the distribution of SPT closer than for w_c = 1 and w_d < 1. Therefore, for the following simulations, we fix w_d=1 and w_c = 0.7, in which case the delay and cost inefficiencies are both 1.07 compared to the best MC algorithm for either metric. (See figure 9).

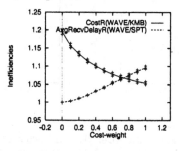

Figure 9: AvgRecvDelayR and CostR as a function of the cost weight
w_c for w_d=1 (200 nodes, outdegree = 3, MC group size = 40).

In summary, we can say that depending on the constraints (cost, delay) imposed, the weights for WAVE can be chosen in such a way that either the cost efficiency of KMB or the delay efficiency of SPT is achieved. An intermediate choice of the weights allows to achieve both, very

For outdegrees that vary from 3 to 8, we produced 500 random networks each with 200 nodes.

To obtain a performance value, we fix all parameters and apply a MC algorithm to all 500 networks. Executing the MC algorithm for all 500 networks gives 500 samples for each performance metric. For the 500 samples, we then calculated the mean values and the 95% confidence intervals. The plots of the means are given with their confidence intervals.

When we consider the case that the MC group may evolve dynamically by nodes joining or leaving we use the function $P_A(k)$ introduced by Waxman [4]:

$$P_A(k) = \frac{\gamma(n-k)}{\gamma(n-k) + (1-\gamma)k}$$

where n denotes the total number of nodes, k the current number of receivers in the MC tree, and γ is a parameter between (0,1). γ represents the ratio #receivers/#nodes. For $\gamma = k/n$ we have $P_A(k) = 1/2$. To determine whether the next modification will be a join or leave, we compute a random number r, $0 \leq r < 1$ to compare with $P_A(k)$. If $r > P_A(k)$, the modification is **leave** and randomly one of the receivers that will leave the MC group is determined. For $r \leq P_A(k)$, the modification is **join** and a node is randomly selected as new receiver.

2.3 Results

We first consider scenarios where the MC group is **static**, i.e. the MC tree is constructed for a fixed group of receivers that does not change.

2.3.1 Choice of the weights

Before comparing the MC algorithms, we need to choose the values for the weights w_c, and w_d. In figure 7 and figure 8 we present the impact of the weights on the average cost and delay of the MC tree. The value of one weight is set to 1 while the value of the other weight varies between 0 and 1.

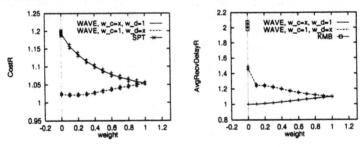

Figure 7: CostR and AvgRecvDelayR as a function of the weights
(200 nodes, outdegree = 3, MC group size = 40).

The average cost of the MC tree for WAVE is between 2% (for $w_c = 1$ and $w_d = 0$) and 20% (for $w_c = 0$ and $w_d = 1$) higher than the cost of the MC tree for KMB. The higher the ratio between the cost weight and the delay weight, the closer the cost performance for WAVE approaches the cost performance of KMB. The delay performance of WAVE for $w_d > 0$ is at worst 22% higher than for SPT. An exception is $w_d = 0$, where the delay increases significantly. Even good cost and delay efficiency.

2.3.2 Impact of MC group size and outdegree

We see in figure 10 the cost and delay efficiency as a function of the outdegree for two different MC group sizes of 5 and 40. The cost inefficiency for WAVE and SPT increases with increasing outdegree. This is due to the fact, that both, WAVE and SPT, use the shortest path to connect a new receiver to a node in the existing MC tree. As the outdegree increases the probability that at least part of this shortest path overlaps with the existing MC tree becomes lower (The decreasing number of neighbor overlaps in figure 11 for increasing outdegree corroborates this.) Since WAVE takes for $w_c > 0$ the cost of the new path into account, its cost inefficiency does increase slower than that of SPT.

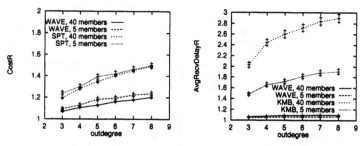

Figure 10: CostR and AvgRecvDelayR as a function of the outdegree for MC group sizes of 5 and 40 (200 nodes).

The delay inefficiency of WAVE stays the same, independent of the outdegree and MC group size. For KMB however, the inefficiency increases with the MC group size and with the outdegree because, as either one increases, KMB has more alternatives for constructing the minimal-cost MC tree. Therefore, the differences between the MC tree constructed by KMB as compared to SPT or WAVE become more pronounced with increasing MC group size or outdegree.

In Table 1 we see the distribution of the delays as a function of the outdegree for two different MC group size. The distributions for WAVE are very close to the ones for SPT. As the outdegree increases for a fixed MC group size, the delay distribution for WAVE and SPT becomes much narrower, i.e. the delays between the source and the receivers become smaller. For KMB, the reduction of the delay values is much less pronounced. A higher outdegree means richer connectivity, since each node has more neighbors. While WAVE and SPT use the richer connectivity to (predominately) optimize the delay, KMB optimizes the cost.

2.3.3 Overhead reduction due to neighbor overlap and other overlap

The following figure 11 shows the overhead incurred by WAVE. We see that there is a significant potential to reduce the overhead by eliminating Rsp messages that incur a neighbor overlap. Depending on the outdegree, the elimination of messages with neighbor overlap reduces the total number of messages that arrive at the receiver between 60% and 80%. The reduction is highest for low outdegrees. As the outdegree increases, more paths exist to connect a new receiver with the MC tree, therefore probability that the path chosen overlaps with the MC tree decreases. Also, the overhead reduction is more effective for larger MC groups for which the probability that the shortest path overlaps with the MC tree increases.

Table 1: Delay histograms (200 nodes).

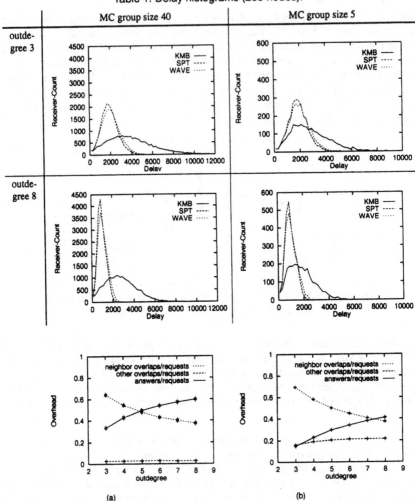

Figure 11: Answers received and overhead reduction for (a) MC group size = 5 and (b) MC group size = 40 (200 nodes).

2.3.4 Dynamic MC Groups

In many cases, the MC group changes when during the existence of a session new receivers join or leave the MC group. A MC algorithm should be able to allow for changes in the MC group without disrupting the communications -- by changing the paths -- between the source and existing members of the MC group. An algorithm such as KMB does not meet this requirement. Any change in the MC group members ship will require to recompute the complete MC tree. Changes in the MC tree therefore affect existing members. To compare WAVE and KMB with respect to the cost inefficiency, we recompute the MC tree using KMB after every 50 MC group modifications. The cost of the MC tree obtained for KMB was then compared with the cost of the MC tree for WAVE that was dynamically evolving with each modification. When interpreting the results, we therefore must keep in mind that this comparison is in some respect "unfair" towards WAVE because KMB is not able to "smoothly" grow the MC tree each time a change in the group membership occurs.

We see in figure 12 the cost and delay efficiency as a function of the outdegree for two different dynamic MC groups of size of 5 and 40. The cost inefficiency for WAVE increases slightly during the first 50 modifications and stays then at the this level for the remaining several hundred modifications. The average delay for WAVE is not affected at all by the modifications.

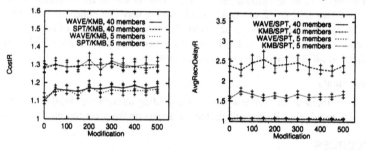

Figure 12: CostR and AvgRecvDelayR as a function of the number of modifi cation for MC group sizes of 5 and 40 (200 nodes outdegree=4).

In Table 2, we see the distribution of the delays as a function of the outdegree for two different MC group sizes after 500 modifications of the MC group (join and leave requests). The

Table 2: Delay histogram for different outdegrees and MC group sizes after 500 modifications.

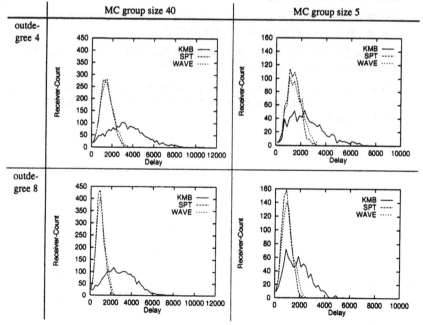

shape of the delay distribution for WAVE remains for all scenarios very close to the delay distribution of SPT that is not subject to any destination at all, because it extends for each new MC group member the MC tree by the shortest path from the source to the new member.

These results confirm that WAVE retains its excellent cost and delay properties for the important case where the MC group evolves dynamically.

3 Conclusion

WAVE is a flexible MC algorithm that allows to optimize the MC tree according to different criteria and achieves close to optimal performance. Depending on the constraint (cost, delay) imposed, the weights for WAVE can be chosen in such a way that either the cost efficiency of KMB or the delay efficiency of SPT is achieved. An intermediate choice of the weights allows to achieve both, very good cost and delay performance. The performance of WAVE is not affected, when the MC tree is subject to modifications.

Acknowledgements

We would like to thank John Matthew Doar for providing us with the simulation code for the KMB algorithm and Antoni B. Przygienda for comments on the presentation.

4 References

[1]   T. H. Cormen, C. E. Leiserson and R. L. Rivest, *Introduction to Algorithms*, The MIT Press, 1990.

[2]   M. Doar and I. Leslie, *How Bad is Naïve Multicast Routing?* Proc. INFOCOM 1993, 82ff.

[3]   L. Kou, G. Markowsky, and L. Berman, *A Fast Algorithm for Steiner Trees*. Acta Informatica, Vol. 15:141-145, 1981.

[4]   B. M. Waxman, *Routing of Multipoint Connections*. IEEE J. Selected Areas in Communications, Vol. 6, No. 9, December 1988, p.1617 ff.

[5]   L. Wei and D. Estrin, *The Trade-offs of Multicast Trees and Algorithms*. Proc. Int. Conf. on Computer Communications and Networks, 1994.

[6]   R. Widyono, *The Design and Evaluation of Routing Algorithms for Real-time Channels*, University of California at Berkeley & International Computer Science Institute, TR-94-024, June 1994.

Connection Establishment for Multi-Party Real-Time Communication

R. Bettati, D. Ferrari, A. Gupta, W. Heffner,
W. Howe, M. Moran, Q. Nguyen, R. Yavatkar

The Tenet Group
University of California, Berkeley, and
International Computer Science Institute

Abstract. There is considerable interest in the network community in supporting real-time multi-party applications, such as video conferencing. The Tenet Group at UC Berkeley and ICSI has designed and implemented protocols that provide *quality of service* (QoS) guarantees for real-time traffic on packet switching networks. Suite 2 of the Tenet protocols provides scalable, flexible and efficient network support for real-time multi-party connections. We outline our method of connection establishment and describe the design issues and alternatives, and our decisions. Preliminary measurements confirm the viability of our approach for real-time multicast connection establishment.

1 Introduction

The design goals and principles of multicast real-time channel establishment in the Tenet Suite 2 are described, along with the mechanisms that support the establishment procedure. The suite described in this paper is based on the Tenet Suite 1 [1]. Therefore, the approach taken in Suite 1 is described in Section 2. The changes made to that approach to adapt it to the multicast abstraction in Suite 2, and a step-by-step example of Suite 2 channel setup are give in Section 3. The performance measurements of a Suite 2 prototype reported in Section 4 show that establishment times are likely to be quite reasonable, even if this approach is used in a wide-area context. Section 5 discusses some other connection establishment methods proposed in the literature.

2 The Tenet Unicast Channel Establishment Procedure

The basic communication abstraction in the Tenet real-time schemes and protocol suites is the *real-time channel*, to be simply called *channel* in the rest of this paper. In the Tenet Scheme 1, which is the set of algorithms and procedures on which the Tenet Suite 1 [1] is based, a channel is a simplex *unicast* connection with QoS guarantees [4]. Since guaranteeing performance and reliability bounds requires admission control (and keeping track of how much of each resource is still available for additional channels, an operation usually called somewhat improperly "resource reservation"), channels are established prior to their use for data transport; in other words, real-time communication has the basic characteristics of a connection-oriented service.

The main design objectives of the Tenet channel establishment procedure since the beginning of our investigation in 1987 were:

- **Speed:** Many real-time clients cannot afford long waits for their transmissions to start [5].
- **Scalability:** The procedure must work also in very large networks and internetworks [6].
- **Mathematical provability of the guarantees:** Real-time clients must be offered firm contractual commitments by the service provider [4, 11].
- **Flexibility in the specification of QoS and traffic parameters:** The network-layer clients must be given as much freedom as possible in specifying their QoS requirements and traffic descriptions; service classes can be easily defined and easily added on top of a flexible interface, while extending the classes around which a channel establishment procedure is built may be very difficult.

To achieve the goal of fast establishment, we needed a relatively simple traffic model and a relatively simple set of QoS parameters, so that the admission tests could be rapidly executed. To be easily scalable, the procedure had to be fully distributed; a centralized approach was likely to be a scalability, reliability, and performance bottleneck. Thus, we decided that an establishment message would be sent out by the source, carrying the QoS and traffic parameters of the requested channel, and that it would follow a pre-computed route, (or build one in a hop-by-hop way), triggering the execution of admission tests in each node it traversed, and tentatively "reserving" resources in the node if all tests were passed therein. Any test failure would cause a *channel reject* message to be sent back to the source; this message would release all the resources tentatively set aside for the channel in each upstream node. To make channel establishment fast, the number of round trips required to complete the establishment procedure was limited to one, even though allowing for more round trips could often decrease the amounts of resources to be set aside for a channel. A consequence of this constraint was the need for the final acceptance or rejection decision to be made in the destination host. If the channel is accepted and enough information is available, this host can also decide the amounts of resources to be allocated to the new channel in each node, and can inform the nodes about these amounts through the *channel accept* message; alternatively, the adjustment (or *relaxation*) of the allocated amounts can be left to the individual nodes, which will inform the upstream nodes about the effects of these adjustments via the same message. After completing the initial design of Scheme 1, we realized that two simple modifications allowed channels to be established in the reverse direction (i.e., starting from the destination) and as duplex connections, respectively.

A crucially important aspect of the procedure was the derivation of local (node) performance bounds from the end-to-end bounds. Admission tests must verify that a new channel will not endanger the guarantees given to the channels already established in each node. For speed and scalability, these tests must be performed locally, i.e., without requiring additional messages (to, for example, the sources of all those channels). Thus, local bounds contain all the information admission tests need to know about each channel, allowing the establishment procedure to be much faster and less expensive; the price that is paid for these advantages is the reduction in the real-time capacity of the network due to the worst-case assumptions to be made in subdividing some end-to-end bounds. For instance, the minimum probability of timely delivery is broken into the product of the local probabilities, which is equivalent to assuming that a packet's timely delivery to the destination requires that the packet be transmitted by each node before the local deadline expires, a clearly pessimistic assumption. The derivation of local bounds, besides localizing the admission tests, is also extremely useful for interoperability: the Tenet establishment procedure works in networks in which different nodes use different packet scheduling policies, as long as it uses in each node the admission tests suitable for that node.

For guarantees to be mathematically provable, the worst-case philosophy must be applied to all admission tests and to the traffic model. Any traffic model to be used for admission control must be a *bounding* model, i.e., a worst-case description of the traffic on the requested channel. However, *worst-case* does not necessarily mean *deterministic*: from the outset, the Tenet Scheme 1 included *statistical* bounds for delays and packet losses, which were based on statistical worst-case techniques. Mathematical provability was also responsible for the decision to allocate buffers statically to each channel in each node [8].

3 Multi-Party Connection Establishment

We first discuss our goals for multi-party communication and their implications for channel establishment. We then illustrate these concepts with a brief example.

3.1 Changes in Establishment for Multi-Party Communication

Implementation of the first-generation real-time protocol suite enabled us to demonstrate the feasibility of providing guaranteed performance communication with real-time connections and admission control. To support multi-party communication, we have extended our goals as follows:

- **Scalability and Efficiency:** In moving to multi-party communication, we have extended the notion of scalability to include the number of *participants* in a given multi-party interaction; achieving such scalability requires efficient allocation of network resources.
- **Flexibility:** The notion of flexibility is extended to include support for dynamic changes in the set of destinations receiving data on a channel, and support for the use of heterogeneous traffic specifications and scheduling algorithms.

- **Apportionment of resources:** The network should *be able* to apportion network resources between user groups according to the "share" that may be specified for each group by the network manager(s).
- **Ease of use:** Facilities must be provided to assist clients in creating and managing real-time channels; for example, clients must be able to book channels in advance of their use.

In keeping with the connection-oriented design of the first Tenet scheme, most of the changes for multi-party communication have affected channel establishment, so that data forwarding remains relatively simple and fast. However, two changes are required in the data forwarding system: to support multicast channels, packets must be copied at branching nodes, and, to support resource sharing, the packet scheduling mechanism must be modified [9].

Implementing multi-party communication with unicast channels would be cumbersome and inefficient in the use of network resources. On the other hand, a single $M \Rightarrow N$ channel abstraction either would be very complex or would fail to match the requirements of all types of multi-party communication, and might introduce inefficiencies for $1 \Rightarrow N$ or unicast communication. Therefore, we obtain an efficient equivalent of an $M \Rightarrow N$ channel by combining $1 \Rightarrow N$ multicast channels (hereafter called simply *multicast channels*) and *resource sharing* among them. The $1 \Rightarrow N$ multicast channel provides a natural abstraction for the delivery of data from a single source to all intended receivers. Performance bounds are defined as in the case of the unicast service. Utilization of network resources is reduced by using a multicast tree, so that multiple copies of the same data are not forwarded across a link.

Naive use of multicast channels would result in over-allocation of resources, since in most multi-party communication scenarios, only a small subset of potential senders are active at a given time. For example, in a typical multimedia conference, only one person will speak at a time. We have introduced a *sharing group* abstraction to allow clients to describe such behavior to the network, allowing the network to share resource allocations between such related channels. The client specifies the channels in the sharing group, and a *group traffic specification*, which indicates the maximum combined traffic entering the network from *all* channels in the group. Admission control tests and packet scheduling mechanisms use the group traffic specification rather than the traffic specifications for the individual channels. More details on resource sharing and results of simulation experiments can be found in [9]. Those experiments indicate that resource sharing significantly improves the scalability of multi-party communication.

In Scheme 2, the real-time channel is a multicast connection. Therefore, the channel establishment procedure attempts to produce a multicast connection from the source to all destinations. *Partial establishment* is allowed, whereby a channel is successfully established even if one or more destinations could not be reached by the channel. Scheme 2 supports the dynamic addition and deletion of destinations to a multicast channel by an *incremental establishment and teardown* mechanism. This mechanism can be exploited in Suite 2 to achieve *receiver-initiated establishment*. In receiver-initiated establishment, the receiver first establishes (in the reverse direction) a channel from the sender to itself. Once this channel is established, other receivers can join it dynamically using the incremental establishment capability. We expect that receiver-initiated establishment will prove to be more scalable in the number of receivers than sender-initiated establishment. However, we should note that in the current prototype, receiver-initiated establishment would not fully realize this scalability gain, since, for ease of implementation, incremental join and leave are implemented in terms of sender-initiated mechanisms. To achieve the expected scalability gains for receiver-initiated establishment, we must first implement receiver-to-source establishment and distributed target set, channel and routing objects.

Local establishment tasks are divided between a component that handles signalling (e.g., parsing, updating, and forwarding establishment messages) and one or more components that manage a single resource (i.e., by performing admission control and resource allocation), with a well-defined interface between the two. This architecture supports the use of heterogeneous scheduling algorithms, since the algorithms and the state information are encapsulated in the resource managers.

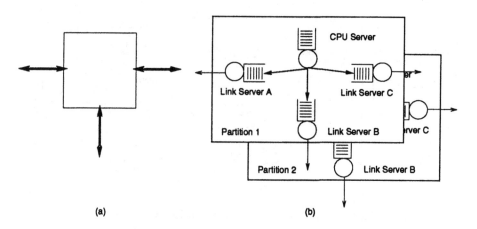

Fig. 1. Node model for node with three interfaces and two partitions

Resource partitioning allows network managers to specify how resources should be divided among user groups. In particular, network resources are apportioned into independent, disjoint partitions, so that channels can be established in one partition without affecting (or being affected by) channels in any other partition. A node model including resource partitioning is shown in Figure 1. We define a *server* as a schedulable network resource (e.g., CPU, link). A node (e.g., a router) with a CPU and three network interfaces, then, consists of four servers. Figure 1(b) shows the node model in the case where the node supports two partitions. Resource partitioning is completely supported through changes in channel establishment, and therefore requires no change in the data forwarding mechanisms. One or more resource partition(s) can be dedicated for channels that reserve resources in advance of their use. Admission control is somewhat more complicated for these "advance-booked channels"; [7] describes these admission control mechanisms.

Several long-lived objects have been introduced to ease the creation and management of multi-party communication in Scheme 2. *Channel objects* maintain channel state. *Target set objects* maintain information related to data receivers, and provide a rendezvous point between senders and receivers. A target set is similar to a host group in IP multicast [2], except that a target set specifies performance requirements for each destination.

When a destination joins (leaves) a target set, the target set requests the channel objects associated with it to add (remove) the destination to (from) their respective multicast trees.

3.2 Example of Channel Establishment

Figure 2 illustrates the steps taken to establish a typical channel. For the sake of

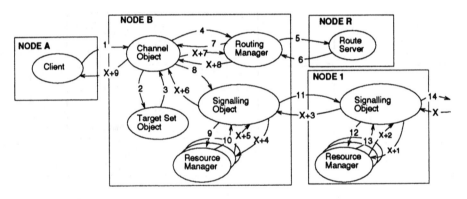

Fig. 2. Steps taken in typical channel establishment

brevity, we describe here only a source-initiated channel establishment. When a client requests the channel object to establish its channel (1), the channel object gets the list of destinations from the target set object (2, 3). The channel object sends this list to the routing manager, which gets a multicast route from the route server (4 – 7). This route is included in the establishment message, which is then sent to the (local) signalling object (8). The signalling object parses the establishment message; it requests the necessary resource manager(s) to run the admission control tests, and (if successful) to make the reservations (9, 10). If the tests fail, a *channel reject* message is sent back along the path. Otherwise, the signalling object updates and forwards the establishment message to the signalling object(s) of the next node(s) in the tree (11,...). The establishment continues hop-by-hop until no other destinations exist along that branch. At each destination, end-to-end admission control tests are performed to ensure that the destination's performance requirements are met. Depending on the results, either a *channel accept* or a *channel reject* message is sent back to the originator of the establishment request $(\ldots, X, \ldots, X + 9)$. At each node along the return path, resources are committed for each branch along which at least one destination was reached, and released otherwise (e.g., $X + 1, X + 2$). When replies have been received from all downstream branches (or a timeout has occurred), a *channel accept* or *channel reject* message is sent back along the path. The first signalling object then reports the result to the channel object $(X + 6)$, which reports the results to the routing manager and to the client $(X + 7, X + 9)$.

4 Performance Measurements

One concern often expressed about admission control is that the admission tests might add considerably to the cost of connection establishment. To address this issue, we measured round-trip delays, per-node latencies, and the times spent in running admission tests on a Suite 2 prototype. Round-trip delay was defined in this context as the duration of the interval between the time the channel object received the request to set up a channel, and the time the results of that establishment attempt were returned by the channel object. In Figure 2, this would correspond to starting measurement at the completion of Step 1 and stopping immediately at the beginning of Step $X + 9$.

The measurements were collected using the logical topology shown in Figure 3, which contains one branch node and three destination nodes; the maximum number of hops is four. All six machines are variants of Sun Sparc 1 class workstations, and are connected to an Ethernet. A total of 35 channels were established successively. The numbers presented in Table 1 are typical ranges of the measured establishment delays.

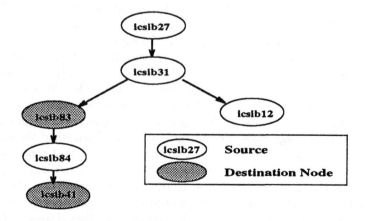

Fig. 3. Network topology of the experiment

Round-trip times had a maximum of 180 milliseconds and a minimum time of 103 milliseconds. On the average, one channel setup took 114 milliseconds. The one-time cost of Step 2 through Step 7 in Figure 2 was 7 ms. For advance-reserved channels, the measurements were similar (total channel setup time was 112 ms, Step 2 through Step 7 was 8 ms). Note that in the prototype that was measured we had messages to and from the routing server, but the route had been pre-computed; thus, route calculation times are not included in our measurements. We are currently integrating the routing server with our prototype, and anticipate that route calculation will generally add a small overhead to the measured 7 milliseconds. The remaining time (107 ms) was spent in the forward and reverse passes of channel establishment. This time will grow with the number of nodes on the longest of the paths from the source to each destination. In our experiments, the 5-node path from icsib27 to icsib41 was the longest.

Measure	Round-trip delay	Start-up latency	Per-node latency	Overhead	Communication	TCP/IP connect
Single Node	–	–	6.8	–	9	Tot: 4-5 Send: 0.4
Aggregate	114	7	34	73	72	Tot: 32-40 Send: 3-4

Table 1. Average channel establishment times (ms)

We can further break down our measurements into per-node latencies. These costs reflect the time spent in the signalling object and resource manager at each node on the longest path. On the forward pass, the resource manager sets up state information for the new channel and performs admission control (4.8 ms per node). During the reverse pass, the resource manager commits the resources for that channel (2 ms). Admission control consumes approximately 0.7 of the 4.8 milliseconds measured for the forward pass. Combining times for both passes, we obtain a total average per-node latency of 6.8 ms.

We can perform a rough calculation of message overhead by summing up the per-node latencies for each node on the longest path (34 ms) and subtracting this from the forward and reverse pass time (107 ms). This difference (73 ms) reflects the the costs of sending messages from one node's signalling object to the next. There are 8 inter-node messages on our longest path. To gain insights into inter-node message costs, we measured the time from when the signalling object requests that a message be sent to the time when that send completes (9 ms). Given this measurement, the aggregate cost along the longest path for the 8 messages is 72 ms, which is close to the difference calculated above.

In our initial prototype, we are sending control messages reliably via TCP/IP by opening a TCP connection, sending the message, and then closing it. To gauge the TCP overhead, we measured several successive attempts to open a TCP connection, send a small message and close that connection, and we found that these operations cost between 4 and 5 ms. We can reduce the communication overhead by caching TCP connections (i.e., keeping connections open between adjacent nodes). This was done in the implementation of Suite 1. The TCP/IP component of the message overhead would be reduced from 4-5 ms to 0.4 ms (per hop) by caching connections, potentially reducing the aggregate overhead from 73 ms to 36-44 ms.

Considering that we do not cache TCP connections, these results are not too different from the connection establishment latencies measured for the unicast Suite 1 [1]. For the latter, the time for channel establishment was measured to be between 80 and 90 ms for unicast channels with six hops between Berkeley and San Diego, California. Also, simulations show that the computational overhead associated with admission control does not increase appreciably with the addition of resource sharing [9] and advance reservations mechanisms [7].

As a final note, we performed the same experiment on a similar topology of DECstations and measured an average round-trip time of 100 ms. The average start-up cost (i.e., Step 2 through Step 7) was 3.5 ms with an average per-node cost of 4 ms at each signalling object. The relative breakdown of time is quite similar to that seen in the Sparc experments, except that the DECstations are newer and faster machines, thus resulting in faster computation times.

5 Related Work

Connection establishment in the Tenet Suite 2 differs in a number of points from the approaches taken by other multi-party resource reservation protocols, such as RSVP or ST-II. [1] RSVP is strictly a reservation protocol; it does not include routing or data transport functions, and has been designed to be used as a companion to IP. ST-II is a network-layer protocol that includes data transport, resource reservation, and routing.

The establishment process in RSVP is strictly receiver-oriented. Receivers establish a connection by sending a *Reservation* request message to the source. The path of the resource reservation message ends when it reaches either the source or a node of the existing distribution tree. The Tenet Suite 2 allows for both sender-initiated and receiver-initiated connection establishment, by either having channels be established to existing target sets or by having destinations join or leave target sets with established channels.

The channel establishment process in RSVP is done in a single pass from the receiver to the first node encountered on the distribution tree. Suite 2 establishes connection in two passes: the first pass tentatively reserves resources on the path from the source to the destinations (in the case of channel establishment) or from the destination to a node on the channel's multicast tree (in the case of a reverse-direction, incremental establishment); the second pass goes back to the origin of the establishment request and either confirms the resource allocation (in case of

---

[1] Although other significant differences exist, in this paper we will focus only on differences in the establishment procedures.

a successful establishment) or frees the temporarily allocated resources (in case of a failure to establish the connection with the required QoS parameters). This return pass informs the originator of the request about the QoS guarantees given to the established connection.

Unlike those made by Suite 2, RSVP reservations are considered "soft-state" and must be periodically refreshed. This approach allows RSVP connections to adapt to network load and router failures, but allows for disruption in real-time service due to underlying route changes.

Both ST-II and the Tenet Suite 2 are connection-oriented. This allows for routing to be performed at connection establishment time. Moreover, since the routing function is a part of, or interacts with, the respective setup protocol, resource availability is known at routing time. This allows for QoS guarantees to be given whenever a connection has successfully been established.

Originally, connection establishment in ST-II was rigorously sender-oriented [10]. In order for receivers to join, they had to inform the sender out-of-band, prompting it to generate a connection request for the receiver wishing to join. The limitations of the sender-initiated scheme have been identified, and two extensions for receiver-initiated connection establishment have been proposed in the IBM ENC ST-II implementation [3]. The first extension ("Join Stream at Router") moves the join request in-band and allows routers that are part of the multicast tree to act as senders and to issue a *connect* request to the new receiver. The second extension ("Create Path Backwards") allows receivers to initiate reverse connection establishments to either the origin or routers in the multicast tree. The second approach is similar to the approach used in Suite 2, where a join by a new receiver causes the routing server to be contacted, which returns a route that is used by the new receiver to establish a connection to the most convenient router in the multicast tree.

6 Summary

When designing the connection establishment component of a multi-party real-time communication protocol, the following issues must be addressed: scalability and efficiency, to provide service to a potentially large number of participants; flexibility, to cope with dynamic changes in the underlying media or in the set of participants; and manageability, to control resource usage. In this paper we described a number of design decisions made when addressing these issues in the design of the Tenet Suite 2, which provides multicast connections, resource sharing, partial and incremental establishment, resource partitioning, and advance reservation.

The preliminary results we have obtained by measuring a prototype implementation of Suite 2 show that Tenet-style multicast channels can be established with delays that are comparable to WAN propagation delays. Even when including relatively long propagation latencies and a relatively large number of hops, multicast channel establishment should appear nearly instantaneous to human users.

250

Acknowledgement

This research was supported by the National Science Foundation and the Defense Advanced Research Projects Agency (DARPA) under Cooperative Agreement NCR-8919038 with the Corporation for National Research Initiatives, by AT&T Bell Laboratories, Digital Equipment Corporation, Hitachi, Ltd., Mitsubishi Electric Research Laboratories, Pacific Bell, Tektronix, and the International Computer Science Institute. The views and conclusions contained in this document are those of the authors, and should not be interpreted as representing official policies, either expressed or implied, of the U.S. Government or any of the sponsoring organizations.

References

1. Anindo Banerjea, Domenico Ferrari, Bruce Mah, Mark Moran, Dinesh Verma, and Hui Zhang. The Tenet real-time protocol suite: Design, implementation, and experiences. Technical Report TR-94-059, International Computer Science Institute, Berkeley, CA, November 1994. To appear in *IEEE/ACM Transactions on Networking*.
2. S. Deering. Host extensions for IP multicasting. RFC-1112, August 1989.
3. Luca Delgrossi, Ralf Guido Herrtwich, Frank Oliver Hoffmann, Sibylle Schaller. Receiver-Initiated Communication with ST-II, Technical Report 43.9314, IBM European Networking Center, Heidelberg, 1993.
4. Domenico Ferrari. Real-time communication in packet switching wide-area networks. Technical Report TR-89-022, International Computer Science Institute, Berkeley, California, May 1989.
5. Domenico Ferrari. Client requirements for real-time communication services. *IEEE Communications Magazine*, Vol. 28, No. 11, pp. 65–72, November 1990.
6. Domenico Ferrari, Anindo Banerjea, and Hui Zhang. Network support for multimedia: a discussion of the Tenet approach. *Computer Networks and ISDN Systems*, Vol. 20, pp. 1267–1280, 1994.
7. Domenico Ferrari, Amit Gupta, and Giorgio Ventre. Distributed advance reservations of real-time connections. *Proceedings of NOSSDAV 95*, Durham, NH, April 1995.
8. Domenico Ferrari and Dinesh Verma. Buffer allocation for realtime channels in packet switching networks. Technical Report TR-90-022, International Computer Science Institute, Berkeley, CA, June 1990.
9. Amit Gupta, Wingwai Howe, Mark Moran, and Quyen Nguyen. Resource sharing in multi-party realtime communication. *Proceedings of INFOCOM 95*, Boston, MA, April 1995.
10. Claudio Topolcic. Experimental Internet Stream Protocol, Version 2 (ST-II). RFC 1190, October 1990.
11. Dinesh Verma. Guaranteed performance communication in high speed networks. Ph.D. Dissertation, Technical Report UCB/CSD 91/663, University of California, Berkeley, December 1991.
12. Lixia Zhang, Steve Deering, Deborah Estrin, Scott Shenker, and Daniel Zappala. RSVP: A New Resource Reservation Protocol. *IEEE Networks Magazine*, Vol. 30, No. 9, pp. 8–18, September 1993.

The Role of Multicast Communication in the Provision of Scalable and Interactive Video-On-Demand Service

Kevin C. Almeroth and *Mostafa H. Ammar*

College of Computing, Georgia Institute of Technology, Atlanta, Georgia 30332-0280
{kevin,ammar}@cc.gatech.edu

Abstract. Multicast delivery can improve the scalability of Video-On-Demand (VOD) systems by allowing multiple customers to share one set of video server and network resources. In such a system, providing customer interactivity can be difficult. In this paper we overview our work which addresses how interactivity may be accomplished in a multicast delivery environment and analyzes the performance of such systems.

1 Introduction

Video-On-Demand (VOD) systems which provide guaranteed interactivity typically allocate one set of video server and network resources for each customer movie request. Such systems may not be scalable because resource usage is directly proportional to the number of customers being served. One alternative is to use multicast communication to share resources and provide service to multiple customers simultaneously. A multicast VOD system servicing multiple customers cannot provide the same individualized, interactive service as a unicast system, but the illusion of one-to-one servicing can still be provided. Typically, when multicast communication is used, some of the "on-demand" nature of VOD may need to be sacrificed[5]; the level of interactivity may need to be reduced; and/or the complexity of system operation and hardware may need to be increased. This paper overviews techniques we considered for using multicast in VOD systems, and summarizes the insights we gained from analyzing such systems.

2 Unicast Video-On-Demand

A unicast VOD system operates by allocating resources and providing interactivity to customers on an individual basis. A customer makes a movie request which is sent to a video server. If a set of video server and network resources are available, the request is satisfied, and playout begins immediately. This type of VOD system services customers in a one-to-one or *unicast* fashion. Resources are reserved on an individual basis, and reservations are typically made independent of other customer requests. Interactivity is provided through VCR functions which can be used to pause, rewind, or fast forward the movie. When a customer initiates a VCR action, a request is sent to the video server where the appropriate change in the playout is made. The advantage of a unicast VOD system is the ability to guarantee the availability of VCR functions. However, because there is a one-to-one relationship between resources and customer requests, the system does not scale well. Furthermore, providing VCR functions may require additional bandwidth[4] and video resources.

3 Multicast Video-On-Demand

One way to more efficiently use resources is to deliver the same movie to multiple customers at the same time. Some of our earlier work examined some of the issues in using multicast communication as an information delivery mechanism[6, 7]. While multicast communication offers the advantage of being scalable, the interactive nature of VOD logically demands individualized service. Several solutions have been suggested which group requests for the same movie. We have investigated solutions based on the use of fixed-length time slots to satisfy multiple requests simultaneously[1, 2]. Others have independently investigated the use of batching and temporal proximity of requests to service multiple requests[3]. In either case, multiple customer requests are satisfied using one set of video server and network resources. Providing interactivity is more difficult in these systems because the video stream multicast to the group cannot be modified because of the VCR actions of one member. Unless tradeoffs in the level of interactivity or system complexity are made, a multicast VOD system must handle VCR actions individually thereby reducing the advantages of using multicast.

3.1 Reducing the On-Demand Nature of the System

In part of our work on VOD systems using fixed-length time slots[1, 2], we examine the tradeoff between the on-demand nature of a system and its scalability. Continuous time is divided into equal length time slots in which customer requests will be grouped. Requests that arrive in the same time slot are serviced together at the end of the time slot. The video server will group the requests, and begin playout of the movie at the end of the time slot. It has been observed that among the set of available movies, a small percentage will be requested very often. For such popular movies, and during prime time, it is likely that many requests for the same movie can be accumulated in each slot. Assuming resources are available, customers need only wait until the end of the time slot in which they make their request and, therefore, the maximum customer wait time is equal to the length of the time slot. Anything more than a small wait time means customers do not experience true VOD. Shorter slot times mean customers will not wait as long which implies a level of service closer to true VOD. However, short time slots also mean that fewer customer requests will arrive during the slot, and that fewer customers will be serviced by one set of resources. Longer slot times mean more customers can be serviced with one set of resources, but the wait time will be longer.

3.2 Providing Interactive VCR Functions

In order to maintain scalability, and create the illusion of one-to-one service, a multicast VOD system must make certain tradeoffs. Because there might be more than one customer in a multicast group, modifying the video stream as a result of one customer's VCR actions in not feasible. Interactivity must be provided through another mechanism. We have developed two ways of providing VCR functions: (1) increasing set-top complexity; and (2) changing the semantics of interactivity.

Increasing Set-Top Box Complexity. Interactive VCR functions can be provided in a multicast VOD system by requiring the set-top box to play the correct frames while still continuing to receive frames multicast by the video server. In most cases, the set-top box can use buffering to handle VCR requests. For example, if a customer wishes to pause a movie, the set-top box can stop playout but continue to receive frames. In the extreme case when the set-top buffer fills up, the customer can be removed from the multicast group and either serviced individually, or added to another existing multicast group. The detailed operation of a system which provides pause-only using set-top box buffering is described in [1].

Changing the Semantics of Customer Interactivity. Interactive VCR functions can also be achieved by modifying the semantics of VCR functions. For example, instead of providing the ability to pause for any duration, a different level of service could offer functions for predetermined time increments. For example, if the base time increment is 2 minutes, a discontinuous pause function would allow a customer to pause for 2,4,6,... minutes. For rewind and fast forward, the customer could move the current playout point by periods of 2,4,6,... minutes in the reverse and forward direction respectively. By making the base time increment equal to the slot time, no additional buffering is needed in the set-top box. A customer initiating a VCR action is removed from the current multicast group, and added to a newly created group, or a previously existing group. A detailed description of a system which provides discontinuous pause, rewind, and fast forward without using set-top box buffering can be found in [2].

4 Simulation and Analysis of a Multicast System

The performance of a VOD system using multicast communication was analyzed by comparing a unicast system; a multicast system with continuous pause; and a multicast system with discontinuous pause, rewind, and fast forward. The performance analysis was based on three measures: (1) *Initial Request Blocking*: the percentage of initial requests that were blocked; (2) *VCR Action Blocking*: the percentage of VCR action attempts that were blocked; and (3) *Undesired VCR Action Length*: the amount of time that a discontinuous VCR action functions beyond what is desired by the customer.

Simulations for all three systems were conducted[1, 2] using a six hour prime-time period. A number of requests were uniformly distributed over the simulation period and for each request a movie was chosen using Zipf's Distribution. Each customer initiated VCR actions according to an exponential distribution, and the duration of each action was uniformly distributed. From the simulations we observed several important results. First, as the number of customers making requests was increased, the initial request blocking probability in the unicast system increased more rapidly. Even for large numbers of customers the initial request blocking probability was acceptable in both multicast systems. Second, as the number of channels was increased, initial request blocking probabilities in the multicast system decreased more rapidly, and approach an acceptable level more quickly. This was true regardless of the level of interactivity provided. Small slot lengths (around 5 minutes) gave good performance and do not significantly affect the on-demand characteristics of the system. As the slot length was increased, the ability of the multicast systems to group and satisfy more requests improved dramatically. The table below summarizes our observations about the three VOD systems. VCR action blocking, which occurs when no resources are available to handle group changes, can be made acceptable in all cases by allocating a sufficient number of emergency channels. Table 1 summarize the numerical results reported in [1, 2].

System	Buffering in the Set-Top Box	On-Demand Nature Of Movies	VCR Actions	Initial Request Blocking	VCR Action Blocking	System Complexity
Unicast w/ Cont VCR	Not Required[1]	True	Continuous	High	Lowest (0%)	Low
Multicast w/ Cont Pause	Required	Near	Continuous Pause Only	Low	Lower	High
Multicast w/ Disc VCR	Not Required[1]	Near	Time Increments	Low	Low	Moderate

Table 1. Results summary of the performance analysis of the three multicast systems.

References

1. K. Almeroth and M. Ammar. Providing a scalable, interactive video-on-demand service using multicast communication. In *ICCCN '94*, San Francisco, CA, Sep 1994. file://ftp.cc.gatech.edu/pub/coc/tech_reports/1994/GIT-CC-94-36.ps.
2. K. Almeroth and M. Ammar. On the performance of a multicast delivery video-on-demand service with discontinuous VCR actions. In *ICC '95*, Seattle, WA, Jun 1995. file://ftp.cc.gatech.edu/pub/coc/tech_reports/1994/GIT-CC-94-49.ps.
3. A. Dan, D. Sitaram, and P. Shahabuddin. Scheduling policies for an on-demand video server with batching. In *ACM Multimedia '94*, San Francisco, CA, Oct 1994.
4. J. Dey, J. Salehi, J. Kurose, and D. Towsley. Providing VCR capabilities in large-scale video servers. In *ACM Multimedia '94*, San Francisco, CA, Oct 1994.
5. T. Little and D. Venkatesh. Prospects for interactive video-on-demand. *IEEE Multimedia*, pages 14–23, Fall 1994.
6. J. Wong and M. Ammar. Analysis of broadcast delivery in a videotex system. *IEEE Transactions on Computers*, pages 863–866, Sep 1985.
7. J. Wong and M. Ammar. Response time performance of videotex systems. *IEEE Journal on Selected Areas in Communications*, pages 1174–1180, Oct 1986.

[1] Minimal buffering is required to handle jitter and provide continuous playout.

Session VIII: Network Scheduling and Real-Time Networking

Chair: Steve Pink, Swedish Institute of Computer Science

Network scheduling and real-time networking has been a core issue for this workshop since its inception. Traditionally, there have been two kinds of networks. The first carries data traffic for computer applications, is statistically multiplexed, is concerned with high throughput and perhaps low-delay, and provides a service for applications that are not interested in low delay-variance (or jitter). The second network carries predominately voice traffic in real time and is circuit switched. Economy of scale argues for one network with integrated services that can carry both kinds of traffic. This has presented a major challenge for network designers since the global network will have to be both efficient in terms of utilization and capable of providing services to both real-time and non-real time applications. The papers in this session address this challenge.

This session was made up of two presentations based on full papers, three shorter presentations based on adjunct papers, and a round table discussion made up of the presenters and an invited panelist, James Kurose.

The first paper, by Hui Zhang and Edward Knightly, presented by Zhang detailed a new resource reservation scheme for variable bit rate video in an integrated services network. According to the authors, there have been three types of solutions posed for this problem: deterministic, predictive and statistical. Deterministic schemes allocate bandwidth at the peak rate of the flow. This provides the best quality of service (QOS) but the worst utilization. Predictive and statistical solutions have better utilization but the QOS suffers from uncontrollable overloads in the network. The solution posed in this work depends neither on statistical multiplexing at the packet level nor resource reservation at the connection level, but resource reservation at the segment level.

A segment of a VBR flow is an interval in the flow that demands constant resources. Thus, a stable reservation can be made for that segment, and a new reservation can be renegotiated for the next segment if its demand for resources is different. The characterization of traffic sources used is the Deterministic Bounding Interval (D-BIND) model. D-BIND characterizes sources as having a bounding rate that decreases over longer interval lengths. An analysis of a number of segments of MPEG video over some seconds shows the drop-off in the bounding rate for these intervals. If the bounding rate drops off quickly, high utilization can be achieved through multiplexing with other flows. If the bounding rate decreases slowly, less gain will be achieved through multiplexing.

Resources are negotiated on a per-segment basis. Since applications themselves decide segmenting policies for themselves, degradation can be controlled gracefully by the application trading off QOS for price-of-service. The authors claim that the renegotiation puts the onus of this scheme on the latency of signaling in the network. But work on the Tenet Real-Time Protocol Suite (at UC Berkeley) has shown that in the wide area the dominant latency for signaling is propagation time and that can be kept down to tens of milliseconds. Since this is equivalent to the loss of only one or two frames, most applications will work well. An analysis is then given to show that certain "on-line" algorithms for segmenting are capable of providing high utilization with good QOS.

The second paper, by Pawan Goyal, Simon S. Lam, and Harrick M. Vin, and presented by Pawan Goyal, attempts to provide a method for deriving an end-to-end delay bound for a number of differently shaped sources in a network of switches that have different scheduling algorithms but all provide guaranteed rate. First, the notion of guaranteed rate is defined for the Virtual Clock, Packet Generalized Processor Sharing, and Self Clocked Fair Queuing algorithms. It is shown that all of these provide a guarantee on the upper bound of packet delay. The next step is to show that end-to-end packet delay, for a network that combines any of these algorithms in the switches can be gotten by analyzing the path as a whole. The goal in this step is to show that by deriving a delay guarantee for a network of servers, the problem can be reduced to determining delay at a single server.

To complete the analysis of a heterogeneous network, the authors attempt to show that the sources for these end-to-end delays need not be restricted to one shaping algorithm. Two shaping algorithms are then plugged into the analysis, Leaky Bucket and Exponentially Bounded Burstiness, and it is argued that the end-to-end delay bounds, whose derivation method was presented in the earlier section, hold for a network using sources shaped by both of these.

The presentations of the adjunct papers in this session complemented those for the full papers. The paper by Bansal, Siracusa, Harn, Ramamurthy, and Raychaudhuri, presented by Bansal, described a new ATM application programming interface (API) called the "ATM Service Manager" (ASM). This API allows an application to use a number of different transport services and choose between varying qualities of service. The architecture for the ASM allows a customizable transport protocol stack, provides the application with the ability to express demands for quality of service to the network, and allows the application to take action when quality degrades. The architecture is layered over ATM and its adaptation layers, the Q.2931 protocol is used for signaling and ABR, VBR, and CBR services are provided to the user.

The second adjunct paper, by Simon S. Lam and Geoffrey G. Xie and presented Lam, describes a burst scheduling network, that provides guaranteed service. The network uses virtual clock scheduling and provides an efficient scheduling algorithm since only the first packet of a burst needs to have its virtual clock updated, the others getting theirs in the same increment. The authors claim that their network provides performance guarantees independent of any source control on the flow, as well as providing a firewall against any misbehaving flow. When taken together with the results of the second full paper in this session (of which Lam is also an author) the above properties of burst scheduling networks can be shown to hold end-to-end.

The last adjunct paper by M. Grossglauser, S. Keshav, and D. Tse and presented by Keshav, argues against the notion of a variable bit rate (VBR) service and argues for a new scheme that uses a constant bit rate (CBR) service with fast renegotiation. VBR with leaky bucket regulators suffer either from loss (when the buffer is too small), long delays (when the buffer is too big), expensive (i.e., the cost of large buffers) or poor protection or isolation from competing flows. CBR service can be augmented with fast renegotiation (RCBR) to provide a statistical multiplexing gain. With the right set of algorithms to provide signaling, RCBR can be used to provide more efficient service to compressed video than VBR. The position argued for in this adjunct paper, one notes, is supported by the results given in the first full paper of the session by Zhang and Knightly. Although this paper was presented at the workshop, it has been excluded from the proceedings by request of the authors.

RED-VBR: A New Approach to Support Delay-Sensitive VBR Video in Packet-Switched Networks

Hui Zhang
School of Computer Science
Carnegie Mellon University
hzhang@cs.cmu.edu

Edward W. Knightly
EECS Department
University of California at Berkeley
knightly@eecs.berkeley.edu

Abstract. Previous approaches to supporting video on packet-switched networks include deterministic service, statistical service, predicted service, and feedback-based schemes. These schemes represent different trade-offs in quality of service (QOS), achievable network utilization, and method of dealing with overload. In this paper, we propose a new service called REnegotiated Deterministic Variable Bit Rate Service (RED-VBR) that attempts to strike an efficient balance with the above trade-offs. The approach is based on deterministic guarantees with client controlled renegotiation of QOS parameters and graceful adaptation during overload periods. We evaluate the scheme using two traces of MPEG-compressed video and show that, even with simple renegotiation polices and relatively low renegotiation frequencies, high network utilization in the range of 50% to 80% can be achieved. For traffic that is bursty over long intervals, this represents a 100% to 150% improvement in network utilization compared to deterministic service. Compared to statistical and predicted service, our approach allows more graceful and client-controlled QOS degradation during overload period.

1 Introduction and Motivation

Future integrated services networks will have to support applications with diverse traffic characteristics and performance requirements. There are three important types of traffic for future integrated services networks: constant bit rate CBR traffic, delay-sensitive variable bit rate or VBR traffic, and best-effort ABR or available bit rate traffic. Among these, delay-sensitive VBR traffic poses a unique challenge. While resource reservation schemes work best for CBR traffic, and there are many congestion control algorithms based on feedback and re-transmission for best-effort traffic, there is no consensus on which strategy should be used for VBR traffic, in particular, compressed video. This is due mainly to two conflicting design goals: good quality of service and high network utilization.

Achieving both goals with bursty traffic is fundamentally difficult. Since a bursty source may generate various amounts of data during different time periods, the aggregate amount of traffic generated by many sources sharing the same network resources also varies over time. When the amount of aggregate incoming traffic is greater than the outgoing link speed, packets have to be buffered. If the situation persists, packets will be dropped due to buffer overflows, which will in turn cause the application's quality of service (QOS) to suffer. This problem is compounded by the nature of VBR video traffic: depending on the underlying information content of the video stream, bursts of high rate can persist for time scales on the order of many seconds over the duration of an entire complex, high-motion scene. Bursts of this time scale cannot be absorbed by network buffers or smoothed at the source because of the excessive delay that this would introduce and the excessive buffer sizes that it would require.

Thus, the fundamental problem is that when bursts from many sources collide inside the network, if the rate of the aggregated traffic is greater than the link speed and the situation persists for a certain period, the QOS of some or all connections will suffer. Various solutions have been proposed to address the problem, and they represent different ways of dealing with the tradeoff between QOS and network utilization. Previous solutions can be classified according to the following four categories: deterministic service with peak-rate allocation [3], statistical service with probabilistic allocation [5, 9, 13] predicted service with observation-based admission control [2], and feedback based scheme with no resource reservation [4, 6].

Previously proposed solutions for deterministic service *eliminate* the occurrence of overload situations by reserving resources at the sources' peak rates. While this approach provides the best QOS, it does so at the expense of having low network utilization when peak-to-average rate ratios are high. In various ways, the other three approaches trade a higher network utilization for a potential degradation of QOS. However, they all suffer from some limitations. Statistical and predicted services try to *control* the frequency of the overload situation by exploiting statistical multiplexing (respectively using knowledge of source statistics and queue measurements). However, the overload situation may still happen, and at unexpected times. Additionally, during the overload period, QOS is likely to suffer significantly for all connections in an uncontrolled and difficult-to-predict way. As well, the QOS may drop significantly due to *consecutive* packet losses. This last problem is exacerbated for VBR *video* since VBR video may have very long burst lengths, on the order of scene lengths, possibly causing a persistent degradation in service when the bursts do collide. Feedback schemes with no reservations try to *adapt* and *react* to overload situations by using network congestion signals to reduce the rates of sources. Such schemes have the advantage that they can *gracefully* degrade QOS during an overload situation by exploring an important property of the compressed video: most of video compression algorithms have a quality control parameter that, when tuned, will output compressed video at different rates and qualities. The drawback of a feedback-based scheme is that, without some round robin type of scheduler at the switch, it won't work unless *all* sources cooperate. Even with switch support, it still has the fundamental problem that it is impossible to provide different types of QOS to different applications.

In this paper, we study a new approach to support VBR video that utilizes the following two important observations. The first one is that although compressed video is bursty, it is much more structured than data traffic. While compressed video is bursty because the size of a compressed frame varies from one frame to the next, there is an underlying structure in that a new frame is generated every 33 msec. More importantly, for an MPEG source, the largest local variation between frame sizes is due to the alternation of inter-frame coded frames with intra-frame coded frames. That is, a larger (intra-frame coded) I-frame is immediately followed by a smaller (inter-frame coded) B-frame so that the micro-level burst does not persist for very long. In addition to such burstiness on a shorter time scale, there is also burstiness on a longer time scale due to scene changes [10]. The second observation is that most of the video compression algorithms have some type of quality control factor (Q-factor). By tuning this factor, a video source can tradeoff its bit rate for perceptual quality.

In order to characterize the property that VBR video has different bounding rates over different interval lengths, we use the Deterministic Bounding Interval-Dependent (D-BIND) traffic model [8] to characterize sources. With the D-BIND model and the new admission control algorithms derived recently [12], we show that, contrary to common belief, no-loss deterministic service can be provided without reservation based on peak-rate. We study the average network utilization that can be achieved for two 10-minute MPEG compressed video sequences. We observe that, for video sequences that have smaller burstiness over longer time intervals, high average network utilization can be achieved even for deterministic services.

We also observe that if there are large traffic-rate variations over longer interval lengths, deterministic service will result in *low* average network utilization. To increase network utilization in this case, we propose a new service called REnegotiated Deterministic Variable Bit Rate or RED-VBR service. With such a service, the application renegotiates its traffic parameters and QOS with the network when there is a *significant* change of long term traffic rate. Such a scheme is possible for two reasons: (1) since renegotiations need to happen only when the traffic rate changes over long term, such renegotiation is not very frequent; (2) even if the renegotiation request for more resources cannot be satisfied, the application can *adjust* the Q-factor of its compression algorithm, and gracefully degrade its QOS based on the currently available resources.

While traditional reservation-less approaches do statistical multiplexing at the packet level (packets may be dropped), and traditional reservation-based service can be viewed as doing statistical multiplexing at the connection level (connection requests may be denied), our approach can be seen as doing statistical multiplexing at the segment level — resources are reserved on a per segment basis and reservation requests for a *segment* may be denied when the network is overloaded. An important feature of such an approach is that each individual application *determines for itself* the tradeoff between QOS and price-of-service by defining its own segmenting algorithm. The approach is statistical in that a renegotiation request for more network resources can be denied. However, compared to statistical service and predicted service, we avoid the uncontrollable and unpredictable packet drop behavior and the extended drop periods by introducing graceful degradation during overload situations.

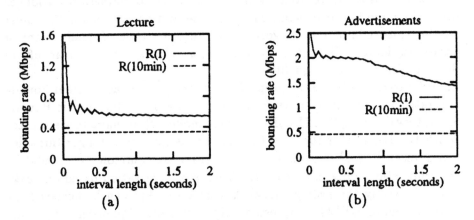

Fig. 1. D-BIND Characterization for Lecture and Advertisements

2   Deterministic Variable Bit Rate Service

While the conventional wisdom has been that a deterministic service requires peak rate allocation and thus achieve the same network utilization as a CBR service, we will show in this section that this is not necessarily the case. A deterministic service will ensure that no packets are dropped or excessively delayed, even in the *worst case*. As alluded to in Section 1, compressed MPEG video has the important property that micro-level bursts do not persist very long. By developing a more accurate traffic model to capture such a property and utilizing this information in the connection admission control algorithm, a Deterministic Variable Bit Rate or D-VBR service can achieve a considerably higher network utilization compared to a peak-rate-allocation scheme.

In [8], we propose a Deterministic Bounding Interval Dependent (D-BIND) traffic model to characterize sources. This model captures the intuitive property that over longer interval-lengths, a source's bounding rate decreases. With the D-BIND model, source j is described by the curve $R_j(I)$ where $R_j(I)$ is the bounding rate over an interval of length I. Dropping the source j subscript, if $A[t_1, t_2]$ represents the total number of bits transmitted by a source in the interval $[t_1, t_2]$, then $A[t, t + I]/I \leq R(I)$, $\forall\, t, I > 0$. Thus, the source is constrained to transmit no more than $I \cdot R(I)$ bits during any interval of length I. In practice, a traffic source must be able to specify its traffic with a small number of parameters. For this reason, the D-BIND *model* consists of N rate-interval pairs, i.e., $\{(R_n, I_n)|n = 1, 2, \cdots N\}$, with an appropriate interpolation between pairs.

Figure 1 shows the D-BIND $R(I)$ curve for two 10-minute traces of MPEG compressed video: a lecture and a series of advertisements. The horizontal axis is interval length and the vertical axis is the bounding rate over the interval length as defined above. As shown in the figure, the general trend of the curves is that the bounding rates approach the source's peak rate for small interval lengths and the long-term average rate for longer interval lengths. Of note is the difference between the two curves. For the lecture sequence of Figure 1(a), there is not a great deal of action, mostly the camera panning and zooming between the speaker and his transparencies. As a result, the $R(I)$ curve drops sharply from

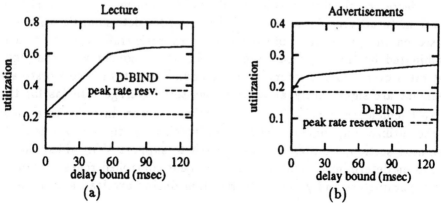

Fig. 2. Achievable Utilization for Lecture and Advertisements

the peak rate to close to the long-term average rate indicating that its high-rate bursts are of limited duration. Because of the shape of the D-BIND curve, one expects that this source will be a good candidate for achieving a reasonable utilization for deterministic service. Alternatively, because of the fast motion and many scene changes of the advertisement sequence, its $R(I)$ curve, shown in Figure 1(b), shows that the bounding rate very slowly decreases from the peak rate to the long-term average rate. This indicates that it will be difficult to achieve high utilization when multiplexing such a source since bursts of high rate and duration cannot be effectively absorbed by network buffers.

Figure 2 shows the achievable multiplexer utilization when a number of such sources are multiplexed. The figure shows deterministic delay bound on the horizontal axis and achievable utilization on the vertical axis. Points on the curve represent the maximum average utilization that can by achieved multiplexing homogeneous connections so that no packets are dropped or violate their delay bounds (details of the admission control algorithm may be found in [7, 8, 12]. As expected from the D-BIND $R(I)$ curves of Figure 1, there is a considerable difference in achievable utilization for the two streams that is caused by the inherent information content of the different videos. For example, for a delay bound of 60 msec, the multiplexed lecture sequence can achieve an average utilization of 60%. However, for the same delay bound, the advertisement sequence achieves an average utilization below 25%. Even with a more accurate traffic model, a more elaborate admission control algorithm, and a more sophisticated scheduling algorithm, the increase of network utilization for a deterministic service will be very small for the advertisement sequence. In fact, there is a fundamental limit to the utilization that can be achieved by a deterministic service, and the limit for the advertisement sequence is very close to the curve shown in Figure 2 [7].

Thus, if a source has long-duration bursts of high rate (i.e., a $R(I)$ curve that decreases slowly), it will be difficult to achieve high network utilization. Intuitively, since resource allocation for deterministic service is based on an upper bound of the source, a source's traffic specification is dominated by the worst-case segment, i.e., the segment with the highest rates over a longer interval. If the bounding rates in the worst-case segment are significantly above the long-term average rate (as for the advertisement sequence), low utilization may occur. In order to achieve higher utilization, some statistical multiplexing has to be introduced. In the next section, we present an approach to support VBR video that is based on deterministic guarantees with client-controlled renegotiation of QOS parameters and graceful degradation during overload situations.

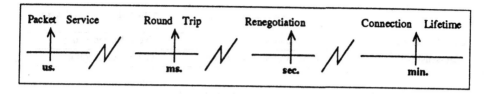

Fig. 3. Important Control Time Scales

3 RED-VBR: REnegotiated Deterministic Variable Bit Rate Service

As discussed in Section 2, there are at least two levels of burstiness of VBR video that are important for a resource allocation algorithm: burstiness on a shorter time scale due to the coding algorithm and small-time-scale variations in picture information content, and burstiness on a longer time scale due to scene changes. Burstiness on shorter time scales is effectively taken into account with the D-BIND model and the tighter admission control algorithms. It is burstiness on longer time scales that will result in a low network utilization for deterministic service.

To increase the network utilization in this case, we propose that the application renegotiate its traffic specification and QOS with the network on a per segment basis, where the policy of choosing segments is decided by each individual application. Between each pair of negotiating points for each application, a D-VBR service is provided. If a request for more resources is denied, the application will adjust the Q-factor of its compression algorithm and lower the transmission rate, which will gracefully lower the perceptual quality of the compressed video. Renegotiations are accomplished via the signaling mechanism such as the Dynamic Connection Management scheme in the Tenet Protocol Suite [11] or via an ATM signaling protocol in an ATM network. We name this scheme REnegotiated Deterministic Variable Bit Service or RED-VBR.

The scheme can be better understood by considering the timescales that are important for network control as shown in Figure 3. Packet service disciplines at the switches operate at the timescale of a packet transmission time by determining which packet to service next when there is more than one packet in the queue. Connection admission control algorithms operate at the timescale of the connection life-time by deciding whether there are enough network resources to accept a new connection. While traditional resource reservation algorithms effect control at these two timescales, and feedback algorithms do control at the timescale of multiple round-trip times, our approach introduces a new control timescale

	traffic known in advance	traffic unknown in advance
not delay-sensitive	video playback	live video recording
delay-sensitive	interactive video browsing	video conferencing

Fig. 4. Classification of Video Transmission

that is between the round-trip time and connection life-time. It corresponds to the time scale over which the rate of compressed video changes significantly, where "significantly" is defined by the individual application.

An important feature of this approach is that each individual application *determines for itself* the tradeoff between QOS and price-of-service by defining its own segmenting algorithm. In one extreme, a video source which does not want to compromise its QOS at any time may have only one segment for the entire sequence. This is equivalent to the traditional deterministic service with no renegotiations. In the other extreme, a video source that wants to minimize reserved resources may want to renegotiate very frequently. Assuming that there is a pricing policy based on the amount of resources reserved, the first source will have the highest quality but more expensive service while the second source will have a cheaper service with the risk that it may have to degrade its QOS during periods of network overload if a renegotiation fails. If most applications are willing to pay for a more expensive service for better quality, the network may operate at a relatively low utilization. Alternatively, if most applications prefer a cheaper service but are willing to risk that they may have to gracefully degrade their QOS, the network will be able to operate at a relatively high utilization. In contrast, a deterministic service allows only the most expensive service with the best QOS.

Thus, the approach provides a *statistical* service on the level of user-defined *segments* in that it is possible that at a transition from a low-bit-rate to a high-bit-rate video segment, the renegotiation request for more network resources will fail. However, unlike traditional statistical service, this approach gives a higher level of control to individual users and avoids uncontrollable packet drop behavior and extended drop periods by using a *deterministic* VBR service as its foundation.

Regarding the speed of renegotiation, our experience with the Tenet Real-Time Protocol Suite indicates that the latency of signaling is dominated by propagation delay [1]. Even for a wide-area network, this latency is on the order of tens of milliseconds which is equal to one or two frame times. We expect that this will be acceptable for most applications.

4 Empirical Evaluation of RED-VBR

In this section, we evaluate the proposed solution by examining the following questions: (a) how much network utilization can be achieved with RED-VBR? (b) how often should a source renegotiate, or what is its segmenting algorithm? (c) how can a source derive its D-BIND parameters for each segment *before* a renegotiation?

To address these questions, Figure 4 shows how compressed video transmission can be classified according to whether the traffic is known in advance and whether the transmission is delay-sensitive. The degree of difficulty in solving the above problems varies according to which categories an application belongs to. For applications with traffic known in advance, problems (b) and (c) can be solved by off-line algorithms. For this case, Section 4.2 describes a a heuristic *off-line* algorithm that illustrates the effectiveness of renegotiations in increasing network utilization. These problems become harder when the traffic is delay-sensitive and unknown in advance. Specifying traffic parameters for live video is a difficult problem that is shared by most of the existing resource allocation schemes. In Section 4.3, we present a heuristic *off-line* algorithm that adaptively chooses traffic parameters for an unknown sequence. Both of the schemes are evaluated according to the performance metric described in the next section.

4.1 Performance Metric

In order to evaluate the renegotiation schemes, we use a weighted average performance metric that is computed as follows. If a trace, T is segmented into S segments (by either an off-line or on-line algorithm), each segment j that is of duration t_j will have its own D-BIND traffic specification $spec_j$, and delay bound d_j (for the experiments presented here we keep d_j the same for all segments). The QOS guarantee is deterministic for the duration of the segment in that no packets will be delayed beyond d_j and none will be dropped due to buffer overflows. Given the link speed, scheduling algorithm (assumed to be FCFS for connections with guaranteed QOS), and buffer size, we can calculate (using the admission control equations in [7, 8]) N_j, the maximum number of connections with $spec_j$ that can be multiplexed so that all packets of all connections meet their desired QOS. A measure of the efficiency of the segmenting algorithm is a weighted average of the number of admissible connections across all of the segments, i.e., $\eta_T = \dfrac{\sum_{j=1}^{S} N_j \cdot t_j}{\sum_{j=1}^{S} t_j}$.

Note that if a user does not want to do any renegotiations, there will be one segment ($S = 1$) so that $spec_1$ (the only traffic specification) is the worst case parameterization over the entire stream. In this case, the corresponding number of admissible connections is as shown in Figure 2. Alternatively, if an application or user is willing to renegotiate its parameterization, more connections can be accepted during periods where $spec_j$ is less bursty. The equation above can be extended to the case of heterogeneous sources by summing over multiple streams or traces T. The number of connections η_T is then converted to average utilization with knowledge of the source's long term average rate and the link speed. An alternative view of the metric above is that if a number of homogeneous streams with trace T are multiplexed at a queue with each stream having a uniformly random start time, then η_T represents the average number of connections that could be simultaneously established with no denied renegotiations. The reason for this is that at a random time τ, the length of a segment t_j corresponds to how likely it is that the randomly offset source is transmitting segment j at time τ, i.e., $Pr\{source transmitting segment j at $\tau\} = t_j / \sum_{i=1}^{S} t_i$. Thus, at time τ the different streams will be transmitting a different segment of the trace and will therefore have a different negotiated traffic specification.

4.2 Off-line Algorithm

The off-line algorithm segments the video sequence assuming the entire sequence is known in advance. Such an algorithm is interesting not only because it can be used for video playback applications, but also because it can serve as a benchmark for comparing the performance of on-line algorithms. Various algorithms are possible to decide if the difference be-

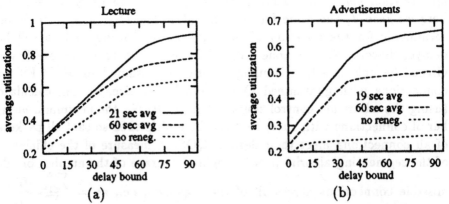

Fig. 5. Achievable Utilization for Off-line Segmenting Algorithm

tween the actual future traffic and the current traffic specification is large enough to merit a renegotiation. For the experiments presented here, we use a recursive algorithm that segments a video sequence according to a fixed QOS and a target network utilization.

The off-line algorithm may be described in the following manner. The algorithm takes as its input a sequence of frame sizes and a parameter ψ $(0 \leq \psi \leq 1)$ that indicates how aggressively to segment. A higher ψ will generate more segments and thus will potentially achieve a higher network utilization and less expensive service for the user. First, the algorithm calculates the D-BIND parameters for the entire sequence. It then identifies the worst-case segment as the segment that achieves this worst-case parameterization. This segment is then extended to the left and right until the average rate of that segment has decreased to $\psi \cdot R_N$, where R_N is the bounding rate over the longest parameterized interval length I_N. With this segment isolated, the procedure is iteratively repeated over the remaining two segments until the sequence is completely segmented.

For the two video traces, Figure 5 depicts the achievable network utilization (as defined in Section 4.1) for the off-line segmentation algorithm. For various values of ψ, the figure shows utilization vs. delay bound as in Figure 2. The lower curves depict the case of no renegotiations or $\psi = 0$ as in Figure 2. In Figure 5(a) for the lecture sequence, the upper curves represent higher values of ψ such that higher utilizations are achieved. However, this is at the expense of requiring a smaller average renegotiation interval. For example, for a 50 msec delay bound, without renegotiations, a 56% utilization is achievable. Alternatively, using renegotiations with an average renegotiation interval of 60 seconds a 67% utilization is achieved. With more frequent renegotiations averaging 21 seconds apart, a 75% utilization is achieved.

For the advertisement sequence of Figure 5(b), the improvements for using the renegotiations are even more pronounced. For example, without renegotiations and a delay bound of 50 msec, the average utilization is 24%. Alternatively, using renegotiations, average utilizations of 48% and 60% are achieved for respective average renegotiation intervals of 60 and 19 seconds. This represents respective improvements of 100% and 150% over the utilization achievable with deterministic service.

4.3 On-line Algorithm

In the off-line algorithm, we assume that the entire video sequence is known advance before transmission starts. In this section, we consider the more difficult case such as live video transmission where traffic parameters are not known in advance. We call the algorithm that dynamically computes traffic specification and issues renegotiation requests an on-line algorithm. As in the case of the off-line algorithm, many algorithms are possible for detecting scene changes or significant changes in traffic parameters. For this experiment, we again present a heuristic algorithm to obtain insight into achievable utilizations for different renegotiation intervals.

The on-line algorithm maintains the currently reserved D-BIND parameters and dynamically computes the D-BIND parameters of the previous N frames. The algorithm needs to make the following policy decisions based on the two sets of D-BIND parameters: (a) when to ask for more resources, and how much more? (b) when to ask for less resources, and how much less? In our heuristic algorithm, three parameters α, β ($\geq$ 1) and K are used to control the policies. If any rate in the measured D-BIND curve exceeds the corresponding rate in the reserved D-BIND curve (i.e., not enough resources are reserved), a renegotiation immediately takes place. The new traffic specification is chosen so that each bounding rate R_n is α times its currently measured value. Thus, in the case of increasing reserved resources, we reserve beyond the current requirements by a factor α so that numerous consecutive increases are not required. If the measured D-BIND parameters have fallen below the currently reserved D-BIND parameters by a factor of β for K consecutive frames, the algorithm will renegotiate to a lower reserved D-BIND parameterization. In the current heuristic algorithm, the lower D-BIND parameters are computed as the average of the currently reserved and currently measured D-BIND parameters.

Figure 6 shows the performance of the on-line algorithm for the lecture and advertisement sequences. As shown, the on-line algorithm can achieve utilizations similar to that of the off-line algorithm. However, the on-line algorithm must renegotiate more frequently to achieve a utilization similar to that achieved by the off-line algorithm. This is as expected since the on-line algorithm does not have knowledge of "future" frame sizes. The figure shows that for the on-line algorithm to achieve utilizations similar to those achieved by the off-line algorithm with an average renegotiation interval of 60 seconds, the lecture sequence must renegotiate with an average interval of 23 seconds and the advertisement sequence must renegotiate with an average interval of 11 seconds.

In the above experiments, there were no denials of requests for resources so that no sources were required to scale back their Q-factor. By allowing sources to gracefully adapt, even higher network utilization can be achieved.

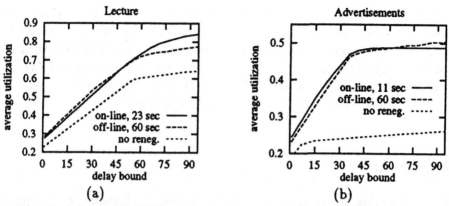

Fig. 6. Achievable Utilization for On-line Segmenting Algorithm

5 Conclusions

We have proposed a new service called REnegotiated Deterministic Variable Bit Rate or RED-VBR service for supporting transmission of delay-sensitive VBR video in packet-switched networks. The service is based on flexible renegotiation of traffic parameters with graceful degradation of QOS in the case where renegotiations fail. Each client determines its own renegotiation policies (when to renegotiate and what parameters are used). Between two adjacent renegotiation points, a deterministic network service is provided. We have shown that such an approach can achieve significant multiplexing gains without requiring an excessive signaling overhead. For example, with the D-VBR service, the network can only achieve 24% utilization when the video traffic is highly bursty over long intervals. However, using RED-VBR with a simple off-line segmenting algorithm and relatively low renegotiation frequencies (20-60 sec/renegotiation), high network utilization in the range of 48% to 60% (50% to 80% for less bursty traffic) can be achieved for connections with delay bounds between 40 and 80 ms. This represents a 100% to 150% improvement of network utilization compared to the D-VBR service. As well, the on-line algorithm achieves similar improvements but requires a smaller average renegotiation interval. For example, the on-line algorithm required an 11 second average renegotiation interval to achieve utilizations close to those achieved with the off-line algorithm and a 60 second average renegotiation interval. The on-line algorithm also provides a practical solution to address the issue of specifying traffic parameters for live video. Compared to statistical and predicted service, RED-VBR allows more graceful and client-controlled QOS degradation during overload period.

While this paper demonstrates the effectiveness of RED-VBR service, many areas remain to be explored in future works: 1) derive more elaborate on-line and off-line algorithms; 2) design algorithms to deal with rejected renegotiation requests; 3) design a mechanism to retry an increase-rate renegotiation for the case when the Q factor has been decreased by a failed renegotiation; 4) implement and experiment.

References

1. A. Banerjea, E. Knightly, F. Templin, and H. Zhang. Experiments with the Tenet real-time protocol suite on the Sequoia 2000 wide area network. In *ACM Multimedia'94*, SF, CA, October 1994.
2. D. Clark, S. Shenker, and L. Zhang. Supporting real-time applications in an integrated services packet network: Architecture and mechanism. In *ACM SIGCOMM'92*, Baltimore, MA, August 1992.
3. D. Ferrari and D. Verma. A scheme for real-time channel establishment in wide-area networks. *IEEE JSAC*, 8(3):368–379, April 1990.
4. M. Gilge and R. Gusella. Motion video coding for packet switching networks – an integrated approach. In *SPIE Visual Communications and Image Processing '91*, Boston, MA, November 1991.
5. R. Guerin, H. Ahmadi, and M. Naghshineh. Equivalent capacity and its application to bandwidth allocation in high-speed networks. *IEEE JSAC*, 9(7):968–981, September 1991.
6. H. Kanakia, P. Mishra, and A. Reibman. An adaptive congestion control scheme for real-time packet video transport. In *ACM SIGCOMM'94*, SF, CA, September 1993.
7. E. Knightly, D. Wrege, J. Liebeherr, and H. Zhang. Fundamental limits and tradeoffs for providing deterministic guarantees to VBR video traffic. In *ACM SIGMETRICS'95*, Ottowa, Ontario, May 1995.
8. E. Knightly and H. Zhang. Traffic characterization and switch utilization using deterministic bounding interval dependent traffic models. In *IEEE INFOCOM'95*, Boston, MA, April 1995.
9. J. Kurose. On computing per-session performance bounds in high-speed multi-hop computer networks. In *ACM SIGMETRICS'92*, Newport, Rhode Island, June 1992.
10. A. Lazar, G. Pacifici, and D. Pendarakis. Modeling video sources for real-time scheduling. In *IEEE GLOBECOM'93*, Houston, TX, November 1993.
11. C. Parris, H. Zhang, and D. Ferrari. Dynamic management of guaranteed performance multimedia connections. *Multimedia Systems Journal*, 1:267–283, 1994.

12. H. Zhang and D. Ferrari. Improving utilization for deterministic service in multimedia communication. In *1994 International Conference on Multimedia Computing and Systems*, Boston, MA, May 1994.

13. H. Zhang and E. Knightly. Providing end-to-end statistical performance guarantees with bounding interval dependent stochastic models. In *ACM SIGMETRICS'94*, Nashville, TN, May 1994.

Determining End-to-End Delay Bounds In Heterogeneous Networks *

Pawan Goyal, **Simon S. Lam** and **Harrick M. Vin**

Department of Computer Sciences, University of Texas at Austin
Taylor Hall 2.124, Austin, Texas 78712-1188
E-mail: {pawang,lam,vin}@cs.utexas.edu, Telephone: (512) 471-9718

Abstract

We define a class of Guaranteed Rate (GR) scheduling algorithms. The GR class includes Virtual Clock, Packet-by-Packet Generalized Processor Sharing and Self Clocked Fair Queuing. For networks that employ scheduling algorithms belonging to GR, we present a method for determining an upper bound on end-to-end delay. The method facilitates determination of end-to-end delay bounds for a variety of sources. We illustrate the method by determining end-to-end delay bounds for sources conforming to Leaky Bucket and Exponentially Bounded Burstiness.

1 Introduction

Computer networks have advanced to a point where they can support multimedia applications like audio and video conferencing and multimedia information retrieval. Such applications require the network to provide a wide range of Quality of Service (QoS) guarantees (including minimum bandwidth, packet delay, delay jitter and loss). Whereas the minimum guaranteed bandwidth must be large enough to accommodate motion video of acceptable resolution, the end-to-end delay must be small enough for interactive communication. In order to avoid breaks in continuity of audio and video playback, delay jitter and loss must be sufficiently small. Techniques for determining an upper bound on end-to-end delay in a network is the subject matter of this paper.

The end-to-end delay of a packet depends on the source traffic characteristics and the scheduling algorithm at the network switches. In the recent past, several source specifications including Leaky Bucket [12], Exponentially Bounded Burstiness (EBB) [15], Flow Specification [10] and the Tenet model [5] have been studied. The scheduling algorithms that have been proposed include Stop and Go Queuing [6], Delay EDD [17], Jitter EDD [17], Hierarchical Round Robin [9], Rate Control Static Priority Queuing

---

*This research was supported in part by IBM Graduate Fellowship, the National Science Foundation (Research Initiation Award CCR-9409666), National Science Foundation Grant No. NCR-9004464, NASA, Mitsubishi Electric Research Laboratories (MERL), and Sun Microsystems Inc.

[16], Self Clocked Fair Queuing (SCFQ) [7], Virtual Clock [18] and Packet-by-Packet Generalized Processor Sharing (PGPS) [12]. The problem of determining an upper bound on end-to-end delay has also received considerable attention [2, 3, 10, 12, 15]. However, most of the techniques determine end-to-end delay by considering a specific source traffic specification and scheduling algorithm. In an integrated network supporting audio, video and data services, the sources have widely varying characteristics. Moreover, in a wide area networking environment, each switch may employ a different scheduling algorithm. Methods for determining end-to-end delay of packets in such heterogeneous environments have not received much attention.

In this paper, we take a step towards addressing the above limitation by (1) defining a class of *Guaranteed Rate (GR)* scheduling algorithms, and (2) developing a method for determining an upper bound on end-to-end delays for a network of switches each of which employs a scheduling algorithm in the GR class. We demonstrate that many of the scheduling algorithms proposed in the literature (e.g. Virtual Clock, PGPS and SCFQ) belong to the class of GR scheduling algorithms. We also show that the method for determining an upper bound on end-to-end delay is general and can be used to determine delay bounds for various source traffic specifications. We employ the method to derive a deterministic end-to-end delay bound for Leaky Bucket sources (a deterministic source characterization) and an upper bound on the tail distribution of the delay for EBB sources (a stochastic characterization). The end-to-end delay bounds that we derive are parameterized by the scheduling algorithm used at each switch and can be instantiated to derive delay bounds for a specific scheduling algorithm or a combination of scheduling algorithms.

The rest of the paper is organized as follows. In Section 2, we define the class of GR scheduling algorithms. In section 3, we present a method for determining end-to-end delay bounds and finally, Section 4 summarizes our results.

2 Guaranteed Rate Scheduling Algorithms

Each unit of data transmission at the network level is a packet. We refer to the sequence of packets transmitted by a source as a *flow* [18]. Each packet within a flow is serviced by a sequence of servers (switching elements) along the path from the source to the destination in the network. To provide guaranteed performance, the servers reserve a rate for a flow and employ a rate-based scheduling algorithm. Based on this rate reservation, many scheduling algorithms can guarantee a deadline by which a packet of a flow will be transmitted. This guarantee is referred to as *delay guarantee*. We refer to the class of rate based scheduling algorithms which provide such guarantees as *Guaranteed Rate (GR)* scheduling algorithms.

The delay guarantees provided by these algorithms are based on the *guaranteed rate clock*[1] values (intuitively, expected arrival time values) associated with each packet. To define the guaranteed rate clock values, consider a flow f that is associated with

---

[1] The concept of guaranteed rate clock is the same as the concept of virtual clock in [18]. We coin a new term for the virtual clock concept to avoid any confusion between the general concept of virtual clock and as it relates to the Virtual Clock scheduling algorithm.

a rate r_f (in bits/sec). Let p_f^j and l_f^j denote the jth packet of flow f and its length, respectively. Additionally, let $GRC^i(p_f^j)$ and $A^i(p_f^j)$ denote the guaranteed rate clock value and arrival time of packet p_f^j at server i, respectively. Then, guaranteed rate clock value for a packet is given by:

$$GRC^i(p_f^0) = 0 \qquad (1)$$

$$GRC^i(p_f^j) = \max\{A^i(p_f^j), GRC^i(p_f^{j-1})\} + \frac{l_f^j}{r_f} \quad j \geq 1 \qquad (2)$$

We use the guaranteed rate clock value of a packet to define the class of GR scheduling algorithms as follows.

Definition 1 *A scheduling algorithm at server i belongs to class GR for flow f if it guarantees that packet p_f^j will be transmitted by $GRC^i(p_f^j) + \beta^i$ where β^i is a constant which depends on the scheduling algorithm and the server.*

The concept of delay guarantee to a packet based on its expected arrival time was introduced in [10, 14]. As is evident from the definition (also observed in [10]), a key property of the class of GR scheduling algorithms is that they provide a delay guarantee for a source independent of the behavior of other sources in the network, and hence isolate the sources. Isolation of sources has been considered to be a very desirable property of scheduling algorithms, especially in large heterogeneous networks where sources may be malicious [1, 4, 10, 13]. This property is the basis for development of a conceptually simple method for determining end-to-end delay bounds in section 3.

In the next few subsections we demonstrate that the GR class includes Virtual Clock, PGPS and SCFQ with certain rate assignments.

2.1 Virtual Clock

The Virtual Clock scheduling algorithm assigns each packet a virtual clock value on its arrival and orders the transmission of packets by increasing virtual clock values. If flow f is assigned rate r_f at server i, then the virtual clock value for packet p_f^j of flow f at server i, denoted by $VC^i(p_f^j)$, is computed as follows [18]:

$$VC^i(p_f^0) = 0 \qquad (3)$$

$$VC^i(p_f^j) = \max\{A^i(p_f^j), VC^i(p_f^{j-1})\} + \frac{l_f^j}{r_f} \quad j \geq 1 \qquad (4)$$

The following delay guarantee was presented in [14]. Define a flow to be active at time t if $VC^i(p_f^j) \geq t$ where p_f^j is the last packet of flow f that has arrived before time t. Let $a^i(t)$ denote the set of active flows at server i at time t. Server i with capacity C^i is defined to have exceeded its capacity at time t if $\sum_{n \in a^i(t)} r_n > C^i$. Let l_{max}^i be the maximum length of the packet served by server i and $L_{VC}^i(p_f^j)$ be the time at which the transmission of packet p_f^j is completed. Then, if a server's capacity has not been exceeded and flow f is assigned rate r_f,

$$L_{VC}^i(p_f^j) \leq VC^i(p_f^j) + \frac{l_{max}^i}{C^i} \qquad (5)$$

Since the equations for virtual clock and guaranteed rate clock are the same, it can be easily observed that if rate r_f is assigned to flow f, then the Virtual Clock scheduling algorithm belongs to GR for flow f with $\beta^i = \frac{l^i_{max}}{C^i}$.

2.2 Packet-by-Packet Generalized Processor Sharing

The Packet-by-Packet Generalized Processor Sharing scheduling algorithm is a practical realization of Generalized Processor Sharing(GPS) service discipline [12]. In fact, PGPS simulates GPS such that

$$L^i_{PGPS}(p^j_f) \le L^i_{GPS}(p^j_f) + \frac{l^i_{max}}{C^i} \tag{6}$$

where $L^i_{PGPS}(p^j_f)$ and $L^i_{GPS}(p^j_f)$ are the times at which packet p^j_f leaves server i employing the PGPS scheduling algorithm and the GPS service discipline, respectively, and l^i_{max} is the maximum length of the packet served by server i [12]. Hence, to show that PGPS belongs to the class of GR scheduling algorithms, we establish a relationship between $L^i_{GPS}(p^j_f)$ and $GRC^i(p^j_f)$.

In GPS, each flow f is associated with a constant ϕ^i_f at server i. GPS is defined such that if flow f is backloged at time t, it receives service at the rate of $\frac{\phi^i_f C^i}{\sum_{k \in b^i(t)} \phi^i_k}$ where C^i is the capacity of the server and $b^i(t)$ is the set of backlogged flows at GPS server i at time t. Thus, a GPS server is defined to have assigned rate r_f to flow f if $\frac{\phi^i_f C^i}{\sum_{k \in b^i(t)} \phi^i_k} \ge r_f$ whenever flow f is backlogged. Hence, if flow f has been assigned rate r_f, then

$$L^i_{GPS}(p^j_f) \le \max\{A^i(p^j_f), L^i_{GPS}(p^{j-1}_f)\} + \frac{l^j_f}{r_f} \quad j \ge 1 \tag{7}$$

Let $L^i_{GPS}(p^0_f) = GRC^i(p^0_f) = 0$. From (7) and (2), it can be easily shown that

$$L^i_{GPS}(p^j_f) \le GRC^i(p^j_f) \quad j \ge 1 \tag{8}$$

From (8) and (6), we get

$$L^i_{PGPS}(p^j_f) \le GRC^i(p^j_f) + \frac{l^i_{max}}{C^i} \quad j \ge 1 \tag{9}$$

Hence if rate r_f is assigned to flow f at server i, then the PGPS scheduling algorithm belongs to GR for flow f with $\beta^i = \frac{l^i_{max}}{C^i}$.

2.3 Self Clocked Fair Queuing

The Self Clocked Fair Queuing scheme, proposed in [7], was designed to facilitate the implementation of a fair queuing scheme in broadband networks. The scheme is defined as follows.

1. On arrival, a packet p_f^j is stamped with service tag $F^i(p_f^j)$, computed as:

$$F^i(p_f^0) = 0 \tag{10}$$

$$F^i(p_f^j) = \max\{F^i(p_f^{j-1}), v^i(A^i(p_f^j))\} + \frac{l_f^j}{\phi_f^i} \quad j \geq 1 \tag{11}$$

where ϕ_f^i is a constant associated with flow f at server i.

2. The server virtual time at time t, $v^i(t)$, is defined to be equal to the service tag of the packet being service at time t. $v^i(t) = t$ when the server is idle.

3. Packets are serviced in increasing order of their service tags.

The following theorem proves that SCFQ algorithm also belongs to the class of GR scheduling algorithms. Let c^i be the set of flows serviced by server i employing SCFQ scheduling algorithm.

Theorem 1 *If $\sum_{m \in c^i} r_m \leq C^i$ and $\forall m \in c^i : \phi_m^i = r_m$, then the departure time of packet p_f^j in SCFQ (denoted by $L_{SCFQ}^i(p_f^j)$) is given by*

$$L_{SCFQ}^i(p_f^j) \leq GRC^i(p_f^j) + \sum_{m \in c^i \wedge m \neq f} \frac{l_m^{max}}{C^i} \tag{12}$$

where l_m^{max} is the maximum length for packets in flow m.

Proof: The proof has been omitted due to space constraints, and is presented in [8]. ∎

Hence, if $\sum_{m \in c^i} r_m \leq C^i$ and $\forall m \in c^i : \phi_m^i = r_m$, then SCFQ scheduling algorithm belongs to GR for flow f with $\beta^i = \sum_{m \in c^i \wedge m \neq f} \frac{l_m^{max}}{C^i}$. Note also that theorem 1 provides a tight bound over all rate assignments. An arrival sequence in which the upper bound is realized can be constructed from the proof steps.

3 Determining End-to-End Delay Bounds

3.1 Method

A simple method for determining a bound on end-to-end packet delays is to consider each server in isolation, and compute the summation of the maximum delay at each server along the path from the source to the destination [2, 3]. Though this may be the only feasible approach for many scheduling algorithms, it has the following drawbacks:

- Due to the variability in the delay experienced by packets at a server, the shape of the traffic gets distorted as it traverses through the network. Therefore, even if a source traffic specification is known at the first server on the path of the flow, it is difficult to determine the specification at a server further down on the path. This makes determining the delay at each of the server difficult.

- In many service disciplines, if a packet experiences a high delay at a server, it may experience a lower delay at the next server along the path. If each server is considered in isolation, the dependence between the delay experienced by packets at different servers is not accounted for, and hence the bound on the delay may be very conservative.

In this section, we address these limitations by presenting a method for determining end-to-end delay bound by analyzing the path as a whole. If the scheduling algorithm at each of the server on the path of the flow belongs to GR, then the delay guarantee of the algorithm can be exploited to determine end-to-end delay bound. This was illustrated in [10] for the Virtual Clock scheduling algorithm in Burst Scheduling networks for a particular source specification. Our key insight is that by deriving a delay guarantee for a network of servers, the problem of determining end-to-end delay can be reduced to the problem of determining delay at a single server.

Let K be the total number of servers along the path of a flow, and let the ith server on the path be denoted by i. Also, let server 0 be the source and server $K + 1$ be the destination. Since server K guarantees that packet p_f^j will be transmitted by $GRC^K(p_f^j) + \beta^K$ and the packet arrives at the first server at time $A^1(p_f^j)$, the end-to-end delay of p_f^j is given by

$$d_f^j \leq GRC^K(p_f^j) + \alpha^K - A^1(p_f^j) \tag{13}$$

where $\alpha^K = \beta^K + \tau^{K,K+1}$ and $\tau^{K,K+1}$ is the propagation delay between server K and the destination.

Observe that $GRC^K(p_f^j)$ depends on $A^K(p_f^j)$, which in turn depends on $GRC^{K-1}(p_f^j)$. Applying this argument recursively $GRC^K(p_f^j)$ can be related to $GRC^1(p_f^j)$. Since $GRC^1(p_f^j)$ is completely determined by the arrival characteristics of the source and the rate associated with the flow, the end-to-end delay can be determined if source specification is known. In what follows, we first relate $GRC^{i+1}(p_f^j)$ to $GRC^i(p_f^j)$ and then relate the end-to-end delay to $GRC^1(p_f^j)$.

Lemma 1 *If the scheduling algorithm at server i belongs to GR for flow f, then*

$$GRC^{i+1}(p_f^j) \leq GRC^i(p_f^j) + \max_{k \in [1..j]} \frac{l_f^k}{r_f} + \alpha^i \quad j \geq 1 \tag{14}$$

where $\alpha^i = \beta^i + \tau^{i,i+1}$ and $\tau^{i,i+1}$ is the propagation delay between servers i and $i + 1$.

Proof: The proof is by induction on j.
Base Case: $j = 1$

$$GRC^{i+1}(p_f^1) = A^{i+1}(p_f^1) + \frac{l_f^1}{r_f} \tag{15}$$

Since scheduling algorithm at server i belongs to GR for flow f, $A^{i+1}(p_f^1) \leq GRC^i(p_f^1) + \alpha^i$. Hence

$$GRC^{i+1}(p_f^1) \leq GRC^i(p_f^1) + \frac{l_f^1}{r_f} + \alpha^i \tag{16}$$

$$\leq \quad GRC^i(p_f^1) + \max_{k \in [1..1]} \frac{l_f^k}{r_f} + \alpha^i \tag{17}$$

Therefore (14) holds for $j = 1$

Induction Hypothesis: Assume (14) holds for $1 \leq j \leq m$.
Induction: We need to show (14) holds for $1 \leq j \leq m+1$.

$$GRC^{i+1}(p_f^{m+1}) = max\{A^{i+1}(p_f^{m+1}), GRC^{i+1}(p_f^m)\} + \frac{l_f^{m+1}}{r_f} \tag{18}$$

Since scheduling algorithm at server i belongs to GR for flow f, $A^{i+1}(p_f^{m+1}) \leq GRC^i(p_f^{m+1}) + \alpha^i$. Hence

$$GRC^{i+1}(p_f^{m+1}) \leq max\{GRC^i(p_f^{m+1}) + \alpha^i, GRC^{i+1}(p_f^m)\} + \frac{l_f^{m+1}}{r_f} \tag{19}$$

Thus, there are two cases to consider:

1. If $GRC^i(p_f^{m+1}) + \alpha^i > GRC^{i+1}(p_f^m)$, then from (19) we get

$$GRC^{i+1}(p_f^{m+1}) \leq GRC^i(p_f^{m+1}) + \frac{l_f^{m+1}}{r_f} + \alpha^i \tag{20}$$

Since $\max_{k \in [1..m+1]} \frac{l_f^k}{r_f} \geq \frac{l_f^{m+1}}{r_f}$,

$$GRC^{i+1}(p_f^{m+1}) \leq GRC^i(p_f^{m+1}) + \max_{k \in [1..m+1]} \frac{l_f^k}{r_f} + \alpha^i \tag{21}$$

2. If $GRC^i(p_f^{m+1}) + \alpha^i \leq GRC^{i+1}(p_f^m)$, then from (19) we get

$$GRC^{i+1}(p_f^{m+1}) \leq GRC^{i+1}(p_f^m) + \frac{l_f^{m+1}}{r_f} \tag{22}$$

Using induction hypothesis we get,

$$GRC^{i+1}(p_f^{m+1}) \leq GRC^i(p_f^m) + \max_{k \in [1..m]} \frac{l_f^k}{r_f} + \frac{l_f^{m+1}}{r_f} + \alpha^i \tag{23}$$

Since $GRC^i(p_f^{m+1}) \geq GRC^i(p_f^m) + \frac{l_f^{m+1}}{r_f}$ and $\max_{k \in [1..m+1]} \frac{l_f^k}{r_f} \geq \frac{l_f^{m+1}}{r_f}$,

$$GRC^{i+1}(p_f^{m+1}) \leq GRC^i(p_f^{m+1}) + \max_{k \in [1..m+1]} \frac{l_f^k}{r_f} + \alpha^i \tag{24}$$

From (21), (24) and the induction hypothesis, we conclude that (14) holds for $1 \leq j \leq m+1$. Hence the lemma follows. ∎

Theorem 2 *If the scheduling algorithm at each of the servers on the path of a flow belongs to GR for flow f, then the end-to-end delay of packet p_f^j denoted by d_f^j is given by*

$$d_f^j \leq GRC^1(p_f^j) - A^1(p_f^j) + (K-1) \max_{n \in [1..j]} \frac{l_f^n}{r_f} + \sum_{n=1}^{n=K} \alpha^n \tag{25}$$

where $\alpha^n = \beta^n + \tau^{n,n+1}$ and K is the number of servers on the path of the flow.

Proof: Since server K guarantees that packet p_f^j will be transmitted by time $GRC^K(p_f^j) + \beta^K$ and the packet arrives at the first node at time $A^1(p_f^j)$,

$$d_f^j \leq GRC^K(p_f^j) + \alpha^K - A^1(p_f^j) \tag{26}$$

Since the scheduling algorithm at each server on the path of the flow belongs to GR, by repeated application of lemma 1, we conclude that:

$$GRC^K(p_f^j) \leq GRC^1(p_f^j) + (K-1) \max_{n \in [1..j]} \frac{l_f^n}{r_f} + \sum_{n=1}^{n=K-1} \alpha^n \tag{27}$$

The theorem follows from (26) and (27). ∎

Notice that $\alpha^n = \beta^n + \tau^{n,n+1}$. Hence, it is completely characterized by the scheduling algorithm and the propagation delay in the network. The remaining terms in (25) depend on the source traffic specifications, and are evaluated in the next section.

3.2 Source Traffic Specifications

A source traffic is specified by characterizing the number of bits that arrive at the network over an interval of time. Let $AP_f^j(t_1, t_2)$ be a function that denotes the flow f bits that arrive in the interval $[t_1, t_2]$ at server i. The bits of a packet are considered to have arrived only after the arrival of the last bit of the packet. Hence, the arrival function consists of an impulse at each packet arrival instants and is right continuous. Also $AP_f^i(t, t)$ is the length of the packet that arrives at time instant t.

As may be evident from theorem 2, to determine an upper bound on end-to-end packet delays, we must relate the guaranteed rate clock value of a packet to its arrival time at the first server. To achieve this objective, we define set S_f^i for flow f at server i as follows:

$$S_f^i = \{n | n > 0 \wedge GRC^i(p_f^{n-1}) \leq A^i(p_f^n)\}$$

From the definitions of guaranteed rate clock and set S_f^i, it can be shown that for each packet p_f^j

$$GRC^i(p_f^j) = A^i(p_f^k) + \sum_{n=0}^{n=j-k} \frac{l_f^{k+n}}{r_f} \tag{28}$$

where $k \leq j$ is the largest integer belonging to set S_f^i. Since $\sum_{n=0}^{n=j-k} l_f^{k+n} = AP_f^i(A^i(p_f^k), A^i(p_f^j))$, we get

$$GRC^i(p_f^j) = A^i(p_f^k) + \frac{AP_f^i(A^i(p_f^k), A^i(p_f^j))}{r_f} \tag{29}$$

Using theorem 2 and (29), we will now determine deterministic end-to-end delay bound for Leaky Bucket sources (a deterministic source characterization) and upper bound on the tail distribution of the delay for EBB sources (a stochastic characterization).

3.2.1 Leaky Bucket

A flow f conforms to Leaky Bucket [12] with parameters (σ_f, r_f) if

$$AP_f(t_1, t_2) \leq \sigma_f + r_f(t_2 - t_1) \quad t_1 \leq t_2, \quad t_1 \geq 0 \tag{30}$$

Theorem 3 *If flow f conforms to a Leaky Bucket with parameters (σ_f, r_f) and the scheduling algorithm at each of the server on the path of a flow belongs to GR for the flow, then the end-to-end delay of packet p_f^j denoted by d_f^j is given by*

$$d_f^j \leq \frac{\sigma_f + (K-1) \max_{n \in [1..j]} l_f^n}{r_f} + \sum_{n=1}^{n=K} \alpha^n \tag{31}$$

where $\alpha^n = \beta^n + \tau^{n,n+1}$ and K is the number of servers on the path of the flow.

Proof: Let $k \leq j$ be largest integer belonging to set S_f^1. Clearly, such a k must exist. Since flow f conforms to Leaky Bucket specification, we get

$$AP_f^1(A^1(p_f^k), A^1(p_f^j)) \leq \sigma_f + r_f(A^1(p_f^j) - A^1(p_f^k)) \tag{32}$$

Hence, from (29) we get,

$$GRC^1(p_f^j) \leq \frac{\sigma_f}{r_f} + A^1(p_f^j) \tag{33}$$

which implies

$$GRC^1(p_f^j) - A^1(p_f^j) \leq \frac{\sigma_f}{r_f} \tag{34}$$

Theorem 3 follows from (34) and theorem 2. ∎

We note that the if the scheduling algorithm used at each of the servers is either of Virtual Clock and PGPS , then bound in (31) is tighter than the bound in [11, 12] for Rate Proportional Processor Sharing (RPPS) rate assignment of PGPS networks when the sources conform to Leaky Bucket.

3.2.2 Exponentially Bounded Burstiness

A flow f conforms to an Exponentially Bounded Burstiness (EBB) [15] process with parameters $(r_f, \Lambda_f, \gamma_f)$, if

$$Pr\left(AP_f^i(t_1, t_2) \geq r_f(t_2 - t_1) + x\right) \leq \Lambda_f e^{-\gamma_f x} \quad x \geq 0 \ t_1 \leq t_2 \tag{35}$$

Theorem 4 *If flow f conforms to EBB with parameters $(r_f, \Lambda_f, \gamma_f)$ and the scheduling algorithm at each of the server on the path of a flow belong to GR for the flow , then the end-to-end delay of packet p_f^j denoted by d_f^j is given by*

$$Pr\left(d_f^j \geq x + (K-1)\frac{\max_{n \in [1..j]} l_f^n}{r^j} + \sum_{n=1}^{n=K} \alpha^n\right) \leq \Lambda_f e^{-\gamma_f x r_f} \quad x \geq 0 \tag{36}$$

where $\alpha^n = \beta^n + \tau^{n,n+1}$ and K is the number of servers on the path of the flow.

Proof: Let $k \leq j$ be the largest integer belonging to set S_f^1. Clearly such a k must exist. By the definition of EBB process, we have

$$Pr\left(AP_f^1(A^1(p_f^k), A^1(p_f^j)) \geq r_f(A^1(p_f^j) - A^1(p_f^k)) + y\right) \leq \Lambda_f e^{-\gamma_f y} \quad y \geq 0 \quad (37)$$

which implies

$$Pr\left(\frac{AP_f^1(A(p_f^k), A^1(p_f^j))}{r_f} + A^1(p_f^k) - A^1(p_f^j)\frac{y}{r_f}\right) \leq \Lambda_f e^{-\gamma_f y} \quad y \geq 0 \quad (38)$$

From (29 we have

$$Pr\left(GRC^1(p_f^j) - A^1(p_f^j) \geq \frac{y}{r_f}\right) \leq \Lambda_f e^{-\gamma_f y} \quad y \geq 0 \quad (39)$$

The theorem follows from (39) and theorem 2. ∎

3.3 Discussion

Theorem 2 demonstrates that a heterogeneous network of servers, each of which employs a scheduling algorithm in the GR class, can provide an upper bound on end-to-end packet delays for heterogeneous sources. Additionally, the salient features of the class of GR scheduling algorithms and the method for determining end-to-end delay bounds include:

- An end-to-end delay bound can be determined for any source traffic specification for which a bound on difference between the guaranteed rate clock and the arrival time of a packet at the first server can be determined. Since this difference is only a function of the source traffic characteristics and the rate associated with the flow, it is simple to determine an end-to-end delay bound. Moreover, this difference can be interpreted as delay experienced by a packet at a single queue server with capacity r_f. Hence, queuing analysis can also be used to determine a bound on the tail distribution of delays experienced by packets for a conventional stochastic process characterization.

- A source can determine end-to-end delays without specifying the shape of the traffic to the network by keeping track of guaranteed rate clock values associated with it's flow at the first server. Such a capability is important as the source may not have a good characterization of the traffic or the characterization may not be known a priori. Moreover, even if the characterization is known, it may not conform to the set of characterizations supported by the network. Finally, this capability allows the source to decide when to renegotiate the reserved rate.

The method derives it's simplicity from the constraint placed on the rate assignments in the scheduling algorithms. Note that the constraint we have placed on rate assignments for PGPS so that it belongs to GR is similar to Rate Proportional Processor Sharing (RPPS) [12]. Such constraints allow each flow to be considered in isolation and hence facilitate the determination of delay bounds for each flow independently. If this constraint is relaxed to derive delay bounds for more general rate assignments, assumptions about the behavior of the other sources in the network may have to be made. In such scenarios, however, the QoS guarantees provided to each flow may be conditional since sources may be greedy and not conform to the specifications [13]. Moreover, if hardware traffic enforcement mechanisms are used, the probability of failure of one of the numerous pieces of enforcement hardware may not be negligible, thereby weakening the guarantees. Hence, we believe that the constraints on rate assignments described above are not a limitation, but in fact are highly desirable.

4 Conclusions

In this paper, we have defined a class of Guaranteed Rate scheduling algorithms. The GR class includes Virtual Clock, Self Clocked Fair Queuing and Packet-by-Packet Generalized Processor Sharing. For networks that employ scheduling algorithms belonging to GR, we have presented a method for determining an upper bound on end-to-end packet delays. The method facilitates determining end-to-end delay for a variety of sources. We have illustrated the method by determining end-to-end delay for sources conforming to Leaky Bucket and Exponentially Bounded Burstiness. The delay bounds that we have derived are parameterized by the scheduling algorithms which when instantiated with Virtual Clock and SCFQ scheduling algorithms, lead to many new results.

REFERENCES

[1] D.D. Clark, S. Shenker, and L. Zhang. Supporting Real-Time Applications in an Integrated Services Packet Network. In *Proceedings of ACM SIGCOMM*, pages 14–26, August 1992.

[2] R.L. Cruz. A Calculus for Network Delay, Part I : Network Elements in Isolation. *IEEE Transactions on Information Theory*, 37:114–131, Jan 1991.

[3] R.L. Cruz. A Calculus for Network Delay, Part II : Network Analysis. *IEEE Transactions on Information Theory*, 37:132–141, Jan 1991.

[4] A. Demers, S. Keshav, and S. Shenker. Analysis and Simulation of a Fair Queueing Algorithm. In *Proceedings of ACM SIGCOMM*, pages 1–12, September 1989.

[5] D. Ferrari and D. C. Verma. A Scheme for Real-Time Channel Establishment in Wide-Area Networks. *IEEE Journal on Selected Areas in Communications*, 8(3):368–379, April 1990.

[6] S.J. Golestani. A Framing Strategy for Congestion Management. *IEEE Journal on Selected Areas in Communications*, pages 1064–1077, September 1991.

[7] S.J. Golestani. A Self-Clocked Fair Queueing Scheme for High Speed Applications. In *Proceedings of INFOCOM*, 1994.

[8] P. Goyal, S.S. Lam, and H.M. Vin. Determining End-to-End Delay Bounds in Heterogeneous Networks. Technical report, Department of Computer Sciences, University of Texas at Austin, (available by anonymous ftp from ftp.cs.utexas.edu in directory pub/multimedia), March 1995.

[9] C.R. Kalmanek, H. Kanakia, and S. Keshav. Rate Controlled Servers for Very High-Speed Networks. In *Proceedings of IEEE GLOBECOM'90, San Diego, CA*, pages 300.3.1–300.3.9, December 1990.

[10] S.S. Lam and G.G. Xie. Burst Scheduling: Architecture and Algorithm for Switching Packet Video. In *Proceedings of INFOCOM*, April 1995.

[11] A. K. Parekh and R. G. Gallager. A Generalized Processor Sharing Approach to Flow Control in Integrated Services Networks: The Multiple Node Case. *IEEE/ACM Transactions On Networking*, 2(2):137–150, April 1994.

[12] A.K. Parekh. *A Generalized Processor Sharing Approach to Flow Control in Integrated Services Networks*. PhD thesis, Department of Electrical Engineering and Computer Science, MIT, 1992.

[13] S. Shenker. Making Greed Work in Networks: A Game-Theoretic Analysis of Switch Service Disciplines. In *Proceedings of ACM SIGCOMM*, pages 47–57, 1994.

[14] G.G. Xie and S.S. Lam. Delay Guarantee of Virtual Clock Server. Technical Report TR-94-24, Dept. of Computer Sciences, UT-Austin, October 1994. Presented at 9th IEEE Workshop on Computer Communications, October 1994.

[15] O. Yaron and M. Sidi. Generalized Processor Sharing Networks with Exponentially Bounded Burstiness Arrivals. In *Proceedings of INFOCOM*, 1994.

[16] H. Zhang and D. Ferrari. Rate Controlled Static Priority Queueing. In *Proceedings of INFOCOM*, volume 2, pages 227–236, 1993.

[17] H. Zhang and S. Keshav. Comparison of Rate-Based Service Disciplines. In *Proceedings of ACM SIGCOMM*, pages 113–121, August 1991.

[18] L. Zhang. VirtualClock: A New Traffic Control Algorithm for Packet Switching Networks. In *Proceedings of ACM SIGCOMM*, pages 19–29, August 1990.

Adaptive QoS-Based API for ATM Networking

V. Bansal, R. J. Siracusa, J. P. Hearn, G. Ramamurthy and D. Raychaudhuri

NEC, USA, C&C Research Laboratories

4 Independence Way, Princeton, NJ 08540.

This paper describes work-in-progress on a new adaptive QoS-based application programming interface (API) for ATM networking. This ATM API, referred to as the "ATM Service Manager (ASM)" is motivated by the observation that current transport interfaces do not provide QoS features necessary for multimedia applications to achieve desired performance/cost objectives on multiservice ATM networks. In general, an application connected to ATM has a choice of transport protocols (e.g. TCP, UDP, alternative multimedia stream protocols), ATM service class (e.g. ABR, VBR, CBR) and QoS parameters for each media type. It is our view that application software should be shielded from the complexity of QoS-based service management by an adaptive API which is responsible for mapping the application requirements to ATM.

1 Design Objective for ATM Service Manager

Current transport network APIs do not provide mechanisms for the application to specify the QoS[1] that they can expect from the network. The ASM addresses this deficiency providing a new API and takes the responsibility of satisfying the applications QoS by using the following mechanisms:

Dynamic renegotiation of traffic and QoS parameters

The current notion that the negotiated QoS for a connection remains the same for the lifetime of the connection is not always valid for multimedia applications. Applications should be able to renegotiate QoS during the lifetime of the connection. Based on the quality perceived by the user, the application may want to change its QoS requirements, thus directly influencing the resources needed and the associated transmission cost. For example, in a video-on-demand application the user might want to change the quality (resolution) of the picture while the session is in progress.

Customized Transport Stack

The transport system architecture in this framework is a vertical process architecture [2], in which, a separate protocol stack is associated with each media belonging to a higher level connection. The advantage of this architecture is that, it takes into account the traffic characteristics and the QoS requirement of the connection. Each media has a separate customized transport stack based on its QoS requirements. For example audio streams have stringent real time requirements and do not require error control. Medical image retrieval applications on the other hand, require error free delivery even at the expense of some additional delay. Based on the knowledge of the media and its QoS requirement, the ASM determines the appropriate transport protocol options to be used for the media.

Characterization of Application Traffic Parameters

The network cannot provide guarantees on QoS without knowing the characteristics of the traffic it has to carry. On the other hand one cannot expect all applications to specify their traffic characteristics and the QoS requirement, since the application 1) may not know them in advance, 2) the characteristics may change during the life-time of the connection, 3) the applications may not be sophisticated enough to provide this information. Hence, system utilities are necessary that will monitor the traffic streams and determine their characteristics on a dynamic basis. The traffic characteristics are determined by making appropriate measurements on the traffic stream and mapping them into suitable stochastic or deterministic parameters.

Map application parameters to network parameters and vice versa

The set of higher level traffic and quality of service parameters specified by the application have to be mapped into a set of lower level network related parameters that the underlying network can interpret[3]. This feature provides a separation between the application and the network, and allows the application to specify these parameters in a language [4] that is most convenient and natural to the application. The QoS parameters specified at the application layer are used by the transport system to:

1) Map the parameters into a set of bounds on the delay and error the network can introduce. These parameters will be specified at connection setup time.

2) Take corrective actions during the protocol execution, to maintain the connection at an acceptable level of quality.

3) Inform the application (upper layer) in case of QoS degradation so that the application can take appropriate action.

Respond to network congestion notification signals

A control path between the ASMs and the signaling module allows dynamic QoS control, connection setup and modification, and exchange of network congestion messages. When congestion occurs in the network the signaling module receives congestion notification signals from the network which, after processing by the signalling module are forwarded to the ASMs. The ASM is programmed to take a variety of actions depending on the type of media it is serving. Actions taken by the ASM include renegotiation of bandwidth, traffic shaping, and even communication with the application to modify the generated traffic (e.g. change the quantization step in a video coder).

2 Prototype Implementation:

An outline of the structure of the ATM Service Manager software is shown in Fig. 1. The basic flow in this architecture is as follows: Higher layers (Media daemons and/or applications) request connection setup to the ATM Service Manager's *Connection Manager* using the new APIs in which they specify the proper traffic and QoS parameters. Once the connection is setup the ASM's *QOS Monitoring module* estimates the quality-of-service of the connection using the quality-of-service reports that it receives and also the connections long term statistics. This module also takes different action if it decides that the QoS for the connection is not been met. Also the *Traffic estimation module*, estimates the traffic characteristics of the connection by continuously monitoring the data stream as it flows through the data plane. The *Renegotiation module* is invoked by either the QoS Monitoring module or the Traffic estimation module if they decide to renegotiate resources for the connection with the network.

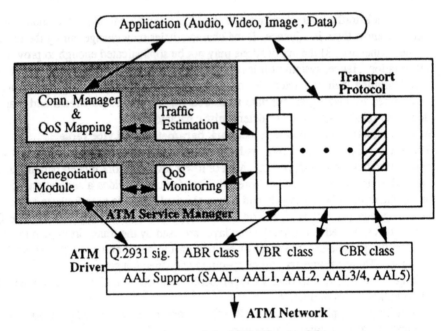

Fig. 1: Implementation model of ATM Service Manager

2.1 Connection Setup procedure

The connection setup procedure separates the control and data channel between the peers. The connection request from an application is intercepted by the connection management module of the ASM. It determines the traffic parameters and/or QoS parameters for the connection, and sets up an *ASM control* VC to the destination. Once the ASM Control VC is established, the source and the destination ASMs can communicate with each other and the application, and determine the actual traffic and QoS parameters (which either side of the connection might know). The ASMs can now determine the ATM service class and the type of AAL it must choose at the ATM layer, and the transport options that must be assembled at the transport layer. After the connection related QoS parameters and transport options are determined and mutually agreed upon by the two ASMs, the ASMs sets up the *data* VCs between the source and destination with the help of signalling module, assembles the required transport stack, on either end and then inform the application that it can commence transmission of data on that data VC. The ASM control VC between the corresponding ASMs is maintained throughout the life of the connection, thus enabling the applications and their respective ASMs to communicate with each other as and when the need arises.

2.2 QoS Monitoring

Monitoring the QoS of the connection is an important feature of this framework. The ASM provides QoS Monitoring by defining a QoS Report (QSR) packet that is exchanged between the two ASMs on either end of a connection. The VC Quality Monitoring mechanism measures packet data loss, packet delay and delay jitter. For example in a video server application where the ASM at the receiver end monitors the QoS on its inbound link, if the ASM detects any degradation in the QoS, it communicates this information through a QSR packet to the ASM at the server end. The ASM at the server end can now take appropriate action to restore the QoS on its outbound link. This could include, renegotiation for additional bandwidth, a change of class, or reduction in the resolution by switching to a lower bit rate. The VC Quality Monitoring process associated with the ASM sends QoS Reports periodically, as well as when there is a deviation of the QoS from a set threshold.

2.3 Transport options selection

Based on the QoS requirements of the application the ASM decides the transport options that must be configured for a connection. ASM decides which transport options are needed from the multimedia transport protocol (MTP) that we have implemented. Presently the transport options include:

Error Detection, Loss Recovery Mechanisms, Flow Control Mechanisms, Encryption, Segmentation and Reassembly and AALs.

There are also logical dependencies between different modules which would make pairing of different modules mandatory. Once the application's requirements are interpreted, the right set of transport modules for the connection can be configured. Below we list some transport options based on the condition of the link:

1. *Choose Error Detection*:
a) If the route to the destination is not reliable and bit errors can occur frequently.
b) If the route to the destination go over non-ATM links
2. *Choice of Loss Recovery Mechanisms*:
a) Choose Selective repeat is used if the cell loss/error rate of the VC is low.
b) Choose go-back-n is used if the error loss/error rate is high.
c) Choose loss detection only, if application wishes to do its own error recovery.
3. *Flow Control Mechanisms*: Use pacing or rate control at the packet level to prevent receiver over run.
4. *Encryption*: If application requires security features.
5. *Segmentation and Reassembly*: Use fixed length TPDUs if application requires the frame boundaries to be preserved. Normally fixed TPDUs are required when the application performs high level error recovery.
6. *ATM Adaptation Layer selection*:
a) If application requires CBR service and has delay stingent requirements use AAL1
b) If application requires VBR service and has delay stringent requirements use AAL2
c) else use AAL5 (AAL3/4 in cases where use of MID field is required)

References

[1] Andrew Campbell, Geoff Coulson and David Hutchison, " A Quality of Service Architecture", Computer Communication Review, April 1994.
[2] Douglas C. Schmidt and Tatsuya Suda. "Transport System Architecture Services for High-Performance Communication Systems", IEEE JSAC, May 1993.
[3] Nahrstedt, K. and J. Smith, "Revision of QoS Guarantees at the Application/ Network Interface", Technical Report, University of Pennsylvania, 1993.
[4] Patricia G.S Florissi and Yechiam Yemini , "QuAL:Quality Assurance Language", ITS'94.

Burst Scheduling Networks:
Flow Specification and Performance Guarantees[*]

Simon S. Lam and Geoffrey G. Xie

Department of Computer Sciences
The University of Texas at Austin
Austin, Texas 78712-1188

1 Introduction

We present a class of packet switching networks, called Burst Scheduling Networks, designed to provide throughput, delay, and delay jitter guarantees. These performance guarantees are derived from the delay guarantee of a VC server, and a new traffic model called Flow Specification [2, 3].

The delay guarantee of a VC server has several desirable properties, including the following *firewall* property: The guarantee to a flow is unaffected by the behavior of other flows sharing the same server. There is no assumption that sources are flow-controlled or well-behaved.

Each guaranteed flow is modeled as a sequence of bursts, each of which is a sequence of packets. Bursts are needed to specify two types of jitter bounds: over the delays of packets in a burst, and over the delays of bursts in a flow. For video flows, each encoded picture is naturally modeled by a burst. The model is also appropriate for audio and data flows that require delay and delay jitter guarantees.

With the new traffic model, a flow can be partitioned into intervals (bursts) that have substantially different average rates; the first packet of a burst carries information on the size and average rate of the burst. Switches are designed to process flows efficiently in bursts [2].

2 Delay guarantee and its properties

Consider a number of traffic sources and a service facility (a single server or a network). Each source generates a sequence of packets, called a *flow*. Prior to generating packets, the source of flow f requests for a reserved rate from the facility. Let $r(f)$ bits/second be the reserved rate allocated to flow f. For an arbitrary packet p, its length in bits is denoted by $l(p)$, its arrival time by $A(p)$, and its departure time by $L(p)$. The delay of packet p is $L(p) - A(p)$. The maximum packet size is l_{max}.

[*] Research sponsored in part by National Science Foundation grant no. NCR-9004464 and by the NSA INFOSEC University Research Program. Papers of the Networking Research Laboratory are available from http://www.cs.utexas.edu/users/lam/NRL.

Our concept of a delay guarantee is based upon the *virtual clock of a flow*. Let *priority(f)* denote the virtual clock of flow f. It can be implemented as a variable, which is zero initially and updated as follows [4] whenever a flow f packet, say p, arrives to the facility:

$$priority(f) := \max\{priority(f), A(p)\} + \frac{l(p)}{r(f)} \qquad (1)$$

The new value of *priority(f)* in (1) is assigned to packet p as its virtual clock value, denoted by $P(p)$. Note that the virtual clock values of flow f are determined by the sequence of packet arrival times of f, and are independent of the design of the service facility. For example, if the service facility is a single server, we have not yet specified its service discipline.

A *VC server* is a priority server that uses the virtual clock value of a packet as its priority. The service discipline is work-conserving and nonpreemptive. Let C denote the capacity, in bits/second, of a VC server. The following delay guarantee is presented in [2] and proved in [3].

Theorem 1. If the capacity of a VC server has not been exceeded for a nonzero duration since the start of a busy period, then the following holds for every packet p that has been served during the busy period:

$$L(p) \leq P(p) + \frac{l_{max}}{C} \qquad (2)$$

We next explain the condition of not exceeding the capacity of a VC server. At time t, a flow f is *active* iff the service facility (queue and server) is not empty and the flow's virtual clock is running faster than real time (i.e., $priority(f) > t$). The server capacity is not exceeded at time t iff $C \geq$ sum of the *reserved rates* of flows that are active at time t.

Note that the condition of not exceeding C can always be satisfied by the server because the allocation of reserved rates is under server control.

Source control not required. In proving Theorem 1, there is no assumption that sources are flow-controlled or well-behaved. While the source of a flow, say f, has a reserved rate of $r(f)$, the source can misbehave, i.e., generate traffic at a rate much larger than $r(f)$.[2] The delay guarantee in Theorem 1 holds even when sum of the *actual rates* of active flows is larger than C.

Conditional guarantee. Source control is not required because the delay guarantee is not a bound on $L(p) - A(p)$. A delay guarantee of the form, $L(p) \leq P(p) + \beta$ where β is a constant, is a conditional guarantee. Specifically, if a source is well-behaved, its packets incur a bounded delay. But if a source generates traffic much faster than its reserved rate, its packets may incur large delays.

Firewall property. The delay guarantee to packets in a flow is independent of the behavior of other traffic flows sharing the same server (obvious conclusion from (1)).

---

[2] It is assumed that each flow is allocated its own buffers, so that if a source misbehaves, it will fill up its own buffers but not those of other flows.

Role of source control. If a source is flow-controlled or known to be well-behaved such that for packet p in the flow, $P(p) - A(p)$ is bounded by a constant, then the delay guarantee becomes a delay bound. For example, $P(p) - A(p)$ is bounded if the source is leaky-bucket controlled.

3 New traffic model

In the balance of this paper, we consider networks with a fixed packet size (such as ATM networks). Consider a flow that requires performance guarantees from a network. Such a flow, which may be video, audio, or data, is called a guaranteed flow. Each guaranteed flow is assumed to satisfy the following Flow Specification when entering the network. For burst i in the flow, let n_i denote its size, in number of packets, and δ_i the maximum duration of its packet arrivals. The average rate of burst i is $\lambda_i = n_i/\delta_i$. (The actual rate is not constrained, e.g., all n_i packets can arrive at the same time.) The jth packet in burst i is denoted by (i,j) and its arrival time at a service facility is denoted by $A(i,j)$.

Flow Specification:

– Each flow is a sequence of bursts, each of which is a sequence of packets. The first packet of burst i carries information on λ_i and n_i.
– Packets in burst i satisfy a *jitter* timing constraint, namely: for $j = 1, 2, \ldots, n_i$,

$$0 \leq A(i,j) - A(i,1) \leq \frac{j-1}{\lambda_i} \tag{3}$$

– Bursts in the flow satisfy a *separation* timing constraint, namely: for $i \geq 1$,

$$A(i+1,1) - A(i,1) \geq \frac{n_i}{\lambda_i} \tag{4}$$

Adaptive rate allocation. In Burst Scheduling networks, the reserved rate allocated to a flow at a channel adapts to the average rate λ_i of burst i when its first packet arrives. The separation timing constraint in (4) ensures that each active flow contains at most one active burst (property used by the server to check that its capacity is not exceeded). (4) also ensures that Theorem 1 holds for a VC server that performs adaptive rate allocation.[3]

Efficiency. In Burst Scheduling networks, the virtual clock of a flow is updated very efficiently. Specifically, the algorithm in (1) is executed only for the first packet of a burst. When any other packet in the burst arrives, the virtual clock is updated by a single increment operation. Furthermore, only one virtual clock value is stored per flow. For a sorted priority queue implemented as a heap, updating a priority value incurs $O(\log N)$ worst-case time where N is the number of active flows (not the number of queued packets).

---

[3] With adaptive rate allocation, (4) is a sufficient condition which can be relaxed.

4 End-to-end delay bounds

Consider a sequence of nodes, indexed by $0, 1, 2, \ldots, K+1$, where node 0 denotes the source, node $K+1$ the destination, and the other nodes packet switches. The following end-to-end delay bounds provided to a guaranteed flow are based upon several assumptions, all of which can be relaxed [2]. Consider an arbitrary packet (i, j) of the flow. Let $D(i, j)$ denote its end-to-end delay, which is measured from the time the packet leaves node 0 to the time it arrives at node $K + 1$. Define

τ_s propagation time from node s to $s + 1$, in seconds, $s = 0, 1, \ldots, K$

γ_s channel capacity from node s to $s + 1$, in packets/second, $s = 1, 2, \ldots, K$

Theorem 2. The end-to-end delay of the first packet of burst i, for $i = 1, 2, \ldots$, has the following lower and upper bounds:

$$D(i, 1) \geq \frac{K - 1}{\lambda_i} + \sum_{s=1}^{K} \frac{1}{\gamma_s} + \sum_{s=0}^{K} \tau_s$$

$$D(i, 1) \leq \frac{1}{\lambda_i} + (K - 1) \max_{1 \leq h \leq i} \{\frac{1}{\lambda_h}\} + \sum_{s=1}^{K} \frac{1}{\gamma_s} + \sum_{s=0}^{K} \tau_s \qquad (5)$$

A proof of Theorem 2 can be found in [2]. Because the jitter timing constraint in (3) is preserved by every switch [2], the delay D_i of burst i is bounded as follows

$$D_i \leq D(i, 1) + \frac{n_i}{\lambda_i} = D(i, 1) + \delta_i \qquad (6)$$

Concluding remarks. (i) The concept of delay guarantee to a packet based upon its virtual clock value was proposed in [2, 3] and recently extended to an end-to-end path [1]. (ii) VC servers and PGPS servers provide the same end-to-end delay bound [1]. But computing virtual clock values is substantially more efficient than computing virtual-time finishing times for PGPS. (iii) With the firewall property, the impact of a source-controller malfunction is limited. This is a significant advantage not found in FIFO and static-priority service disciplines.

References

1. Pawan Goyal, Simon S. Lam, and Harrick M. Vin. Determining end-to-end delay bounds in heterogeneous networks. In *Proceedings NOSSDAV*, April 1995.
2. Simon S. Lam and Geoffrey G. Xie. Burst Scheduling: architecture and algorithm for switching packet video. Technical Report TR-94-20, July 1994. An abbreviated version in *Proceedings INFOCOM '95*, April 1995.
3. Geoffrey G. Xie and Simon S. Lam. Delay guarantee of Virtual Clock server. Technical Report TR-94-24, October 1994. Presented at 9th IEEE Workshop on Computer Communications, October 1994.
4. Lixia Zhang. VirtualClock: A new traffic control algorithm for packet switching networks. In *Proceedings of ACM SIGCOMM '90*, pages 19–29, August 1990.

Session IX: Storage Architectures

Chair: Jonathan Walpole, Oregon Graduate Institute of Science and Technology

This session covered a range of issues in storage system design. Most of the papers and discussions focused on the problems of building high performance Video on Demand (VOD) systems, and consequently focused on large-scale network-based parallel storage systems. Optimal data placement and I/O request scheduling in this environment were the topic of several papers in the session.

The key research problems that came up in the session included the following:

- Constant frame-rate service does not necessarily translate to constant bit-rate retrieval (because of compression techniques such as MPEG). This characteristic greatly reduces the number of concurrent requests that can be guaranteed in a VOD system, and hence reduces commercial viability.
- Data layout and scheduling approaches that are optimized for normal playback are generally not appropriate for VOD systems that must support additional functionality such as interactive, variable-rate fast-forward.
- New compression approaches will support video playback at various quality levels (such as reduced spatial resolution). Such approaches add a new dimension to the problem of admission testing and scheduling in VOD servers. Similarly, VOD servers may support varying degrees of interactivity QOS.
- Should a storage service be generic across video data types or specific to a data type such as MPEG or JPEG data? In a generic server how should the information necessary to support variable rate fast forward and rewind on different data types be stored? For example, to support fast forward in an MPEG stream, how would the server know where the I frames are? Are external index files a satisfactory solution? Can fast forward and rewind streams be stored separately from the normal playback streams?

At the end of the panel discussion, the question of how to compare various proposals for VOD servers arose. Should we compare them purely on performance, on the maximum number of concurrent streams they can support, on the range of QOS options they support, or on their functionality (such as their degree of interactivity)? It was suggested that so long as minimal VCR functionality is supported, then the only true metric is "dollars per stream." However, for some specialized applications the panel agreed that functionality can be more important that cost per stream.

A Novel Video-On-Demand Storage Architecture for Supporting Constant Frame Rate with Variable Bit Rate Retrieval

S.W. Lau
swlau@cs.cuhk.hk

John C.S. Lui*
cslui@cs.cuhk.hk

Department of Computer Science, The Chinese University of Hong Kong

Abstract. One of the quality of service (QOS) factors in video-on-demand (VOD) applications is to provide high resolution quality to end users. One way to achieve this is to provide a constant display frame rate (e.g., 30 frames/sec) at the display station. However, due to the nature of video files and compression technique applied, video frame sizes vary significantly from frame to frame. Therefore, although the display frame rate is fixed, data retrieval is a variable bit rate process. Conventional VOD storage servers assume a peak rate retrieval of video files. Therefore, the number of concurrent requests to the VOD server cannot be maximized. In this paper, we consider a VOD storage server which can support a fixed frame rate at the display and at the same time, variable bit rates retrieval of compressed video files. We describe 1) video files layout strategy, 2) request scheduling algorithm, 3) buffering issues and, 4) various VCR features support such that the number of concurrent requests can be maximized.

1 Introduction

With recent advances in networking technologies and vast improvement of storage systems, it is now feasible to provide multimedia services such as multimedia mail, news distribution, computer animation advertisement, library information system and home entertainment to users via high bandwidth network. Due to this reason, research in multimedia storage systems has received a lot of attention in the past few years.

Usually video object, by itself, has large storage and large bandwidth requirement. For example, a 100 minutes HDTV video object requires an average of 800 megabits per second (Mbps) bandwidth and around 60 Gbytes of storage [1]. Typically, compression (e.g, MPEG) is used to reduce the storage as well as the network bandwidth requirement so that video object can be delivered to end users. However, it is important to observe that the frame size (bits) varies significantly from frame to frame. This is due to:

- Variations of information content among frames. For example, if there is a sudden change of scene in the video file, then the size of a group of frames from one scene may be much larger than the size of group of frames in another scene.
- Nature of the compression algorithm. For example, MPEG compression files have three types of frames, namely, I-frame, P-frame, and B-frame. I-frames are coded independent of any other frames. On the other hand, B-frames are coded by interpolating between previous and a future I or P-frame. Therefore, the I-frames might have size which is 100 to 200 times the size of the B-frame[6].

* This work was supported in part by the Croucher Foundation Research Grant and the CUHK Direct Grant.

Most recent research works [12, 11, 1, 10] concentrated on the study of multimedia storage systems which support the retrieval of a multimedia object at a *peak* display bandwidth (bits/sec); for example, assuming that the display bandwidth of object is fixed at $B_{display}$ Mbps throughout the duration of the display, the storage server retrieves object using $B_{display}$ Mbps disk I/O bandwidth. This approach may be applicable for low-quality video files, for example, if the frame size of these video objects is not highly variable, or if users do not require a high quality video display at their viewing stations.

However, designing a multimedia storage server using a peak display bandwidth assumption has the following drawbacks:

- It is often desirable to provide users with high speed browsing functions such as *fast forward* or *fast rewind* with viewing. To support these type of functions, the retrieve rate may be much higher than regular display bandwidth. If designers use the worst case bandwidth allocation[2], then storage I/O bandwidth is not efficiently utilized.
- For HDTV typed of video applications, there will be a high variability in the display bandwidth. For example, the MPEG-III for supporting HDTV has display bandwidth that can range from 5 to 20 Mbps [3]. Again, storage I/O bandwidth is not efficiently utilized if the peak bandwidth allocation policy is used.
- Using the worst case display bandwidth allocation as the disk I/O retrieval rate, it is possible to have *buffer build up problem*. For example, if buffer is allocated for *each* disk retrieval, since the object display bandwidth is less than the retrieval rate, the number of allocated buffer will build up, thereby demanding more buffer from the storage server. Since the total number of buffers in the storage server is finite, this implies that the number of concurrent requests that the system can support is reduced.

In this paper, our aim is to design a VOD storage server which can support a fixed frame rate at the display station and at the same time, variable bit rate retrieval in the storage subsystem. In this way, I/O bandwidth is efficiently utilized and therefore, the number of concurrent requests to the VOD storage server can be increased compared to traditional VOD architectures. Also, the VOD storage server is implemented on parallel disks such that load balancing can be achieved. We also illustrate 1) video files layout policy, 2) parallel disk scheduling policy for incoming request, 3) admission control policy and, 4) how to support VCR typed function such as fast forward with viewing.

It is interesting to point out that in [4], authors described different ways of reducing I/O demand for the VOD storage server. The class of techniques used is based on *dynamically merging* of requests to the same video object during their display periods such that system resources (e.g., disk I/O operations, buffers ... etc) can be reduced. The main idea is to dynamically adjust the frame rates of similar requests so that there is possibility to merge two or more requests into one system request. It is important to point out that the VOD storage server we describe in this paper can support this interesting I/O reduction techniques with zero storage overhead. For more information about dynamic merging techniques, please refer to [4].

The organization of the paper is as follows. In Section 2, we describe the architecture of VOD storage server and video file layout policy. In Section 3, we describe a request scheduling algorithm that optimizes disk utilization and

---

[2] worst case bandwidth allocation is defined as taking the peak display bandwidth requirement during the duration of display, including possibility of support fast forward or fast rewind with viewing.

buffer space. In Section 4, we describe how to support VCR typed function such as fast forward with viewing. Section 5 describes some related work in VOD storage server and performance study is carried out in Section 6. Conclusion is given in Section 7.

2 The VOD Storage Server Architecture

The VOD storage architecture we consider is a hierarchical storage architecture with a tertiary tape storage device and a parallel disk array as illustrated in Figure 1. All video objects reside permanently on the tape cartridge in the

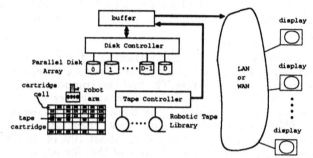

Fig. 1. Cost-effective multimedia storage server

tape system. This type of two-tier storage architecture provides a cost-effective solution for VOD since the size of each video file may be very large and it is prohibitive (in terms of cost) to store all of them in a magnetic disk storage system.

Upon request arrival to the VOD storage server, if the video file is not available in the disk storage system, then the video object is retrieved from the tape system, via the robot arm, to the disk storage system. Efficient tape scheduling algorithms for VOD storage system have been studied in [8]. Upon retrieval from the disk storage system, video frames are put into the buffer so that they can be packetized and be delivered through the network (either in form of LAN or WAN) to different display stations. In this study, we focus on the I/O bottleneck phenomena and we assume that the bandwidth of the network exceeds the display bandwidth requirement of a video object. The assumption is justified considering the current high-speed networking technologies.

Before we talk about the video file layout policy. We assume that there is a database within the video filesystem such that upon encoding and compression of video object, the size of each frame of the video object is kept in the database for future access and reference. This database is important so later on we can have an efficient parallel disk scheduling algorithm.

A file layout policy is as follow. The compressed video file $\mathcal{F}$ is broken down into equal size fragments F_i, such that $\mathcal{F} = \{F_0 \cup F_1 \cup \ldots \cup F_n\}$ and $F_i \cap F_j = \emptyset$. Fragments are then assigned to the parallel disk in a round-robin manner, for example, fragment F_i is assigned to disk $i \pmod{D}$ where D is the number of disks in the storage subsystem. Upon request, retrieval is done in unit of fragment. The size of the fragment F_i is currently chosen to be two cylinders. Note that the rationale for choosing this size is to minimize each seek and rotation overhead for each fragment transfer[3]. For simplicity of presentation, we assume that each frame is stored in exactly one fragment. That is, a frame will not be split such that part of it is stored in fragment F_i and remaining part of the frame

---

[3] Based on the parameters we used in our study, the seek overhead for each fragment transfer is about 10%.

is stored in fragment F_{i+1}. Also, due to compression applied, different fragments may contain different number of video frames.

A multimedia object is retrieved by reading fragments of the object in a pipe-lining manner, for example, the retrieval of fragment i will be completed before the end of the playback period of fragment $i - 1$. Since the file system has a database containing frame sizes of video object and the fragment size is fixed. To support a constant frame rate at the display station, playback time for each fragment can be easily computed. Therefore, once the start time of a request is determined, the deadline of a fragment retrieval of the request can be determined by adding up the playback periods of all preceding fragments and the request start time. We term the above scheme as *round-robin striping*.

3   Round-robin Striping

We define a *task* as an operation of retrieving a fragment from a disk. The execution time of a task has three components: the seek time, the rotational latency and the fragment transfer time. The first two components are the overhead within a task. Since our goal is to design a storage server which supports high display bandwidth multimedia objects, we bound the task's overhead such that it is less than 10% of the transfer time of a task. For a typical 1.2 Gbytes hard disk, when the fragment size is two cylinders, about 10% of the disk bandwidth is wasted in switching overheads. In the rest of the discussion, we assume that the execution time of a task is a constant of τ seconds.

The algorithm we propose, the round-robin striping algorithm, has several components. It first finds an optimal *execution order* for the tasks in each disk in the parallel disk subsystem. With the execution order, the *execution schedule* of the tasks in a disk is then determined in a way such that the fragment buffer requirement is minimal. This execution schedule defines the start time of the request and the retrieval and completion time of each task in a request.

Upon arrival of a request, the algorithm *ScheduleRequest* will be executed to test whether the storage server can accept this new request. If the system can accept this new request, it finds the execution order and execution schedule of all tasks within the request. The algorithm ScheduleRequest is defined as follows.

Algorithm ScheduleRequest *Assume the number of buffer (which is used for storing fragment after its retrieval) in the storage server is B. Given a new playback request R for a multimedia object O and the latest time, t, such that the requester can wait until, the algorithm determines whether object O can start to display on or before time t and the earliest possible start time of the playback request R.*

```
1 procedure ScheduleRequest(R : request;
          var starttime : real; var success : boolean);
   { If object O can start on or before t, success is set to
     TRUE and starttime is set to the earliest start time
     of the request, otherwise, success is set to FALSE. }
2 begin
3    call StartTime() to find the earliest start time of R
     and the optimal execution order of tasks in each disk
     without considering the fragment buffer requirement;
4    If the earliest start time ≤ t then
5    begin
6       call ScheduleTask() to find the execution
        schedule of all tasks in the system which
        minimizes buffer requirement;
```

```
7        while (the maximum required number of
         buffer > B) and(the earliest start time ≤ t) do
8        begin
9            increment the start time of R by a fixed value;
10           call ScheduleTask() to find the execution
             schedule of all tasks in the system which
             minimizes buffer requirement;
11       end
12   end;
13   if the earliest start time ≤ t then
14   begin
15       success := TRUE;
16       starttime := earliest start time;
17   end
18   else
19       success := FALSE;
20 end
```

We propose two algorithms for routines in line 3 and line 6 (or line 10) of algorithm *ScheduleRequest*. They are the *StartTime* and *ScheduleTask* algorithms respectively.

3.1   Algorithm StartTime

Algorithm *StartTime* is responsible to find the earliest start time of a request R as well as the execution orders of all tasks in R in the parallel disks subsystem. To schedule tasks within a disk, the earliest deadline first (EDF) algorithm is used. We choose the EDF algorithm because the EDF algorithm is found to be optimal for scheduling tasks in a single disk[9]. Temporal relation for related tasks (belong to the same request) that were assigned to different disks are maintained by the algorithm (via each fragment deadline). The system maintains a doubly linked-list which contains all tasks scheduled for the particular disk. Tasks are arranged in an ascending order of deadlines. Algorithm *StartTime* determines the start time of a new request R by the following steps: 1) set the start time of request R to the current time; 2) given that current start time and execution time of each tasks, determines the deadlines of each tasks of R; 3) find the earliest completion time for each task of R by scheduling the task in the unused period between the scheduled tasks (of other requests) in the disk; 4) let LT_i be the late time task i as:

$$LT_i = (\text{completion time of task } i - \text{deadline of tasks } i)^+$$

then the start time of request R is:

$$\text{current time} + \text{execution time of the first task of } R + \max_{i \in R}\{LT_i\}$$

Algorithm StartTime *Given the linked lists of scheduled tasks in the disk (pointed by p_1) and the linked lists of tasks of a new request R (pointed by p_2), the following algorithm finds the earliest start time of request R. Please refer to [7] for the detail of algorithm.*

function StartTime(): **real**;
begin
  i : **integer**;
  S : Set of Task;
  {MaxDelay is equal to $\max_{i \in R}\{LT_i\}$ }
  MaxDelay, RemainTime : **real**;
  p_1, p_2 : pointer to a task in a linked list;
  MaxDelay := 0.0;
  for i := 1 **to** D **do**
  begin
      p_1 := points to the head of the list L_1 of all scheduled task of other
         requests not equal to R in disk i in ascending order of deadlines;
      p_2 := points to the head of the list L_2 of tasks in R for disk i in ascending
         order of deadlines;
    while p_1 <> **nil do**
    begin
        $S = \emptyset$;
        put task pointed by p_1 into set S;
        RemainTime := deadline of task pointed by p_1 - current time -
           the total execution time of all tasks in set S;
        while((RemainTime >= execution time of task pointed by p_2)
           and (p_2 <> **nil**) **do**
        begin
           put task pointed by p_2 into set S;
           MaxDelay = max {MaxDelay,Late Time(LT) for task pointed by p_2};
           update p_2 to point to next task in L_2;
        end;
        if RemainTime < 0 **then**
           move p_2 to a previous task and remove minimum number of
           tasks in R from set S such that RemainTime $\geq$ 0 ;
        update p_1 to point to the next task in L_1;
    end;
    while (p_2 <> **nil**) **do**
    begin
        put p_2 into the set S;
        MaxDelay = max {MaxDelay,Late Time(LT) for task pointed by p_2};
        update p_2 to point to next task in L_2;
    end;
  end;
  return (current time + execution time of the first task of R + MaxDelay)
end

Lemma 1. *Algorithm StartTime requires* $\Theta(2N_{\overline{R}} + N_R)$ *link traversals to find the earliest start time of request* R *where* $N_{\overline{R}}$ *and* N_R *are the total number of tasks of other requests not equal to* R *in the parallel disks and the number of tasks of the new request* R *respectively.*

Proof: please refer to [7]. ∎

3.2 Algorithm ScheduleTask

    Given the execution order of tasks, Algorithm *ScheduleTask* minimizes the required buffer space by scanning the task list of each disk in the reverse order of task deadlines and determines the latest retrieval time of each task. The retrieval time of a task is the time at which the task starts to execute.

Algorithm ScheduleTask Let N_i be the number of tasks in disk i. Let $J_{i,1}, \ldots,$ J_{i,N_i} be the tasks in disk i listed in ascending order of deadlines. The retrieval time of all tasks in the disks are determined by the following procedure:

```
procedure ScheduleTask();
begin
  i, j : integer;
  CurTime : float;
  for i:= 1 to D do
  begin
    CurTime := +∞;
    for j := Nᵢ down to 1 do
    begin
      if (CurTime > deadline of Jᵢ,ⱼ) then
        CurTime := deadline of Jᵢ,ⱼ;
      CurTime := CurTime - execution time of Jᵢ,ⱼ;
      retrieval time of Jᵢ,ⱼ := CurTime;
    end
  end
end
```

Theorem 2. *Given a set of tasks that can be scheduled by the EDF algorithm, Algorithm ScheduleTask finds a feasible schedule of tasks that requires a minimal buffer space.*

Proof: please refer to [7]. ∎

4 Interactive Playback Support

In this section, we describe how to support VCR typed functions. For simplicity of presentation, we only describe support of fast forward with viewing. Rewind with viewing can be supported using similar technique.

In order to support the fast forward with viewing operation, we can break it up into two sub-operations, 1) viewing fast forward frames when the fast forward button is pushed, and 2) resume normal display after the fast forward button is released.

Let us discuss the second sub-operation first. If the peak rate retrieval policy is used, it is very simple to support resuming the normal display after the fast forward button is released. To illustrate this point, Figure 2 illustrates the frag-

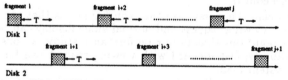

Fig. 2. Fast Forward with Peak Allocation

ment retrieval schedule if the peak rate retrieval policy is used and D (number of parallel disks in the system) is equal to two. Since the system assumes a peak retrieval rate when a request arrives at the system, the time between successive fragment retrieval is fixed with time T. If the fast forward operation is to skip fragment i to fragment $j - 1$, it is a simple operation to re-map the retrieval schedule such that fragment k will move up $\frac{i-i}{D}$ units. For example, for disk 1 in Figure 2, instead of retrieving fragment $\{ i, i+2, i+4, \ldots \}$, fragment $\{ j, j+2, j+4, \ldots \}$ are retrieved instead. This is always possible because:
- the size of each fragment is the same.

- the inter-fragment time is fixed as T (due to peak retrieval rate policy).
- retrieval schedule of fragment can always be re-mapped (e.g., fragment j re-map to fragment i) because all fragments retrieval are scheduled during request arrival. Therefore, we are guaranteed that there is a *slot* available for re-mapping fragment retrieval.

On the other hand, to support variable bit rate retrieval, time between fragments retrieval is not fixed. Figure 3 illustrates a variable bit rate retrieval. Now,

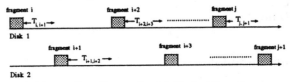

Fig. 3. Fast Forward with Peak Allocation

since the time between fragments is not fixed, direct re-mapping of fragments may not be possible because, 1) since $T_{i,i+1}$ (time between retrieval of fragment i and fragment $i+1$) is not equal to $T_{j,j+1}$, therefore the video continuity may not be capable of being satisfied, 2) disk storage system is servicing other requests (e.g., requests to other video files) and the presence of these requests' schedules (which were determined at each request arrival instant) might make the re-mapping impossible. Therefore, direct re-mapping will create a situation such that after the fast forward button is released, normal video display cannot be continued.

To overcome the problem stated above, we first defined an advanced unit, U_a (e.g., each U_a is equivalent to 30 seconds of normal display time). Note that U_a is a system tunable parameter. User can now specify the number N_a, which indicates the number of U_a advance units he/she wants to fast forward. Once this information is entered, the system treats this as a new request and try to schedule it using the algorithm we described in the previous section. If the request can be scheduled, it is accepted and previous allocated resources (e.g., I/O schedule for fragment retrieval) can be deleted. On the other hand, if request cannot be scheduled, the system has the following options:

- reject the request and continue display the video file.
- increment (or decrement) N_a and try to schedule this request again. We can repeat this approach several times. If the system still cannot schedule the request, the system simply informs the user that the fast forward operation cannot be scheduled.

Using this approach, the worst case that can happen is that the system rejects fast forward with viewing request and normal video display can be continued. It is important to point out that in our performance study, we observe that with very high probability, fast forward with viewing request can be accepted for a large range of system load.

Now we are in the position to answer how to support fast forward with viewing operation. In general, there are three approaches: 1. *separated replicated files* in [1]; 2) *fragment sampling* in [2] and 3) *frame sequence resampling*. Each has different degrees of storage overhead and quality of service. For detail description, please refer to [7].

5 Related Work

In [1], staggered striping was proposed for file layout architecture in support of video on demand. We choose staggered striping for comparison because it uses the similar concept of file declustering, that is, splitting up a video file and laying the file across the parallel disk array.

First, let us briefly define the concept of staggered striping. A video object O is split into separate sub-objects $O_1, O_2, \ldots, O_n$ where $O_i \cap O_j = \emptyset$. Each sub-object is composed of M fragments such that fragments of the same subobject are stored in M adjacent disks[4]. A stride is defined to be the distance (in term of number of disk) between the first fragment of sub-object O_i and the first fragment of sub-object O_{i+1}. Request retrieval is accomplished by retrieving a sub-object at a time; therefore, for each sub-object retrieval, M adjacent disks are involved in retrieving M fragments.

Staggered striping suffers from the following problems, 1) *time fragmentation* [1] where there are idle disks but they cannot process waiting requests; 2) it can only support constant retrieval rates; and 3) request may be starved (or be forced to wait forever in the request queue) if non first-in-first-out (non-FIFO) queueing discipline is used for reducing request waiting time.

In contrast, round-robin striping is starvation-free because all requests are scheduled when they arrive. Also, round-robin striping has the advantage that the start time of playback of a request can be determined when the request arrives. This information is very useful for system resource management.

In [10], a storage layout method that optimizes several concurrent requests of the same video object is proposed. With this method, fragments of several requests of different phases of the same object can be retrieved with one disk movement (seek and rotational movement). The phase of a request is the point in time at which the object is being displayed. The method can improve the system performance when several requests retrieve the same objects. However, the approach performs worse when many different video objects are retrieved concurrently because only a small fragment of an object is retrieved for each disk movement. In [10, 2], several ways to support interactive playback function are proposed, such as fast forward and backward functions by skipping fragments. Lastly, there is an on going research work on staggered striping for a compressed video object [5].

6 Performance Evaluation

In this section, we evaluate the performance of round-robin striping and staggered striping by computer simulation for four different cases: Case 1) the required display bandwidth for the playback of an object is constant and it is equal to 5 Mbytes/second; Case 2) The required display bandwidth for the playback of an object varies over time. The playback time is split into intervals of 0.6 seconds. The display bandwidth requirement within an interval is uniformly distributed between 2.5 Mbytes/second and 5 Mbytes/second; Case 3) The required display bandwidth for the playback of an object is constant and it is equal to 10 Mbytes/second; Case 4) The required display bandwidth for the playback of an object varies over time. The playback time is split into intervals of 0.6 seconds. The display bandwidth requirement within an interval is uniformly distributed between 5 Mbytes/second and 10 Mbytes/second. The main parameters of the

Parameter	Cases 1 & 2	Cases 3 & 4
Number of disks	200	400
Disk bandwidth	2.5 MB/s	2.5 MB/s
Number of objects	100	100
Playback period of an object	600 secs	600 secs
Fragment size	1.5 MB	1.5 MB

Table 1. Main Simulation Parameters.

simulation are shown in Table 1. The simulation runs for round-robin striping and staggered striping with various parameters are abbreviated in Table 2.

---
[4] M is also known as the degree of declustering in Staggered Striping

SS(i, k, n)	staggered striping with non-fifo request queueing discipline, stride = k, n fragment buffers in storage server, and the bandwidth requirement is that of case i.
RS(i, n)	round-robin striping with n fragment buffers in storage server and the bandwidth requirement is that of case i.

Table 2. Abbreviations for simulation runs.

We measured the average waiting time of round-robin striping and staggered striping by an open queueing network in which the request arrival process is a Poison process. And we measured the maximum throughput of round-robbin striping and staggered striping by a closed queueing network in which the number of requests is fixed. Tables 3 (Table 4) presents the average waiting time (in seconds) of a playback request for Cases 1 and 2 (Cases 3 and 4). The average response time of a playback request is the average waiting time plus the execution time of the retrieval of the first fragment of an object. Tables 5 and 6 show the maximum throughput of staggered striping and round-robin striping for different bandwidth requirements and different number of fragment buffers.

Arrival rate (req/hr)	100	200	300	400	450	500
SS(1, 1, 400) or SS(2, 1, 400)	0.684	1.368	2.795	7.199	14.049	33.016
SS(1, 2, 400) or SS(2, 2, 400)	0.423	0.669	1.160	2.509	4.325	9.707
SS(1, 3, 400) or SS(2, 3, 400)	0.506	0.916	1.892	5.459	12.574	42.961
RS(1, 400)	0.169	0.462	1.057	3.111	53.626	88.964
RS(1, 480)	0.169	0.462	1.057	2.576	4.945	10.502
RS(1, ∞)	0.169	0.462	1.057	2.572	4.681	10.045
RS(2, 400)	0.142	0.353	0.667	1.304	2.005	10.171
RS(2, 480)	0.142	0.353	0.667	1.304	1.865	3.507
RS(2, ∞)	0.142	0.353	0.667	1.304	1.836	2.721

Table 3. Average waiting times (in seconds) for Cases 1 and 2.

Arrival rate (req/hr)	100	200	300	400	450	500
SS(3, 1, 800) or SS(4, 1, 800)	1.187	2.749	6.314	16.886	35.255	92.823
SS(3, 4, 800) or SS(4, 4, 800)	0.423	0.669	1.160	2.509	4.325	9.707
SS(3, 7, 800) or SS(4, 7, 800)	0.549	1.089	2.593	9.877	27.664	95.110
RS(3, 800)	0.168	0.460	1.034	2.523	4.855	10.685
RS(3, ∞)	0.168	0.460	1.034	2.441	4.800	10.248
RS(4, 640)	0.140	0.355	0.676	1.410	3.525	20.489
RS(4, 800)	0.140	0.355	0.676	1.307	1.872	4.595
RS(4, ∞)	0.140	0.355	0.676	1.307	1.866	2.814

Table 4. Average waiting times (in seconds) for Cases 3 and 4.

For fast forward with viewing, we measured the waiting time of fast forward request of multimedia objects. The main parameters of the simulation is shown in Table 7. Each multimedia object is a 90-minute video object. The playback period of each object is divided into 0.6 second intervals. In each interval, the display bandwidth requirement is uniformly distributed between 2.5 Mbytes/second and 5.0 Mbytes/second. In this simulation, a request will demand a fast forward with viewing operation at time t where t is a random variable uniformly distributed between 0 to 60 minutes. For each fast forward with viewing operation, the object is scanned at 3 times the normal playback speed, and the display time of fast forward with viewing is 1 minute. Hence,

# of Fragment Buffers (n)	400	480	∞
SS(1, 1, n) or SS(2, 1, n)	572.215	572.215	572.215
SS(1, 2, n) or SS(2, 2, n)	593.910	593.910	593.910
SS(1, 3, n) or SS(2, 3, n)	558.361	558.361	558.361
RS(1, n)	510.405	545.433	595.724
RS(2, n)	577.315	623.028	793.334

Table 5. Maximum throughput (in requests/hour) for Cases 1 and 2.

# of Fragment Buffers (n)	800	960	∞
SS(3, 1, n) or SS(4, 1, n)	563.728	563.728	563.728
SS(3, 4, n) or SS(4, 4, n)	594.593	594.593	594.593
SS(3, 7, n) or SS(4, 7, n)	542.630	542.630	542.630
RS(3, n)	568.330	587.028	596.013
RS(4, n)	613.455	655.730	798.090

Table 6. Maximum throughput (in request/hour) for Cases 3 and 4.

the average execution time of a request is equal to the display time × average retrieval bandwidth/disk bandwidth or $(87 + 1) \times 3.75/2.5$minutes $= 132$ minutes Assuming that the VOD server has 200 parallel disks, the theoretical maximum throughput is $60 \times 200/132$requests/hour $= 90.91$ requests/hour.

We measured the waiting time distributions for four combinations of arrival rate and number of fragment buffers. Let $FF(n, r)$ denote a simulation run with n fragment buffers in the storage server and request arrival rate r (unit is in requests/hour). Figure 4 shows probability distribution functions of waiting time for the four combinations.

In general, we see that round-robin striping outperforms staggered striping in most situations. Even under the constant display bandwidth assumption (case 1 and 3), round-robin striping has better response time for low to moderate arrival rate. It is important to point out that video file varies in fragment sizes (as we have argued in Section 1. Therefore, what we are showing is to compare round-robin against staggered striping in some rare cases. For system throughput, round-robin is comparable to staggered striping. For VCR-typed functions such as fast forward, we see the system accepts fast forward with viewing request with high probability.

7 Conclusion

In this paper, we have proposed a VOD storage server that can support constant display frame rate at the display station and at the same time, variable bit rate retrieval. We discussed the video file layout policy, the admission control, request scheduling, buffer management as well as VCR-typed functions support. Performance studies have been carried out and we have shown that it can have good request response and system throughput. Also, the type of VOD can support techniques as described in [4] to reduce the I/O cost.

Parameter	Case 5
Number of disks	200
Disk bandwidth	2.5 MB/sec
Number of objects	20
Normal playback period of an object	90 minutes
Fragment size	1.5 MB

Table 7. Simulation Parameters for Fast Forward Playback.

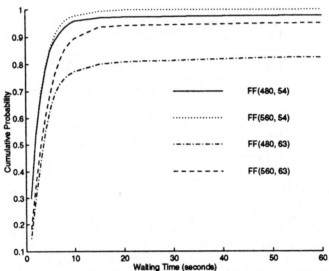

Fig. 4. Probability distribution functions of waiting time.

References

1. S. Berson, S. Ghandeharizadeh, R.R. Muntz, X. Ju. "Staggered Striping in Multi-media Information Systems", In *ACM SIGMOD Conf.*, pp. 79-90, June, 1994.

2. M. S. Chen, D. D. Kandlur, and P. S. Yu, "Support for Fully Interactive Playout in a Disk-Array-Based Video Server." In *Proceedings of the 2nd Annual ACM Multimedia Conference*, October 1994.

3. Borko Furht. "Multimedia Systems: An Overview." In *IEEE Multimedia Magazine*, Spring Issue, 1994.

4. L. Golubchik, John C.S. Lui, Richard Muntz, "Reducing I/O demands in Video-On-Demand Storage Servers." In *Proceedings of the ACM SIGMET-RICS/PERFORMANCE '95 Conference. May, 1995.*

5. L. Golubchik, R.R. Muntz. *Private Communication.*

6. D. Le Gall. "MPEG: A Video Compression Standard for Multimedia Applications" *Communications of the ACM, April, 1991.*

7. S.W. Lau, John C.S. Lui. "A Novel Video-On-Demand Storage Architecture for Supporting Constant Frame Rate with Variable Bit Rate Retrieval", Technical Report CS-TR-94-12, Department of Computer Science, the Chinese University of Hong Kong, 1994.

8. S.W. Lau, John C.S. Lui, P.C. Wong. "A Cost-effective Near-line Storage Server for Multimedia System" *In Proceedings of the 11th International Conference on Data Engineering. March, 1995.*

9. C.L. Liu and J.W. Layland. "Scheduling Algorithms for Multiprogramming in a Hard-Real-Time Environment", *JACM, Vol. 20, No.1, Jan. 1973. pp. 47-61.*

10. B. Ozden, A. Biliris, R. Rastogi and A. Silberschaz. "A Low-cost Storage Server for Movie on Demand Databases", *Proceedings of the 20th International Conference on Very Large Databases, September 1994.*

11. P. V. Rangan and H. M. Vin, "Efficient Storage Techniques for Digital Continuous Multimedia." In *Transactions on Knowledge and Data Engineering*, August 1993.

12. H. M. Vin and P. V. Rangan, "Designing a Multi-User HDTV Storage Server." In *IEEE Journal on Selected Areas in Communication*, Vol. 11, No. 1, January 1993.

The Design and Implementation of a RAID-3 Multimedia File Server

Alan J. Chaney, Ian D. Wilson and Andrew Hopper[*]
Olivetti Research Laboratory
24a, Trumpington Street
Cambridge CB2 1QA
United Kingdom

Tel: +44-1223-343000
Fax: +44-1223-313542

Email: {iwilson,achaney,ahopper}@cam-orl.co.uk

Abstract

The Olivetti Research Laboratory has developed an experimental system based on intelligent peripherals connected directly to an ATM network. As well as multimedia modules (e.g. audio and video) the system also includes a directly connected RAID-3 storage server called the "Disc Brick". This paper describes the architecture of the Disc Brick, and discusses some of the hardware and software issues raised by its design. It also presents measurements taken from a Disc Brick in operation, and discusses how the observations relate to the original design objectives. Finally, the paper attempts to evaluate the Disc Brick as part of ORL's family of directly connected peripherals.

Introduction

An experimental system has been constructed at the Olivetti Research Laboratory which aims to provide a rich multimedia environment for a variety of users [1]. It utilises ATM communications technology as the basic interconnect both for computers and multimedia peripheral modules. Each module is made up of a number of standard component parts: the hardware consists of an ARM CPU, up to 32 Mbytes of memory, and a 100Mbit/s ATM TAXI interface; the low-level software consists of a microkernel called ATMos [2] which provides a mechanism for scheduling processes and controlling low level hardware. In addition there is provision for interoperation with other systems by using protocols such as TCP/IP and XTP, or distributed platforms based on CORBA.

The ATMos framework is used to implement both switches (4x4 and 8x8) and end-point modules (or *direct peripherals*). The modules include ATM video, ATM

---

[*] University of Cambridge and Olivetti Research Laboratory

audio, ATM LCD tile, ATM TV, ATM frame store, ATM processor farm and the Disc Brick, as well as workstations and PCs (see Figure 1).

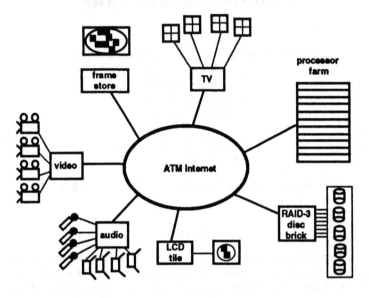

Figure 1

This approach has similarities with the Desk Area Network [3] but also differs from it in important ways. Rather than exploding the workstation, ORL's approach is to treat each direct peripheral module as a first class ATM object; furthermore, most of the traffic from a module will typically flow to points elsewhere in the system and not to a nearby PC or workstation. However, as with the DAN, the approach uses a network as the peripheral interconnect, and hence is scalable.

The system has been deployed in the laboratory and has been in use for about 18 months. Some two hundred modules and switches are available for experimentation. A typical office has four cameras, four speakers, four microphones, a display tile and a workstation as its multimedia infrastructure. In addition, there are five Disc Bricks available on the network for use as multimedia fileservers. Applications in use include a video-mail system, which takes advantage of the Disc Brick's performance by recording several video and audio channels simultaneously. Other applications include a multi-way video-phone which uses four video streams and an audio stream between the corresponding parties.

The rest of this paper concentrates on one particular directly connected ATM peripheral: the RAID-3 Disc Brick.

The Disc Brick Filing System

The Olivetti Research Laboratory has been working in the multimedia area for many years. One of its earlier systems, Pandora [4], relied on a fileserver for the storage of audio and video objects. It is the filing system which was originally designed for the

Pandora Video Repository which now runs on the Disc Brick, since the overall requirements for both systems are virtually identical.

The main aims of the filing system design were:

- simple, hierarchical directory structure;

- efficient use of intelligent disc drives;

- efficient handling of both large and small filing system objects; and

- optimisation for sequential, as opposed to random, access.

The use of a conventional filing system for multimedia data differs from the approach taken by other people. For example, Berkeley's Filing System for Continuous Media [5] makes no attempt to lay the disc out, and relies on pre-allocating contiguous areas for data storage. Lancaster's Continuous Media Storage Server [6] is more sophisticated, in that it keeps a separate directory disc to hold meta-data, but still uses fixed contiguous areas on its data discs. The approach described in this paper has the advantage that all data types can be stored using the same filing system, without sacrificing the performance benefits of the simpler architectures.

Disc Layout Issues

There are two important factors when it comes to making efficient use of intelligent disc drives. Firstly, there is no point in attempting to optimise accesses based on a drive's physical geometry. Indeed, it is often not possible to find out the real drive geometry: track and sector sparing, automatic sector reassignment etc. all conspire to make the drive's physical characteristics irrelevant. Secondly, the actual disc layout (taking into account sector interleave and track skew) is completely hidden from the user, and optimised for large sequential accesses. Most drives nowadays have large data buffers and perform read-ahead and write-behind. This, combined with "read on arrival" which reduces the effect of rotational latency, means that the best way to get optimum performance from them is to *stream* large amounts of sequential data in very much the same way as handling a tape. The repercussions on the filing system design are:

- to lay the disc out so that objects are in large, sequential chunks;

- to allocate I/O buffers so that transactions are as large as possible; and

- to minimise the amount of disc seeking.

The algorithm used is straightforward: assume all new files are going to be large, and reserve disc space accordingly. In other words, when allocating space for a file, reserve a large contiguous chunk at the beginning, and then use up the reservation as necessary. As a file grows extra contiguous chunks are reserved as required, and when the file is closed the unused space is freed. This scheme has a tendency to fragment the space available, but this is not a problem since the spare blocks are mopped up as a side-effect of the filing system's housekeeping operations.

In order to minimise the amount of disc seeking, there is an attempt to store all the blocks which comprise an object as close together on the disc as possible. For this to work in practice, when a new object is created, it must be positioned on the disc in an area where there is a reasonable amount of contiguous free space. Obviously, there is a trade-off between having to seek a *small* amount while handling an object, and having to seek a *large* amount in order to get to it in the first place. To find an appropriate place for a new object, the filing system searches outward from a known disc position looking for the area with the largest amount of contiguous free space, but weighting the results of the search using the inverse square of the seek distance. In this manner, disc fragmentation is kept low, as are seek distances between related filing system objects. Also, head scheduling (either "elevator" or "least seek") is performed by the disc device driver, reducing the effects of seeking still further.

File Structure
In order to handle large and small objects in an efficient manner, a modified version of the UNIX *inode* structure is used. Each object is represented by a *header* block which contains its length, protection mode, last modification date and so on. Only a small portion of the header block is used for this information, and the remainder is used to hold pointers to the object contents. As with the inode structure, there are data blocks which are directly accessible, and those accessible via one, two or three levels of indirection. To all intents and purposes, this allows objects to grow arbitrarily, with a maximum of three levels of indirection before reaching the object contents.

Optimisation For Sequential Access
Many studies have been made in the past about the nature of general purpose filing systems and how they are used in practice. Two results are of particular significance:

- the majority of accesses are read operations; and

- the majority of accesses are sequential.

It was an essential part of the filing system design that it should be optimised for this type of use, even though this can result in a performance degradation when random accesses are performed. To this end, the filing system performs *read-ahead* and *write-behind* at the object level, so that disc operations can, hopefully, be overlapped with user data manipulation. The pipelining effect obtained by this technique means that, assuming the object is reasonably contiguous in its disc layout, the required streaming effect can be achieved.

Cache Strategy
One of the more radical decisions taken when the filing system was being designed was to cache header/indirection blocks and directory contents, but *not* to cache object contents. The justification is that the disc performance is worst when the ratio of seeking to data transfer is very high, and best when performing large sequential accesses. The former mode of operation is typical of general filing system

housekeeping (for example, when picking up a set of header blocks during a directory listing), and is something which is relatively easy to optimise using a cache. The latter, however, is typical of accesses to object contents—the layout of which has been arranged to be as contiguous as possible. Using buffer memory for read-ahead and write-behind rather than as a data cache allows the discs to operate in their most efficient manner, with the added bonus that it is not necessary to perform a cache search or invalidation for each data transfer—not an insignificant overhead.

The final vindication of the "everything but data" cache strategy is seen when the filing system is used with multimedia objects. Video files, in particular, are often tens or hundreds of megabytes in length, and are usually accessed sequentially. Such usage is guaranteed to flush any kind of data cache, and maintaining a cache can only add overhead to what is, essentially, a disc streaming operation. Performance figures for the filing system running on the Disc Brick are given later in this paper.

Which RAID Version?

RAID is an acronym for Redundant Array of Inexpensive Disks and was first presented in [7]. The methods of organising the data on a RAID array are of interest. The aggregate capacity of several drives was desired, and the maximum transfer rate possible would be achieved by accessing all drives concurrently. The two RAID configurations considered applicable were:

> RAID-3: Byte striping, where words are read/written in parallel to several discs, each byte going to a separate disc; and

> RAID-5: Sector striping, where each drive has one logical sector.

Previous work [8] has indicated that the optimum performance should be given by a RAID-5 system. However, this is only applicable:

- for wide arrays (say 9 or more drives); and

- for small transfers (one or two sectors).

In our case it was felt that the comparative simplicity of RAID-3, coupled with our need to transfer very large files, made the RAID-3 architecture the most suitable.

Design Criteria for the Disc Brick Hardware

The main design criterion was to balance the available disc drive transfer performance with that provided by the network interface. At the time work started, a typical high performance disc drive was capable of sustaining transfers of 2.7Mbyte/s. Four such drives in parallel would give an overall transfer rate of around 10.8 Mbyte/s (approximately 90Mbit/s). The ATM network interface had a raw transfer rate of 100Mbit/s. There was a good match between these two figures, although it was realised that other factors (such as the overhead of managing the discs and the network protocol) would make it impossible to achieve this maximum. It was also a design criterion that there should be no performance loss when operating with one failed drive.

Hardware Architecture

The Disc Brick has the following major sub-systems:

- ARM 610 RISC processor with a 32MHz clock and 32 MB of memory;
- 5 x SCSI interface controllers, each with an 8 bit SCSI-2 interface;
- 5 x SCSI disc drives;
- parity generation/decoding logic;
- a DMA controller;
- a 2k x 32 bit bi-directional FIFO;
- an ATM network interface.

A physically compact design was produced utilising a number of components already developed for other ORL direct peripherals. Five 3.5" SCSI disc drives are used for the storage of data in the Disc Brick—typically these are Seagate ST12550N Barracuda drives, each of 2GB capacity.

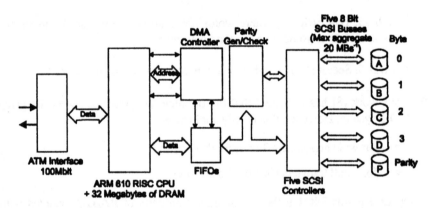

Figure 2

The array is 32 bits wide and requires five separate SCSI ports. Four of the drives hold user data (with the fifth holding parity information) giving an effective capacity of 8GB with 2GB discs. The four data drives are shown as A,B,C and D in Figure 2. Hardware was designed to generate parity information and reconstruct drive data in the event of failure.

Parity is generated during write operations with simple *exclusive OR* logic. If the data from one of the drives A to D is to be regenerated, then the data from the remaining three available drives is passed through the regeneration logic together with the data from the parity drive. This "reconstructs" the data for the unavailable drive.

A FIFO is used to buffer data to and from the SCSI ports. There are two possible data transfer methods: polled I/O transfers using the block transfer mode of the ARM; and DMA. In order to reduce the interference between the ATM network and disc I/O, a fine grain bus sharing scheme is used where block operations are split into a number of small transfers by the logic of the DMA controller.

This technique relies on the utilisation of the memory bus by the ARM CPU being much less than 100% (due to the presence of its on-chip cache). Observations indicated that typically only 30% to 50% of the available memory bandwidth was being used. The DMA controller was designed to perform a 32 bit word transfer in 125ns. In the Disc Brick design, the ARM has a memory transfer clock (MCLK) of 16MHz. The DMA controller is allowed access to the bus for 1μs (16 MCLK ticks) and then the transfer is suspended for a further 1μs. Allowing for arbitration delays, this gives an effective sustained DMA transfer rate of about 20 Mbyte/s—a good match for the maximum SCSI bus transfer rate. In the Disc Brick each SCSI port has a maximum transfer rate of 4 Mbyte/s, which gives a theoretical aggregate of 16 Mbyte/s for 32 bit data words. The data for the parity drive is never transferred to or from the ARM memory, and thus has no effect on overall performance.

Disc Brick Performance

To evaluate the performance of the Disc Brick, it is necessary to do more than just measure disc and network throughput. Each subsystem is controlled directly by the ARM, and hence carries a CPU and memory bandwidth overhead. Similarly, because of the nature of the devices, there are possible interference effects (interrupt latency, for example) which determine the behaviour of the system as a whole. To be able to understand these interference effects, it is first necessary to understand how each of the subsystems performs in isolation.

Each ATMos system has an idle process which is executed whenever there is nothing else which can be scheduled. The idle process is written in such a way that, by noting the value of a single memory location at the beginning and end of a performance measurement, it is possible to infer the average "idleness" of the processor and memory during that time. All the measured timings that follow are also accompanied by an indication of the system idleness, shown as a percentage.

Raw RAID Array Performance

Figure 3 shows the performance of the "raw" RAID array. Measurements were taken of the time to read/write 50, 100 and 1000 Mbytes of contiguous disc, and the results averaged. Each set of timings were made for *polled* access mode (where the ARM is responsible for the FIFO data transfer) and *DMA* mode (where transfers are handled by an external DMA controller). In order to illustrate that there is no performance penalty in data reconstruction, the timings were repeated for a system in which drive A had been disconnected.

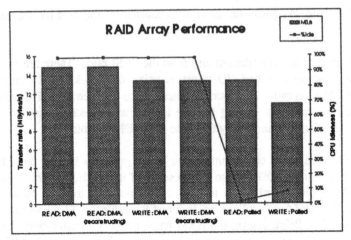

Figure 3

- The *read* transfers are entirely SCSI bus limited, since the theoretical maximum data rate from each drive is only 4Mbyte/s.

- The fact that *write* operations are slower than *read* operations is an artefact of the disc drives themselves—not of the RAID system.

- The effective transfer rates from both *polled* and *DMA* modes are very similar, but the variation in CPU loading is dramatic.

Raw Network Performance

Figure 4 shows the effect on overall system performance of various amounts of ATM traffic, in the absence of disc activity. Measurements were taken for approximately 10, 20, 30 and 40 Mbit/s of continuous network activity, user process to user process.

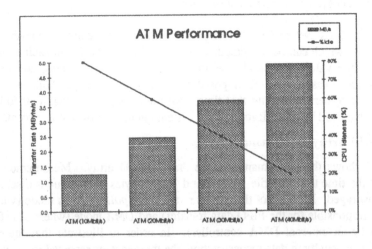

Figure 4

Actual bandwidth requirements at the ATM physical layer are some 10% larger than these figures, primarily because of the 5 byte header overhead for every 48 bytes of ATM cell payload. As can be seen, CPU saturation would be reached significantly before the theoretical 100Mbit/s limit. This is due to the fact that the prototype ATM interface in the Disc Brick generates an interrupt for every cell received or transmitted, and that the adaptation layer processing is performed exclusively in software.

Filing System Performance

To evaluate the performance of the filing system, measurements were taken of the time to read/write files of 5, 10, 50 and 100 Mbytes, and the results averaged. Because creating a file carries with it a significant block allocation overhead, measurements were also taken of the time to *re-write* (i.e. write in place) the same files. Timings were also taken of the filing system performance when an extra data copy is involved, for example by using the ANSI C functions *fread* and *fwrite* through a "buffered" interface. The results are shown in Figure 5.

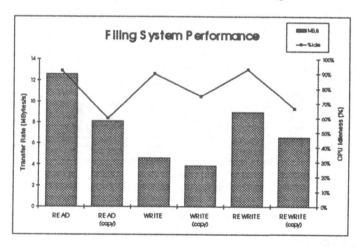

Figure 5

- The CPU overhead of using the filing system rather than the raw disc is not large—especially for *read* operations.

- Comparison of the write and re-write timings gives some idea of the overhead involved in block allocation. The filing system always performs block allocation synchronously to preserve disc integrity, and this has an obvious knock-on effect.

- The overhead of the extra data copy in each of the operations is highly significant. Not only is the CPU less idle, but the overall filing system performance is much lower.

Combined Network And Filing System Performance

The measurements in Figure 6 are identical to the *read* timings described above, but with the added overhead of 10, 20, 30 and 40 Mbits of network traffic occurring in parallel. These values reflect the conditions which would be found in a real multimedia file server, and indicate the extent to which disc and network operations interfere with each other.

As can be seen, the filing system performance degrades gradually as the network load is increased. This is not unexpected, but it is worth observing the difference between the raw measurements and those which involve an extra data copy: here the performance has become significantly worse, indicating that both the network traffic *and* the data copy are interfering with disc activity.

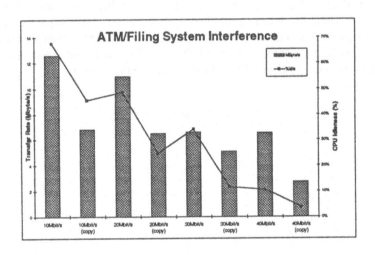

Figure 6

Other Applications

The Disc Brick is currently being exploited commercially in a collaborative agreement between *Conner Peripherals Inc.* and *ATM Ltd.* A range of RAID based ATM direct peripherals is envisaged. It is also part of a "Video on Demand" field trial in the Cambridge area [9]. Connectivity is being provided by *Cambridge Cable*, TV set-top decoder boxes are being provided by *Online Media*, programme material is being provided by *Anglia Television*, and networking infrastructure is being provided by *ATM Ltd.* Disc Bricks are also being used in a collaborative project with the University of Lancaster [10] which is investigating the issues of storage server scalability.

Further Developments

Since the conception of the Disc Brick, the media transfer rate from 3.5" disc drives has increased due to new coding techniques and greater rotational speed. Newer, faster, higher capacity drives are regularly becoming available, and it is essential that the design of the Disc Brick hardware and software should keep pace with these developments. Similarly, network technology is changing sufficiently rapidly that it may soon be necessary to re-evaluate the current 4+1 RAID configuration.

It will be possible both to reduce the cost and improve performance of future systems. Cost reduction can be achieved by integration: the ARM CPU has a very small core which can be integrated together with other components on a single chip. Thus ATM modules, including the Disc Brick, can be much reduced in cost. At the same time a StrongARM is under development which is based on the DEC Alpha CMOS process. This will make available a component with a clock speed of about 200MHz and will provide a performance upgrade path. Similarly, chipsets are becoming available to reduce the overhead of handling the ATM network—the interface to which is the main bottleneck in the current system.

Conclusion

This paper set out to show that a combined network and storage object could be produced which provided a good balance between the performance of the storage and the network. The prototype system was built to demonstrate this—the results show that the disc sub-system works well, and the ARM processor makes an excellent RAID storage controller. However, there is a performance bottleneck in the ATM network interface. New technology will shortly be available to improve the ATM performance.

The Disc Brick fits well into the ORL family of distributed ATM peripherals. With 8GB of capacity, it provides storage for a reasonable amount of multimedia data (e.g. approximately 12 hours of MPEG-1 encoded video). The network interface can support about 40-50Mbit/s of continuous traffic concurrently with high performance disc accesses.

The redundancy provided by the RAID-3 approach has proved important. The usage of multimedia data in the office environment is such that most objects are large, but have a short life. It is expensive and very time consuming to implement a comprehensive backup strategy for such data—the added reliability and availability of the RAID system is helpful.

In conclusion, the ORL Disc Brick provides an efficient and cost effective storage solution in an ATM networked multimedia environment.

Acknowledgments

The work described is the end result of the efforts of a large number of people. In particular, Philip Elwell provided invaluable assistance with the design of both the hardware and software of the Disc Brick. Caroline Bardelay wrote a test suite for the Disc Brick; Ian Crowe, Ernie Wisner and Sharon Grant helped to produce the prototype systems.

References

1. Wray, S.C., Glauert, T. H. and Hopper, A., *Networked Multimedia: The Medusa Environment*, IEEE Multimedia, Winter 1994.

2. French, L. J., Wilson, I. D. and Girling, C. G., *The ATMos Reference Manual*, Olivetti Research Laboratory, 1993-1995.

3. MacAuley, D. R., *Operating System Support for the Desk Area Network*, Proceedings of the 4th International Workshop on Networking and Operating Systems Support for Digital Audio and Video, 1993.

4. Hopper, A., *Pandora - An Experimental System for Multimedia Applications*, ACM Operating Systems Review, Vol. 24 No. 2, April 1990.

5. Anderson, D. P., Osawa, Y. and Gorindan, R., *A File System for Continuous Media*, ACM Transactions on Computer Systems 10(4), November 1992.

6. Lougher, P., and Shepherd, D., *The Design of a Storage Server for Continuous Media*, The Computer Journal (special issue on multimedia), February 1993.

7. Patterson, D. A., Gibson, G., Katz, R. H., *A Case for Redundant Arrays of Inexpensive Discs (RAID)*, Proceedings of ACM SIGMOD, June 1988.

8. Lee, E. K. and Katz, R. H., *Performance Consequences of Parity Placement in Disc Arrays*, Proceeedings of ASPLOS, April 1991.

9. Online Media Ltd., *The Cambridge Interactive Television Trial*, Press Release, September 1994; Daily Telegraph, 11th October 1994.

10. Lougher, P., Pegler, D., and Shepherd, D. , *Scalable Storage Servers for Digital Audio and Video*, Proceedings of IEE International Conference on Storage and Recording Systems, April 1994.

Efficient Data Layout, Scheduling and Playout Control in MARS*

Milind M. Buddhikot and Gurudatta M. Parulkar

Washington University in St. Louis
Computer & Communications Research Center
Dept. of Computer Science
St. Louis, MO 63130-4899

Abstract. Large scale on-demand multimedia servers, that can provide independent and interactive access to a vast amount of multimedia information to a large number of concurrent clients, will be required for a wide spread deployment of exciting multimedia applications. Our project, called Massively-parallel And Real-time Storage (**MARS**), is aimed at prototype development of such a large scale server. This paper primarily focuses on the distributed data layout and scheduling techniques developed in this project. These techniques support a high degree of parallelism and concurrency, and efficiently implement various playout control operations, such as *fast forward, rewind, pause, resume, frame advance* and *random access*.

1 Introduction

The primary focus of this paper is on the distributed data layout, scheduling and playout control algorithms developed in conjunction with our project, called the *Massively-parallel And Real-time Storage* (MARS). This project is aimed at the design and prototyping of a high performance large scale multimedia server that will be an integral part of the future multimedia environment. The five main requirements of such servers are: support potentially thousands of concurrent customers all accessing the same or different data; support large capacity (in excess of terabytes) storage of various types; deliver storage and network throughput in excess of a few Gbps; provide deterministic or statistical *Quality Of Service* (QOS) guarantees in the form of bandwidth and latency bounds; and support a full spectrum of interactive stream playout control operations such as *fast forward (ff), rewind (rw), random access, slow play, slow rewind, frame advance, pause, stop-and-return and stop*. Our work aims to meet these requirements.

1.1 A Prototype Architecture

Figure 1 shows a prototype architecture of a MARS server. It consists of three basic building blocks: a cell switched ATM interconnect, storage nodes, and the

---

* This work was supported in part by ARPA, the National Science Foundation's National Challenges Award (NCA), and an industrial consortium of Ascom Timeplex, Bellcore, BNR, Goldstar, NEC, NTT, Southwestern Bell, Bay Networks, and Tektronix.

central manager. The ATM interconnect is based on a custom ASIC called *ATM Port Interconnect Controller* (APIC), currently being developed as a part of an ARPA sponsored gigabit local ATM testbed [4]. The APIC is designed to support a data rate of 1.2 Gbps in each direction. Each storage node provides a large amount of storage in one or more forms, such as large high-performance magnetic disks, large disk arrays or a high capacity fast optical storage. The nodes that use optical storage can be considered as off-line or near-line tertiary storage. The contents of such storage can be cached on the magnetic disks at the other nodes. Thus, the collective storage in the system can exceed a few tens of terabytes. Each storage node may also provide one or more of the resource management functions, such as media processing, file system support, scheduling support, and admission control.

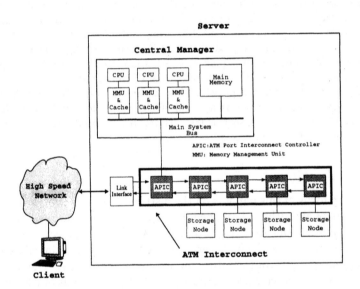

Fig. 1. A prototype architecture

The central manager shown in Figure 1 is responsible for managing the storage nodes and the APICs in the ATM interconnect. For every multimedia document,[2] it decides how to distribute the data over the storage nodes and manages associated meta-data information. It receives the connection requests from the remote clients and based on the availability of resources and the QOS required, admits or rejects the requests. For every active connection, it also schedules the data read/write from/to the storage nodes by exchanging appropriate control information with the storage nodes. Note that the central manager only sets up the data flow between the storage devices and the network and does

---

[2] A movie, a high quality audio file, an orchestrated presentation etc. are a few examples of a multimedia document.

not participate in actual data movement. This ensures a high bandwidth path between the storage nodes and the network.

Using the prototype architecture as a building block (called a *"storage cluster"*) and a multicast ATM switch, a large scale server can be realized. Both these architectures can meet the demands of future multimedia storage servers and have been described in greater detail in [1].

Note that these architectures easily support various on-demand multimedia service models, such as Shared Viewing (SV), Shared Viewing-with-Constraints (SVC) or *"near-video"*, and Dedicated Viewing (DV). However, in this paper, we assume that the server supports a retrieval environment using the DV service. This service model is a natural paradigm for highly interactive multimedia applications, as it treats every client request independently and does not depend on spatial and temporal properties of the request arrivals. Also, in this paper, we assume that each storage node uses magnetic disks or a disk array, such as commercial Redundant Arrays of Inexpensive Disks (RAID).

2 Distributed Data Layout

A data layout scheme in a multimedia server should possess the following properties: 1) it should support maximal parallelism in the use of storage nodes and be scalable in terms of number of clients concurrently accessing the same or different document, 2) facilitate interactive control and random access, and 3) allow simple scheduling schemes that can ensure periodic retrieval and transmission of data from unsynchronized storage nodes.

We use the fact that the multimedia data is amenable to spatial striping to distribute it hierarchically over several autonomous storage nodes within the server. One of the possible layout schemes, called *Distributed Cyclic Layout* (DCL_k), is shown in Figure 2. The layout uses a basic unit called *"chunk"* consisting of k consecutive frames. All the chunks in a document are of the same size and thus, have a constant time length in terms of playout duration. Different documents may have different chunk sizes, ranging from $k = 1$ to $k = F_{max}$, where F_{max} is the maximum number of frames in a multimedia document. In case of MPEG compressed streams, the group-of-pictures (GOP) is one possible choice of chunk size. A chunk is always confined to one storage node. The successive chunks are distributed over storage nodes using a logical layout topology. For example, in Figure 2, the chunks have been laid out using a ring topology. Note that in this scheme, the two consecutive chunks at the same node are separated in time by kDT_f time units, D being the number of storage nodes and T_f the frame period for the stream. Thus, if the chunk size is one frame (DCL_1 layout), the stream is slowed down by a factor of D from the perspective of each storage node or the throughput required per stream from each storage node is reduced by a factor of D. This in turns helps in masking the large prefetch latencies introduced by very slow storage devices at each node.

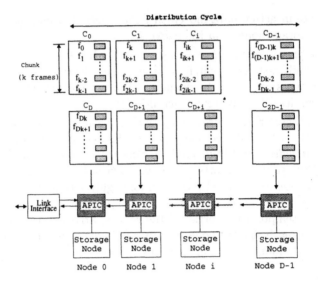

Fig. 2. Distributed Chunked Layout

2.1 Load Balance Property of Data Layouts

In the simple DCL$_1$ layout (recall chunk size $k = 1$), when a document is accessed in a normal playout mode, the frames are retrieved and transmitted in a linear $(\bmod D)$ order. Thus, for a set S_f of any consecutive D frames (called "frame set"), the set of nodes S_n (called "node set") from which these frames are retrieved contains each node only once. Such a node set is called a balanced node set. A balanced node set indicates that the load on each node, measured in number of frames, is uniform[3]. However, when the document is accessed in an interactive mode, such as ff or rw, the load-balance condition may be violated. In our study, we implement ff and rw by keeping the display rate constant and skipping frames, where the number of frames to skip is determined by the ff rate and the data layout. Thus, ff may be realized by displaying every alternate frame, every 5th frame, or every d^{th} frame in general. We define the fast forward (rewind) distance d_f (d_r) as the number of frames skipped in a fast forward (rewind) frame sequence. However, such an implementation has some implications for the load balance condition. Consider a connection in a system with $D = 6$ storage nodes, a DCL$_1$ layout, and a fast forward implementation by skipping alternate frames. The frame sequence for normal playout is $\{0, 1, 2, 3, 4, 5, \ldots\}$, whereas for the fast forward the same sequence is altered to $\{0, 2, 4, 6, 8, 10, \ldots\}$. This implies that in this example, the odd-numbered nodes are never visited for frame retrieval during ff. Clearly, it is desirable to know in advance what frame skipping

---

[3] The load variation caused by the non-uniform frame size in compressed media streams is compensated by adequate resource reservation and statistical multiplexing.

distances a layout can support without violating the load-balance condition. To this end, we state and prove the following theorem[4].

Theorem 1. *Given a* DCL₁ *layout over D storage nodes, the following holds true:*

- *If the fast forward (rewind) distance d_f (d_r) is relatively prime to D, then*
  1. *The set of nodes S_n, from which consecutive D frames in fast forward (rewind) frame set S_f (S_r) are retrieved, is load-balanced.*
  2. *The fast forward (rewind) can start from any arbitrary frame (or node) number.*

Proof. We give a proof by **contradiction**. Let f be the number of the arbitrary frame from which the fast forward is started. The D frames in the transmission cycle are then given as:

$$\{f, f + d_f, f + 2d_f, f + 3d_f, \ldots, f + id_f, \ldots f + jd_f + \ldots f + (D-1)d_f\}$$

If the frame f is mapped to node n_f, the set of nodes from which these D frames are retrieved is as follows:

$$f \mapsto n_f,$$
$$f + d_f \mapsto (n_f + d_f) \bmod D,$$
$$\vdots$$
$$f + (D-1)d_f \mapsto (n_f + (D-1)d_f) \bmod D \quad (1)$$

Without any loss of generality, assume n_p to be one of the D storage nodes that appears at least more than once in this node set. This means two frames, say $f + id_f$ and $f + jd_f$, are mapped to the same node n_p. If we carefully study the layout, we can see that the set of frames assigned to the node n_p can be defined as follows:

$$F_p = \{\forall \ell \in \mathcal{N} : (p + \ell \times D) \mapsto n_p\} \quad (2)$$

Clearly, any two frames mapped to the same node differ by an integral multiple of D. Hence,

$$(f + jd_f) - (f + id_f) = kD$$
$$(j - i) = k \times \frac{D}{d_f} \quad (3)$$

Two cases that arise are as follows:

---

[4] The result was first pointed out in a different form by Dr. Arif Merchant of the NEC Research Labs, Princeton, New Jersey, during the first author's summer research internship.

- **Case 1: k is not a multiple of d_f:** If D and d_f are relatively prime[5], then, $\frac{D}{d_f}$ cannot be an integer. The left hand side (L.H.S) of Equation 3 being a difference of two integers, is also an integer. Hence, the left hand side and the right hand side of the above equation cannot be equal. Thus, the Equation 3 cannot be true, which is a contradiction.
- **Case 2: k is a multiple of d_f:** If this condition is true, then $(j - i) = k_1 \times D$, where $k_1 = \frac{k}{d_f}$. However, this contradicts our assumption that the two selected frames are in the set which has only D frames and hence, can differ at the most $D - 1$ in their ordinality.

Since, the frame f from which fast-forward begins is selected arbitrarily, the claim 2 in the Theorem statement is also justified. The proof in the case of a rewind operation is similar and is not presented here.

Thus, as per this theorem, if $D = 6$, skipping by all distances that are odd numbers $(1, 5, 7, 11 \ldots)$ and are relatively prime to 6 will result in a balanced node set. We can see that if D is a prime number, then all distances d_f that are not multiples of D produce a balanced node set.

2.2 Staggered Distributed Cyclic Layouts

Now we will briefly describe a more general layout called *Staggered Distributed Cyclic Layout* (SDCL) and characterize the fast forward distances it can support without violating load balance. Figure 3 illustrates an example of such a layout. We define a distribution cycle in a layout as a set of D frames, in which the first frame number is an integral multiple of D. The starting frame in such a cycle is called an anchor frame and the node to which it is assigned is called an anchor node. In the case of a DCL$_1$ layout described earlier, the anchor node for successive distribution cycles is always fixed to the same node. On the other hand, for the layout in Figure 3, anchor nodes of the successive distribution cycles are staggered by one node, in a $(\bmod D)$ order. This is an example of a staggered layout with stagger factor of $k_s = 1$, and other staggered data layouts with non-unit stagger distance are possible. Note that DCL$_1$ is a special case of SDCL layout with the stagger distance of $k_s = 0$. In general, the SDCL can be looked upon as a family of distributed cyclic layouts, each with different stagger distance k_s and with different load-balance properties. The following theorem illustrates the load-balance properties of SDCL with $k_s = 1$. A similar result for the general case with non-unit stagger distance is not presented here.

Theorem 2. *Given a SDCL layout with $k_s = 1$ over D storage nodes, and numbers $d_1, d_2, d_3, \cdots d_p$ that are factors of D, the following holds true:*

- **Load balance condition for fast forward:** *If the fast forward starts from an anchor frame f_a, with fast forward distance d_f, then the node set S_n is load-balanced, provided:*

---

[5] If two numbers p and q are relatively prime, then their greatest common divisor is 1.

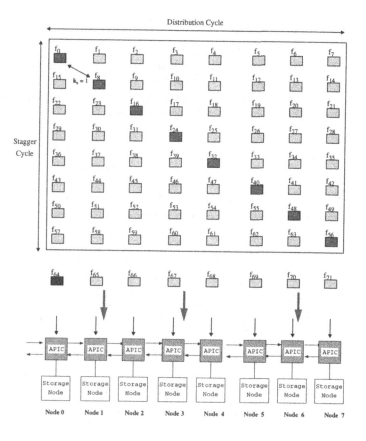

Fig. 3. Staggered Distributed Cyclic Layout(SDCL) with $k_s = 1$

1. $d_f = d_i$ (where $1 \leq i \leq p$) or
2. $d_f = m \times D$ where m and D are relatively prime or
3. $d_f = d_i + kD^2$ ($k > 0$)

- **Load balance condition for rewind:** *The same result holds true for rewind if the rewind starts from a frame $2D - 1$ after the anchor frame.*

A detailed proof of this theorem can be found in the current version of [2, 3]. The aforementioned two theorems together allow the server to provide clients a rich choice of *ff* (*rw*) speeds. Also, both these theorems are equally valid for a chunked layout with non-unit chunk size, if the *ff* (*rw*) is implemented by skipping chunks instead of frames. These results are useful in implementing *ff* (*rw*) on MPEG streams that introduce interframe dependencies and make it difficult to realize arbitrary frame skipping distances.

3   Distributed Scheduling

In this section, we illustrate the basic scheme and data structure used to schedule periodic data retrieval and transmission from storage nodes. Note that in addition to this scheme, each storage node has to schedule reads from the disks in the disk array and optimize disk head movements.

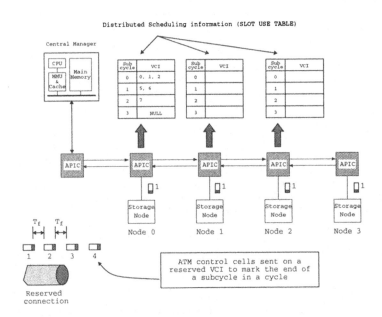

Fig. 4. Distributed scheduling implementation

In a typical scenario, a client sends a request to the server to access a multimedia document at the server. This request is received and processed by the central manager at the server, shown in Figure 1. Specifically, the central manager consults an admission control procedure, which based on current resource availability, admits or rejects the new request. If the request is admitted, a network connection to the client, with appropriate QOS, is established. The central manager informs the storage nodes of this new connection, which in response create or update appropriate data structures such as *Slot Use Table*, *Connection State Block*, *Transmission Map*, etc. and allocate sufficient buffers. If an active client wants to effect a playout control operation, it sends a request to the server. The central manager receives it, and in response, instructs the storage nodes to change the transmission and prefetch schedule. Such a change can add, in the worst case, a latency of one scheduling cycle[6].

---

[6] A cycle is typically a few hundreds of milliseconds duration.

The global schedule consists of two concurrent and independent cycles: the "prefetch cycle" and the "transmission cycle", each of length T_c. During the prefetch cycle, each storage node retrieves and buffers data for all active connections. In the overlapping transmission cycle, the APIC corresponding to the node transmits the data retrieved in the previous cycle, that is, the data transmitted in the current i^{th} cycle is prefetched during previous $(i-1)^{th}$ cycle. A ping-pong buffering scheme facilitates such overlapped prefetch and transmission. Each storage node and associated APIC maintain a pair of ping-pong buffers, which are shared by the C_a active connections. The buffer that serves as prefetch buffer in current cycle is used as a transmission buffer in the next cycle and vice-versa. The APIC reads the data for each active connection from the transmit buffer and paces the cells, generated by AAL5 segmentation, on the ATM interconnect and to the external network, as per a rate specification. Note that the cells for all active connections are interleaved together.

Table 1. Prefetch information at a node

VCI	No. of Frames	Frame IDs	Frame Address	Buffer Descriptor
VCI_1	1	8	$addr_8$	$bufdescr_1$
VCI_2	2	4,5	$addr_{4,5}$	$bufdescr_{4,5}$
VCI_3	1	1000	$addr_{1000}$	$bufdescr_{1000}$
$\vdots$	$\vdots$	$\vdots$	$\vdots$	$\vdots$
VCI_{100}	1	8500	$addr_{8500}$	$bufdescr_{8500}$

Each storage node has its own independent prefetch cycle, in which it uses the prefetch information, illustrated in Table 1, for each active connection to retrieve the data. Specifically, the prefetch information consists of the following basic items: 1) Number of frames to be prefetched in the current cycle, 2) identification (ID) numbers of the frames to be fetched, 3) metadata required to locate the data on the storage devices at the storage node, and 4) the buffer descriptors that describe the buffers into which the data retrieved in the current cycle will be stored. Thus, for the example of Table 1, for $VCI = 2$, two frames $f = 4, 5$ need to be fetched using addresses $addr_4$ and $addr_5$ into the buffer described by $bufdescr_{4,5}$. Typically, the buffer descriptors and the buffers will be allocated dynamically in each cycle.

The transmission cycle consists of D identical sub-cycles, each of time length $\frac{T_c}{D}$. The end of a sub-cycle is indicated by a special control cell sent periodically on the APIC interconnect. As shown in Figure 4, the APIC associated with the central manager reserves a multicast control connection, with a unique VCI, that is programmed to generate these control cells at a constant rate $\frac{T_c}{D}$. Each of the remaining APICs in the interconnect, copies the cell to the storage node controller and also multicasts it downstream on the APIC interconnect. The storage node counts these cells to know the current sub-cycle number and the start/end of the cycle.

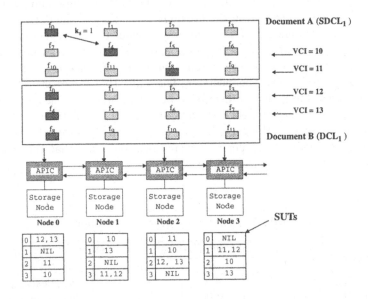

Fig. 5. An example of connections in different playout states

One of the main data structures used by each node to do transmission scheduling is the **Slot Use Table** (SUT). The ith entry in this table lists the set of VCIs for which data will be transmitted in the ith sub-cycle. This table is computed by the storage node or the central manager at the start of each cycle, using simple modulo arithmetic and load-balance conditions described earlier.

Table 2. Frame and node sets for all connections

VCI	Frame set S_f	Node set S_n
10	4, 5, 6, 7	1, 2, 3, 0
11	8, 9, 10, 11	2, 3, 0, 1
12	0, 3, 6, 9	0, 3, 2, 1
13	4, 5, 6, 7	0, 1, 2, 3

Figure 5 illustrates distributed scheduling with an example. This example shows two documents: Document A stored using the SDCL layout and Document B stored using DCL$_1$ data layout. Of the four active connections indicated, the connections with $VCI = 10, 11$ are accessing the document A and the connection with $VCI = 13$ is accessing document B in a normal play mode. On the other hand, $VCI = 12$ is accessing the document B in *ff* mode by skipping every third frame. Table 2 illustrates for each connection, the transmission frame set and ordered set of nodes from which it is transmitted during current transmission cycle. Using this table, the SUT at each node can be constructed. For example, node 0 transmits for connections $12, 13$ in slot 0, for connections 11 in slot 2, for connection 10 in slot 3, and remains idle during slots 1. The SUT at node 0 in Figure 5 records this information. Also, note that the SUTs at all the nodes contain exactly four non-zero entries and one NIL entry per cycle, indicating that the load is balanced over all the nodes. In this example, the documents have the same chunk size, however, the case when documents have different chunk sizes can be easily accommodated.

4 Implications of MPEG

Empirical evidence shows that in a typical MPEG stream, depending upon the scene content, I to P frame variability is about 3:1, whereas P to B frame variability is about 2:1. Thus, the MPEG stream is inherently variable bit rate. Clearly, when retrieving MPEG stream, the load on a node varies depending upon the granularity of retrieval. If a node is performing a frame-by-frame retrieval, the load on a node retrieving an I frame is 6–8 times that on a node retrieving a B frame. Hence, it is necessary to ensure that certain nodes do not always fetch I frames and others fetch only B frames. The variability of load at the GOP level may be much less than at the frame level, and hence selecting appropriate data layout and retrieval unit is crucial. In presence of concurrent clients, it is likely that each storage node can occasionally suffer overload, forcing the prefetch deadlines to be missed and thus, requiring explicit communication between the storage nodes to notify such events. The modifications to the basic scheduling required to realize this are not described here. Also, note that if the disk arrays used at the storage nodes are commercial RAIDs, the scheme for striping the data at each node is in effect fixed and may be inefficient for the statistical multiplexing of MPEG streams.

Another problem posed by MPEG like compression techniques is that they introduce inter-frame dependencies and thus, do not allow, frame skipping at arbitrary rate. This in effect means that *ff* by frame skipping can realize only a few rates. For example, the only valid fast forward frame sequences are IPP···IPP··· or [IIII...]. However, both these sequences increase the network and storage BW requirement enormously during *ff* and *rw*. The two ways to rectify this problem are as follows:

– **Store a intra-coded version of the movie along with a interframe coded version:** This option offers unlimited fast forward/rewind speeds, however, it increases storage and throughput requirement. There are three optimizations possible that can alleviate this problem to some extent: 1) Reduce the quantization factor for the intra-coded version, but this may lead to loss of detail. 2) Reduce the display rate, however, this may cause jerkiness. 3) Store the spatially down-sampled versions of the frames, that is, reduce the resolution of the frames. This requires the frames to be up-sampled in real-time using up-sampling hardware. We believe that all three optimizations will be necessary, especially at high ff rates, to keep the network and storage throughput requirements unaltered.

- **Use the interframe coded version but instead of skipping frames skip chunks:** In this option, the skipping granularity is increased to chunks instead of frames, and chunks are transmitted from the individual storage nodes similar to the normal play mode (but in a different order). The load balance results illustrated earlier are valid for chunk skipping, with the frames skipping distance d_f replaced by chunk skipping distance d_{cf}. This option has the advantage that it keeps the storage and throughput requirements unchanged from the normal play, however, it may prove to be visually unappealing, especially with large chunk sizes.

The tradeoffs associated with these two options are currently being evaluated.

5 Conclusions

In this paper, we described data layout and scheduling options in our prototype architecture for a large scale multimedia server currently being investigated in the project **MARS**. We illustrated a family of hierarchical, distributed layouts called *Staggered Distributed Data Layouts* (SDCLs), that use constant time length logical units called chunks. For some of these layouts, we defined and proved a load-balance property that is required for efficient implementation of playout control operations such as fast-forward and rewind. Finally, we illustrated a distributed scheduling framework that guarantees orderly transmission of data for all active connections in any arbitrary playout state and addresses the implications of MPEG. These schemes and the associated tradeoffs are currently being evaluated using simulations.

References

1. Buddhikot, M., Parulkar, G., Cox, Jerome, R. Jr.: Design of a Large Scale Multimedia Storage Server. *Journal of Computer Networks and ISDN Systems (1995) 504-517.*
2. Buddhikot, M., Parulkar, G.: Scheduling, Data Layout and Playout Control in a Large Scale Multimedia Storage Server. Technical Report **WUCS-94-33**, Department of Computer Science, Washington University in St. Louis (1994).
3. Buddhikot, M., Parulkar, G.: Load Balance Properties of Distributed Data Layouts in MARS. Technical Report (in preparation), Department of Computer Science, Washington University in St. Louis. (1995).
4. Dittia, Z., Cox., J., Parulkar, G.: Design of the APIC: A High Performance ATM Host Network Interface. Proceedings of IEEE INFOCOM'95 (to appear) Boston (1995).

Storage Replication and Layout in Video-on-Demand Servers

Scott D. Stoller[1]* and John D. DeTreville[2]

[1] Dept. of Computer Science, Cornell University, Ithaca, NY 14853-7501, USA.
stoller@cs.cornell.edu
[2] Digital Equipment Corporation, Systems Research Center
130 Lytton Avenue, Palo Alto CA 94301-1044, USA.
jdd@pa.dec.com

Abstract. We propose and analyze an architecture for storage servers in large Video on Demand (VoD) systems. We describe a method for distributing the collection of titles among the levels of the storage hierarchy, based on estimates of the mean demand for each title. The resulting distribution minimizes cost for a given level of performance. Since high availability is desirable in VoD systems, we consider the use of mirroring or parity-based redundancy (*à la* RAID) and estimate the effect on the system's cost and availability. In the very-large-scale storage systems needed for VoD, the placement of disk arrays on the pool of computers must be chosen carefully to provide high availability for the least cost. We propose a strategy for arranging disk arrays on a pool of PCs; our strategy is inspired by Holland and Gibson's work on parity declustering for RAID.

1 Introduction

A Video on Demand (VoD) system provides access to a library of video (*e.g.*, digitized movies) by multiple independent subscribers in homes or offices. Large VoD systems would have been impossible to deploy cost-effectively with the technology of two decades ago; two decades from now they should seem easy. VoD systems should be a common application on the coming "information superhighway."

To better anticipate future design issues, we create analytical models of VoD systems and their cost and performance. We concern ourselves with large systems and with very high performance, the better to illustrate the challenges in engineering VoD systems.

* This work was performed in part at the Digital Equipment Corporation Systems Research Center. This material is based on work supported in part by the Office of Naval Research under contract N00014-91-J-1219, the National Science Foundation under Grant No. CCR-9003440, DARPA/NSF Grant No. CCR-9014363, NASA/DARPA grant NAG-2-893, and AFOSR grant F49620-94-1-0198. Any opinions, findings, and conclusions or recommendations expressed in this publication are those of the author and do not reflect the views of these agencies.

A VoD system in a large metropolitan area might serve 10^4 to 10^5 simultaneous viewers (N_V) at its busiest. The library of movies, *etc.*, might easily contain 10^3 to 10^4 titles (N_T). Although home viewers might tolerate significant delays in starting or restarting a movie, we require a latency of at most a few seconds for such operations; this allows stored video also to be used in interactive applications. We assume that the popularities of the titles follow a Zipf-like distribution, *i.e.*, that the popularity of the ith title is proportional to $1/i$.

1.1   General Architectural Assumptions

Each title is striped across an array of G storage devices (*i.e.*, G is the group size). During playback, the data stream must enter the distribution network at the same rate r it is to be viewed: a few Mb/s. As this is an order of magnitude slower than disks can read, each disk array can serve roughly $10G$ streams. We choose to concentrate equipment at a central site, where it can be shared, such that each viewer needs only a network connection and a simple set-top unit (STU) to decode the stream and provide a user interface.

We assume a number of server computers at the central site, each with its own disks, interconnected via a high-speed network, and attached to the distribution network. Since the limiting factor at the servers is the bandwidth of the memory-I/O bus, we choose the PC architecture for the servers, as commodity hardware minimizes cost per bandwidth.

In a large VoD system, component failures will be common. We say that the servers can *tolerate* a failure if, despite that failure, the servers can continue to provide nearly uninterrupted service to all N_V viewers. (We allow a small hiccup in scheduling that could be masked by a buffer in the STU.)

1.2   Focus: High-level Server Design

We restrict our attention to the physical and logical architecture of the servers. We seek the optimal distribution of titles between disk and RAM, and the optimal layouts of titles among disks and PCs, in order to minimize cost and maximize availability at a given level of performance.

In a VoD system, unlike a general-purpose file system, the data are large and static, real-time response is required, bandwidth can be pre-allocated, and the usage patterns of the viewers are partly known. We base our design on these features.

2   Placing Titles in the Storage Hierarchy

The function of the servers is playback of stored video data. Various storage media are available, each with different cost and performance. The available storage media are called the *storage hierarchy*. Descending the hierarchy corresponds to *decreasing* cost per unit capacity and *increasing* cost per unit throughput.

Server design includes deciding where in the hierarchy to store each title. Multiple copies of a title may be needed to serve all of the requested streams for that title; this is *replication for throughput*. We arrange titles in the storage hierarchy with more popular titles in higher levels; storing a popular title at a lower level would require more copies of that title, counterbalancing the lower cost per unit capacity at the lower level. For concreteness, we assume that the storage hierarchy comprises RAM, (magnetic) disk, and (magnetic) tape, in that order. Generalizing our analysis to accommodate additional storage media is straightforward.

We quantify the above placement argument for the particular case of allocating titles between RAM and disk. The number of streams that can be served from each copy of a title depends on the layout of the data—in particular, it can be increased by striping a title across an array of storage devices. We assume a title in RAM is striped across G PCs; a title on disk is striped across G disks. (Relaxing the assumption that the same group size is used for both media does not affect our conclusions.) Let t_D and t_{PC} denote the mean throughput of a disk and (the I/O-bus of) a PC, respectively. Let p_D and p_{PC} denote the cost of a disk and PC, respectively. If s streams are needed, then the number of copies needed for bandwidth if the title is stored in RAM or on disk is approximately $i_{RAM} = \frac{sr}{Gt_{PC}}$ or $i_D = \frac{sr}{Gt_D}$, respectively.

Assume, for now, that the disks are *throughput-limited* (*i.e.*, the total required disk throughput equals the total available disk throughput). Then the total costs of serving this title from RAM or disk are approximately $P_{RAM} = \lceil i_{RAM} \rceil dr p_{RAM} + i_{RAM} G p_{PC}$ or $P_D^t = i_D G p_D + \frac{t_D}{t_{PC}} i_D 2 G p_{PC}$, respectively, where d is the duration of the title.[3] The second summands are the cost of the needed PC throughput; the factor of 2 in P_D^t reflects data on disk crossing the PC's I/O-bus twice before transmission. Viewing these costs as functions of s, we see that they intersect at some value of s, which we denote s_{RAM}^t. The system cost is minimized by storing titles with $s \geq s_{RAM}^t$ in RAM, and titles with $s < s_{RAM}^t$ at a lower level.

The above calculation assumes the disk system is throughput-limited; note that no such assumption was made for RAM. If the disk system is sufficiently *capacity-limited* (*i.e.*, the total required disk storage space equals the total available disk storage capacity), then the cost of serving the streams for this title from disk is just the cost of the storage space; roughly, $P_D^c = i_D \frac{dr}{c_D} p_D$.

Of course, the intersection of P_{RAM} and P_D^c defines a different cut-off between RAM and disk. Since we don't know *a priori* which cut-off is correct, we compute the cut-off s_{RAM} as follows. We calculate an initial estimate for s_{RAM} by assuming the disk system is throughput-limited—this estimate is s_{RAM}^t. We then check whether the resulting disk system is actually throughout-limited. If so, we are done; if not, we increment s_{RAM} repeatedly until the disk system *is* throughput-limited. This method often leads to a final configuration where the disk system is at the balance-point of being capacity-limited *and* throughput-limited. The examples in Section 5 illustrate this.

---

[3] Slight modifications are required if redundancy is used. For example, if titles in RAM are mirrored, then the storage cost per title in RAM doubles.

Distributing Titles Between Disk and Tape. It is tempting to store the least popular titles only on tape when they are not being viewed and copy them to disk as needed. However, calculations similar to those above show that, except in VoD systems with low ratios of viewers to titles, the tape throughput needed for on-demand copying costs (almost) as much as the disk capacity that is saved. We conclude that using tape in this way is generally not worthwhile, especially if the additional complexity of supporting on-demand loading of titles from tape is taken into account.

3 Redundancy in RAM

Another major design decision for VoD servers is the form of redundancy to use. Different redundancy schemes may be more attractive at different levels of the storage hierarchy, so we discuss the choices separately for RAM and disk. In this section, we discuss briefly the resources needed for titles in RAM for no redundancy, parity, and mirroring. Availability is analyzed in Section 6.

The use of parity for fault-tolerance is well-known from RAID [1]. The resource requirements depend on where missing data is reconstructed. Reconstruction in the STU instead of the servers has some benefits (*e.g.*, reducing the net cost of the servers and STUs) and some drawbacks (*e.g.*, increasing the performance requirements for the STUs).

If reconstruction is done in the STU, then the STU must be fast enough to reconstruct the missing data in real-time. Since the STU is processing a single video stream, this requirement is modest.

If reconstruction is done in the server, extra PC throughput is required for the PCs to exchange data to reconstruct the missing data. The task of reconstruction can be distributed among many PCs (not just those in the affected array) to reduce the additional PC throughput needed.

The cost of mirroring is dominated by the cost of the extra RAM needed for storage.

4 Disk Organization and Redundancy

After deciding which titles to store on disk, we must still choose the layout of the titles on the disks and the layout of the disks on the PCs. For the former, we continue to assume that each copy of a title on disk is striped across exactly G disks. The arrangement of these disk arrays on the PCs affects the availability. The best choice depends on the form of redundancy.

In this section, we determine the resource requirements for titles on disk with each redundancy option; availability is analyzed in Section 6. The requirements depend on both the form of redundancy and the *tolerated failures, i.e.,* the types of failures the system tolerates. For example, using mirroring when the system must tolerate any single disk failure requires doubling the disk capacity.

Two principles help determine the best organization. For economy, the organization should minimize the resources needed to tolerate tolerated failures. For availability, it should minimize the number of viewers affected by non-tolerated failures.

4.1 Organizations with No Redundancy

A system with no redundancy tolerates no failures. Availability is maximized by distributing each disk array onto as few PCs as possible, since this minimizes the number of viewers affected by each PC failure.

4.2 Organizations with Parity: Declustered Disk Arrays

We use parity to tolerate failure of a single disk or PC.[4]One simple organization is to arrange the PCs into arrays of size G. Each array of disks is spread across an array of PCs; each PC has at most one disk from each disk array. This makes it possible for the system to tolerate a PC failure.

The resource requirements for the servers depend on where reconstruction is done. Reconstruction in the STU requires few additional resources. The resources needed for reconstruction in the servers depend on the transmission schedule in the event of failure. One simple schedule has each PC in the affected array synchronously read data from disk, exchange the data with the other PCs, reconstructs its part of the missing data, then transmits its data to the STUs according to the normal transmission schedule. In the event of a failure, PCs read data earlier than normal but transmit it at the usual time, so additional buffer RAM is needed.[5]The main costs of parity-based redundancy are this buffer RAM and the extra PC throughput needed for reconstruction.

With the organization sketched above, in the event of the failure of a PC with n_{PC}^{D} disks, the extra load on the surviving PCs in the affected array of PCs is n_{PC}^{D} times the extra load resulting from a single disk failure, as is the extra RAM and throughput needed. The resource requirements can be significantly reduced by better distributing the extra load caused by a PC failure. Intuitively, we think of the PCs as a large homogeneous pool and arrange the disk arrays on the PCs to minimize the average number of disk arrays "shared" by each pair of PCs.

More precisely, we say that two PCs *share* a disk array iff both of the PCs have a disk in that disk array. Let $\sigma_i = \max(\{shared(i,j) \mid j \neq i\})$, where i and j name PCs and $shared(i,j)$ is the number of disk arrays shared by i and j. A *declustered disk array* organization is one that (nearly) minimizes $\bar{\sigma} = N_{PC}^{-1} \sum_i \sigma_i$, where N_{PC} is the number of PCs in the system. These organizations are closely analogous to those proposed by Holland and Gibson for arranging data stripes among a pool of PCs [5]. Using the formulas in their Section 4.2, we

---

[4] Our availability analysis takes into account that some double disk failures can also be tolerated.

[5] This buffering can be eliminated by reading the data from disk twice, but our calculations show that the extra disk throughput generally costs more than the buffer RAM.

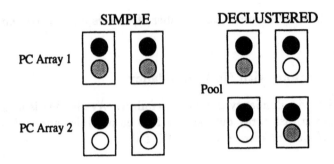

Fig. 1. Example of declustering. The rectangles are PCs; the circles, disks. Shading represents disk arrays. Note that $\bar{\sigma} = 2$ for the simple organization and $\bar{\sigma} = 1$ when declustered.

expect $\bar{\sigma} \approx (n_{PC}^{D})^2 (G-1)/(N_D - n_{PC}^{D})$, where N_D is the number of disks in the system. It suffices to use an organization with approximately this value of $\bar{\sigma}$.

Figure 1 contains a simple example of declustering. Section 5 illustrates the cost savings from declustering disk arrays. Declustering reduces availability, but only slightly.

4.3 Organizations with Mirroring

As with parity, the system tolerates the failure of a single disk or PC. As in the first organization with parity, the PCs are divided into arrays of size G, and disk arrays are striped across arrays of PCs. To minimize the PC throughput needed to handle a PC failure, we again use a form of declustering: the backups of different disk arrays on a PC array are placed on different PC arrays. The resource analysis for mirroring is similar to that for parity.

5 Hardware Cost

We estimate hardware costs for various server designs, based on the analysis sketched above. We adopt many simplifications of reality, so our figures are rough estimates of actual cost. For example, although the video streams may be variable-bit-rate, we use just the mean bit-rate in our calculations. We adopt only simplifications that are roughly "orthogonal" to the design issues under consideration, so our analysis should reflect the *relative* costs for different designs.

We assume that the network can multicast data; for example, an ATM network based on the AN2 switch [9] can multicast. This is useful for the most popular titles: multiple viewers can receive the same stream, so the servers need never to supply more than (say) one stream per second per title.

Our calculations are based on the expected hardware cost and performance figures for late 1995 given in Table 1. We take the mean bit-rate of a stream

Table 1. Expected hardware cost and performance figures for late 1995.

RAM	Disk Controller
Cost: $p_{RAM} = \$14/MB$	Throughput: $t_{ctrlr} = 20$ MB/s
Disk	Cost: $p_{ctrlr} = \$250$
Striping unit: $B = 200$ KB	PC
Capacity: $c_D = 4.3$ GB	I/O Throughput (PCI bus): $t_{PC} = 90$ MB/s
Mean Throughput: $t_D = 4$ MB/s	Cost: $p_{PC} = \$4000$
Cost: $p_D = \$1600$	

Table 2. Cost and availability of a medium VoD system ($N_T = 10^4, N_V = 10^5$)

Redundancy Organization	None	Parity Simple	Parity Declus.	Mirror	Mir/Par Declus.	ParSTU Simple	ParSTU Declus.
N_T^{RAM}	18	18	18	0	18	18	18
RAM (GB)	50	390	73	5	119	395	73
Disk-cap. (10^3)	6.2	6.3	6.3	12.4	6.3	6.3	6.3
Disk-tput.(10^3)	6.2	6.3	6.3	9.5	6.3	6.3	6.3
Disk Ctrlr(10^3)	1.6	1.6	1.6	3.1	1.6	1.6	1.6
PC	700	1800	1000	860	810	720	710
Network (10^3\$)	0	110	110	0	70	0	0
Cost (10^6\$)	13.8	23.3	15.7	24.1	15.5	18.9	14.4
ir (year^{-1})	.14	.027	.021	.019	.015	.015	.015

to be $r = 3$ Mb/s; this corresponds to VHS-quality video encoded with MPEG-2. Increasing the group size G improves load-balancing and reduces replication of titles but reduces availability. We take $G = 50$; this is just large enough to require negligible replication of titles for throughput. Thus, by storing titles in RAM, striping widely, and taking advantage of network multicast, we nearly eliminate replication for throughput; we use redundancy primarily for enhancing availability.

Tables 2 and 3 describe a "medium" VoD system ($N_T = 10^4, N_V = 10^5$) and a "large" VoD system ($N_T = 10^4, N_V = 4 \times 10^5$), respectively. The three sections of each table give the design, its hardware requirements, and the resulting availability. The "Redundancy" row gives the forms of redundancy used for RAM and for disk (in that order, if two forms are given), or for both (if only one form is given). "Par(ity)" denotes parity with reconstruction in the servers; "ParSTU" denotes reconstruction in the STU. N_T^{RAM} is the number of titles stored in RAM.

The "Disk-cap." and "Disk-tput." rows count the disks required for capacity and for throughput; the number of disks needed is the maximum of these. The "PC" row counts the PCs needed. The "Network" row estimates the cost of the internal network used by the servers to interchange reconstruction data. The cost of the external network is not included, since it is constant among these

Table 3. Cost and availability of a large VoD system ($N_T = 10^4$, $N_V = 4 \times 10^5$)

Redundancy Organization	None	Parity Simple	Parity Declus.	Mirror	Par/Mir	ParSTU Simple	ParSTU Declus.	ParSTU/Mir
N_T^{RAM}	193	193	193	96	193	193	193	193
RAM (GB)	517	1388	546	516	528	1388	546	528
Disk-cap. (10^3)	6.2	6.3	6.3	12.3	12.3	6.3	6.3	12.3
Disk-tput.(10^3)	15.6	15.9	15.9	18.7	15.9	15.9	15.9	15.9
Disk Ctrlr(10^3)	3.9	4.0	4.0	4.7	4.0	4.0	4.0	4.0
PC	2190	5550	3630	2360	3390	2220	2190	2220
Network (10^3\$)	0	442	442	0	0	0	0	0
Cost (10^6\$)	41.9	68.5	49.0	47.7	47.6	54.7	42.8	42.7
ir (year^{-1})	.15	.062	.057	.037	.052	.029	.033	.035

designs. The row labeled "ir" is discussed in Section 6.

In the medium system, the optimum value of N_T^{RAM} results in the disk system being both throughput-limited and capacity-limited. In the large system, the disk system is throughput-limited but not capacity-limited.

Comparing "Parity" and "Mir/Par" for the medium system shows that the reduced storage cost from parity in RAM is offset by the cost of the PC throughput needed for reconstruction. The same effect can be seen in the large system by comparing the columns "Mirror" and "Par/Mir."

For titles on disk, we see that parity is more attractive in the medium system, while mirroring is more attractive in the large system. For titles in RAM, parity is more attractive than mirroring if we reconstruct in the STUs; otherwise, parity and mirroring are about equally expensive and mirroring has slightly better availability. For both systems, the cheapest redundancy option increases the system cost by about 3% for reconstruction in the STUs, and by about 13% otherwise.

6 Availability

Redundancy can increase availability. We quantify availability as ir, the "mean rate of observed interruptions due to server failures, per STU." "Observed interruptions" do not include failures when the STU is not in use. To quantify this, we introduce two parameters: the mean fractional load on the system, denoted $meanFL$; and the maximum fraction of STUs active at once, denoted $maxFA$. Note that the total number of STUs is $N_V/maxFA$, and that the mean number of active STUs is $N_V meanFL$. We take $meanFL = 1/4$ and $maxFA = 1/3$. As a sanity check on these values, note that each STU is in use $(meanFL)(maxFA)$ of the time, i.e., 14 hours/week. These values represent a future time when VoD has largely supplanted broadcast TV and videotape rental in the U.S. It is easy to see the effect of choosing other values for these parameters, since ir is directly proportional to each.

Our availability calculations are based on a classification of failures by cause. Following Gray and Reuter [4], we take the set *Causes* of possible causes of failures to be: hardware (subdivided into RAM, disk, and PC), operations, maintenance, environment, and software. In equations, we abbreviate the last four causes by their first letter. Let $r(c)$ denote the rate of failures with cause c.

To estimate the effect of redundancy on availability, one must consider the tolerance to failures of each cause. We propose the following model. Each failure is assumed to have the effect of rendering inoperative one physical or *logical* component of the system. In this model, the set *CType* of types of components that a failure may affect are: RAM (one word of RAM), D (one disk), DA (one disk array), PC (one PC), PCA (one PC array), or SYS (the entire system). For a given system design, for each component type t, let $\tau(t)$ denote the number of viewers whose streams are interrupted by a given failure of type t.

Our model postulates that, of all the failures with a given cause c, some fraction λ_t^c render inoperative a component of type t. For example, a software error in the OS will probably crash a single PC, while a software error in a scheduling module is likely to affect an entire array of PCs, so λ_{PC}^S and λ_{PCA}^S are both non-zero. The mean number of viewers interrupted by a failure with cause c is the weighted sum

$$\kappa(c) = \sum_{t \in CType} \lambda_t^c \tau(t) \ . \tag{1}$$

Multiple Failures. To model multiple failures, we generalize the above definitions slightly, by taking the domains of κ and r to be non-empty subsets of *Causes*. For example, $r(\{D, D\})$ is the rate of double disk failures, and $\kappa(\{D, D\})$ is the mean number of viewers interrupted by a double disk failure. Each of these rates $r(C)$ is a parameter of the model; for example, we are free to choose $r(\{D, D\})$ to reflect correlations between disk failures. The earlier discussion is still valid, when occurrences of $r(c)$ and $\kappa(c)$ are interpreted as abbreviations for $r(\{c\})$ and $\kappa(\{c\})$, respectively. Thus, we continue to use equation (1) to define κ on singleton sets. In contrast, we do not assume any particular form for the equations defining κ on sets of cardinality greater than one; these equations are derived using probabilistic arguments and contain only the parameters introduced above. Finally, the mean rate of observed interruptions due to server failures, per STU, is

$$ir = \frac{(meanFL)(maxFA)}{N_v} \sum_{\emptyset \subset C \subseteq Causes} r(C)\kappa(C) \ . \tag{2}$$

6.1 Availability Calculations

The availabilities in Tables 2 and 3 were obtained using the model sketched above. Table 4 contains the failure rates used in our calculations. They are based primarily on data from surveys of Tandem customers [3, 4] and on product information (*e.g.*, [7]). The failure rates reported in the Tandem surveys are *per*

Table 4. Failure rates by cause.

$r(\{\text{RAM}\})$	$= (3 \times 10^7 \text{ hour})^{-1}$	per 2MB bank (selected)
	$(3 \times 10^8 \text{ hour})^{-1}$	per 2MB bank (unselected)
$r(\{\text{D}\})$	$= (3 \times 10^5 \text{ hour})^{-1}$	per disk
$r(\{\text{PC}\})$	$= (50 \text{ year})^{-1}$	per PC
$r(\{O\})$	$= (75 \text{ year})^{-1}$	per 100 PCs
$r(\{M\})$	$= (420 \text{ year})^{-1}$	per 100 PCs
$r(\{E\})$	$= (170 \text{ year})^{-1}$	per system
$r(\{S\})$	$= (30 \text{ year})^{-1}$	per 3 PCs
$r(\{\text{D}, \text{D}\})$	$= 10(N_\text{D}r(\{\text{D}\}))^2 MTTR_\text{D}$	per system
$r(\{\text{D}, \text{PC}\})$	$= (N_\text{D}r(\{\text{D}\}))(N_\text{PC}r(\{PC\}))$	per system
	$(MTTR_\text{D} + MTTR_\text{PC})$	
$r(\{\text{PC}, \text{PC}\})$	$= 10(N_\text{PC}r(\{PC\}))^2 MTTR_\text{PC}$ per system	

system, for systems with an average of three processors. Therefore, we scale their software failure rate by $N_\text{PC}/3$ and (somewhat arbitrarily) their operations and maintenance failure rates by $N_\text{PC}/100$. Following Gray's comments [3], we compensate for underreporting of failures by increasing the reported rates for operations, environment, and software failures by 100%, 100%, and 5%, respectively. The factors of 10 in $r(\{\text{D}, \text{D}\})$ and $r(\{\text{PC}, \text{PC}\})$ account for correlated failures. Assuming a pool of spare disks is available, $MTTR_\text{D}$ is dominated by the time needed to fill one of the spare disks with the appropriate data. With mirroring, this is just the time needed to fill the spare disk with data, so $MTTR_\text{D} \approx c_\text{D}/t_\text{D}$. Reconstructing data from parity requires more work, so with parity, we take $MTTR_\text{D} \approx 1$ hour. Replacing a PC may require human intervention, so we take $MTTR_\text{PC} = 1$ day.

Unfortunately, we are not aware of any empirical studies on which to base the values of the parameters λ_t^c, so for our present calculations, we merely chose values that seem plausible, namely

	RAM	D	DA	PC	PCA	SYS
λ^O	0	0	0.3	0.6	0.09	0.01
λ^M	0	0	0.05	0.89	0.05	0.01
λ^E	0	0	0.05	0.05	0.05	0.85
λ^S	0	0	0.3	0.6	0.09	0.01

The values of λ^t for hardware failures (*i.e.*, $t \in \{\text{RAM}, \text{D}, \text{PC}\}$) are obvious; for example, $\lambda_\text{D}^\text{D} = 1$ and $\lambda_\text{PC}^\text{D} = 0$.

The formulas for $\tau(t)$ and $\kappa(C)$ depend on the form of redundancy and the disk organization. For illustration, we give the formulas for parity with the simple (not declustered) organization. Let N_V^D denote the number of viewers served from disk. With parity, the system can tolerate the failure of a word of RAM, a disk, or a PC, but not the failure of an entire disk array or PC array, so

$$
\begin{aligned}
\tau(\text{RAM}) &= 0 & \tau(\text{DA}) &= N_\text{v}^\text{D}/N_\text{DA} \\
\tau(\text{D}) &= 0 & \tau(\text{PCA}) &= N_\text{v}/N_\text{PCA} \\
\tau(\text{PC}) &= 0 & \tau(\text{SYS}) &= N_\text{v} ,
\end{aligned}
\tag{3}
$$

where $N_\text{DA} = N_\text{D}/G$ and $N_\text{PCA} = N_\text{PC}/G$ are the numbers of disk arrays and PC arrays, respectively. These formulas, together with equation (1), determine the contributions of single failures to ir.

Multiple failures involving more than two causes are so infrequent that their contribution to ir is negligible. Compared to single failures, double failures make a modest but non-negligible contribution to ir. Since the total contribution of double failures to ir is modest, we keep only the largest double-failure terms. The largest rates of single failures are for software, disk, and PC, so we consider only the six combinations of these.

Since the redundancy schemes discussed here do not provide (complete) tolerance to software failures, the contribution to ir from single software failures dominates contributions from double-failure terms involving software failures.[6]Thus, it suffices to include contributions from the three double-failure terms involving combinations of disk and PC. Simple probabilistic arguments yield the following estimates:

$$
\kappa(\{\text{D}, \text{D}\}) = ((G-1)/(N_\text{D}-1))\tau(\text{DA}) \tag{4}
$$
$$
\kappa(\{\text{D}, \text{PC}\}) = (n_\text{PC}^\text{D}G/N_\text{D})\tau(\text{DA}) \tag{5}
$$
$$
\kappa(\{\text{PC}, \text{PC}\}) = ((G-1)/(N_\text{PC}-1))\tau(\text{PCA}) . \tag{6}
$$

Similar reasoning is used to obtain formulas for other organizations and other forms of redundancy. These calculations yield the figures for ir in Tables 2 and 3. We conclude that parity or mirroring provide comparable increases in availability: adding either form of redundancy reduces the interruption rate by 75–90%.

7 Conclusions

We have examined high-level design of VoD servers. Our designs and analysis contain novel features. We have described a method for distributing the collection of titles among the levels of the storage hierarchy. Our method is specific to VoD only in that it requires estimates of the mean demand for each file. This problem has also been studied by Tetzlaff et al. [8] and by Doğanata and Tantawi [2].

In a very-large-scale storage system, the placement of entire disk arrays is an important issue. If parity-based redundancy is used, we propose arranging disk arrays on a pool of PCs using techniques similar to those used to arrange data stripes on a pool of disks [5]. This idea is not specific to VoD. Choosing the placement of disk arrays is complementary to allocating titles to disk arrays [6].

---

[6] Since our redundancy schemes provide *partial* tolerance to software failures, this claim is not obvious, but it is easily checked by estimating a few of these terms.

Our availability analysis reflects the increased tolerance to failures *of all kinds* that redundancy provides. For example, mirroring provides tolerance to some software failures, as well as tolerance to certain hardware failures. We estimate tolerance to non-hardware failures by modeling the effects of non-hardware failures as failures of *logical components*.

Numerical studies of our model show that intelligent use of redundancy in a VoD system increases cost moderately (by about 13%) and improves availability significantly (reducing interruptions by 75–90%). In some systems, it is attractive to use different redundancy schemes for titles in different levels of the storage hierarchy.

More work is needed to study the interaction between the storage architectures proposed here and other crucial elements of VoD systems, such as admission control, scheduling, and full VCR-like functionality.

Acknowledgments

The authors thank Ed Lee for helpful discussions.

References

1. P. M. Chen, E. K. Lee, G. A. Gibson, R. H. Katz, and D. A. Patterson. Raid: High-performance, reliable secondary storage. *ACM Computing Surveys*, 26(2):145–185, June 1994.
2. Y. N. Doğanata and A. N. Tantawi. Making a cost-effective video server. *IEEE Multimedia*, 1(4):22–30, Winter 1994.
3. Jim Gray. Why do computers stop and what can be done about it? In *Proc. Fifth Symposium on Reliability in Distributed Software and Database Systems*, pages 3–12, 1986.
4. J. Gray and A. Reuter. *Transaction processing: concepts and techniques*. Morgan Kaufmann, 1993.
5. M. Holland and G. Gibson. Parity declustering for continuous operation in redundant disk arrays. In *Proc. Fifth International Conference on Architectural Support for Programming Languages and Operating Systems (ASPLOS-V)*, pp. 23–35. ACM Press, 1992.
6. T. D. C. Little and D. Venkatesh. Probabilistic assignment of movies to storage devices in a video-on-demand system. In *Proc. Fourth International Conference on Network and Operating System Support for Digital Audio and video (NOSSDAV '93)*, pp. 213–224, 1993.
7. Micron Semiconductor, Inc. *DRAM Data Book*, 1993.
8. W. Tetzlaff, M. Kienzle, and D. Sitaram. A methodology for evaluating storage systems in distributed and hierarchical video servers. In *COMPCON 94*, pp. 430–439. IEEE Computer Society Press, Spring 1994.
9. C. P. Thacker. *AN2 Switch Overview*. Digital Equipment Corporation, Systems Research Center, August 1994. In preparation.

Scalable MPEG2 Video Servers with Heterogeneous QoS on Parallel Disk Arrays.

Seungyup Paek, Paul Bocheck, and Shih-Fu Chang.

Department of Electrical Engineering & Center for Telecommunications Research,

Columbia University, New York, NY 10027.

{syp, bocheck, sfchang} @ctr.columbia.edu

ABSTRACT

In this paper we focus on the video storage unit of a video server. We present a new, flexible data placement strategy for independent parallel disk arrays. The trade-off between utilization efficiency and interactive delay is investigated for this data placement strategy. Based on this trade-off, we show the advantage of video servers supporting a range of *interactivity QoS*. For our data placement strategy, we show that using scalable video improves the utilization and interactivity performance of a video server. We use three-layer, scalable MPEG2 digital video to support *resolution QoS* at a video server. Finally, we show that the data placement strategy reduces the complexity of admission control at the video server to that of a single disk system.

1. Introduction

In designing Columbia's Video On Demand testbed system [1,2] we are investigating advanced image and video technologies as components of a VoD system. One critical component is the design of an optimized real time video storage unit in the video server. Previously, we presented a disk partitioning technique to reduce the access delay for a single disk based single resolution video storage unit [5]. In this paper, we present a flexible strategy for the placement of video data on a parallel array of disks. For this placement strategy, we show that using scalable video improves the overall utilization and interactivity performance of a video server. Work on scalable video data placement in which utilization of the disk system is maximized is studied in [4]. However, the proposed scheme incurs large maximum start up and interactivity delays. In [3], a multiresolution video data placement scheme is presented in which fewer disks service low resolution requests and all disks in a parallel array service high resolution requests. We show that the performance of the low resolution requests is the same as in [4], whereas the performance of high resolution requests is not maximized. In real time retrieval of multiple video streams, we show that there is a trade-off between maximum interactive delay and utilization of disks. For the placement strategy that we present, different videos can have a range of interactivity and utilization performance based on this trade-off. On one end of the spectrum, the utilization of the disks is maximized (hence increasing the number of concurrent connections) and on the other end, the maximum interactivity delay is minimized. The flexibility of our strategy is that different videos can operate at different points of this retrieval performance spectrum to provide a range of interactivity QoS. We investigate the use of scalable video in a video server. It is shown that using scalable video based on the proposed data placement strategy improves the overall utilization and interactivity performance of a video server. The data placement strategy is optimized for the MPEG2 video coding structure (conforming to both main profile and high profile of MPEG2) to reduce the quality degradation during congestion. An admission control strategy based on the proposed data placement strategy is developed. It is shown that our data placement strategy reduces the complexity of admission control to that of a single disk system.

Section 2 describes the MPEG2 scalable video compression technology [7]. We show the advantage of supporting video resolution QoS at a video server. Section 3 briefly describes the system operation of the video storage unit. In section 4, a new strategy for the placement of video data on a parallel array of disks is presented. The trade-off relations based on this placement strategy show the advantage of supporting interactivity QoS in video servers. It is shown how scalable video can improve the overall utilization and interactivity performance of a video server based on the proposed data placement strategy, which provides further advantages of supporting resolution QoS in video servers. Finally, we present the admission control strategy for the video server based on the placement strategy that is presented.

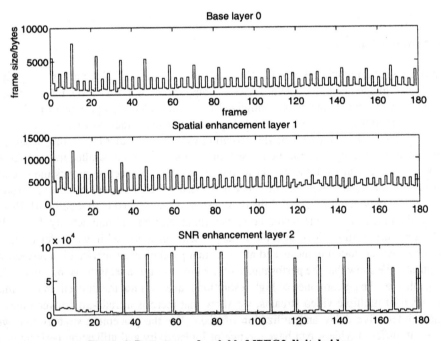

Figure 1. Data trace of scalable MPEG2 digital video.

2. MPEG2 Scalable Digital Video for Video Resolution QoS

In this section we overview the scalable MPEG2 digital video technology that we propose to use in our video server, and we show the advantage of supporting video resolution QoS based on scalable video at a video server. In section 4 we present further advantages of using scalable video in video servers. In scalable MPEG2 video coding, a subset of the full resolution bitstream can be used to obtain a subset of the full resolution video [6]. The MPEG2 standard allows a hybrid spatial and SNR scalability for three layer coding of video sequences. In such a scheme, the base layer provides the initial resolution of video, an additional spatial enhancement layer allows for the upsampling and hence increase in frame size of the base layer, and a further SNR enhancement layer provides for an increase in the visual quality of the base+spatial enhancement layers of video. For our video server design, a possible allocation of bit rates for each layer of scalable video can be chosen as in table 1. In this paper, we focus on constant bit rate, variable quality MPEG2 video. Optimal allocation of bit rates for constant bit rate and variable bit rate scalable MPEG2 is being researched as part of the video server research, and will be covered in a separate paper.

Table 1: Bitrate allocation for scalable MPEG2 video (All frame rates are 24fps)

Layer	Avg. Bit Rate (Mbps)	Frame Size	Visual Quality	Avg. PSNR (dB)
Base	0.32	304 x 112	VHS	35
Spatial Enhancement	0.832	608 x 224	Super VHS	34
SNR Enhancement	1.856	608 x 224	Super VHS	37

The values in table 1 and figure 1 above are from a sequence of 3,000 frames from the movie Ben Hur. The burstiness in the trace data comes from the encoding structure of MPEG2 [7]. For simulation, trace data for MPEG2 scalable video was prepared for 15,000 frames, by using Columbia's full-profile, standard-conforming MPEG2 software encoder. The selection of the bit rates for each layer was based on the approximation that, for video of frame size 720x480 and 30 fps, a bit rate of 4.0 Mbps provides VHS quality video. For video frame sizes of m x n, at f fps, we approximate the required bit rate b Mbps for VHS quality in the following way: $\frac{m \times n}{720 \times 480} \times \frac{f}{30} \times 4.0 = b$. The bit rates in the table are incremental bit rates (not accumulated rates).

In advanced video server systems it will be necessary to support different video resolutions and video stream data rates to accommodate clients with different network bandwidth, display resolutions and processing power. Storing multiple independent video streams of the same video in order to support different video resolutions will be inefficient in terms of video storage requirements. Scalable video provides an effective way to store multiple resolutions of videos with the same storage requirements of single resolution videos.

3. Overview of System Operation

We consider a parallel array of independent disks each connected in parallel to a central memory. When a request for an I/O operation from a single disk is placed, two types of overhead are incurred: the time it takes for the head to move to the appropriate cylinder (referred to as the *seek time*), and the time it takes for the first sector to appear under it (referred to as the *rotation latency*). Following this overhead, the transfer of the video data begins. The transfer time is a function of the data requested. For every cycle of the video server, one 'retrieval block' of video data has to be retrieved for every video stream. For a larger retrieval block, a higher utilization efficiency can be achieved, but a larger buffer size will be required. Each video stream is serviced in a round robin fashion during each cycle. The retrieval block is a fixed number of frames that is referred to as a *group of frames* (gof).

4. Data Placement Strategy for Interactivity QoS

In this section, two extreme strategies for the placement of video data on a parallel array of disks is compared. These strategies are presented to provide a framework to evaluate various placement strategies. For each scheme, advantages and disadvantages are compared, and a new, flexible strategy for the placement of video data is presented. The new scheme is shown to support a range of interactivity QoS for a parallel array of disks.

In advanced digital video systems of the future, we reconsider the commonly accepted notions of interactivity. Our goal for interactivity in the video server is not to 'simulate' VCR functions exactly but to achieve effective search mechanisms while efficiently utilizing the limited resources of a video server. We propose that the critical functions of interactivity that are required for video servers are location of specific scenes and multiple rate 'scanning' of video segments (fast/slow forward/reverse). For our data placement strategy, the maximum interactivity delay values of all the interactivity functions (start, request gof, resume) (figure 2) are equal and will be shown to depend on a single parameter (segmentation level). The scan granularity (the minimum gof interval between consecutive gof retrieved during a scan) is directly dependent on this same parameter.

4.1 Balanced placement.

This scheme represents one end of the interactivity QoS. The interactivity delay (defined in figure 2) of this scheme is one cycle, but the utilization of each disk is low. For example, if a user pauses the playback of a video stream and after some time requests that the video stream be resumed, the video stream would be able to resume in the following round robin cycle. In this scheme, each group of frames (gof) of each resolution of video is divided into N_d equal segments and placed over all N_d disks. In

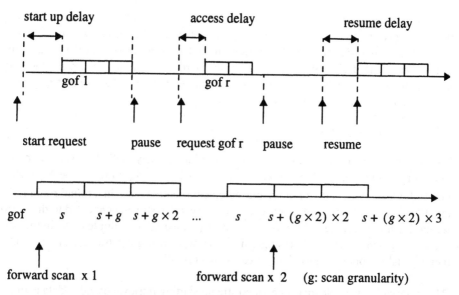

Figure 2: Interactivity functions of video server.

[3] a similar data placement strategy is presented, in which the full resolution gof is segmented to N_d segments. For the balanced placement strategy, the excessive number of disk seeks leads to under utilization of the disks. For an approximate analysis, we first consider all video streams in the scheduler round robin to be of one resolution. For our analysis, each disk is assumed to use the SCAN disk scheduling algorithm during each round robin cycle. It is shown that utilization $\rho = \dfrac{R_p \times S_{max}}{N_d \times R_d}$ (S_{max} is the maximum number of video streams of a given resolution that the parallel array of disks can support, R_p is the video playback rate and R_d is maximum disk transfer rate). As shown in our prior work [5], S_{max} can be derived from the following equation, where T_{cycle} is the round robin cycle time, T_{sx} is maximum seek time, T_{sm} is minimum seek time and T_{rx} is maximum rotation latency.

$$T_{cycle} = S_{max} \times \left(\frac{T_{cycle} \times R_p}{N_d \times R_d} + T_{rx} + T_{sm} \right) + 2 \times T_{sx}.$$

In the SCAN scheduling algorithm, the scanning cycle consists of two phases. During the first cycle, the head scans the disk from the inner most track to the outer most track. While scanning the disk, data blocks belonging to different streams are read from the disk. Upon reaching the outer most track, the head is returned to the initial position. Several assumptions are made in the above analysis. Firstly, any stream accessed during the first phase will add to the total retrieval cycle the maximum rotational latency, the data reading time and the minimum seek time. Secondly, since the retrieval cycle consists of two phases of head movement, we add two maximum seek delays to the total cycle time. Based on this analysis, we show the trade-off between utilization of the disk array and interactivity delay in figure 6. This will be explained further in section 4.3. The analysis shows that increasing the retrieval block size (gof) increases the utilization of the disks, but also results in an increase in the maximum interactivity delay. The analysis above is also used to evaluate the periodic placement strategy and the multiple segmentation strategy.

4.2 Periodic placement [4].

This scheme represents the opposite side of the interactivity QoS. This scheme maximizes disk utilization, and the maximum access delay will be shown to be N_d cycles. For each video, consecutive gof are placed on consecutive disks in a round robin fashion. For every cycle, one gof is retrieved for every video stream connected to the video server. Each gof is retrieved from a single disk (compared to multiple disks in the balanced placement scheme). If a single disk can support n gof retrievals in one cycle, then N_d disks support $(N_d.n)$ video streams concurrently.

The observation is made that for a video stream starting retrieval of video data at cycle r, the video stream accesses a different single disk during each cycle. However, the video stream accesses the same single disk during each cycle as all video streams with start cycles in the following set: $\{r_i, i=1,2,...N_s \mid (r_i \bmod N_d = r \bmod N_d)\}$, where r_i denotes the start cycle of video stream i and we assume the first gof of all videos are stored on the same disk. This observation shows that for all video streams connected to the video server, we can group the video streams into N_d *video stream sets*.

All video streams in a video stream set retrieve data from the same disk during any given cycle (figure 3). Based on this, it can be shown that the worst-case interactivity delay for a video stream is N_d cycles for any of the equivalent interactivity functions. To prove this, we first note that each of the interactive functions are equivalent in that a *specific required gof* must be retrieved from the array of disks. The number of video streams being serviced on the disk that contains the required gof is the number of video streams in the video stream set that is accessing the disk during a particular cycle. The required gof cannot be accessed until a video stream set that can accommodate a new video stream is accessing the appropriate disk. Since the total number of sets are N_d, the maximum access delay before retrieval is N_d. We can also show that the scan granularity for this scheme is N_d. It has been shown that for regular playback, a video stream j accesses consecutive disks to retrieve consecutive gof. If video stream j requires a forward scan while only utilizing the resources reserved in its video stream set, we can show that the scan granularity is $g=N_d+1$ i.e. consecutive gof retrieved for a scan starting at gof s are: s, $(s+g \times 1)$, $(s+g \times 2)$,... In other words, the finest forward scan this scheme can support is (N_d+1).

4.3 Multiple Segmentation

In this section, we present a new flexible strategy for the placement of video data on a parallel array of disks. This scheme allows videos to take on a range of maximum interactive delay and scan granularity values. It is shown that decreasing interactivity delay can be achieved at the cost of decreasing utilization efficiency. Therefore, there is a design range for the placement of video data. In this section we also show how scalable video has advantages for video servers based on this placement strategy. We also develop an admission control framework based on this data placement strategy. The new scheme presented here uses different degrees of segmentation of gof blocks for the placement of gof blocks across a parallel array of disks.

Multiple segmentation (MS) scheme:

1. For a parallel array of N_d disks, we define $(log_2\ N_d) + 1$ segmentation levels: $S = \{S_i = 2^i,\ i=0,1,...log_2\ N_d\}$

2. For a given segmentation level S, divide each gof into S equal segments.

3. For a given segmentation level S, specify (N_d / S) sets of disks.

4. For each video sequence, the consecutive retrieval blocks (gof) which were each divided into S equal segments are stored on consecutive sets of disks as in table 2.

Table 2: Multiple Segmentation N_d=8 disks

Disk	1	2	3	4	5	6	7	8
S=1	gof 1	gof 2	gof 3	gof 4	gof 5	gof 6	gof 7	gof 8
S=2	gof 1	gof 2	gof 3	gof 4	gof 1	gof 2	gof 3	gof 4
S=4	gof 1	gof 2	gof 1	gof 2	gof 1	gof 2	gof 1	gof 2
S=8	gof 1	gof 1	gof 1	gof 1	gof 1	gof 1	gof 1	gof 1

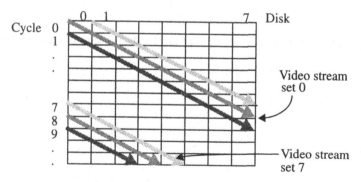

Figure 3: Video stream sets for periodical placement strategy.

Balanced placement is a special case of multiple segmentation with S =8, while peri-odical placement is a special case with S=1. We can show that increasing the segmen-tation S reduces the maximum interactivity delay at the price of utilization efficiency.

For a segmentation level S, a video stream accesses S disks during each cycle. Extending the structure of video stream sets, we develop the structure of *component video stream sets*. For a parallel array of N_d disks, we define N_d component video stream sets. For a video j that is stored with segmentation level S, we say that S com-ponent video streams are required for a single video stream of video j. Therefore, resources are reserved on S component video stream sets for the retrieval of a single video stream for video j. Figure 4 shows which component video stream sets are used for the retrieval of a given video stream at cycle r stored with segmentation level S.

All component video streams in a video stream set retrieve data from the same disk during any given cycle. Based on this, it can easily be shown that the worst-case inter-activity delay for a video stored with segmentation level S is N_d/S cycles for any of the equivalent interactivity functions. Suppose that a video j is stored with segmentation level S=2 on an N_d=8 disk array (figure 5). Consider a video stream that has reserved resources on component video stream sets (0, 4), with all other video stream sets exhausted by other video streams. Assume a request for a gof stored on disks (0,4) is

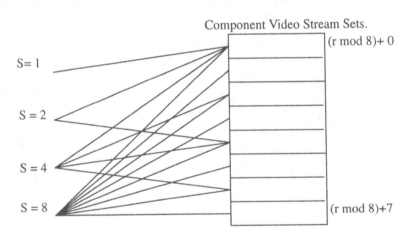

Figure 4: Component video streams sets for the retrieval of video stream at cycle r

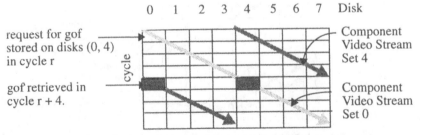

Figure 5: Example to demonstrate maximum interactivity delay.

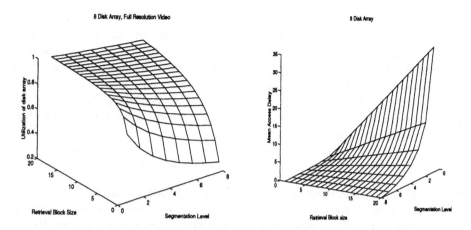

Figure 6: Performance of utilization and mean access delay vs retrieval block size and segmentation level

made during cycle r, and the desired start gof is stored on the disk(s) which have just been accessed during cycle r. The delay before the desired gof can be accessed from the appropriate disk(s) is $N_d/S=4$. In summary, a video stored with segmentation level S requires S component video streams. If resources are reserved on S component video stream sets, a maximum of N_d/S cycles are required before a given set of S component video stream sets has accessed all disks. Using a similar analysis, we can also show that the scan granularity for this scheme is N_d/S.

This scheme has advantages in flexibility in that videos with high interactivity delay tolerance can be stored with a smaller segmentation level, and videos requiring low interactivity delay are stored with higher segmentation levels. Multiple levels of segmentation can be supported on the same array of disks in a video server to provide a range of interactivity QoS.

4.4 Multiple Segmentation Based on scalable MPEG2 Video

We use the proposed multiple segmentation scheme to segment each gof of each layer of scalable video into S segments. The specific value of S to use is a design parameter that can be chosen by the system designer for each video in the video server, depending on its access requirements. We now consider how to divide each gof of each resolution (layer) of video into S segments. Each gof of each layer consists of a sequence of I, B, P frames of MPEG2 video. There are two basic ways to segment the gof of a given layer, as shown in figure 7. Using method 1, we see that if one segment is not retrieved, all frames of a gof will be affected. Method 2 is clearly a better option. Furthermore, based on method 2, we may group together frames of the same type (I, P, B) before segmentation. In this way, we assign the highest priority to segments containing I frames, intermediate priority to segments containing P frames, and the lowest priority to segments containing B frames. Segmentation does not occur exactly at frame boundaries. Each segment has an associated priority, and the priorities can be used in the video server scheduler to selectively drop segments to achieve *graceful degradation* in the case of congestion. In addition, further granularity in interactive scan functions can be easily achieved by skipping B and/or P frames. In many real time applications or near real time applications for which fast responses are critical, lower layers may be segmented with a higher level (method 3, figure 7) so that lower layers can be retrieved with shorter delays for a high degree of interactivity. This can be used for progressive retrieval in which lower layers are displayed before full resolution layers are fully retrieved (figure 8).

4.5 Admission Control Framework Based on Multiple Segmentation.

Given the multiple segmentation placement strategy presented above, we develop an admission control framework for the video server. It was shown that each incoming video stream can be decomposed into a number of *component video streams*. Higher segmentation levels require more component video streams for a single video stream. Admission control at the video server is an operation at the call establishment level for a video stream request at a video server. Given an incoming request with a specific QoS requirement, the admission control must decide to accept or reject the call. The policy has to determine if the request can be serviced by the video server while maintaining heterogeneous QoS requirements of all video streams already connected to the video server. The challenge is to maximize the utilization of the video server resources while ensuring heterogeneous QoS requirements of connected video streams. For a parallel array of N_d disks, we define N_d component video stream sets (CVSS). All component streams in a given CVSS retrieve video data from the same single disk during a given cycle. The component video streams in a CVSS are said to be connected to the same *logical disk*. The CVSS simplification provides a strategy for admission control in the video server. In the video server, we maintain a single CVSS admission control table. For each incoming video stream, we update the corresponding CVSS entries accordingly. Note that depending on the resolution of the video stream, we calculate whether the incoming video stream can be supported on the each logical disk associated with each CVSS. All logical disks are assumed to be identical with the same disk characteristics.

5. Conclusion and Future Work.

We have presented a new video data placement strategy for scalable video. In our testbed, the data placement strategy was applied specifically three layer, scalable MPEG2 video. The new strategy is a more flexible strategy than those proposed previously, and can accommodate a wide spectrum of video access characteristics in video servers. We have also showed the advantages of using scalable video based on the proposed data placement strategy. We have also presented a framework for admission control in a video server based on this new data placement strategy. The complexity of the admission control was shown to be reduced to that of a single disk system, even for parallel array of disks. Simulations are being to test the video storage unit design presented here using discrete event simulation [10]. In our simulation (figure 9), we model each disk in a disk array with specific disk characteristics to test our simplified approxima-

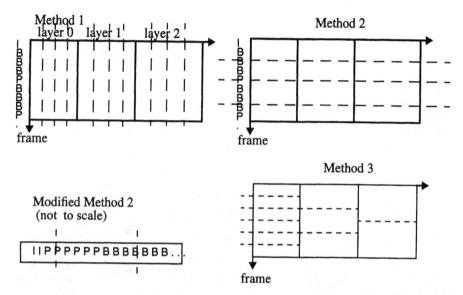

Figure 7: Multiple segmentation based on scalable MPEG2 video.

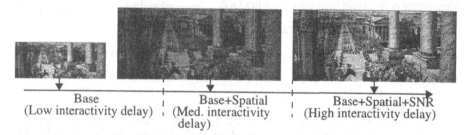

Figure 8: Improved utilization/interactivity performance using scalable MPEG2 video

tions. The simulations are based on actual trace data for three layer scalable MPEG2 video coding. Based on poisson arrival statistics of clients and simple interactivity request models, we are testing utilization and interactivity performance of our multiple segmentation data placement strategy for independent parallel disk arrays. Future plans include implementation of the video storage unit design into the video server for the Columbia campus-wide Video On Demand testbed.

For guaranteed delivery of video streams from the video server, we can deterministic or statistical service. In general, statistical service achieves higher utilization of the disk array. In our current research, we are focusing on a statistical and deterministic service for the retrieval of variable bit rate (VBR) video streams from the disk array. Providing guaranteed service requires resource reservation at the disk array. For constant bit rate video streams, we can achieve a high utilization of the disk array resources. However, reservation of resources for VBR video based on the peak rate leads to low utilization of resources. We are developing schemes to increase the utilization of disk resources for VBR video based on multiple buffer management to sup

Arrival requests for video with resolution QoS
modeled with poisson statistics.

Disk model based on disk drive
specifications
to simulate
disk
latencies.

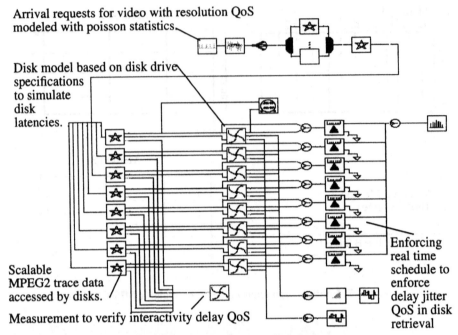

Scalable
MPEG2 trace data
accessed by disks.

Measurement to verify interactivity delay QoS

Enforcing
real time
schedule to
enforce
delay jitter
QoS in disk
retrieval

Figure 9: Parallel Disk Array Simulation

port delay jitter. This will introduce a *delay jitter QoS* dimension to the heterogeneous
QoS suite of a video server.

References:

1. S.-F. Chang, D. Anastassiou, A. Eleftheriadis, J. Meng, S. Paek, S. Pejhan, J. Smith, "Development of Advanced Image/Video Servers in the Video On Demand Testbed," IEEE Visual Signal Processing & Communications Workshop, Sept. 1994, New Brunswick, NJ.

2. S. -F. Chang, A. Eleftheriadis, and D. Anastassiou, "Some Interoperability Issues in Columbia's Video on Demand Testbed", Contribution to International Digital Audio/Visual Council, June 1994

3. K. Keeton and R. Katz, "The Evaluation of Video Layout Strategies on a High-Bandwidth File Server," Intern. Workshop on Network and Operating System Support for Digital Audio and Video, Lancaster, England, UK, Nov. 1993.

4. E. Chang and A. Zakhor, "Scalable Video Data Placement on Parallel Disk Arrays," SPIE Symposium on Imaging Technology, San Jose, 1994.

5. P. Bocheck, H. Meadows, and S.-F. Chang, "A Disk Partitioning Technique for Reducing Multimedia Access Delay," Intern. Conference on Distributed Multimedia Systems and Applications, Honolulu, Aug., 1994.

6. Tihao Chiang and Dimitris Anastassiou, "Hierarchical Coding of Digital Television," IEEE Communications Magazine, May 1994.

7. ISO/IEC 13818-2 Committee Draft (MPEG2)

8. "The Almagest," Manual for Ptolemy, University of California at Berkeley, 1992.

The Design of a Variable Bit Rate Continuous Media Server

Gerald Neufeld, Dwight Makaroff and Norm Hutchinson

Department of Computer Science,
University of British Columbia
Vancouver, Canada

Abstract. This paper describes the design and implementation of a file server for variable bit rate continuous media. Most continuous media file servers have been designed for constant bit rate streams. We address the problem of building a server where each stream may have a different bit rate and, more importantly, where the bit rate within a single stream may vary considerably. Such servers will be come increasingly more important because of Variable Bit Rate (VBR) compression standards such as MPEG-2.

1 Introduction

The motivation for the design of a specialized file server for continuous media such as video and audio is well established. Most existing work in this area has assume constant bit rates for the media stream. Recent work has been done in analyzing variable rate servers[1]. However, such analysis still assumes that each *individual* stream has a constant bit rate. Compression methods such as motion JPEG or MPEG-2 produce streams whose bit rates vary considerably within the stream. The server describe here is intended to support such variable streams. The primary area of complexity is in the admissions control algorithm and in I/O scheduling. As well, the server described here does not assume any single syntax such as MPEG-2.

2 Architecture

The design of the file server is based on a set of server nodes, each with a processor and disk storage on multiple local SCSI Fast/Wide buses. Each node is connected to the ATM network for delivering continuous media data to the client systems (See Figure 1).

Reading a media stream from the server is done via three RPC requests: *open*, *prepare* and *read*. The open request provides basic administration support, while the prepare request primes the connection in preparation for subsequent reads by transmitting an initial amount of data.

For example the client application issues open requests for a video, audio and text streams. Each open request will create an XTP[2] connection – which is rate

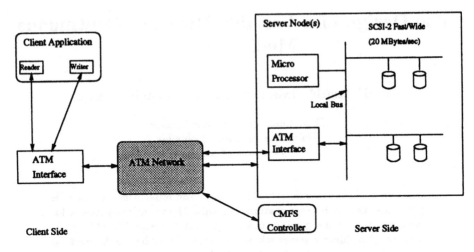

Fig. 1. Organization of System

controlled but without error recovery – from the server node containing the file to the client. The XTP connect request (FIRST packet) contains information about the minimum size of the window and the required bit rate. If the client accepts the request window size (i.e., reserves that amount of buffer space) then the subsequent local read operations will not be delayed. During the transmission of the media over the XTP connection, the client periodically sends RESERVE packets back to the server indicating that it has more buffer space available. The client must send a RESERVE packet if the amount of media data buffered at the client falls below the minimum required for continuous operation.

3 Admissions control algorithm and I/O scheduler

In order to schedule variable bit rate (VBR) streams, the server defines fixed length cycles or slots for all streams[1]. Each disk stream is then divided into these slots. A stream vector is created which contains the number of blocks which must be read for each slot for the stream. Because the stream may be VBR, the values for the vector may vary considerably.

The admissions control algorithm must know what is the minimum and maximum number of blocks that the server can read in a single slot. These values are calculated by running a calibration program. The minimum number is calculated by uniformly spacing the blocks across the disk thus maximizing the seek times (assuming a SCAN algorithm). The maximum number of blocks which can be read is simply the number of contiguous blocks which can be read in a slot time. These values more accurately reflect the actual capacity of the server since they include all transfer delays (through SCSI bus and I/O bus to memory as well as server software overhead).

---

[1] A reasonable time for such a slot may be 500 milliseconds.

A simple admissions algorithm then is simply to sum the vectors for the active streams plus the new stream. If any slot in the resulting vector is greater than the minimum number of blocks the server can read per slot, the admission fails. This is a very conservative estimate however. Any single slot may have less blocks to read than the server could read. In this case, the server is idle at the end of a slot. In order to admit more streams, we permit the server to read ahead as fast as it can subject to buffering constraints. By permitting the server to read ahead we can admit a stream where the total number of blocks required to be read within a slot is greater than the minimum number of blocks the server can read for a slot. The amount of such over allocation is proportional to the number of blocks the server has read ahead. The maximum number of blocks a server can read per slot is required for accurately calculating the buffering requirements.

The following example illustrates this method. Assume that the server is capable of reading a minimum of 10 (fixed size) disk blocks per slot. Figure 2 shows the current schedule for the server and a new stream to be admitted. In

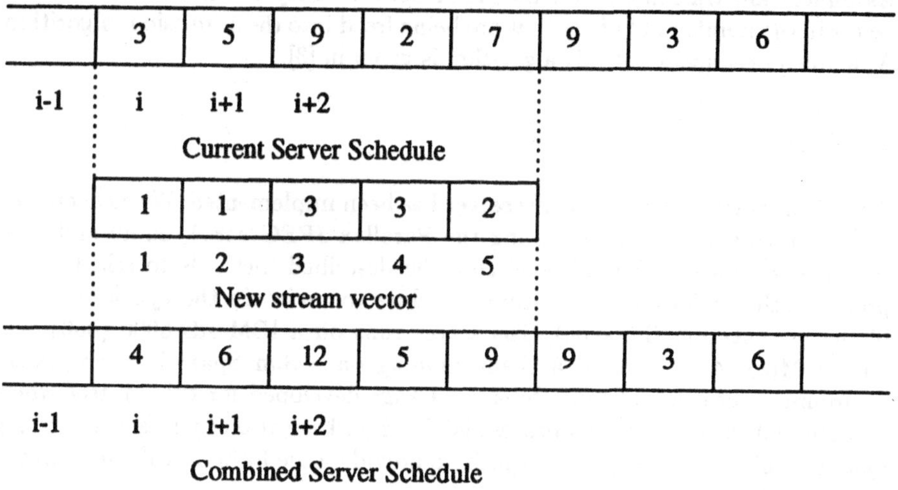

	3	5	9	2	7	9	3	6	

$i-1$ i $i+1$ $i+2$

Current Server Schedule

	1	1	3	3	2	

1   2   3   4   5

New stream vector

	4	6	12	5	9	9	3	6	

$i-1$ i $i+1$ $i+2$

Combined Server Schedule

Fig. 2.

these vectors, the numbers represent the number of disk blocks that must be read in each slot. For instance, in the current server schedule, at slot i the server must read 3 disk blocks, at slot $i + 1$ the server must read 5 disk blocks etc. These blocks represent the total number of blocks for all active streams. The vector for the new stream to be admitted represents the blocks which must be read just for that new stream. For instance, in the first slot for the new stream the server must read 1 block, then 1 again for the next slot, etc.

In the conservative admissions control algorithm, we would simply add the new stream vector to the current schedule. In this case, the $i + 2^{nd}$ slot would have a value of 12 which is higher than the minimum number of blocks the server can read in that slot (10). However if we permit the server to read more than a single slots worth, the first two slots worth of disk blocks would be read in one slot time. This read-ahead permits the given schedule to be accepted. By the time the server reads slot $i + 2$ it will still be in the 2nd slot of time assuming the server reads at the minimum number of blocks per slot.

The server in practice reads more than the minimum blocks per slot. This read-ahead is taken into account when a new vector is added. The number of blocks that were read-ahead are the actual number of blocks the server was able to read per slot (between minimum and maximum blocks per slot). The algorithm starts with this number of actual read-ahead blocks and then continues assuming the server will read a minimum number of blocks.

So far in this discussion we have assumed that there are an arbitrary number of buffers. That is, the server can read ahead with out fear of running out of buffers. Clearly this is not the case. We therefore have to stop read-ahead in the admissions algorithm once we have run out of buffers. For purposes of buffer consumption we assume the server reads a *maximum* number of blocks per slot. As buffers are transmitted on the ATM network they are freed. We therefore factor in the number of buffers that are being freed into the admissions algorithm. A detailed description of this algorithm is given in [3].

4 Conclusions

A multiple node version of the file server has been implemented. We have created a client that supports video (using the Parallax JPEG card), audio and text. Synchronization is accomplished using the described methods to schedule the prepare calls and using a real-time schedule to maintain the synchronization of the presentation (lip-sync). The server runs on a IBM RS 6000 (350) over an 100 Mpbs ATM link to a client running on a Sun Sparc II. The system environment uses a real-time threads package developed for this project which operates within a single Unix process [4]. This package also provides an operating system shield to native systems which do provide some form of real-time threads such as AIX 4.1.

References

1. Bikash, S., Ito, M. and Neufeld, G.: The Design and Performance of a Continue Media Server for a High-Speed Network *to appear* IEEE MultiMedia Conference, Boston, (May 1995)
2. Strayer, W. T., Dempsey B. J., and Weaver A. C.: XTP: The Xpress Transfer Protocol, Addison Wesley Publishing, 1992
3. Neufeld, G., Makaroff, D., Hutchinson, N.: Internal Design of the UBC Distributed CMFS, Technical Report, (1995)
4. The UBC Real-Time Threads package, Technical Report, July,1994

Lecture Notes in Computer Science

For information about Vols. 1–945

please contact your bookseller or Springer-Verlag

Vol. 981: I. Wachsmuth, C.-R. Rollinger, W. Brauer (Eds.), KI-95: Advances in Artificial Intelligence. Proceedings, 1995. XII, 269 pages. (Subseries LNAI).

Vol. 982: S. Doaitse Swierstra, M. Hermenegildo (Eds.), Programming Languages: Implementations, Logics and Programs. Proceedings, 1995. XI, 467 pages. 1995.

Vol. 983: A. Mycroft (Ed.), Static Analysis. Proceedings, 1995. VIII, 423 pages. 1995.

Vol. 984: J.-M. Haton, M. Keane, M. Manago (Eds.), Advances in Case-Based Reasoning. Proceedings, 1994. VIII, 307 pages. 1995.

Vol. 985: T. Sellis (Ed.), Rules in Database Systems. Proceedings, 1995. VIII, 373 pages. 1995.

Vol. 986: Henry G. Baker (Ed.), Memory Management. Proceedings, 1995. XII, 417 pages. 1995.

Vol. 987: P.E. Camurati, H. Eveking (Eds.), Correct Hardware Design and Verification Methods. Proceedings, 1995. VIII, 342 pages. 1995.

Vol. 988: A.U. Frank, W. Kuhn (Eds.), Spatial Information Theory. Proceedings, 1995. XIII, 571 pages. 1995.

Vol. 989: W. Schäfer, P. Botella (Eds.), Software Engineering — ESEC '95. Proceedings, 1995. XII, 519 pages. 1995.

Vol. 990: C. Pinto-Ferreira, N.J. Mamede (Eds.), Progress in Artificial Intelligence. Proceedings, 1995. XIV, 487 pages. 1995. (Subseries LNAI).

Vol. 991: J. Wainer, A. Carvalho (Eds.), Advances in Artificial Intelligence. Proceedings, 1995. XII, 342 pages. 1995. (Subseries LNAI).

Vol. 992: M. Gori, G. Soda (Eds.), Topics in Artificial Intelligence. Proceedings, 1995. XII, 451 pages. 1995. (Subseries LNAI).

Vol. 993: T.C. Fogarty (Ed.), Evolutionary Computing. Proceedings, 1995. VIII, 264 pages. 1995.

Vol. 994: M. Hebert, J. Ponce, T. Boult, A. Gross (Eds.), Object Representation in Computer Vision. Proceedings, 1994. VIII, 359 pages. 1995.

Vol. 995: S.M. Müller, W.J. Paul, The Complexity of Simple Computer Architectures. XII, 270 pages. 1995.

Vol. 996: P. Dybjer, B. Nordström, J. Smith (Eds.), Types for Proofs and Programs. Proceedings, 1994. X, 202 pages. 1995.

Vol. 997: K.P. Jantke, T. Shinohara, T. Zeugmann (Eds.), Algorithmic Learning Theory. Proceedings, 1995. XV, 319 pages. 1995.

Vol. 998: A. Clarke, M. Campolargo, N. Karatzas (Eds.), Bringing Telecommunication Services to the People – IS&N '95. Proceedings, 1995. XII, 510 pages. 1995.

Vol. 999: P. Antsaklis, W. Kohn, A. Nerode, S. Sastry (Eds.), Hybrid Systems II. VIII, 569 pages. 1995.

Vol. 1000: J. van Leeuwen (Ed.), Computer Science Today. XIV, 643 pages. 1995.

Vol. 1002: J.J. Kistler, Disconnected Operation in a Distributed File System. XIX, 249 pages. 1995.

Vol. 1004: J. Staples, P. Eades, N. Katoh, A. Moffat (Eds.), Algorithms and Computation. Proceedings, 1995. XV, 440 pages. 1995.

Vol. 1005: J. Estublier (Ed.), Software Configuration Management. Proceedings, 1995. IX, 311 pages. 1995.

Vol. 1006: S. Bhalla (Ed.), Information Systems and Data Management. Proceedings, 1995. IX, 321 pages. 1995.

Vol. 1007: A. Bosselaers, B. Preneel (Eds.), Integrity Primitives for Secure Information Systems. VII, 239 pages. 1995.

Vol. 1008: B. Preneel (Ed.), Fast Software Encryption. Proceedings, 1994. VIII, 367 pages. 1995.

Vol. 1009: M. Broy, S. Jähnichen (Eds.), KORSO: Methods, Languages, and Tools for the Construction of Correct Software. X, 449 pages. 1995. Vol.

Vol. 1010: M. Veloso, A. Aamodt (Eds.), Case-Based Reasoning Research and Development. Proceedings, 1995. X, 576 pages. 1995. (Subseries LNAI).

Vol. 1011: T. Furuhashi (Ed.), Advances in Fuzzy Logic, Neural Networks and Genetic Algorithms. Proceedings, 1994. (Subseries LNAI).

Vol. 1012: M. Bartošek, J. Staudek, J. Wiedermann (Eds.), SOFSEM '95: Theory and Practice of Informatics. Proceedings, 1995. XI, 499 pages. 1995.

Vol. 1013: T.W. Ling, A.O. Mendelzon, L. Vieille (Eds.), Deductive and Object-Oriented Databases. Proceedings, 1995. XIV, 557 pages. 1995.

Vol. 1014: A.P. del Pobil, M.A. Serna, Spatial Representation and Motion Planning. XII, 242 pages. 1995.

Vol. 1015: B. Blumenthal, J. Gornostaev, C. Unger (Eds.), Human-Computer Interaction. Proceedings, 1995. VIII, 203 pages. 1995.

Vol. 1017: M. Nagl (Ed.), Graph-Theoretic Concepts in Computer Science. Proceedings, 1995. XI, 406 pages. 1995.

Vol. 1018: T.D.C. Little, R. Gusella (Eds.), Network and Operating Systems Support for Digital Audio and Video. Proceedings, 1995. XI, 357 pages. 1995.

Vol. 1019: E. Brinksma, W.R. Cleaveland, K.G. Larsen, T. Margaria, B. Steffen (Eds.), Tools and Algorithms for the Construction and Analysis of Systems. Selected Papers, 1995. VII, 291 pages. 1995.

Vol. 1020: I.D. Watson (Ed.), Progress in Case-Based Reasoning. Proceedings, 1995. VIII, 209 pages. 1995. (Subseries LNAI).

Vol. 1021: M.P. Papazoglou (Ed.), OOER '95: Object-Oriented and Entity-Relationship Modeling. Proceedings, 1995. XVII, 451 pages. 1995.

Vol. 1022: P.H. Hartel, R. Plasmeijer (Eds.), Functional Programming Languages in Education. Proceedings, 1995. X, 309 pages. 1995.

Vol. 1023: K. Kanchanasut, J.-J. Lévy (Eds.), Algorithms, Concurrency and Knowlwdge. Proceedings, 1995. X, 410 pages. 1995.

Vol. 1024: R.T. Chin, H.H.S. Ip, A.C. Naiman, T.-C. Pong (Eds.), Image Analysis Applications and Computer Graphics. Proceedings, 1995. XVI, 533 pages. 1995.

Vol. 1025: C. Boyd (Ed.), Cryptography and Coding. Proceedings, 1995. IX, 291 pages. 1995.